Outcomes Measurement in the Human Services

Outcomes Measurement in the Human Services
Cross-Cutting Issues and Methods

EDWARD J. MULLEN
JENNIFER L. MAGNABOSCO
EDITORS

Center for the Study of Social Work Practice—
A joint program of Columbia University School of Social Work
and the Jewish Board of Family and Children's Services

NASW PRESS

National Association of Social Workers
Washington, DC

Jay J. Cayner, ACSW, LISW, *President*
Josephine Nieves, MSW, PhD, *Executive Director*

Linda Beebe, *Executive Editor*
Nancy A. Winchester, *Editorial Services Director*
Patricia D. Wolf, Wolf Publications, Inc., *Project Manager*
Marcia A. Metzgar, Wolf Publications, Inc., *Copyeditor*
Susan J. Harris, *Proofreader*
Louise Goines, *Proofreader*
Melissa D. Conroy, Wolf Publications, Inc., *Proofreader*
Robert Elwood, *Indexer*

First impression June 1997
Second impression February 1998

Library of Congress Cataloging-in-Publication Data

Outcomes measurement in the human services : cross-cutting issues and methods / Edward J. Mullen, Jennifer L. Magnabosco, editors.
p. cm.
Includes bibliographical references and index.
ISBN 0-87101-275-8
1. Human services—United States—Evaluation. 2. Human services—Evaluation—Methodology. 3. Social service—United States—Evaluation. 4. Outcome assessment (Medical care). 5. Family social work—United States—Evaluation. I. Mullen, Edward J., 1937– . II. Magnabosco, Jennifer L.
HV91.097 1997
361'.0068'4—dc21 97-7824
CIP

Printed in the United States of America

DEDICATION

This book is dedicated to Mitchell I. Ginsberg and Carol H. Meyer. Mitchell Ginsberg contributed immeasurably to social welfare policy and international social justice. As a member of the Center for the Study of Social Work Practice's Development Council, he helped to shape both the Center's mission and its program, including the symposium on which this book is based. Carol Meyer provided brilliant leadership in the development of practice theory. Both Mitch and Carol will be missed deeply, but their contributions to the Center and to social welfare will continue to be felt by all who knew them.

—EJM

Joining EJM in his dedication to Mitchell Ginsberg and Carol Meyer, I dedicate this book also to Tony, my parents and brother, and my close friends—all of whom have been instrumental in helping me achieve positive life outcomes this past year.

—JLM

CONTENTS

Part II Outcomes Measurement in Mental and Behavioral Health

Part III Outcomes Measurement in Child and Family Services

Part V Concluding Observations

FIGURES

TABLES

FOREWORD

Outcomes measurement has received scant attention in the human services and especially in social work. Perhaps we have avoided the subject because we do not believe it is possible to obtain valid, objective outcomes data in our field. Or perhaps the high value we place on confidentiality and privacy makes it difficult for us to expose our work to the scrutiny of "outsiders." Although some publications about outcomes measurement exist, few major conferences have focused on this topic. Even fewer conferences have yielded a major volume that reflects the status of current thinking about outcomes measurement in the human services.

Social work, in particular, has a dearth of scholarly work about outcomes measurement. Few, if any, national social work conferences have addressed this topic. If the human services professions had known to confront this challenge several decades ago, they might have directed their wisdom and resources toward the creation of educational programs about outcomes measurement, and they probably would not be plagued now by a continuous barrage of skepticism and budget cuts.

As a rule, the current attacks on the human services professions are not supported by empirical data that demonstrate deficiencies or failures but rather by the absence of reliable data that can either affirm or reject their promises of efficacy. In such a vacuum, public debates are shaped more on ideology, rhetoric, and political muscle than by systematic empirical data.

Managed care, for example, has the capacity to advance social work in important ways but also to interfere, in some cases, with appropriate service delivery. When social work providers have challenged certain of the unrealistic expectations of managed care organizations, they have done so without sufficient research and documentation to support their arguments. If social work providers could prove their effectiveness using certain theoretical frameworks and modalities of treatment, managed care organizations would respond accordingly. These same arguments could help alter the tone of public policy debate.

Social work and allied human services professions are aware of the challenges that confront them. In social work, the newly revised accreditation standards of the Council on Social Work Education now require that professional schools train students on how to evaluate the outcomes of their own practice. Although the requirement is welcome at this stage of the profession's development, the scant attention given to outcomes measurement at social work conferences suggests that the profession's talent may not yet be developed to fulfill it. Nevertheless, it is only through such formal requirements that sufficient impetus is gained to ensure significant advances on the part of any profession. To the degree that this requirement provides the motivation to create better evaluation tools, it should be viewed as a positive step for the social work field.

Accordingly, *Outcomes Measurement in the Human Services* constitutes a timely and welcome addition to the literature of social work and the helping professions. The symposium that generated it represents the first large-scale effort by social workers to assemble scholars, educators, and practitioners to address outcomes measurement. The book does not represent an insular effort that draws solely on social workers. Rather, the symposium participants and the contributors to this book are experts from various helping professions who worked together for two days in intensive and collegial intellectual exchange. This volume is not merely a multidisciplinary product; it is truly interdisciplinary.

The book's contents reflect the interrelated concerns of researchers, educators, and practitioners. Similarly, they reflect the shared interests and interrelated mission of a leading social services agency, the Jewish Board of Family and Children's Services, and of a leading educational institution, the Columbia University School of Social Work. It is under these organizations' joint auspices that the Center for the Study of Social Work Practice, founded in 1987, sponsored the National Symposium on Outcomes Measurement in the Human Services in 1995, which resulted in this book.

Thanks to the dedicated and skillful work of Edward J. Mullen and Jennifer L. Magnabosco, *Outcomes Measurement in the Human Services* reflects an important milestone for human services practitioners and educators in strengthening their services and demonstrating—both to themselves and to the public—the ways in which the human services are beneficial and cost-effective on the one hand or in need of refinement and improvement on the other. It constitutes a major advance in the gradual and arduous process of building and improving the helping professions.

The authors elucidate how knowledge about outcomes measurement is essential both for educating professionals in the human services and for shaping practice in a wide range of human services agencies. The book helps integrate education and practice and highlights how these two realms depend on each other. It also demonstrates that agency practice cannot be improved without better professional education or in-service training and, in turn, that professional education cannot advance in the absence of valid, reliable, and continuous information from agencies and practitioners. It is our expectation that future publications about outcomes measurement will regard this book as a noteworthy contribution.

Many human services professionals know that they are successful in relieving the pain that so many people experience because of poverty, social stress, or mental illness. However, self-perceptions are no longer enough. The development of valid outcomes measures will help attract the resources and community recognition our work so richly deserves.

Ronald A. Feldman
Dean
Ottman Centennial Professor
Columbia University School of Social Work

Alan B. Siskind
Executive Vice President
Jewish Board of Family and Children's Services

ACKNOWLEDGMENTS

This book is an outgrowth of the National Symposium on Outcomes Measurement in the Human Services held on the campus of Columbia University and convened by the Center for the Study of Social Work Practice on November 9–10, 1995. An interdisciplinary group of nearly 300 practitioners, administrators, and researchers from across the United States as well as from Canada and Great Britain assembled to examine outcomes measurement in the human services. The chapters in this book are based on the symposium papers and discussions. We are grateful to all who participated and contributed to the rich discussions occurring at the symposium.

This symposium is the third national conference sponsored by the Center for the Study of Social Work Practice. In 1987 the nation's largest voluntary social services agency, the Jewish Board of Family and Children's Services (JBFCS), and the nation's oldest school of social work, the Columbia University School of Social Work (CUSSW), formed an affiliation that included sponsorship of the Center for the Study of Social Work Practice. A joint program of the two organizations, the Center has assembled faculty, agency administrators, practitioners, and students in partnerships to develop and disseminate social work practice knowledge. The organizational partnership expressed through joint sponsorship of the Center has been personalized through the outstanding executive leadership provided by Ronald A. Feldman, CUSSW dean, and Alan B. Siskind, JBFCS executive vice president. Their combined leadership and support made the symposium and this book possible.

The symposium was supported by gifts from the Virginia and Leonard Marx Foundation, the Beatman Foundation, and David S. Lindau. For their generous support and encouragement, we thank Virginia W. Marx, Francis Beatman, Josie and David S. Lindau (development council chair), and other members of the Center's development council.

A subcommittee of the Center, including Robert Abramovitz, Rita Beck Black, Grace Christ, Steve Cohen, Bruce Grellong, André Ivanoff, Rami Mosseri, Lawrence Martin, Brenda McGowan, Anne O'Sullivan, Helen Rehr, Doris L. Rosenberg, and Annaclare van Dalen, joined us in planning the symposium. For the symposium's outstanding quality and great success, we are thankful to each of these planning committee members.

We gratefully acknowledge the special assistance of those who served as symposium rapporteurs: Michael Arsham, Mark Cameron, Paul Cavanaugh, Joseph Frisino, Yvonne Johnson, Katina Georgopolas, Louisa Gilbert, Mark Holter, Dara Kerkorian, Gary Mallon, Anne O'Sullivan, Michael Powell, Jeanette Schiff, Karun Singh, Julia Rothchild-Stewart, and Elaine Walsh.

We thank each of the book's contributors. They gave generously of their time and wisdom by preparing symposium papers and subsequent chapters for this book. We appreciate their patience with our requests for revisions and for our need to meet stringent deadlines. Their expert knowledge and great enthusiasm for outcomes measurement has been expertly expressed both in this book and at the symposium.

Many others have contributed to the symposium and to the book's success, including Joseph Tobin, Kathy Wilke, Jane Waldfogel, Jane Hoffer, Jeanne Connor, Gary Katcher, Donald McVinney, Mary Francis De Rose, Steven Sher, and Patrick Villeneuve.

The professional editorial assistance of Gretchen Borges was critical to the timely and successful completion of this book. Finally, we would like to thank Linda Beebe and Nancy Winchester of the NASW Press and Patricia Wolf, Marcia Metzgar, and Melissa Conroy of Wolf Publications, Inc., for their skillful work in editing and publishing the book.

Edward J. Mullen
Jennifer L. Magnabosco

INTRODUCTION

Outcomes Measurement in the Human Services has been written to consider issues and methods in outcomes measurement as the nation re-examines social welfare interventions and desired outcomes.* National debates regarding human services policy and program reform have addressed and will continue to address intended and unintended outcomes into the 21st century. For researchers and an array of other stakeholders, there is a need to contribute more significantly to these discussions. Outcomes measurement requirements initiated in the public and private sectors are reshaping clinical and administrative practice in the human services. Of special interest to us is the effect that demands for accountability have had and will continue to have on social work practice, social agency programs, and organized human services systems. Issues related to outcomes measurement are relevant to the social work profession because the profession will continue to be a core human services provider group.

This book is the first to present state-of-the-art theory and practice regarding outcomes measurement in human services with a specific focus on social work. The book expands on the National Symposium on Outcomes Measurement in the Human Services sponsored by the Center for the Study of Social Work Practice, a joint program of the Columbia University School of Social Work and the Jewish Board of Family and Children's Services. The symposium was held at Columbia University in November 1995. Most of the chapters in this book are based on materials presented at that symposium, although original material was developed and significant reorganization has been done to make the content suitable for a book.

Our intention for the symposium and the book was to bring together prominent thinkers, researchers, practitioners, administrators, and policymakers to discuss issues relevant to the current impetus for accountability and measuring outcomes in health, mental and behavioral health, and child and family services. We recognize that such a review is interdisciplinary, requiring perspectives that are not driven primarily by social work. Accordingly, the symposium was attended by human services professionals from many disciplines and fields. Similarly, the book includes chapters written by human services specialists with expertise in practice, policy, or research.

Given that outcomes measurement is a broad topic, the book reflects how this topic has been defined—and is being redefined—in public policy, clinical and administrative practice (for example, management theory, managed care, empirical

*Although initially awkward, the term *outcomes* rather than simply *outcome* implies that normally the reference is to many measures rather than one, especially when placed in the framework of a system of measures.

clinical practice), and evaluation research. Social work and other human services disciplines have been concerned with the evaluation of social intervention effectiveness for a long time. Recently, however, public policy and managed care initiatives have increasingly mandated measures of accountability as an integral part of service delivery. This book provides the human services profession an opportunity to re-examine outcomes measurement in these contexts. It also gives students and professionals information to begin creating a comprehensive framework and to understand better the implications of outcomes measurement for the human services. To accomplish this end, the book (like the symposium) has been designed to examine the following questions:

- How can outcomes measurement be usefully reconceptualized and placed in historical, public policy, administration, practice, and research contexts? What is the legislative and public policy context of outcomes measurement? Why should outcomes be addressed in a measurable way?
- What approaches to outcomes measurement are being promulgated? What can be said about the reliability, validity, and quality of existing approaches to outcomes measurement and their relevance to social work interventions?
- What are the implications for future research?
- What are the implications for social programs and for practitioners of the increasing attention being given to outcomes measurement?

The Book's Organization

The drive for increased accountability or push to measure quantifiable outcomes in the human services is a movement with diverse origins. We are in the midst of an unusual merging (and potential conflict) among diverse interests, agendas, and approaches. It is out of this context that the outcomes measurement movement will grow into its developed form in the early part of the 21st century. This diverse parentage is reflected in the book's content and its contributors.

Dealing effectively with outcomes measurement and accountability in the human services is, as stated previously, interdisciplinary. Consequently, chapter authors are experts who discuss outcomes measurement from particular theoretical or applied contexts, representing the human services fields of health, mental and behavioral health, and child and family welfare. The contributing authors present specialized materials relevant to aspects of outcomes measurement, and their chapters touch on various aspects of the orienting questions. In this introduction as well as the conclusion, the editors and discussants draw from these chapters as well as from the rich symposium discussions to address the orienting questions.

This introduction focuses on the first orienting question, drawing on the thinking expressed in subsequent chapters. It outlines the theoretical and applied context and issues of outcomes measurement that may be helpful when reading the text. Part I of the book addresses general overarching issues and cross-cutting themes of outcomes measurement, and parts II through IV examine three fields of human services in which outcomes measurement has become a strong force: (1) health, (2) mental and behavioral health, and (3) child and family services. Part V presents concluding observations, including chapters written by specialists in the three fields of practice examined in parts II through IV. Authors of these concluding chapters were invited to review the chapters in their respective areas, to examine symposium recordings and their participatory experience at the symposium, and to prepare concluding observations including consideration of implications. These authors were members of the originating symposium planning committee, and they chaired or attended symposium sessions; thus, they are well suited to provide the needed perspective and expertise. Part V concludes with a commentary prepared by the editors with their assessment of possible answers to the last three orienting questions.

The following subsections introduce the book's parts and chapters. Because of the diversity of the perspectives and the breadth of the book's parts, we provide some detail in these descriptions to give a comprehensive view and to place each part and chapter in context. The concluding section of this introduction describes our view of the current context of outcomes measurement.

Part I

Part I examines the overarching issues and methods that apply to all human services disciplines. In chapter 1 Hatry describes the current status of outcomes measurement in the public and private social services and examines outcomes measurement at all government levels, in the private sector, in performance partnerships, and in community foundations. He distinguishes among types of outcomes measurement, arguing that *regular* outcomes measurement, rather than *in-depth, ad hoc* evaluations, is most appropriate. Hatry proposes a human services outcomes measurement research agenda specifying four technical issues that researchers should address to make outcomes measurement in the human services more effective: (1) breadth of focus (that is, should human services measurement focus on all aspects of the client's condition or focus more narrowly on outcomes relating to specific services?), (2) timing of follow-up (when should follow-up of individual clients be done to determine what the outcomes have been?), (3) response rate (how can adequate response rates be obtained?), and (4) prevention (how should prevention—an important outcome for a substantial number of human services programs—be measured?). Hatry believes that although outcomes measurement is popular, one should be mindful of its limitations, especially because most approaches fail to specify outcomes causation. Despite these limitations, he argues that outcomes measurement has considerable value in providing those responsible for human services policies and programs, as well as consumers, with timely performance indicators.

In chapter 2 Rossi provides his most extensive treatment to date of conceptual and measurement issues relating to human services program outcomes. He reviews definitions of outcomes, distinguishing among types that are characteristic of human services programs, and he examines associated measurement problems and gives guidelines for specifying outcomes. Like other contributors, Rossi notes that evaluations are contingent on stakeholder perspective (for example, policymaker, administrator, and service recipient). He makes the useful distinction between *gross outcomes* (those outcomes observed after the program) and *net outcomes* (those outcomes left after removing what would have occurred without the program). This distinction is important to consider when reading subsequent chapters. Rossi also cautions that the popular emphases on process measurement or on client satisfaction should not be substituted for outcomes measurement.

Rossi's conceptual and methodological guidelines are based in a well-established social sciences evaluation research tradition. However, many contributors to this book offer alternative perspectives. For example, although Rossi argues for impact evaluations, some view impact evaluations as impractical for ongoing outcomes measurement systems.

Chapters 3 and 4 provide in-depth analyses of key developments in outcomes measurement that have emerged from extensive research programs in health and behavioral health. Although these developments are field-specific, the authors address cross-cutting ideas that are generalizable to other human services fields. Both chapters focus on patient outcomes assessment. (In these chapters the term *outcomes assessment* implies *outcomes measurement.* Furthermore, field-specific terms such as *patient* often carry specialized meanings that should be considered when generalizing to other human services fields that use different terms such as *client* or *customer*.)

In chapter 3 Booth and Smith assess the science of outcomes assessment by examining issues of scientific debate, success to date of developments in outcomes assessment, and current and future challenges for the field. Booth and Smith write that the objective of patient outcomes assessment is to monitor and improve treatment and treatment outcomes by assessing patient characteristics, the processes of treatment, and the outcomes of routine care. The authors describe several important advances in the science of patient outcomes assessment, including increased precision and reliability in quantifying the elements of treatment, agreement on what constitutes the critical outcome domains (that is, functioning, disability, quality of life, patient satisfaction, general health status, and mental health status), the ability to measure important outcome domains confidently, use of outcomes assessment to link people receiving various treatments to the outcomes of those treatments, and use of outcomes assessment results to improve services and support accountability. Booth and Smith conclude by posing important challenges for outcomes assessment. Like other contributors, they identify what is perhaps the greatest challenge to outcomes measurement: determination of whether the technology of outcomes assessment improves human services outcomes and the quality of service.

In chapter 4 Ware examines the measurement of health care outcomes from the patient's point of view. Although Ware is known for work on the SF-36 and the RAND Health Insurance Experiment and Medical Outcomes Study research programs, for the first time he addresses outcomes measurement and patient assessment in the context of social work and the human services. Ware critically examines conceptual and methodological dimensions of patient-based assessments and provides guidelines for their use. He reports that consumers' views of their health care are associated with features of their health plans and features of services received (for example, access and quality), with measures of quality being the most important predictor. He suggests that whether or not clients are regarded as valid judges of their care important consequences exist regarding what people think about their health care, such as continued use of services and compliance with treatment.

Ware cautions that serious methodological flaws exist in much patient assessment work, with a problematic lack of standardization. He points out that the field must determine the validity of measures because health care decisions and comparisons among services, treatments, and patient groups are increasingly based on findings from patient assessments.

In chapter 5 Hudson presents the ways in which assessment tools and computerized outcomes measurement systems can be used in clinical practice. The issues and perspective presented in this chapter are of fundamental importance as the human services professions move into the use of computers for outcomes measurement. Hudson notes that the implications for using measurement tools in computerized quality assurance and outcome effectiveness evaluation systems are important and urgently needed. He is skeptical about using computerized information systems that do not provide information of direct use to clients and practitioners. He argues that if these tools are used to help clients and practitioners on an individual basis, there can be significant potential benefits. If these tools are not used, client needs will be ignored, with disappointing and harmful consequences. Hudson's discussion of using computerized outcomes measurement in the service of direct practice offsets other views emphasizing large databases (which aggregate thousands of cases) for health care decision making.

Hudson distinguishes among terms commonly used in outcomes measurement including *measurement* (purely descriptive), *assessment* scales (evaluative), *outcomes* measurement (either regarding the problem for which the client seeks help or regarding the intervention effects), and *effectiveness* (change over time). He focuses on the notion that outcomes represent a *change* in the status of the client's problem. He believes that it is this type of outcome for which social work practitioners and administrators should accept accountability under managed care. He believes that data regarding outcomes in terms of *intervention effects* (that is, causal) should be of concern to social work researchers and should not be expected of practitioners or administrators by managed care organizations.

In chapter 6, Berman and Hurt describe conceptual and practical issues in the development and implementation of clinical outcomes systems. Drawing from their academic and industry experiences at Behavioral Health Outcomes Systems (BHOS, Inc.), they provide an example of a continuous quality improvement approach to the design and implementation of an outcomes measurement management system. Although it is not our intent to promote any particular firm or measurement protocol, the BHOS Manager Outcomes Information System is highlighted here for illustrative purposes.

Berman and Hurt propose that the development of an outcomes system requires that seven questions be answered: (1) Who is the customer? (2) What domains will be evaluated? (3) What types of data are desired? (4) Where will the data come from? (5) What time frame is to be used? (6) What predictors are to be studied? (7) What processes will be examined? They recommend that outcomes measurement systems include four interrelated components: (1) services outcomes that measure program structures and processes, (2) cost outcomes that stress cost-containment values, (3) satisfaction outcomes, and (4) clinical change outcomes or effectiveness. These distinctions are particularly useful because they propose that each component can be used as a tool for quality improvement in human services organizations. Berman and Hurt believe that outcomes measurement systems can help clinicians and administrators streamline practice and organizational design.

Part II

The contributors to part II examine mental and behavioral health services outcomes measurement. The terms *mental health* and *behavioral health* are sometimes used interchangeably when discussing outcomes measurement. However, the term *behavioral health* typically is used when the reference designates services that apply to people with substance abuse and mental health problems in a managed care context (Freeman & Trabin, 1994). Some use the term to connote measurability or an emphasis on behavioral functioning.

This section begins with an overview chapter by Shern and Trabin that examines system changes and accountability for private and public behavioral health services. Shern and Trabin note that rapid changes are occurring in the financing and oversight of behavioral health care and that these changes are motivated by the growth of health and behavioral health care expenditures. Some purchasers have sought to eliminate coverage for behavioral health care, and others have sought to achieve cost containment through managed care devices. The authors suggest that without standardized comparative measures of service value, cost considerations become paramount. They view the growing emphasis on service value, quality, and accountability as a counterpoint to this cost-containment trend. Accordingly, they highlight strategies that have been or should be considered by the public and private sectors in designing outcomes measures to assess value, quality, and accountability structures and identify areas of particular relevance to human services practice and research.

Manderscheid and Henderson focus on federal and state legislative and program directions for managed care in chapter 8. They describe current and anticipated federal and state legislative and regulatory activities of relevance to managed behavioral health care, including insurance reform, the Medicaid and Medicare programs, performance partnership grants, specification of essential community providers, definition of mandated benefits, development of licensure and accreditation procedures for utilization review firms, community rating of health insurance premiums, and definition of specialty providers as primary care providers. They also explore the implications of current developments for the future including changes in case management. They suggest that case management will continue as part of a "carve out" for people with severe problems and that attention should be given to associated payment mechanisms. They urge that action be taken quickly if case management is to be successful.

The next two chapters examine *specific* approaches that receive attention in mental and behavioral health care: outcomes modules and rapid assessment instruments (RAIs).

In chapter 9 Smith, Rost, Fischer, Burnam, and Burns review the components, administration, and application of outcomes modules in routine clinical practice. Such modules have been developed and tested at the Center for Outcomes Research and Effectiveness at the University of Arkansas for Medical Sciences in Little Rock. This work is among the most sophisticated and impressive efforts to develop outcomes measures that are specific to behavioral health conditions. In chapter 3 Booth and Smith, also members of this research group, include outcomes modules in their assessment of the state of the science of outcomes measurement. These chapters can be reviewed together.

Chapter 9 describes outcomes modules as recently developed measurement tools used to assess how treatment affects outcomes in patients with specific psychiatric disorders. The authors describe how these measures can be used to inform administrative decisions about improving care quality and how they can affect decisions by patients, providers, and payers. The components of outcomes modules and their administration and applications are described for several illustrative psychiatric conditions. The authors see outcomes modules as providing an approach that is standardized, comprehensive, adaptable, and low burden. They argue that such standardization facilitates comparisons across studies. Another benefit is facilitation of continuous quality improvement efforts in routine clinical practice.

In chapter 10 Corcoran examines the use of RAIs as outcomes measures. This is an important extension of RAIs given the influence of managed care on social work clinical practice. RAIs have become popular in social work clinical practice, and they have been described in detail elsewhere (Fischer & Corcoran, 1994). Their development also is examined by Hudson in chapter 5. RAIs have been used alone and together with single-case designs by many clinicians from the empirical practice school. They also are used by clinicians in psychology, psychiatry, and others in the helping professions.

Corcoran notes that since the mid-1970s, despite the marked growth of measurement tools available to practitioners, these tools have generally not been adopted and incorporated into routine practice. He argues that the typical practitioner continues to rely on practice wisdom, clinical judgments, and intuition to make decisions. Corcoran believes this reliance will change with the advent of managed care because managed care is requiring that providers systematically measure client problems and goals, monitor treatment, and evaluate its effectiveness. Corcoran describes how RAIs can be used to assess the need for treatment and to measure treatment outcomes.

In chapter 11 Nurius and Vourlekis examine issues and questions from the perspective of social work practice and social work education. Their chapter complements the discussion by Corcoran in chapter 10 pertaining to the use of measures of direct relevance to individual case planning. In particular, they focus on the link between process and outcomes measures that they consider key to case-level accountability as well as to program improvement and effectiveness. Their discussion examines important questions about outcomes measurement and managed care such as how to harness the accountability and cost-containment engine into a strategic system-changing tool.

Chapters 9, 10, and 11 focus primarily on patient- and client-level outcomes measurement. In chapter 12 Segal gives equal importance to program- or organization-level performance. He provides an examination of outcomes measurement systems in mental health appropriate to this program-level perspective. He and many contributors to this book believe that because of the current emphasis on cost-cutting and managed care, mental health programs are now being asked to justify their existence with measurable outcomes. Segal views these current forces as different from the earlier ones focusing on outcomes and effectiveness because these new forces now tie outcomes to program financing.

Segal examines organizational performance in governance, accessibility, human resources development (that is, personnel practices, staffing, consumer representation, training), maintenance of fiscal stability, community relations, and organizational respect in the community of agencies. He notes that an excellent program may founder on the political mistakes of any of these components. As is true throughout outcomes measurement at all levels, Segal examines how important desired outcomes differ for individual stakeholders and describes the best available outcomes measurements (that is, "soft" and "hard" measures and organizational performance measures). Although he describes several impediments to the current use of outcomes measures, he proposes ways in which programs can increase their use of such measures. He argues that outcomes measurement will occur to the extent that measurement systems are linked to organizational survival and views such systems as potentially providing an impetus for the development of new and more effective forms of service.

In chapter 13 Wasow discusses some recent developments in mental health consumer advocacy, some changes occurring in the relationship of professionals and consumers, and some core values that underlie the consumer movement. Although she does not address outcomes measurement directly, Wasow assumes that outcomes measurement must incorporate consumers as key stakeholders. In addition to the exemplary work of the National Alliance for the Mentally Ill, the Center for Mental Health Services and the Mental Health Statistics Improvement Program have sponsored a major effort to develop outcomes measures, report cards, and guidelines explicitly focused on consumer perspectives (for example, see chapters 7 and 8; also see Hall, 1996; Mulkern, Leff, Green, & Newman, 1995; Sherman & Kaufman, 1995).

Part III

Part III examines the common and unique aspects of outcomes measurement in child and family services. Although the move toward outcomes measurement has been most evident in health and mental and behavioral health, the field of child and family services is rapidly moving in that direction. Child and family services share many of the same contexts that have shaped outcomes measurement in other fields, yet the current force of managed care is only beginning to be evident.

In chapter 14 Weiss critically assesses results-based accountability for child and family services. She notes that during the 1990s significant changes occurred in child and family services as a result of major government shifts (for example, President Clinton's reinvention initiative, devolution, privatization). Consequently, there has been an increased focus on organizational responsibility and accountability for program results. In this context Weiss notes a significant move toward the implementation of organizational management theories that stress continuous improvement and the idea of the "learning organization." Weiss views this framework as useful because child and family services must change to be publicly accountable. She examines in detail results-based accountability in child and family services and provides a national perspective. And she considers why a need exists for results-based accountability, what the need is, and the use and challenges of results-based accountability efforts. She considers several examples, including Oregon's Benchmarks and Minnesota's Milestones initiatives, to assess how results-based accountability is working.

Complementing Weiss's broad conceptual overview of results-based child and family services, Wulczyn describes in chapter 15 methodological issues that have inhibited system-level outcomes measurement in child and family welfare. Wulczyn examines emerging technologies and research methods that could have a dramatic impact on outcomes measurement and outcomes research in child and family welfare. He argues that outcomes research would be improved by contextualizing child and family services through "changing the reductionist conceptualization in current outcomes research, using statistical models that reveal the structure and pattern in the experiences of children, avoiding selection bias in cross-sectional research, and creating geographic sensitivity" (p.187).

Developing outcomes measures has proved to be a difficult and time-consuming process. In chapter 16 McCroskey describes two noteworthy and successful efforts to build outcomes measures in Los Angeles County. Her discussion is especially firmly based because she has been a participant over a 10-year period in the development of the measures that she describes. She reports that this 10-year process included developing consensus about outcomes for public child welfare services, defining outcomes measures for a countywide children's scorecard, working with practitioners to develop a new measurement instrument to assess changes in family functioning, and evaluating child and family services programs. She notes that in child and family services little experience has occurred with the development and use of outcomes measures. In this chapter, she describes two applications of outcomes measurement systems: development of a countywide children's scorecard to support planning for systemwide services integration, and development of a Family Assessment Form to support practitioner-based program-level research and evaluation.

McCroskey and many other contributors distinguish among levels of outcomes measures for use in decisions at the policy, program, and direct practice levels. In chapter 17 Benbenishty proposes combining program and direct practice outcomes levels in support of empirical practice. Benbenishty advocates for a move to a position between the program and the practitioner, a middle ground that focuses on practitioners within organizations. In this context he sees a requirement for gathering, processing, and interpreting information by all practitioners within an agency and addressing the information needs of agency personnel involved in shaping services: practitioners, supervisors, administrators, managers, and policymakers. Like Weiss, Benbenishty views this combination as necessary to create a learning environment that facilitates effective practice. He describes several principles to guide this formulation of effective empirical practice and presents a case illustration of implementation of these principles in a child welfare agency that provides foster care. The case illustrates the use of a computerized outcomes measurement system. Benbenishty argues that an agency with such an information system environment will be better prepared to face the challenge of accountable practice, be better able to provide quality service, and be better positioned to survive despite shrinking political and financial support.

Part IV

Perhaps no field of human service practice has been more affected by outcomes measurement than health. Several chapters have provided descriptions and analysis of important developments in outcomes measurement emanating from health research (chapter 4) and the closely associated fields of mental and behavioral health (chapters 3 and 6 and the chapters in part II). The chapters in part IV of this book are complemented by those chapters. In particular, the work of Ware and his colleagues is frequently referenced by authors in the following chapters.

Part IV is composed of two sections. The first section includes five chapters that address conceptual and methodological dimensions of outcomes measurement in health. The second section includes chapters that provide case examples of practice–research outcomes studies in health and social work.

Perhaps no single organization has contributed more to outcomes measurement in health than has RAND. Accordingly, the opening chapter in this part of the book reviews the RAND research. In chapter 18 Coulter examines the development of health-related quality-of-life measures at RAND. He traces the historical development of health-related quality-of-life (HRQL) measures with respect to patient-reported outcomes at RAND. He examines current work and focuses on patient satisfaction as an exemplar of the development and evolution of specific instruments. He reviews the major psychometric demands made for reliable and valid instruments. He proposes that the work on HRQL at RAND has attempted to answer two broad questions left unanswered by the landmark Medical Outcomes Study and the Health Insurance Experiment: (1) Were the instruments, as developed, reliable and valid for other populations? (2) Could more efficient scales that are shorter be developed with similar psychometric properties? Coulter notes that as this research continues, new challenges in outcomes measurement are emerging. Increasing attention is focused on the use of cross-cultural measures in countries around the world, including issues of item-translation, operational, scale, and order equivalence. Of equal importance, according to Coulter, is work on the development of culturally sensitive instruments for various racial and ethnic groups in the United States. Coulter views the development of reliable and valid culturally sensitive instruments tested over a wide spectrum of patient and social categories as important goals.

Building on the work of HRQL and the work of Ware and his colleagues, in chapter 19 Berkman examines outcomes measurement for social work research and practice in health care. In particular, Berkman focuses on the measurement of social work patient outcomes in health care. She notes that because it is impossible to determine the specific effects of most social work services on patients, outcomes research that uses standardized HRQL measures is necessary. She notes that too frequently health outcomes have been defined narrowly and have focused on biological dimensions; these measures should be extended to include psychosocial components of social work relevance. Berkman views HRQL measures as first steps in multidimensional, multistage diagnostic screening to facilitate provision of needed services.

Berkman discusses issues in the selection of HRQL measures as well as in the analysis of data gathered in outcomes measurement using such measures. She describes a study she has conducted with elderly patients in primary care at Massachusetts General Hospital in which the SF-36 was used with the addition of questions to assess social work–relevant dimensions. She posits that measurement tools must become more convenient and acceptable to patients and practitioners by being brief, having ease of administration and scoring, and permitting simple interpretations.

In chapter 20 Epstein, Zilberfein, and Snyder examine the use of available information for practice-based outcomes research. To illustrate their idea, they describe the design for a case study of psychosocial risk factors and liver transplant outcomes. The authors, drawing from their experiences at Mt. Sinai Hospital, examine the merits of using available health information for outcomes measurement in effectiveness studies. They review recent literature comparing outcomes studies based on available data with those based on randomized, controlled trials (RCT) in medical effectiveness research. A methodological debate within social work research is examined, and the authors suggest that rather than obsess about failures to achieve the "gold standard" of RCT social work research, more practice-based research should be conducted with available health information. As an example, a study is described that uses routinely available information.

In chapter 21 Zabora examines the use of prospective psychosocial interventions with oncology patients, using this setting as an example of how clinical and research techniques can be merged to enhance effectiveness. He notes that early problem identification and resolution not only enhances treatment but also provides clinicians with an opportunity to collect baseline data for outcomes measurement. He observes that managed care requires comprehensive services, and in addition to outcomes indicators such as survival and overall cost, patient satisfaction and quality of life are important. He believes that psychosocial providers can take the lead in collecting and providing such data, positioning psychosocial services for inclusion in global contracts. To do so, human service professionals should learn skills in outcomes measurement by joining research and clinical methods.

In chapter 22 Dimond and Roca describe examples of outcomes measurement in social work health services with reference to continuous quality improvement principles. This chapter draws from their experiences in these two health care settings. They discuss financial and quality outcomes variables in both inpatient and ambulatory services. To illustrate the ideas discussed, the authors describe two studies: (1) an interdisciplinary outcomes study examining timely discharge of patients from inpatient units and (2) a study designed to establish care pathways including costing out of inpatient mental health services.

Further illustrating applications of outcomes measurement in social work health services, the next four chapters constitute a section of hospital social work practice–research case examples. Together they illustrate how outcomes research is being conducted in hospital social services settings. These case chapters include chapter 23 by Fahs and Wade, in which a study of hospital discharge planning comparing two social work models of service to patients with acquired immune deficiency syndrome (AIDS) is described; chapter 24 by Gitelson, Russo, and Caraisco, in which an intensive case management community residential care program for patients discharged with mental illness is examined; chapter 25 by Royle and Moynihan, in which an application of the use of outcomes measures with low-income, ethnically diverse clients with multiple diagnoses is presented; and chapter 26 by Gorin presenting a university-based breast cancer program support service. These case studies illustrate current practice–research focused on outcomes measurement in social work health settings and the significant challenges to outcomes measurement in health.

Part V

Part V presents concluding observations with discussion of implications for policy, clinical and administrative practice, and outcomes research. It begins with chapters written by specialists in each of the three fields of practice examined in parts II, III, and IV. The authors of these concluding chapters were invited to review the chapters in their respective areas, to reflect on their participation at the originating symposium, to examine symposium recordings, and to prepare concluding observations. As noted, these authors were members of the originating symposium planning committee, chairing or participating in the symposium, so they are well suited to provide the needed perspective and expertise. Part V ends the book with a concluding commentary prepared by the editors.

In chapter 27 Abramovitz, Ivanoff, Mosseri, and O'Sullivan comment on the outcomes measurement in mental health and behavioral health. In chapter 28 McGowan and Cohen provide comments on outcomes measurement in child and family services. In chapter 29 Christ and Black comment on outcomes measurement in health. Part V ends with our concluding thoughts regarding outcomes measurement in the human services, including our assessment of four of the book's orienting questions:

- What approaches to outcomes measurement are being promulgated? What can be said about the reliability, validity, and quality of existing approaches to outcomes measurement and their relevance to social work interventions?

- What are the implications for future research?
- What are the implications for social programs and for practitioners of the increasing attention being given to outcomes measurement?

Context of Outcomes Measurement in Social Work and the Human Services

As the description of the book's chapters suggests, the contributing authors provide a wide view of outcomes measurement in the human services. We have asked each contributing author to comment on how outcomes measurement can be usefully reconceptualized and placed in historical, public policy, administration, practice, and research contexts. We asked them to consider the legislative and public policy context of outcomes measurement including why outcomes should be addressed in a measurable way. These chapters provide useful insights into the context that has made outcomes measurement so important. The following paragraphs draw from the contributing authors' ideas and include our thoughts regarding the current context of outcomes measurement.

The context of human service outcomes measurement has been shaped by several recent and evolving developments. We believe that the most profound and enduring influence shaping outcomes measurement in the human services that will continue well into the next century is in the accountability–performance–results movement as reflected in public and private sector policy. This context is described first and in greatest detail. Although the four other developments are historically distinct, we view them as having secondary importance and perhaps in the long run being subsumed by the broader forces behind the accountability–performance–results movement. Nevertheless, these more specialized contexts each contribute to an understanding of the current outcomes measurement framework, especially in particular human service fields. We briefly comment on each secondary context: administrative and clinical practice theory, managed care, the consumer interest and advocacy movement, and evaluation research. Beginning with the broad context of accountability–performance–results as expressed in policy, these developments are described next.

Accountability–Performance–Results: The Public and Private Sectors

In their influential bestseller *Reinventing Government: How the Entrepreneurial Spirit Is Transforming the Public Sector,* Osborne and Gaebler (1993) captured the current context of outcomes measurement when they wrote "words like accountability, performance, and results have begun to ring through the halls of government" (p. 141). This ring has grown to a clamor. The demand for accountability, performance, and results has been translated into requirements for evidence of outcomes by funding sources, accrediting bodies, and accounting standards. The Governmental Accounting Standards Board (GASB), which sets standards for most state and local governments, has included performance measurement among their requirements.

Martin and Kettner (1996) view the GASB Service Efforts and Accomplishments (SEA) initiative as affecting the human services into the next century by requiring performance measurement as a generally accepted accounting standard. (For a review of how the human services will be affected by the Government Performance and Results Act of 1993 [GPRA; P.L. 103-62] and the SEA initiative as well as how various types of accountability may be viewed, see Martin & Kettner, 1996.) In chapter 1 Hatry cites evidence of this development even before implementation of the new standards. He refers to a recent issue of *Financial World* magazine that rated state and city governments on management practices and that included "managing for results" as a performance measurement. (See *Financial World* [March 14 and September 26, 1995].)

As noted by Martin and Kettner (1996), the influential GPRA and the related National Performance Review (NPR) initiative of the Clinton–Gore administration were heavily influenced by the accountability–performance–results context, with its emphasis on outcomes measurement. Both GPRA and NPR will affect human services into the next century. As subsequently noted by Hatry, GPRA requires that by fiscal year 1999 each major federal program be required to identify its mission, general goals, and the way that progress toward those goals should be measured, including outcomes indicators. GPRA requires programs to set annual output and outcome performance indicator targets. At the end of each year, results for each performance indicator are to be reported to Congress and the president. As Hatry notes, although national outcomes measures have been generated for years by federal agencies, GPRA will now require that outcomes data be provided at the program level. Because of the impact of federal agency requirements on other government levels and on nongovernment agencies, the effect of GPRA and NPR requirements will ultimately be felt throughout the human services.

As Hatry notes, the move toward outcomes measurement and benchmarking already has occurred at state, county, and city levels. Oregon's Benchmark program is a well-known and closely watched example of a state outcomes measurement initiative. Texas, Minnesota, Iowa, Arizona, Virginia, and Florida have introduced results-based regular measurement processes. Although GPRA and NPR have been federally initiated, these efforts have been typically legislated by the states, with some states requiring annual performance reporting (for example, Maine and Arkansas) and exploring the use of performance contracting that builds indicators of outcomes into contracts of service provision.

Another expression of the influence of developments such as those represented by GPRA and NPR is the rapidly developing idea of performance partnerships that can bring together different levels of government agencies and private organizations. Oregon Options is an example of a federal–state performance partnership. Partnerships involve joint selection of performance indicators, time-based targets for the indicators, and, in some instances, incentives such as monetary rewards or penalties.

In mental health and substance abuse, in chapter 8, Manderscheid and Henderson describe how Performance Partnership Grants (PPGs) may replace

Department of Health and Human Services' state block and categorical grants. In chapter 1, Hatry elaborates, noting that the proposed Public Health Service combination of 108 programs into 16 categories in performance-based partnerships would require grantees to report on progress toward performance targets. Proposed incentives include a small pool of funds for provision of rewards for successful performance and a state incentive allowance when outcome performance is high. A key option in performance partnerships is to give lower-level governments more flexibility in exchange for more results-based accountability.

The impact of results-based accountability on child and family services is as evident as in other human service areas. In chapter 14 Weiss views results-based accountability as a key feature of systems reform in child and family services. Weiss states that in child and family services, promising systems reform models have been results-oriented and that planning and articulating expected results and outcomes indicators are key components.

Hatry and McCroskey describe private sector outcomes measurement efforts that also pertain to child and family services, such as Kids Count, Kansas City's Partnership for Children, and the Los Angeles County Children's Planning Council efforts. Beyond child and family services, Hatry and Rossi report in chapters 1 and 2, respectively, that such regional and even neighborhood-level outcomes measurement efforts occur in various parts of the United States. An example cited by Hatry is the seven-city National Neighborhood Indicator Project administered by The Urban Institute in Washington, DC, measuring indicators that cut across programs, agencies, organizations, and levels of government.

The goals of the accountability–performance–results initiatives—whether expressed through devices such as performance contracting, performance partnerships, initiatives to group categorical programs into block grants, report cards, or results-based accountability in the human services—share a common focus on outcomes measurement for human service program improvement. These efforts all stress the need for linking outcomes to service improvement. All are motivated in part by cost containment and quality improvement. The debates regarding outcomes measurement in the context outlined in the previous paragraphs will continue to increase in force into the next century. Human service professionals should be aware of these contextual forces and the trends that push outcomes measurement into the focus of service delivery and the formulas on which funds are allocated. As Hatry points out, human service professionals must learn the game that is being played. Otherwise, the ability to direct human service policy from an offensive, as opposed to a defensive, stance may be seriously diminished. Consequently, human services for those in need will be jeopardized.

Although many forces have contributed to the push toward outcomes measurement, it is this recent accountability–performance–results context with its subthemes of cost containment and devolution of decision making that finally may consolidate, reshape, broaden, and institutionalize outcomes measurement in social work and the human services. Subsequent chapters provide a rich and diverse array of perspectives on how this context is playing out in the human services.

Administrative and Clinical Practice Context

TOTAL QUALITY MANAGEMENT

Total quality management (TQM), also referred to as continuous quality improvement (CQI), has provided an important theoretical context for some aspects of outcomes measurement (see Bowles & Hammond, 1991; Deming, 1986). Results-based accountability approaches to outcomes measurement as described earlier have been heavily influenced by the TQM and CQI management theories, such as how public agencies and human service organizations can "reinvent" themselves to monitor service delivery progress and outcomes systematically and to build organizations that can grow and withstand the changes necessary for organizational survival and the provision of more efficient and effective services while keeping costs down (for example, see Martin & Kettner, 1996; Osborne & Gaebler, 1993). Under the assumption that the most efficient economies are associated with improved quality, TQM and CQI are now regarded as a means to cost containment and as a merger of quality assurance efforts, outcomes measurement, and cost-containment goals (Donabedian, 1968).

Perhaps no human service field has been affected more by TQM and CQI theory than health and, more recently, behavioral health. In chapter 6 Berman and Hurt present an example of how a CQI framework can be used for measuring and improving behavioral health services delivery. When used in a CQI framework, they argue that outcomes data can assist in clinical decision making, program development, and the provision of better-quality services at low costs. Berman and Hurt and other authors view the measurement of outcomes as a means to an end, with that end being system improvement and quality outcomes. The TQM/CQI framework is an important context that promises to grow in importance as the human services move toward increasing effectiveness and quality.

Under the assumption that the greatest economies are associated with improved quality, TQM/CQI management theory, although initially applied in business, has now found a receptive home in human service programming. Accordingly, quality improvement is regarded as a means to cost containment, a happy joining of quality assurance and cost containment and of process and outcome. TQM/CQI theories and applications have enhanced and begun to reorient the focus on quality outputs and quality improvement systems, as central to private and public sector management and provision of human services. Fundamental to the TQM/CQI thinking is consumer/client/patient satisfaction. Information pertaining to outcomes and satisfaction should be returned to customers/clients/patients and staff so that improvement and choices can be made in the processes causing those outcomes. This emphasis on the centrality of the customer/client/patient leads directly to what we consider another significant context of human service outcomes measurement: the growth in importance of consumer interests and advocacy.

CONSUMER INTERESTS AND ADVOCACY

Although debate exists regarding whether or not consumer preference or satisfaction measures are to be considered as outcomes measures, few would disregard their importance and the power of consumers/clients/patients in the stakeholder debates regarding human service outcomes. In the face of cost-containment forces, measures of outcomes and service quality are considered by consumer groups to be an important counterbalance. In chapter 13 Wasow discusses recent developments in the mental health consumer advocacy movement, the changes that are occurring between professionals and consumers, and some core values that underlie the movement with reference to mental health. In chapter 8 Manderscheid and Henderson describe efforts that the Center for Mental Health Services have sponsored to develop outcomes measures and guidelines based on consumer perspectives. Other organizations, such as the National Alliance for the Mentally Ill, focus attention on the importance of outcomes measurement for effective service provision and also on the importance of including consumers in developing and monitoring outcomes measures that surpass consumer satisfaction variables. Given that consumer satisfaction influences choice of services and that satisfaction measures are often associated with important outcomes, the consumer perspective takes on new meaning in the marketplace of health care competition for customers in the United States. In chapter 4 Ware underscores the importance of these associations. Consumer satisfaction ratings are generally now required in health delivery systems—being mandated by the National Council on Quality Assurance—and in many large health care purchasers (Winslow, 1995). Increasingly, health insurance, health management, and health maintenance companies include satisfaction measurement in their data systems.

The consumer/client/patient stakeholder perspective and the advocacy of consumer interest groups are forces that will continue to shape outcomes measurement in human services. Although few deny the importance and obvious value of consumer reports regarding their problems, functioning, symptoms, quality of life, and experience with the human services under review, many question whether or not such self-reports should be considered outcomes measures. From this stance outcomes measures are assessments based on objective sources such as independent observers, records, professional judgments, and so forth. Yet, many consumers would consider their own self-assessments to be the most meaningful indicators of human service intervention outcomes.

MANAGED CARE

For us, managed care is a generic term that encompasses expressions of cost-containment efforts in policy or practice arenas in both the private and public sectors. Although originally applied to general health care, managed care is now present in behavioral health, family and child welfare, education, and other human services. (For a consideration of managed care in health and behavioral health, see Corcoran & Vandiver, 1996; MacLeod, 1993; Trabin & Freeman, 1996.) Although cost containment has been central to early managed care thinking, competition for both private and public payers is forcing attention to be paid to quality indicators of service outcomes. Various stakeholders, including consumers of services and their families, are pushing for outcomes and their associated costs to become central issues for managed care and government organizations to address more thoroughly. Given that managed care is an evolving and complex development, the focus in this book is on how outcomes assessment tools and other measures of outcomes and outcomes systems can be used in organizational reform and managed care and other service system reform efforts.

Critical articles by Paul Ellwood (1988) and Kathleen Lohr (1988) describe how work in outcomes assessment and general outcomes have refined thinking regarding the use of instruments to measure and evaluate outcomes and concepts of outcomes management. Booth and Smith, as well as Smith, Rost, Fischer, Burnam, and Burns, describe how outcomes assessment modules can be used as clinically cost-effective screening tools in managed care and other human service organizations. In chapter 8 Manderscheid and Henderson review the development of managed care in mental health and behavioral health.

EMPIRICAL SOCIAL WORK PRACTICE

Since the 1960s social work has been struggling with how to better integrate research into clinical practice methods. To some extent this effort was stimulated by early reports of intervention ineffectiveness. Consequently, many social work educators and researchers argued for strengthening the empirical base of clinical practice by using quantitative measurement for assessment, intervention planning, and outcomes measurement. In addition, the use of single-system designs by practitioners was advocated to monitor change toward mutually desired goals. Intervention validity is sought in empirical research evaluations of effectiveness. Reid (1994) described the development of the empirical practice movement together with its major characteristics.

In chapter 5, Hudson discusses outcomes measurement from the empirical practice context. Corcoran in chapter 10 describes one of the products of the empirical practice model, rapid assessment instruments (RAIs), and notes how they can be used as outcomes measures. The empirical practice movement has stressed the importance of assessment of individual client status changes over time to provide direct information to the client and practitioner for intervention planning. RAIs and single-system designs have been designed for such purposes, and although results from such assessments can be aggregated for group analysis, the primary focus has been at the case level. Such assessments are designed for direct use by the practitioner and client. Yet, outcomes measurement in the context of managed care has typically occurred at the aggregate level, permitting assessment of programs and groups of clients. Such aggregate assessments have been used for program accountability, profiling, development of scorecards, program improvement, and so forth. Many outcomes measures have not been validated for use at the case level, although the data are collected from client or practitioner reports. In chapter 11 Nurius and Vourlekis elaborate on the importance of maintaining the case-level focus in outcomes assessment, and their framework for this argument is influenced by the values of the empirical practice model.

In chapter 16 McCroskey describes activities in Los Angeles that focused on both system and client levels: a systems-level outcomes measurement system used for county-level planning illustrated by the Los Angeles County Children's Score Card and the Family Assessment Form (FAF), a practice-based measurement designed to help practitioners assess the impact of their work at the program level. McCroskey notes that the FAF was developed over 10 years through an interactive process involving direct service practitioners, administrators, and researchers.

For those approaching outcomes measurement from the empirical practice framework, a great concern is how outcomes measurement systems can be designed for use at the case level and at the program and policy levels of aggregation. Questions are raised about how a single outcomes measurement system can satisfy both sets of requirements. In chapter 17 Benbenishty argues for a creative solution, that is, an outcomes measurement system that is focused on a position between the program and the practitioner. He sees as a requirement of this middle-ground approach the gathering, processing, and interpretation of information by all practitioners within an agency combining to create a learning environment supporting effective practice.

Those associated with the empirical practice movement find the current emphasis on outcomes measurement to be consistent with several key components of the empirical practice model. However, as discussed by Hudson, Corcoran, Nurius and Vourlekis, and Benbenishty, given that many areas of common interest exist, significant areas of potential conflict also exist, especially pertaining to the growth of managed care.

EVALUATION RESEARCH

Rossi, in chapter 2, describes developments in evaluation research since the mid-1960s that have heightened the current interest in human service outcomes measurement. Evaluation research has been a major player and strong influence in the current outcomes measurement movement. Rossi views the current emphasis on outcomes measurement as an accelerated extrapolation of a trend originating in the 1960s, a growing emphasis on accountability and evaluation in the assessment of human service policies and programs. Rossi notes that policymakers in the 1960s began to write evaluation requirements into human services–authorizing legislation. He sees a growing skepticism among policymakers about the ability of human service policies and programs to accomplish goals and a parallel requirement that evidence about effectiveness and efficiency be produced (Rossi, 1987). He cites a fit between the remarkable capacity of measurement technology—especially computer technology—and the emphasis on accountability and evaluation. Rossi suggests that as a result of these technological developments, it is now possible to collect and analyze the outcomes data that policymakers seek.

The continuing influence of evaluation research on outcomes measurement is clear. Yet, as Rossi notes, evaluation researchers tend to value a more controlled outcomes measurement methodology than is usually evident in much of current outcomes measurement. It is likely that evaluation research will continue to be a strong force in the outcomes measurement movement, but it is not clear how that influence will be played out because the goals of formal research are not necessarily consistent with less rigourous measurement objectives. Although outcomes measurement for practice and management are typically required to be brief and nonintrusive, those for research should be robust to answer typically complex scientific questions. Higher psychometric standards are required. Social science research values objectivity and collection of data from sources unaffected by the outcomes, yet other uses typically rely on direct client and provider reports, with auditing added for accountability. The continuing role of evaluation research in human service outcomes measurement should be assessed in terms of these sometimes conflicting requirements.

Conclusion

These contextual themes will be examined in subsequent chapters. These themes share a strong push toward the production of quantitative evidence that human service policies and programs are providing some benefit to a valued stakeholder. This is a heavy burden for the human services and social work. To a large extent the ability of the human service field to satisfy the expectations that outcomes measurement initiatives have set will be determined by answers to the questions posed at the beginning of this introduction. These questions assess the approaches to outcomes measurement currently being promulgated as well as their psychometric qualities and their relevance to human service practice. Contributing authors address these questions and others in the chapters that follow.

References

Bowles, J., & Hammond, J. (1991). *Beyond quality.* New York: Berkeley.

Corcoran, K., & Vandiver, V. (1996). *Maneuvering the maze of managed care: Skills for mental health practitioners.* New York: Free Press.

Deming, W. E. (1986). *Out of crisis* (2nd ed.). Cambridge, MA: MIT Center for Advanced Engineering Study.

Donabedian, A. (1968). The evaluation of medical care programs. *Bulletin of the New York Academy of Medicine, 44,* 117–124.

Ellwood, P. M. (1988). Outcomes management: A technology of patient experience. *New England Journal of Medicine, 318,* 1549–1556.

Fischer, J., & Corcoran, K. (1994). *Measures for clinical practice.* New York: Free Press.

Freeman, M. A., & Trabin, T. (1994). *Managed behavioral health care: History, models, key issues, and future course.* Rockville, MD: U.S. Center for Mental Health Services.

Government Performance and Results Act of 1993, P.L. 103-62; 107 Stat. 285.

Hall, L. L. (1996). Report cards accelerate quality and accountability—Impact of managed care on severe mental illness: The role of report cards, consumers, and family members. *Behavioral Healthcare Tomorrow, 5,* 57–61.

Lohr, K. N. (1988). Outcome measurement: Concepts and questions. *Inquiry, 25,* 37–50.

MacLeod, G. K. (1993). An overview of managed health care. In P. R. Pongstvedt (Ed.), *The managed care handbook* (2nd ed., pp. 3–11). Gaithersburg, MD: Aspen Publishers.

Martin, L. L., & Kettner, P. M. (1996). *Measuring the performance of human service programs.* Newbury Park, CA: Sage Publications.

Mulkern, V., Leff, H. S., Green, R. S., & Newman, F. (1995). *Performance indicators for a consumer-oriented mental health report card: Literature review and analysis.* Mental Health Statistics Improvement Program Task Force on the Development of a Mental Health Care Report Card. Rockville, MD: U.S. Center for Mental Health Care Services.

Osborne, D., & Gaebler T. (1993). *Reinventing government: How the entrepreneurial spirit is transforming the public sector.* New York: Plum.

Reid, W. J. (1994). The empirical practice movement. *Social Service Review, 68,* 165–184.

Rossi, P. H. (1987). No good applied research goes unpunished. *Social Science and Modern Society, 25,* 73–80.

Sherman, P., & Kaufman, C. (1995). *A compilation of the literature on what consumers want from mental health services: A report prepared for the MHSIP Phase II Task Force on the Design of the Mental Health Component of a Healthcare Report Card.* Rockville, MD: U.S. Center for Mental Health Services.

Trabin, T., & Freeman, M. A. (1996). *Managed behavioral healthcare: History, models, strategic challenges, and future course.* Tiburon, CA: CentraLink Publications.

Winslow, R. (1995, September 25). Care at HMOs to be rated by new system. *The Wall Street Journal,* B12.

Edward J. Mullen
Jennifer L. Magnabosco

PART I

Overarching Issues and Methods

CHAPTER 1

Outcomes Measurement and Social Services: Public and Private Sector Perspectives

HARRY P. HATRY

This chapter discusses and identifies some of the public sector activity in social services outcomes measurement and encompasses some activities of private nonprofit organizations where significant activity is emerging. This is an exciting time from the viewpoint of outcomes measurement. Much activity has occurred in the past several years. Little of this activity is technically sophisticated, and it does not follow the full-fledged scope that Rossi and Ware address in chapters 2 and 4, respectively. Nevertheless, this new activity has considerable potential for helping management improve services and for providing considerable outcomes information for evaluators and for policy and program analysts.

Types of Program Evaluation

The two types of program evaluation—in-depth, ad hoc and regular outcomes measurement—are contrasted in Table 1-1.

IN-DEPTH, AD HOC EVALUATION

Researchers and professional evaluators prefer in-depth, ad hoc evaluations because such evaluations attempt to identify causes of outcomes to some extent and provide relatively strong evidence on outcomes and impact. In-depth evaluations, if designed appropriately, can also yield direct evidence as to what changes can be made to improve future outcomes. The disadvantages of these evaluations include their high cost and low coverage of agency programs. The typical program may be evaluated once every 20 to 30 years. Governments cannot afford to do many in-depth evaluations each year.

REGULAR OUTCOMES MEASUREMENT

Regular outcomes measurement, an approach in which service outcomes are tracked on a regular basis, is currently the major focus of governments and human service agencies. The advantage of regular outcomes measurement is that it can cover many

Table 1-1

TWO KEY TYPES OF PROGRAM EVALUATION

Type	Pros	Cons
In-depth, ad hoc	Identifies cause of outcomes (to some extent) Provides relatively strong evidence on outcomes and effect	High cost Very low coverage of agency programs
Regular outcomes measurement	Covers many or most agency programs Provides information on a regular basis (for example, annually or quarterly) Lower cost per covered program Hints at improvement actions Makes later in-depth evaluations easier	Provides little information on cause of outcomes Provides little information as to improvement actions

programs and offers a lower cost per covered program. Outcomes measurement also can provide information on a regular and more timely basis to managers, elected officials, and the public. This approach can be helpful in providing timely information that can affect management decisions. Outcomes information usually is provided at least annually and usually quarterly or monthly. A well-conceived outcomes measurement process can also provide program officials with hints as to how programs can be improved. Regular outcomes measurement systems can also be useful for in-depth evaluations by providing historical outcomes data streams and, if evaluators wish, can ease randomized experiments if clients who are included in the outcomes measurement process are identified as belonging either to a control or experimental group. Evaluators can tap into the process and use that readily available source for collecting future data on outcomes for each group.

Regular outcomes measurement programs, however, provide little information but hints on the cause of outcomes and little information as to improvement actions. As Rossi states in chapter 2, measurement provides gross, rather than net, outcomes. This fact has important accountability implications. Accountability issues are beyond the scope of this chapter, but I believe that no human service official can with fairness be held fully accountable for outcomes, because in the real world many other factors in addition to the subject program affect outcomes.

Most of this chapter addresses outcomes measurement that is performed on a regular basis. Regular outcomes measurement is what most governments and private human service agencies are currently considering. It is difficult for anyone to keep up with all the activity on outcomes measurement. Regular outcomes measurement is a major step forward in getting agencies, their personnel, and the public to focus on outcomes—on results—and not solely on activity.

Outcomes measurement is analogous to information commonly available to the manager of any sports team: the score. Managers need to keep track of the score to tell whether their teams are winning or losing. Scores do not provide information on why the teams are winning or losing. However, it is important for managers and the public to be able to track both outcomes and the score. In summary, outcomes measurement should provide vital but limited information. Program officials need to examine the elements of the program if the outcomes data indicate problems to assess why outcomes were low and what particular improvement options should be tried.

Status of Current Outcomes Measurement Practices in Public and Private Agencies

FEDERAL GOVERNMENT

The Government Performance and Results Act (GPRA) of 1993, which was signed into law on August 3, 1993, is important federal legislation, originated by Senate Republicans. Senator William Roth of Delaware was the lead senator in developing this bill when Republicans were in the minority. It was passed during the Clinton administration with support of the U.S. General Accounting Office and Office of Management and Budget. Both houses of Congress passed it unanimously.

GPRA calls for a form of mild strategic planning. Each major program in the federal government, including those of the U.S. Departments of Health and Human Services, Labor, Education, and so forth, is required to identify its mission, general goals, and the way in which progress toward those goals should be measured, including outcomes indicators. Consultation with Congress and other interested entities is required.

The legislation also requires each major program to set targets at the beginning of each fiscal year for each performance indicator. The performance indicators required by GPRA are outcomes and output indicators. Targets are to be set for the coming year for each of these indicators. Finally, after the end of each fiscal year, the program is required to report to Congress and the president on the actual results for each performance indicator.

GPRA wisely does not call for immediate full implementation. Regular outcomes measurement is an enormous piece of business for the federal government, which has been mostly reporting on inputs and outputs, with little outcomes information provided on a regular basis. Full implementation is called for in the act for fiscal year 1999. That time is near. Many federal agencies are already working on outcomes measurement. For example, in the fall of 1994, the Offices of the Assistant Secretary for Planning and Evaluation and the Administration for Children and Families of the Department of Health and Human Services, with the assistance of the author's organization (The Urban Institute), formed two working groups (child welfare and child health services) as pilot demonstrations. The working groups identified a set of performance indicators and attempted to identify how the data might be obtained. The child welfare working group categorized the indicators into four basic dimensions of outcomes for children: (1) safety, (2) permanence (how long the child remains in the household), (3) child development (including health, education, and other aspects of quality of life for a child), and (4) customer service (to include aspects of service quality such as timeliness, accessibility, and courtesy). The groups identified the need to consider state agencies as customers and, thus, to obtain ratings by state agencies of the quality of federal services.

Various national outcomes indicators, such as a wealth of data on health and poverty, have been regularly produced for a number of years by various parts of the federal government. However, these indicators have not provided program-level outcomes data such as data on the outcomes of specific drug control or dropout prevention programs.

STATE GOVERNMENT

Some states addressed outcomes measurement earlier than the federal government. Oregon, with its Benchmark program, is one of the leaders in the effort to identify and track indicators that focus on outcomes. Oregon has had trouble connecting its statewide indicators with the work of specific state government agencies, but state government agencies are working on this. Texas has also been at the forefront in this effort. Minnesota, Iowa, Virginia, and Florida, among others, have also been attempting to introduce results-based regular measurement processes. Most of these efforts have been brought about by the state legislature, requiring annual performance reporting that goes beyond the traditional input and physical output orientation.

Canadian provinces have also been addressing outcomes measurement. For example, Alberta has a new program called "Measuring Up" that requires each provincial agency to provide annual reports to the public that include outcomes information. This idea of annual reports to constituents that include not just which activities have occurred but also what these programs have accomplished in terms of outcomes is beginning to spread.

Examples of outcomes-focused reporting from Texas are given in Table 1-2. These examples mark a radical change in terms of what state agencies are collecting and reporting. In the past, government agencies have reported such information solely as amount of activity provided and number of clients. Reporting outcomes is a change from what states have reported in the past. The example in Table 1-2 of the "percent of mental health clients receiving in-home family support who are admitted to a state facility within two years" is even more unusual because it is expressed as a negative. For a state agency (or a local or federal agency) to report anything negative that it does not have to report is unusual. This is progress. Also of considerable interest is that these outcomes indicators were included in state legislative appropriation documents.

Figure 1-1 presents an example of outcomes reporting from the Adult and Family Services Division of the Oregon Department of Human Services. The percentage of clients getting jobs (monthly in this case) is a classic measure and a good one. Figure 1-1 illustrates the use of targets and comparisons to a baseline (5.1 percent), to

Table 1-2

EXAMPLES OF STATE OF TEXAS HUMAN SERVICE OUTCOMES INDICATORS INCLUDED IN FY 1995 BUDGET

- percentage of JOBS participants entering employment whose salary is at least minimum wage
- percentage of AFDC clients leaving AFDC rolls because of increased employment earnings
- percentage of mental health customers receiving in-home and family support who are admitted to a state facility within two years
- percentage of mental retardation customers who moved to a less restrictive living environment and the percentage who moved to a more restrictive environment
- percentage of adults completing alcohol or drug abuse treatment programs who are abstinent 60 days after discharge

Note: FY = fiscal year; JOBS = Job Opportunities and Basic Skills Training program; AFDC = Aid to Families with Dependent Children.

Source: State of Texas. (1995, May 23). Supplement to House Journal: 74th Legislature, Text of Conference Committee Report, House File No. 1 (Several Appropriations Act), Austin, TX.

a short-term target (5.5 percent), and to a "potential" high goal (10 percent). Divisions also are asked to provide explanatory information on unusual values.

Another development at the state level is *performance contracting,* which builds indicators of outcomes into contracts. For example, some early contracts on drug abuse have included targets in the contracts as to the number and percentage of clients who were off drugs after a specified period of time. The state of Maine legislated the requirement for many human service programs (which already were contracted to the private sector) to use performance contracts (State of Maine, 1994). The state, with the help of the University of Maine, has been wrestling with how to implement this requirement and to include reasonably reliable, valid indicators of outcomes. (Measurement procedures should be worked out with significant input from contractors, at least to obtain agreement on indicators.) The Department of Human Services of Arkansas also was legislated to use performance contracting at about the same time (State of Arkansas, 1993).

LOCAL GOVERNMENT

At the local government level, Sunnyvale, California, is famous as one of the first governments to address performance measurement. (One of the staff developers of GPRA had been mayor of Sunnyvale.) Sunnyvale is a small city and perhaps not of major interest from the viewpoint of human services, but it has been implementing performance measurement for some time.

Many other local governments, some before GPRA, have been working to implement results-based performance measurement. Examples are Prince William

Figure 1-1

OREGON DEPARTMENT OF HUMAN RESOURCES, ADULT AND FAMILY SERVICES DIVISION, PERFORMANCE MEASUREMENT

Measure: Percentage of clients getting jobs.

Definition: Clients getting jobs include all ADC single-parent and ADC two-parent families and all ADC applicants in job search who got a job (full-time or part-time) during the month. This sum is divided by the total caseload in these programs during the month.

Demonstrates: Clients moving into employment is one of the best overall indicators of agency program success in achieving client self-sufficiency.

Potential: The 10 percent placements rate was based on Field Services Section wanting a high goal for this measure, which is consistent with the self-sufficiency concept.

Baseline: The average placement level from October 1990 through June 1991 was used to set the baseline of 5.1 percent.

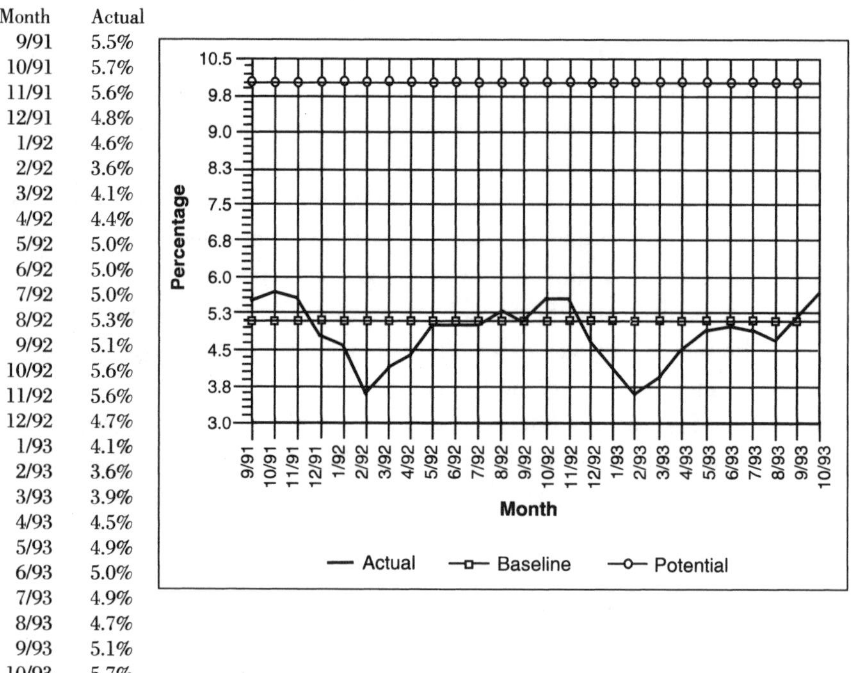

Month	Actual
9/91	5.5%
10/91	5.7%
11/91	5.6%
12/91	4.8%
1/92	4.6%
2/92	3.6%
3/92	4.1%
4/92	4.4%
5/92	5.0%
6/92	5.0%
7/92	5.0%
8/92	5.3%
9/92	5.1%
10/92	5.6%
11/92	5.6%
12/92	4.7%
1/93	4.1%
2/93	3.6%
3/93	3.9%
4/93	4.5%
5/93	4.9%
6/93	5.0%
7/93	4.9%
8/93	4.7%
9/93	5.1%
10/93	5.7%

Source: State of Oregon, Adult and Family Services Division. (1993, December 15). *Agency performance update.* Salem, OR: Author.

County, Virginia; Multnomah County, Oregon; and New York City. New York City has been preparing a Mayor's Management Report annually for many years. Its indicators for health and human services contain some outcomes and services quality data (especially response times).

Table 1-3 lists several human service outcomes indicators from the 1995–96 budget plan of Prince William County, Virginia. These kinds of indicators have seldom been collected or included in county budgets in the past. I have looked at hundreds of budgets in recent decades, and seldom, if ever, have such indicators been included. (As with state budgets, local government agency budgets most often include data on amount of activity and number of customers, rather than data on service outcomes.) Prince William County is tracking and reporting this information. (The budget plan includes data for FY 1994 for those indicators.) Note that, as with the first of the Texas indicators in Table 1-2, several of these indicators are based on data obtained from regular customer surveys.

Table 1-4 displays selected outcomes indicators (called "benchmarks") from Multnomah County, Oregon. Wherever possible, these indicators have been linked to the state's benchmark indicators. This also is the first time that I have seen explicit recognition that more than one agency contributes and shares outcomes and outcomes indicators. It takes many agencies, preferably working together, to produce favorable results on many, of not most, human service outcomes indicators.

Before leaving the government sector, I refer readers to articles in *Financial World* (Barrett & Greene, 1995a, 1995b). The September 26, 1995, article rated state governments, and the March 14, 1995, article rated the 30 largest U.S. cities on several management elements. A distinctive feature of these ratings is that one of the elements of management that the authors examined to develop their ratings was "Managing for Results." Performance measurement status was an important criterion in these ratings.

PRIVATE SECTOR

Much activity is occurring in the private sector. A substantial number of United Way organizations across the United States have begun to require, or at least encourage in a significant way, outcomes data from service agencies. United Way of America (UWA) has recently established a major national project on outcomes measurement. UWA, with participation from many local United Ways, has developed training programs that can be used by United Ways throughout the United States. The package includes training in outcomes measurement for services agencies receiving funding from United Ways. For many, if not most, of these agencies, low-cost data collection procedures are essential. At least 14 "leading edge" United Ways have been in the outcomes measurement business for a few years. For example, the United Ways of Minneapolis, New Orleans, and Milwaukee have made significant progress in working with their services agencies to encourage them and to help them provide regular data on the outcomes of services to clients. UWA (1996b) has recently published *Measuring Program Outcomes: A Practical Approach*, a guide for private nonprofit services agencies, and *Focusing on Program Outcomes: A Guide for United Ways* (UWA, 1996a).

Table 1-3

OUTCOMES/QUALITY INDICATORS

Parent–Infant Education Program

- Children who evidenced developmental concerns at entry not requiring special education preschool programs at discharge
- Families satisfied with the overall quality and effectiveness of services

Mental Health Outpatient Services

- Clients successfully maintained in the program and not discharged to state psychiatric facilities
- Consumers completing a twice yearly consumer satisfaction survey who are satisfied with services

Substance Abuse Adult Outpatient Services

- Clients completing treatment who improve in functioning

Senior Nutrition Program

- Home-delivered meals to clients started within three working days of referral

Planning and Community Programs

- Clients placed in unsubsidized employment who remain in job for three months

Administration Program

- Noncompliance findings in Virginia Department for the Aging monitoring reports

At-Risk Youth and Family Services Program

- Children not convicted of offense within two years of case closure
- Children placed in residential facilities returned to community within nine months of entering facility
- Percentage of parents/guardians participating in Level II Family Assessment and Planning Team staff who are satisfied with service delivery

Mental Retardation Residential Services

- Clients successfully maintained in the residential program and not discharged to a more restrictive environment

Long-Term Care

- Clients whose level of independence has been maintained or improved for three months or more

Senior Centers Program

- Participants who say they have increased understanding of health and lifestyle issues

Adult Day Care Program

- Family caregivers who report improvements in home environment

Source: Prince William County. (1997). *Prince William County 1997 fiscal plan* (Vol. 2). Prince William, VA: Author.

Table 1-4

MATRIX OF BENCHMARKS BY COUNTY DEPARTMENTS

Multnomah County Benchmarks	County Departments with Related Responsibilities									
	Children and Families	Health	Aging	Juvenile Justice	MCSO	DCC	DA	DES	Library	Other
Teen pregnancy— Pregnancy rate per 1,000 females ages 10–17 (by ethnicity)	✓	✓		✓						
Prenatal care— Percentage of babies whose mothers received adequate prenatal care beginning in the first trimester	✓	✓		✓	✓	✓				
Drug-free babies— Percentage of infants whose mothers did not use illicit drugs, alcohol, or tobacco during pregnancy	✓	✓		✓	✓	✓				
Immunization— Percentage of two-year-olds adequately immunized	✓	✓		✓						

Table 1-4 continues

Table 1-4 (*continued*)

Multnomah County Benchmarks	County Departments with Related Responsibilities									
	Children and Families	Health	Aging	Juvenile Justice	MCSO	DCC	DA	DES	Library	Other
Health care access/ economic—Percentage of population with economic access to health care (by ethnicity)	✓	✓	✓							
Health care access/ geographic—Percentage of citizens who have geographic access to basic health care	✓	✓	✓							
Teenagers' sexually transmitted diseases—Rate per 1,000 population ages 10–19	✓	✓		✓						

Source: Multnomah County. (1994, March 4). *Developing benchmarks for Multnomah County: A progress report* (p. 14). Portland, OR: Author.

Community foundations are a newcomer to outcomes measurement (but not necessarily to in-depth, ad hoc evaluations). Community foundations tend to look broadly across the community. The United Way effort, as well as the efforts of most federal, state, and local governments, tends to be aimed at specific programs rather than across sectors. An example of a communitywide focus is the reporting of data on the well-being of children, such as *Kids Count* data assembled in many areas in the United States. Another example is the work of Kansas City, Missouri's Partnership for Children, supported jointly by the United Way and the Greater Kansas City Community Foundation. The Partnership for Children produces a report card and data briefing book on the status of children; the outcomes are not related to specific programs or activities.

Another exciting development is evident in neighborhood indicators. A National Neighborhood Indicator Project administered by The Urban Institute in Washington, DC, currently exists among Atlanta, Boston, Chicago, Cleveland, Denver, Oakland (California), and Providence (Rhode Island). Most participants are community research institutions attempting to define a set of indicators for use by both the public and private sectors and by the neighborhoods themselves that would together be useful for tracking the health and well-being of individual neighborhoods in their cities.

A key characteristic of the neighborhood focus is that the indicators cut across programs, agencies, organizations, and levels of government. It has become clear that to examine a neighborhood or a larger community as a whole, a much broader set of indicators is needed than would be required for one specific government or private agency program. Community and neighborhood indicators need to be more holistically oriented. Data are needed from the state government, the federal government, the local government, the health department, the schools, the welfare department, and so forth. Data are also needed from neighborhood residents on aspects not measured by any of the formal organizations, such as how neighbors get along with one another, the neighborhood environment, accessibility to convenience stores, and numerous other elements that concern neighbors. (Claudia Coulton at Case Western Reserve University has done some fine work on using such neighborhood surveys [see Coulton, Korbin, & Su, 1995].) What makes neighborhood indicators feasible in the 1990s is Geographical Information Systems (GIS) technology. GIS software is now becoming widely available and practical, so that if addresses or other geographic coordinates are available for individual events, the information can be aggregated and mapped into desired neighborhood indicators (assuming the boundaries of the neighborhood can be defined).

PERFORMANCE PARTNERSHIPS

Performance partnerships have generated considerable recent discussion. For example, the U.S. Department of Health and Human Services has proposed several performance partnerships with states. Because of the difficult current political struggle between the executive and legislative branches, the disposition of these partnerships is unclear.

Performance partnerships may be, for example, between a federal agency and states, between states and their local governments, or between a government and private organizations. Performance partnerships involve joint selection of performance indicators and time-based targets for the indicators. Oregon has been a leader in working with federal agencies such as the U.S. Department of Health and Human Services to develop such agreements (the "Oregon Options" program, under development at the time of this writing, is an example of such a partnership). Performance partnerships can include incentives, such as monetary or other rewards, or penalties (monetary incentives can be difficult to include properly). For example, the U.S. Public Health Service has proposed combining 108 programs into 16 categories in performance-based partnerships that require grantees to report on progress toward performance targets (Budget of the United States Government, 1995). Proposed incentives included both a small pool of funds used to provide rewards for successful performance and more flexibility in the use of funds to states showing high performance. A key option in performance partnerships is to give lower-level governments more flexibility in exchange for more results-based accountability.

Potential Products of Outcomes Measurement Efforts

Table 1-5 provides a hypothetical example of one of the principal reports expected to emerge from an outcomes measurement process. This type of table might be produced at any level of government or by private human service agencies. This example is extracted from The Urban Institute work in the 1970s on child welfare programs. Data for the first two indicators would come from agency record data. Data for the third indicator, the percentage of children whose adjustment level improved during the previous 12 months, might come either through client surveys or from procedures called *trained observer procedures*. The fourth indicator would use data from customer surveys (the percentage of clients reporting satisfaction with their living arrangements). The format here also illustrates that outcomes reports can be used to compare previous with current performance and also to compare actual results with targets. For example, the 35 percent achievement figure for the third indicator shows improvement from the previous period but is still well below the targeted level.

Table 1-6 focuses on one key outcomes indicator. (Data are fabricated on the basis of procedures used by the New Hanover County Department of Social Services in North Carolina and the Chesapeake Bureau of Social Services in Virginia in the early 1980s.) Data on client condition levels can be obtained by administering a questionnaire to incoming clients and at a later period to assess change (but not causality). Table 1-6 illustrates consideration of the difficulty of incoming cases to avoid the temptation to cream (focus on easy-to-help clients at the expense of more difficult-to-help clients) and to provide data that can be more fairly interpreted. Difficulty levels for each incoming client can be based on an algorithm derived from each client's responses to the intake questionnaire. It is vital to distinguish client difficulty levels when examining outcomes. Table 1-6 also illustrates comparisons across similar offices while considering different mixes of client difficulty that may exist among them. Agencies can code each client as to the type and level of service each received to help relate outcomes to types and levels of service for clients with various difficulty levels, especially if clients can randomly be assigned to different

Table 1-5

ACTUAL OUTCOMES VERSUS TARGETS

Outcome	Last Period			This Period		
Indicator	Target	Actual	Difference	Target	Actual	Difference
Percentage of children returned to home within 12 months	35	25	–10	35	30	–5
Percentage of children with more than two placements within the past 12 months	20	20	0	15	12	+3
Percentage of children whose adjustment level improved during the past 12 months	50	30	–20	50	35	–15
Percentage of clients reporting satisfaction with their living arrangements	80	70	–10	80	85	+5

Note: + = improved values; – = worsened values.

levels without violating ethical concerns. Note that agencies should establish separate targets on expected outcomes (such as the percentage expected to improve) for each difficulty level. Various statistical approaches can be used to identify relations among these variables. Regular use of such technical procedures is still in the future for human service agencies, who must learn to walk before they can run with the data.

Figure 1-2 illustrates another step that can be used in human service outcomes measurement procedures to establish a causal link between a program and its outcomes. Figure 1-2 is an extract from a questionnaire that was used by the Family Services Association of America to track the results of family services programs. The first question is a basic satisfaction question. Based on the results of numerous past surveys of respondent satisfaction with various human services, I believe that most human service programs should expect to have at least 85 percent to 90 percent of respondents reporting satisfaction. Most clients are happy with human service caseworkers.

The second question addresses the outcome, that is, whether clients are better off. The third question asks respondents for their perceptions as to whether the program's

Table 1-6

OUTCOMES BY ORGANIZATIONAL UNIT BY DIFFICULTY OF PRESERVICE PROBLEMS (CHILD WELFARE PROGRAM)

	Percentage of Clients Whose Adjustment Level Had Improved 12 Months after Intake			
Difficulty of Problems at Intake	**Family Services Unit 1**	**Family Services Unit 2**	**Family Services Unit 3**	**Total**
Minor	52	35	56	47
Moderate	35	30	54	39
Major	58	69	61	63
Total	48	44	57	50

services affected the outcome. By combining the findings from the second and third questions, an agency can calculate the number and percentage of clients who reported improvement and who felt that the service contributed to that improvement. Although clients are limited in their ability to judge these matters fully, clients' perceptions are important. After all, clients are the ones receiving the services.

The public health area probably has been the leader in identifying outcomes indicators and developing data on them. Vocational rehabilitation is another area where extensive outcome measurement has occurred, perhaps because vocational and employment outcomes are readily measurable. The social services, from which I have drawn examples, are probably one of the weakest, if not the weakest, in terms of the availability of outcome information, at any level of government.

Mental health has been the subject of considerable development work, especially during the 1970s and early 1980s. Considerable good work was sponsored by the National Institute of Mental Health. Numerous instruments for assessing the status of clients' mental health were developed. Mental health outcomes appear to be grouped into four dimensions: client distress level, social functioning, client satisfaction with services, and burden on the family. Two principal approaches have been used to obtain data. One has been to use trained clinicians to make ratings. However, it can be expensive to obtain objective information (such as by using clinicians other than the clients' caseworkers to assess client status). The second and probably more popular approach has been through surveys of clients. Questionnaires on client distress have been short, containing as few as nine questions (such as that developed by Dr. James Ciarlo at the Denver Community Mental Health Center [Ciarlo & Reihman, 1974]), or they are lengthy and cover many elements of a client's mental state.

Outcomes data are intended to help people focus on what they should be achieving. Preferably, as such data become regularly available, managers will use the regular reports to call their staffs together for "how are we doing?" sessions. The groups would discuss the outcomes findings to identify where they were doing well and where they were doing poorly, and why, and then they would develop a plan for improvements. Then, perhaps six months or a year later, the groups would look at the

Figure 1-2

MAIL SURVEY QUESTIONS ON FAMILY COUNSELING

1. How satisfied were you with the way you and your counselor got along with each other?

___Very satisfied
___Satisfied
___No particular feelings one way or the other
___Somewhat dissatisfied*
___Very dissatisfied*

*Please tell us why you felt this way: ______________________________

2. Since you started at the agency, has there been any change in the way the members of your family get along with each other?

___Much better
___Somewhat better
___Same
___Somewhat worse*
___Much worse*

*Explain: ______________________________

3. How do you feel the service provided by the agency influenced the changes you have reported?

___Helped a great deal
___Helped some
___Made no difference
___Made things somewhat worse*
___Made things much worse*

*Explain: ______________________________

Source: Beck, D. F., & Jones, M. A. (1980). *How to conduct a client follow-up study.* New York: Family Service Association of America.

latest reports to see whether outcomes had improved and whether to continue, modify, or turn back their previous actions.

A Human Service Outcomes Measurement Research Agenda

BREADTH OF FOCUS

A key issue research should address is whether human service measurement should focus on all aspects of the clients' condition or on outcomes relating to specific services and programs. I have switched back and forth on this issue. The whole-client approach on the surface sounds more desirable. Data collection must cover a wide range of outcomes dimensions, regardless of the services and programs clients receive.

The program-oriented approach focuses on outcomes relevant to an individual program. It has the advantage of being much more useful to individual program managers who want to improve their programs. The outcomes information focuses much more on what an individual program is trying to do. With the whole-client approach, outcomes information can provide greater coverage of the range of client concerns. Ideally, an agency would do some of both if it has the resources.

TIMING OF FOLLOW-UP

Another research issue that should be addressed is when individual clients should be followed up to determine what the outcome has been. How long after, and after what? Should the starting point be the time the client came in for service or the time of discharge (which varies considerably)? Should the follow-up occur at three months, six months, a year, or two years? These choices depend to some extent on the nature of the program. For some programs the principal outcomes are short term (such as emergency food and shelter programs). For other programs the principal outcomes are long term (such as drug and alcohol treatment programs). However, the longer the interval is between the starting point and follow-up, the more other factors can confound the follow-up results, the less useful the information is likely to be to current operating managers, and the more difficult and more expensive it is to find former clients. Can agencies afford to follow up clients and analyze the findings at more than one time?

RESPONSE RATES

Another issue research should address is how to obtain adequate response rates, which can be a major problem. This issue is not only concerned with identifying procedures that encourage responses but also with the question of what is an adequate response rate. How much precision is necessary? If an agency receives responses from a majority of those from whom it seeks responses, is that sufficient? High levels of response provide higher precision and presumably more valid data but at greater cost and effort.

PREVENTION

A final issue is how to assess prevention, an important outcome for many human service programs, on a regular basis. How can prevention success be tracked? We currently track nonprevention. In-depth, ad hoc evaluations, especially experimental designs, are expensive and lengthy. They are not practical for regular outcomes measurement.

Conclusion

Outcomes measurement is a hot topic these days for the human services as well as other public services. It has many limitations, especially in not indicating the causes of the outcomes. However, it also has considerable value in providing human service officials and their staffs with timely evidence about the outcomes they are seeking. If you don't know the score, how can you play the game? Improving the lives of clients over what their lives would have been without the program is the game. Public and private agencies need to know whether, and the extent to which, improvements are occurring, even if these are only rough estimates. Otherwise, they are shooting in the dark on the need for improvements and actions and on the consequences of actions that the agencies have taken.

References

Barrett, K., & Greene, R. (1995a). Ranking the top 30 cities. *Financial World, 164* (7), 56–71.

Barrett, K., & Greene, R. (1995b). State of the state 1995. *Financial World, 164* (20), 36–60.

Beck, D. F., & Jones, M. A. (1980). *How to conduct a client follow-up study.* New York: Family Service Association of America.

Budget of the United States Government. (1995, January). Fiscal Year 1996 (pp. 191–195). Washington, DC: Executive Office of the President of the United States.

Ciarlo, J., & Reihman, J. (1974). The Denver Community Mental Health Questionnaire: Development of a multidimensional program evaluation instrument. Denver: Northwest Denver Community Mental Health Center.

Coulton, C. J., Korbin, J., & Su, M. (1995, June). *Measuring neighborhood context for young children in an urban area.* Research paper, Case Western Reserve University, Cleveland, OH.

Government Performance and Results Act of 1993, P.L. 103-62; 107 Stat. 285.

Multnomah County. (1994, March 4). Developing benchmarks for Multnomah County: A progress report. Portland, OR: Author.

Prince William County. (1997). *Prince William County 1997 fiscal plan* (Vol. 2). Prince William, VA: Author.

State of Arkansas. (1993). An Act to Require the State Hospital Board and the Department of Human Services to Develop and Use Performance Based Contracts, Act 1255.

State of Maine. (1994, April 20). An Act to Establish a System of Performance-Based Agreements for the Provision of Certain Social Services, Public Law 737.

State of Oregon, Adult and Family Services Division. (1993, December 15). *Agency performance update.* Salem, OR: Author.

State of Texas. (1995, May 23). Supplement to House Journal: 74th Legislature, Text of Conference Committee Report, House File No. 1 (Several Appropriations Act), Austin, TX.

United Way of America. (1996a). *Focusing on program outcomes: A guide for United Ways.* Alexandria, VA: Author.

United Way of America. (1996b). *Measuring program outcomes: A practical approach.* Alexandria, VA: Author.

CHAPTER 2

Program Outcomes: Conceptual and Measurement Issues

PETER H. ROSSI

The contemporary emphasis on assessing policies, agencies, and programs by their outcomes appears to be new. However, from a historical perspective, the emphasis on outcomes is no more than an extrapolation of the trend of the past three decades consisting of a growing emphasis on accountability and evaluation in the assessment of human service policies and programs. Social historians have yet to produce a credible account of why policymakers in the 1960s began to write evaluation requirements into legislation authorizing human service programs. One source of the change appears to be that policymakers became increasingly skeptical about whether policies and programs were able to accomplish their goals and began to ask for evidence about effectiveness and efficiency. An important factor in the emphasis on accountability and evaluation probably was that social science research technology was ready to confront the task of providing the needed evidence. Especially important was the ability of social scientists to undertake large-scale data collection and to analyze the findings. Another technical development facilitating the trend was the drastic reduction in the cost of computing: Workstations, personal computers, and accompanying software have made it possible for even the smallest agencies to have their own management information systems. Whether the technical capacity to undertake outcomes research or the growing policy interest was more important in driving the trend is unclear. What is important, however, is that currently it is possible to collect and analyze outcomes data and that policymakers are applying pressure to do so.

If the current emphasis on outcomes is nothing new, why is it worrying some of us? First, the trend appears threatening because we suspect that it is mean-spirited, carrying with it nightmarish visions of demonic policymakers shouting "Gotcha!" when our favorite policies and programs do not achieve their output production quotas. However, these nightmares are self-inflicted. Why can't we imagine the alternative, namely that our policies and programs will turn out to be effective and efficient? Alas, our nightmares also are extrapolations of the past three decades. Evaluations have not found many social programs to be effective and efficient (Rossi, 1987a). If some social program is a "magic bullet," its existence has been carefully concealed. It is not easy to design and implement effective programs. Accordingly, we fear that this discovery will be turned against all programs and not interpreted properly—as a spur to the development of programs that will be more effective and efficient.

There is an alternative to abandoning social programs because they have not turned out to be as good as we had hoped they would be: improve their targeting, delivery, and effectiveness. We need to invent programs that produce positive results and to be able to assemble credible evidence that they accomplish their intended tasks.

Programs are designed to produce results in the form of favorable outcomes. Properly identifying and measuring outcomes, therefore, are central concerns in assessing the worth of social programs. The remainder of this chapter discusses some of the major issues involved.

Defining Outcomes

When used in connection with social programs, the concept of outcomes is deceptively simple. The outcomes of a program or policy are changes, intended or not, in the program's targets that accompany exposure to the program. In human service programs, targets can be people, families, neighborhoods, schools, agencies, and firms to which the program is directed. Programs can cover a variety of activities designed to achieve intended outcomes, including the providing of information, counseling, material support, training, laws and legal sanctions, medical therapy, and so forth.

The simplicity of the definition of outcomes given above is deceptive. There are many obstacles and pitfalls to be encountered in giving specific content to the concept in concrete instances.

IDENTIFYING TARGETS

Identifying the direct targets of most programs may be relatively easy. A job training program targets people who are unemployed for some period of time. An educational program aimed at improving the numeracy of high school students clearly is directed at high school students. However, in some cases, the targets are not obvious. Some programs are directed at so-called at-risk populations whose members are difficult to identify because the at-risk state is not obvious. For example, a program intended to prevent substance abuse among youths at risk for becoming substance abusers is directed at a vaguely defined population mainly because risk factors for substance abuse are not identifiable in precise terms. Programs aimed at poorly defined targets such as communities or neighborhoods present problems because we do not know how to identify neighborhoods or communities. Is *community* properly conceptualized as the collection of people, families, or households with addresses in a given territory; the web of relationships of kinship, sociability, and exchange; or some other set of social objects connected with a given territory? Without some clarity about the definition of neighborhoods, it is difficult to identify the outcomes we should observe as indicators of program effects or outcomes.

There also is the problem of indirect or unintended targets. Most target populations are not isolated entities. School children cannot be reached independently of their schools. Women at risk for having an illegitimate child are enmeshed in relationships with others, such as the men at risk for becoming illegitimate fathers as well as members of the women's families and households. The Food Stamp program involves income maintenance agencies, food stores, and commercial banks as well as the directly targeted Food Stamp recipients. Even homeless people, perhaps the most atomized of targets, are connected with shelters, food kitchens, and medical clinics. Whatever one may do to homeless people necessarily has some impact on the agencies that serve homeless people. As we know, there are real restrictions on where shelters, halfway houses, and other services for homeless people can be placed because of reactions from people and organizations who do not relish becoming indirect targets of these programs. In short, the outcomes of programs extend beyond the entities that are intended and include those entities with close connections to them.

PERSPECTIVES ON OUTCOMES

Program changes that are positively valued are desirable outcomes. Whether an outcome is positive or negative depends on the perspective from which it is viewed. For example, a criminal justice program that is intended to reduce burglary rates has intended outcomes that are positively valued by all members of society except perhaps burglars and those who deal with stolen property. A program intended to reintegrate people discharged from mental hospitals into their families may be regarded as having positive outcomes by the mental health agency running the program if it succeeds, but it may seem to have negative outcomes by the patients or families involved. A program designed to reduce illegitimate births may also increase the use of abortion, an outcome that may be regarded as negative by many.

As in cost–benefit analyses, the perspectives from which the value of an outcome may be viewed include the society as a whole, the agency responsible for the program, and the direct and indirect targets of the program. Perhaps for most programs all perspectives yield approximately the same valuation of outcomes, but for some, different perspectives lead to different valuations of outcomes. Typically, the perspective of society as a whole (that of policymakers) dominates.

The point is that the outcomes of programs can be differentially valued, and programs can accomplish outcomes that are positive in the views of some major actors and negative in the eyes of others. The current controversy over such income maintenance programs as Aid to Families with Dependent Children (AFDC) aptly illustrates this point. For those concerned about the material welfare of single mothers and their children, AFDC outcomes in the form of income maintenance are positive; for others, the reduced work levels of AFDC recipients resulting from income maintenance are viewed as negative outcomes.

In the past decade it has become fashionable to advocate for a definition of outcomes of a program as the negotiated consensus among the major stakeholders. In most cases, this viewpoint leads to few problems because the major stakeholders share the same view of the desired outcomes, but there are some programs in which the views of policymakers, funding organizations, program operators, and target populations differ widely. There are no rules about which perspectives should hold in the case of such conflicts, although I would predict that the views of policymakers and funding organizations typically prevail.

INTENDED AND UNINTENDED OUTCOMES

It is customary to distinguish between intended outcomes—those related to the objectives of a program—and other outcomes, usually designated as *unintended.* Although one might expect that the latter are undesirable outcomes, that is not always the case. Once in a while we get more than we ask for.

By definition, intended outcomes are easily identified because programs usually articulate their intentions, whereas unintended outcomes are more difficult to anticipate. The identification of unintended outcomes often depends heavily on good theoretical understanding and substantive knowledge of the human activity domain with which a program deals. For example, in the income maintenance experiments, an expected but unintended consequence of the program of guaranteed income was a reduction in work effort. This outcome was anticipated on the basis of economic theory that predicted lowered levels of work effort when income guarantees were in place. Basic knowledge concerning the economic ties underlying marriage also led the investigators to anticipate the unintended outcome of higher rates of marital dissolution when the guaranteed income supports rules allowed divorced spouses to divide their entitlements (Robins, Spiegelman, Weiner, & Bell, 1980). Similarly, basic knowledge concerning how "street level" bureaucrats typically circumvent agency rules of which they do not approve led researchers to anticipate that closing down general assistance in Michigan would lead to a compensating rise in Supplemental Security Income rolls as workers shifted former general assistance clients to that program (Danziger & Kossoudji, 1994).

These examples point out that the identification of potential unintended outcomes depends on basic knowledge concerning the social problem in question and the actions of organizations involved. An appropriate example is a study I made some years ago of the outcomes of information programs sponsored by a state Department of Environmental Protection (Rossi & Will, 1989). The information program was designed to heighten public concern about the quality of drinking water and water used for recreational purposes in streams and on the beaches. On the basis of knowledge of other information campaigns, I reasoned that the program might be successful in arousing public concern about water quality but that it might have an offsetting unintended outcome of lowering satisfaction with the activities of the state agency. That turned out to be the case: the more concerned members of the public were about water quality, the less convinced they were that the agency was operating effectively.

In addition, the interests of policymakers often direct attention to possible unintended outcomes about which they have expressed concern. For example, not only did economic theory suggest that income maintenance plans might discourage work effort, but questions were raised about that issue by members of Congress.

There also is a more general point. Social science theory and basic knowledge should be involved in the design of effective social programs and in the identification of outcomes of such programs. However, blind trial-and-error strategies appear to dominate those activities. Perhaps the major reason for the dominance of trial-and-error strategies is the poverty of theory in most social science fields, the possible exception being economics. In addition, programs often are designed by practitioners and policymakers, many of whom are attorneys, both groups far removed from theory and basic social science knowledge.

OVERLY OPTIMISTIC OUTCOMES EXPECTATIONS

Program designers and operators can be expected to advertise their programs as having desirable outcomes. Probably no funding source would provide the means to run a program whose designers and operators did not expect it to be effective. Furthermore, program designers and operators can be expected to claim higher anticipated outcome levels than might be found after careful empirical investigation. In large part, these inflated outcome expectations reflect the enthusiasm of advocates, but they also help to obtain support from sponsors.

The fires of enthusiasm also produce inflated views of the size of the social problem to which a program may be directed. This inflationary tendency has been phrased as "the iron law of vanishing target populations"; as soon as a systematic evaluation is started, target populations shrink by up to a third of prior estimates. In my own work estimating the size of Chicago's homeless population in the mid-1980s, the empirically based estimates of the number of Chicago homeless were little more than one-tenth of the number claimed by advocates for homeless people (Rossi, 1987b).

What this inflation means for those who may try to estimate the size of outcomes of a program is that research designers can often severely underestimate the power needed to demonstrate outcomes. Taking the advocates' guesses seriously, I drew a sample in Chicago that was too small and had to go back to my funding source for additional funds to supplement the initial sample (Rossi, 1989).

It usually is wise to deflate what program advocates expect to be the size of program outcomes to calculate the needed power of a research design for outcome estimation. It probably is safe to expect that outcomes will turn out to be less than one-half of advocates' estimates. Overall, social change usually occurs in small increments: Likewise, changes fostered by social programs typically are small and unspectacular, especially when contrasted with what is expected of them. Although it is important to have strong arguments in advancing a program, perhaps program advocates should exercise more modesty and self-restraint in advancing effectiveness claims for social programs. Those who make outlandish claims may have cause to regret having done so.

GROSS AND NET OUTCOMES

In a simpler world, all the outcomes observed after a program has been implemented can be interpreted as having been caused by the actions of the program. Unfortunately, in the real world, this is not the case. The outcomes of interest often are the results of multiple causes, and the program is just one among many. What typically is observed after a program has been implemented are "gross" outcomes, consisting of the effects of the program plus the effects of all of the other processes that also led to such outcomes. A program targeted to 14-year-olds to reduce the proportion who drop out before high school graduation is bound to find that most participants will graduate high school by age 19. However, that would be the case without any program: Currently, most 14-year-olds will graduate high school by age 19. What is of interest is whether more youths graduate high school after participating in the program than if they had not participated. That is, we are interested in "net" outcomes, changes that would not have occurred without the program.

One illustration of the sometimes dramatic differences between gross and net outcomes is provided by the history of evaluation of family preservation programs (Rossi, 1991). These are programs designed to avoid unnecessary foster care placements of abused or neglected children by six to eight weeks of intensive casework with the families. Early "evaluations" of the program claimed effectiveness rates of more than 80 percent, based on the observation that 80 percent or more of the treated families did not experience foster care placements in the year following completion of the treatment. The implicit assumption underlying this extraordinary effectiveness claim is that all or most of the children would have been sent to foster care if their families had not been exposed to family preservation treatment. However, randomized experiments on family preservation programs showed that participating families and families randomized to control groups experienced the same placement rates, ranging between 10 percent and 25 percent. In short, gross and net outcomes measures were vastly different, meaning that the assumption was false that most or all of the families treated would have experienced a foster care placement without the treatment.

The estimating of net outcomes is one of the most challenging tasks in evaluating social programs. Gross outcomes are easy to obtain: The challenge is in devising credible estimates of what would have happened without the program, estimates that are necessary for the calculation of net outcomes. Although there is not complete consensus on how best to make net outcomes estimates, the preferred mode in the evaluation profession is to conduct randomized field experiments (Rossi & Freeman, 1993). Under a limited set of circumstances, it is possible to conduct randomized field experiments. For instance, it is necessary to have the funds and time to conduct them. All of the alternative approaches, encompassing the various forms of quasi-experiments, yield estimates that are less credible but better than either judgment calls or the assumption that the differences between gross and net outcomes are nonexistent or negligible.

It is likely that in most attempts at outcomes assessment, either randomized experiments or approximations simply are out of the question. The critical issue then lies in identifying the standards against which a given measured level of outcome is to be judged. A common solution is to judge a program or agency against some measure of central tendency computed over some large set of agencies or programs. For example, a hospital's performance in coronary bypass surgery might be judged by its death rate for patients undergoing that procedure compared with the average of death rates for all hospitals in the state or region. A foster care reunification program run by an agency might be judged by the proportion of cases successfully reunited compared with other agencies in the same jurisdiction.

There are serious problems with comparing program or agency outcomes with some statistical norm. The major problem is illustrated by an apocryphal story: When then governor of Georgia, Lester Maddox, was asked by journalists why the Georgia prison system was near the bottom on each of a series of quality measures of prison systems in the 50 states and what he was going to do about improving the Georgia prison system, Maddox is reputed to have responded that he could not improve the prisons of Georgia until they got a better class of prisoners. Maddox's point was that prison system outcomes have to be judged in relation to the difficulty presented by the clients of the system. More generally, comparisons with normative standards uncorrected for the nature of an agency or program's clientele penalizes those who deal with more difficult clients. It is tempting to think that this problem can easily be solved by adjustments that take such differences among agencies or programs into account, but for most programs we may not know enough about how client mixes affect outcomes independent of the programs in question. Accordingly, adjustment schemes can become a matter over which considerable rancorous conflict can develop.

A discussion of the issues involved in the design and interpretation of net effect estimates of various sorts could be the focus of an entire series of books. See Rossi and Freeman (1993) for an introductory discussion of the issues and the references cited there for more technical treatments.

GENERAL WELL-BEING MEASURES VERSUS PROGRAM-SPECIFIC OUTCOMES

Should outcomes be conceptualized as general measures of well-being, or are they tailored to the specific features of social programs? Perhaps the most general well-being measure is "happiness," which is clearly the ultimate goal of every social program. Examples of other general well-being outcomes for clients include self-esteem, family functioning, life satisfaction, and quality of life. In contrast, a program-specific outcome is a specific goal of a social program: For example, family preservation programs have as one of their major specific goals the prevention of out-of-home placement of abused or neglected children. A critical advantage claimed for the general well-being outcomes is that they may provide a kind of general outcome currency allowing for the comparison of many different programs, providing answers to such effectiveness questions as whether AFDC increases the general happiness of AFDC clients more than gainful employment, whether single-gender high school education increases the self-esteem of students compared with coeducational high schools, or whether homeowners experience a higher quality of life than people who rent their homes.

The main difficulty with using general well-being measures as outcomes stems from the fact that they are the result of many influences, the effects of which are likely to overshadow those resulting from any one program. Surely members of a family that can avoid having a child placed in foster care is likely to be happier and have higher self-esteem, but there are many other life processes that may be affecting those general outcomes in much stronger ways, such as employment or substance abuse of a family member, likely drowning out the effects of family preservation. In contrast, family preservation may have had a clear specific effect in the prevention of foster care. In general, a program has a markedly greater chance of affecting its clients in relatively specific ways closely tied to program processes than affecting general well-being outcomes.

Identifying Valid and Useful Outcomes

A valid intended outcome of a program is one that people who are knowledgeable about the program mostly agree that the program seeks to accomplish. A useful outcome can be measured by quantification, either by enumeration or by giving numerical values to empirical observations.

IDENTIFYING PROGRAM OUTCOMES

By definition, a program is a communal action set in place by a communal body to accomplish a specific purpose or set of purposes. For example, a school board may adopt a high school dropout prevention program to reduce the proportion of students who leave school before attaining their high school diplomas, a state child welfare agency may adopt a family preservation program to reduce the number of unnecessary out-of-home placements of abused and neglected children and to ensure the safety of children who are the victims of such abuse and neglect, or a city council may establish a neighborhood development program to improve housing and employment opportunities in specified neighborhoods. The purposes of a program as stated by those who authorized it identify the class of outcomes that are to be associated with the program. It is useful to characterize the stated purposes of a program as its goals or objectives, recognizing that, as usually stated, goals are general and sometimes far removed from measurable outcomes.

Determining the goals of a program has developed into a subspecialty within the discipline of evaluation. For example, the "evaluability analysis" propounded by Wholey (1979) recommends a set of research procedures designed to make program goals explicit. The first place to look for the goals of a program is in its authorizing legislation, broadly construed to include the formal actions of all sorts of organizations including legislatures, governing boards of nonprofit organizations, and so forth. The deliberations that led to the legislation are another source for identifying such goals, objectives, and purposes. The officials responsible for administering a program also are a useful source for this purpose. Only if some definite goals emerge from this research process can the outcomes be identified. Wholey declares a program "unevaluable" if it is not possible to identify its goals: A program without goals in the form of identifiable outcomes cannot be assessed.

In some instances, programs are defined as processes with vague general goals. For example, the Neighborhood and Families Initiative (NFI) of the Ford Foundation has as its goal the improvement of lower-income inner-city neighborhoods, which covers a large and possibly infinite number of outcomes. The Ford Foundation has given grants to four local foundations with the directives to start up community organizations to be known as neighborhood collaboratives that are to design and carry out integrated community programs. The University of Chicago Chapin Hall Center for Children has taken on the task of evaluating the NFI. Identifying NFI outcomes will be a difficult, perhaps impossible, task.

When the goals of a program can be identified, the task of converting goals into outcomes remains. There often are significant gaps between the stated purposes of a program and practical indicators of those goals or outcomes. For example, a family preservation program may have enhancing family functioning as one of its stated objectives. This clearly is a desirable goal, but it must be given specific content in the form of outcomes that can be measured and counted. Good family functioning can be defined as appropriate fulfillment of major family functions, including shelter and food; proper socialization experiences for children including discipline, learning, and physical growth; psychological support for family members; access to medical care and education for children; and so forth. By examining the kinds of casework typically accomplished by family preservation workers, it may be possible to determine which aspects of family functioning the family preservation treatment actually attempts to affect. For example, few such programs attempt to change family income or school achievement, but a great deal of attention may be given to proper discipline of children and prompt attention to their medical needs, suggesting that the specific family functioning outcomes for family preservation programs should include the latter and not the former, as discussed earlier in the section titled "General Well-Being Outcomes versus Program-Specific Outcomes."

There may be broad consensus about what the goals of a program are, but there also may be great disagreement on how to translate those goals into measurable outcomes. Accordingly, program outcomes typically are more controversial than program goals.

MULTIPLE VERSUS SINGLE OUTCOMES

Few programs have single goals or objectives. Typically a program has several goals. Job training programs usually have the goals of fostering employment and higher income; family preservation programs usually aim to reduce unnecessary out-of-home placements and to enhance family functioning, child well-being, and child safety; and the school lunch program aspires to enhance caloric intake, achieve balanced nutrition, and increase the consumption of dairy products. The multiple goals may be closely and positively related, as in the case of employment and wages, or, in other cases, potentially contradictory, as in the school lunch program in which the goal of reducing surplus stocks of cheese and butter may contradict the goal of promoting balanced nutrition by introducing too much fat into the school lunch menu.

Multiple goals inevitably lead to multiple outcomes. That there may be several outcomes occasionally leads to problems because major stakeholders sometimes insist that a given program can only have a single goal or that contradictory outcomes are not acceptable. These controversies usually can be settled by introducing the idea that multiple outcomes can be presented as a profile of outcomes.

Multiple goals cause some technical difficulties. Correlated outcomes often are not independent of one another. The higher earnings of people who have gone through job training programs partially reflect their higher rates of employment. Students' higher grades in mathematics may be closely related to their high grades in language skills. In some cases, such interrelatedness may indicate causal sequences and in other cases may reflect alternative measures of the same underlying phenomenon. In either case, the analysis of outcomes may mean the use of statistical models that can properly capture their meaning. Causally related outcomes may have to be modeled as such and alternative measures combined into a single measure through the use of data reduction methods such as factor analyses.

PROXIMAL VERSUS DISTAL OUTCOMES

Program goals often are stated as long-term changes in program targets. For example, a program directed at enhancing the sense of social responsibility among high school students may express its goal as affecting students' employment behavior as adults, perhaps a decade or more after adolescence. In principle, there is nothing wrong with such a distant objective: In practice, however, goals that are to be achieved years after the program is in place are impractical. The decision-making cycles of policymakers run on short time schedules that cannot accommodate periods longer than a few years at most.

Fortunately, it usually is possible to convert distant objectives into outcomes that can be discerned in the short term. There are few theories of behavior that give much credence to so-called sleeper effects, changes that occur abruptly at some point in time distant from their early causes and without discernible intervening changes. Usually we expect changes to be cumulative and incremental. A socially responsible mature adult typically also has been a socially responsible adolescent and young adult. This means that we can measure outcomes that occur on the way to a final state. If a preschool program intends to affect the earnings of its pupils as adults, it may be possible to measure outcomes that are consistent with that goal but that occur close enough in time to be practical to use in the measurement of that program's effectiveness and efficiency.

Of course, there is another danger that must be confronted. There may be few examples of sleeper effects, but there are many examples of the extinction of behavior over time. Gains in cognitive functioning achieved in preschool may disappear by the second or third grade. Good parenting practice gains after participating in a family support program may diminish after a year or more. A large proportion, perhaps a majority, of successful graduates of alcohol abuse programs experience subsequent bouts of alcoholism. At best, the influences of social programs are minor, easily overshadowed by subsequent experiences. The loss of positive outcomes over time has led some commentators to suggest that programs should be aimed at systemic rather than individual or small group change, reasoning, for example, that recovering alcoholics should not be returned to the environments that fostered their addiction but that programs ought to be concerned with changing underlying conditions rather than repairing individuals harmed by such conditions.

ENDOGENEITY

It also is necessary to avoid endogeneity in specifying program outcomes. An outcome that is equivalent to the program's activities cannot be an acceptable outcome. As stated earlier, a program is an activity directed at achieving some set of outcomes and can be judged only by whether those outcomes are realized. Perhaps the most obvious example of endogenous outcomes would be a program aimed at substance abusers that claims that one of its major goals is the recruitment of drug abusers into the program. Clearly, for a substance abuse program to exist it must recruit substance abusers, but recruitment cannot be an end in itself. Sometimes endogenous outcomes are more subtle. For example, a family preservation program that claims that one of its outcomes is avoiding the out-of-home placement of children while their families are participating in the program is stating an outcome that is close to being the program itself. Typically, a family recruited into a family preservation program is offered participation as an alternative to the agency taking custody of the abused or neglected child, amounting to the promise of a moratorium on placement. The fact that a child in a recruited family is not taken into custody while in the program restates the existence of a moratorium and is not in itself an outcome of the program.

Recent trends in evaluation styles emphasize the study of program processes, some to the point of equating evaluation with the study of program processes. The statements in this chapter about program processes are not to be interpreted as opposition to such views. The close study of how programs are implemented is extremely important in understanding why programs succeed or fail. Such evaluative activities also are critical to the design of programs and their fine-tuning, amounting in many instances to technical assistance and management consultation. However, when it comes to judging whether a program achieves its purposes, outcomes are the criteria. A poorly implemented program most likely cannot achieve its intended outcomes, but a well-implemented program also might not produce positive results.

CLIENT SATISFACTION MEASURES AS OUTCOMES

Some programs have target or client satisfaction as one of their goals, and many program evaluations measure the extent to which the clients of a program are satisfied with the services they have received, the caseworkers assigned to them, or other aspects of the programs being evaluated. Sometimes these measures are presented as evidence of program effectiveness. Sometimes evaluators have asked clients to judge whether the program has been effective for them.

Client satisfaction measures can be useful information for program managers. To the extent that a program needs the goodwill and cooperation of targets to be implemented properly, client satisfaction measures may provide critical feedback useful for fine-tuning. For example, a well-baby medical clinic that finds high levels of dissatisfaction with its hours of operation probably should consider alternative schedules.

For some kinds of programs, client satisfaction is rarely measured (or even contemplated). For example, the evaluation of a law enforcement program designed to deter burglars would likely never consider conducting a satisfaction survey of potential burglars even though evidence of deep dissatisfaction with the program might be viewed as evidence of successful implementation.

Measuring client satisfaction is not a bad idea, but such measures usually are not worthy of being regarded as evidence for program success or failure. Such measures may be regarded as evidence of successful implementation of a program but by themselves cannot be regarded as evidence that the program has caused any changes.

THE INTEGRITY OF OUTCOMES MEASURES

Outcomes are important measures having the potential of affecting the actions of sponsors, the fate of programs, and the well-being of clients. Sponsors may use outcomes measures in their decisions as to whether to continue a program and whether funding levels should be increased or decreased. Program personnel may be rewarded according to program outcomes. Clients, present and future, may benefit from services. Outcomes are numbers suffused with political meaning, in the broad sense of *political*. Accordingly, every precaution needs to be taken to guard their integrity and authenticity. More so than with respect to other kinds of measures, it is important to reduce the possibility of bias and to ensure that the measures are as reliable as social science measures can be.

An elementary precaution against bias in outcomes measures is to locate the collection of observations that go into outcomes measures as far as possible out of the direct control of those directly affected by the outcomes measures. Some programs ask personnel to collect such observations. Although social workers probably are no less honest than members of any other occupational group, their opinions on whether the clients they served have improved because of their program participation may result in outcomes measures that may be biased in favor of the program Similarly, asking clients whether a program in which they have participated affected them is also subject to potential bias.

A subtle example of "interested participant bias" occurred in a large-scale randomized experiment testing the effectiveness in reducing recidivism of unemployment benefits given to felons released from two large state prison systems (Rossi, Berk, & Lenihan, 1980). The experiment relied on two measures of recidivism, self-reports of arrests obtained from interviews with the released prisoners taken at three-month intervals during the year after release and official arrest records as recorded in the files of local police departments and in consolidated records of arrests and convictions recorded in Federal Bureau of Investigation (FBI) files. As anyone might expect, the self-reports yielded arrest and conviction counts that were significantly lower than either police department records or FBI rap sheets.

The same reporting bias was found among high school principals in Taiwan who were asked by the Taiwanese ministry of education to enumerate drug abusers among their students at several points in time (Chen, 1995). The ministry of education used the trends in drug abuse over time in the schools to judge the effectiveness of the high school drug abuse programs run by the principals, rewarding those whose schools showed a decline in drug use and punishing those who did not report declining numbers. As soon as the principals found out how their enumerations were used, the enumerations rapidly converged to approximately the same low proportions of drug users in all Taiwanese high schools. The released felons may have been shading the truth to present a more law-abiding appearance, but there is strong evidence that the principals were "cooking" their data, aided by not having the knowledge or resources to conduct surveys by scientifically acceptable procedures.

A more subtle sort of self-report bias may be at work in the recently reported decline in birthrates of the New Jersey AFDC population after a "family cap" limitation on AFDC payments was imposed. The limitation meant that women on the AFDC rolls who gave birth to additional children would not have their monthly payments increased. The outcomes measure, births occurring to AFDC mothers, is a self-report to the AFDC agency. The suspicion is that placing the family cap provision into place undermined AFDC mothers' motivation to report births because their payments would not be affected one way or the other by such reports (Myers, 1995). The observations on which outcomes measures should be based should not be made the responsibility of organizations or people who can be affected by the outcomes.

It also is possible to go beyond this recommendation, possibly to the point of conducting data audits to ensure the authenticity of data. For example, to use foster care placements as recorded in the administrative database for a child welfare agency, data audits can be conducted to test the authenticity of data entries. Audits might include checking whether data entries indicating a child has been placed in foster care are matched by corresponding entries in foster care records. Similarly, foster care records indicating that children are in foster care should be matched by corresponding records in the administrative database. In any database, we can expect that there will be errors indicated by record mismatches. Whether records are good enough to use depends ultimately on judgment calls concerning what is to be regarded as an acceptable error rate.

Conclusion

First, the current emphasis on program outcomes is not new but is the continuation of a trend starting in the 1960s. However, if you are threatened by it, there is reason to think you are not paranoid because there is someone out there who is out to get you. Furthermore, you know who it is.

Second, there is nothing complicated about the concept of outcomes, but to get to the measurable consequences of programs is difficult and complex. What is most difficult of all is that the focus is not on the changes that occur to the targets of programs after participating in a program but rather on net outcomes that credibly can be attributed to the programs in question, over and above what would have happened without the program.

Third, other difficulties are encountered in identifying target populations. The prime example is presented by at-risk populations, mainly because in the present state of knowledge concerning social problems, we typically do not understand enough to calculate risk with sufficient precision. In some programs it is not possible to identify intended outcomes, and such programs cannot be evaluated.

Fourth, social programs usually have multiple intended outcomes and often several unintended ones as well. Although we usually can identify the intended outcomes of social programs, we need to know more about how programs work to be able to anticipate their unintended consequences.

Fifth, because measured outcomes can have consequences for programs and for their clients or targets, we must strive to measure them reliably and in an unbiased manner. Indicators that measure program processes amount to tautologies in the form of restatements of the program and do not qualify as legitimate measures of its outcomes. Outcomes measures based on observations made by people who have stakes in the outcomes have the potential of being biased. Observations that go into outcome measures should come from sources other than program participants or program personnel. Auditing such observations to be able to certify their authenticity also may be a good idea.

Finally, despite all the difficulties enumerated in this chapter, the effectiveness and efficiency of a program can be assessed only by estimating a program's net outcomes. To improve social welfare, programs must be devised that clearly produce significant increments in positively valued outcomes: these efforts can be guided by measuring the net outcomes of programs and revising them accordingly.

References

Chen, H. (1995). *The "effectiveness" of a drug abuse education program in Taiwan.* Unpublished manuscript, University of Toledo, OH.

Danziger, S. K., & Kossoudji, S. A. (1994). *What happened to former GA recipients?* Ann Arbor: University of Michigan School of Social Work.

Myers, R. (1995). *New Jersey's "family cap": Measuring the effects.* Trenton: New Jersey Department of Human Services.

Robins, P. K., Spiegelman, R. G., Weiner, S., & Bell, J. G. (1980). *A guaranteed annual income: Evidence from a social experiment.* New York: Academic Press.

Rossi, P. H. (1987a). The iron law of evaluation and other metallic rules. In J. Miller & M. Lewis (Eds.), *Research in social problems and public policy: Vol. 4* (pp. 3–20). Greenwich, CT: JAI Press.

Rossi, P. H. (1987b). No good applied research goes unpunished. *Social Science and Modern Society, 25* (1), 73–80.

Rossi, P. H. (1989). *Down and out in America: The origins of homelessness.* Chicago: University of Chicago Press.

Rossi, P. H. (1991). *Evaluating family preservation services.* New York: The Edna McConnell Clark Foundation.

Rossi, P. H., Berk, R. A., & Lenihan, K. J. (1980). *Money, work and crime: Experimental evidence.* New York: Academic Press.

Rossi, P. H., & Freeman, H. (1993). *Evaluation: A systematic approach* (5th ed). Newbury Park, CA: Sage Publications.

Rossi, P. H., & Will, J. A. (1989). *Public opinion on environmental problems and programs in Massachusetts.* (Publication No. 89-5, the Environmental Institute and the Social and Demographic Research Institute). Amherst: University of Massachusetts Press.

Wholey, J. S. (1979). *Evaluation: Promise and performance.* Washington, DC: The Urban Institute.

CHAPTER 3

Outcomes Measurement: Where We Are

BRENDA M. BOOTH

G. RICHARD SMITH, JR.

This chapter presents the state of patient outcomes assessment. Issues discussed include the success of outcomes measurement to date, issues of scientific debate, and challenges present and future. Paul Ellwood (1988) and Kathleen Lohr (1988) described outcomes assessment and outcomes management in general, and their articles were not limited to a particular area of human services. Although most of the research on outcomes assessment and outcomes management conducted by our group at the University of Arkansas and the Little Rock Veterans Affairs Medical Center has been in mental health or behavioral settings, the concepts can be generalized to other health care and services settings. Development of instruments to measure and evaluate outcomes and to refine the concepts of outcomes management is based on the thinking and principles described by Ellwood and Lohr. The principles and issues addressed in this chapter can be applied to health care; primary care and specialty care; and medical, surgical, mental health, or other settings. Where appropriate, these principles can also be generalized to service settings such as child welfare centers.

Objectives of Patient Outcomes Assessment

Clinicians use patient outcomes assessment to evaluate patient characteristics, processes of treatment, and outcomes of routine care to monitor or improve treatment and outcomes. Some key words and concepts here are *assessment; routine care;* and *establishing the linkages among patient characteristics, process of care, and patient outcomes.* Remarkable advances in the science of patient outcomes assessment have occurred. For example, outcomes measurement has become increasingly precise and reliable in quantifying the elements of treatment for a variety of general health and mental health conditions. Critical outcomes domains can be defined for many medical and mental health disorders with a remarkable degree of consensus. These domains can be measured with confidence. Outcomes assessment now is used to link patient self-report data with diagnostic and treatment data, chart review data, and patient outcomes. Concurrently, the results of these assessments are being used to improve care and to hold accountable those who provide care. Health care organizations currently are conducting outcomes assessments with varying degrees of success. At this point, however, although much has been accomplished, there are still many issues being debated and a number of critical challenges ahead.

Areas of Success

It now is clear that patient outcomes assessment is feasible in routine clinical settings in both the public and private sector. Providers, payers, and clinicians are becoming increasingly knowledgeable about outcomes assessment and are demanding outcomes information. Purchasers of health care, such as large employers and public payers, now insist that providers demonstrate that the services they provide are useful and cost-effective. The following are a few examples of successful implementations in the mental health field:

- A large, innovative managed behavioral care company developed its own outcomes assessment program. The company found that a substantial number of clients who were referred for treatment of substance abuse never returned for care after one or two visits. Subsequently, the company initiated a follow-up project to determine the causes and consequences of this nonengagement in treatment.
- The employee assistance program (EAP) of a large service organization initiated an outcomes assessment program to monitor the outcomes and treatment of the employees whom the EAP referred for care. The program revealed that certain providers were incorrectly diagnosing bereavement as major depression. They began to discuss this observation with their network of providers to improve diagnostic accuracy and, consequently, the quality of care provided.

The current reality is that the demand for outcomes assessment may be driven by third-party payers, including managed care organizations, or by employer groups negotiating managed care contracts. Outcomes assessments are being conducted in all areas of health care, as well as in service areas such as family centers, with varying degrees of success and instrumentation.

Major progress has occurred recently in two areas: in defining the domains of outcomes that should be assessed and in developing patient–consumer based scales and indices. These domains have generally been agreed on as the areas of importance by those leading the outcomes movement. Most are relevant across all areas of health including functioning, disability, quality of life, patient satisfaction, general health status, and mental health status. Knowledge of measuring these issues has been considerably advanced by work at RAND and by John Ware and his research group as described in chapters 4 and 18. Many of these accomplishments are now a standard part of most outcomes assessments as reflected in several chapters in this book (chapters 4, 5, 8, 18, and 19) (Ware & Sherbourne, 1992). Much of the work on generic assessment has been conducted during the past 15 years. Part of the achievement in assessment of general domains has been in the development and refinement of shorter measures that require minimal time and resources from clients or clinicians. Advances in technology also have reduced the time and resources required for general outcomes assessment. Other domains are specific to the disorder and have been developed by field experts and professional organizations. These disease-specific domains have been defined for a wide variety of conditions including asthma, cataracts, chronic back pain, substance abuse, and major depression.

High-quality tools now are available for objective measurement of clinical status for many disorders, general health status, quality of life, general mental health status, health care utilization, and patient satisfaction. Most of these tools have demonstrated acceptable reliability and validity (Hollenberg, Rost, Humphrey, Owen, & Smith, 1997; Rost, Ross, Humphrey, Frank, Smith, & Smith, 1996). However, health care use measures generally do not assess the nature or quality of what occurs during treatment but are usually more objective measures such as number of outpatient visits or number of hospital days.

Issues of Scientific Debate

At least five areas of scientific debate about outcomes measurement are important because of their practical and theoretical implications. These areas include disorder-specific versus general assessment, sampling versus assessment of an entire population, assessment of tracer conditions versus assessment of all disorders, brief assessments versus precise, multidimensional studies, and assessment logistics.

DISORDER-SPECIFIC VERSUS GENERAL ASSESSMENT

If the major goal of outcomes assessment is to understand the effectiveness or quality of care, there is not yet consensus as to whether these systems should be specific to the disorder or broadly generic. Conceptually, specific knowledge of a disease, its treatment, and disease-specific outcomes is usually necessary to understand the relationship between treatment and the desired outcomes. However, there is not uniform agreement on this issue. For example, several large, proprietary behavioral outcomes assessment systems use one assessment approach for all patients. These systems generally are designed to measure generic mental health symptoms including symptoms of anxiety, depression, distress, and disordered thinking.

General or generic assessment is logistically and administratively simpler, allowing for use of the same instrument, rather than different tools for different disorders, across all patients, clients, or consumers. One advantage of general assessment is that it allows for direct comparisons among disorders. In addition, generic assessment is a valid method when the end point of this approach is assessment of the general health or functioning of a large population. However, in many or most cases, it is unlikely that general assessment alone will yield productive information on effectiveness or quality of care for specific diseases or health conditions. This lack of specificity exists because the treatment process varies so widely among conditions and critical outcomes domains are generally condition dependent. For example, the treatment and critical outcomes domains for patients with asthma and patients with cataracts are vastly different.

Combination approaches, including both generic and disorder-specific elements, may be both straightforward and specific. One method involves a generic assessment at baseline (or initiation of treatment), which takes advantage of the logistic simplicity of the generic approach, and a disorder- or disease-specific assessment at follow-up when organization into disorder-specific groups can be more easily conducted via administrative or outcomes databases. Another approach is to combine generic and disorder-specific domains both at baseline and at follow-up. This method allows for comparison among disorders for general measures of health and functioning and for more focused measurement of disease-specific outcomes domains and treatments. These approaches are worthy of further debate.

SAMPLING VERSUS ASSESSMENT OF ENTIRE POPULATION

Many experts, including W. E. Deming, the father of total quality management (TQM), argue in favor of collecting data by sampling instead of by universal inspection (Deming, 1982). Deming would say, for example, that the worst method would be to inspect every aspect of every car as it comes off the assembly line, because that approach leads to rework and waste. This criticism has been carried over into health care management, with administrators and clinicians concerned that their clinical mission gets swamped by the burden of data collection.

However, in terms of feasibility, work flow, and management practice, measurement of the entire population is often simpler. Most clinical managers seem to agree that it is easier to survey every patient routinely rather than, for example, one of every five patients. However, the logistical problems become more complex when only certain tracer conditions are being assessed. There is probably no ideal decision in this case, and every organization must design a system to meet its own needs. It is especially important to consider the disadvantages of sampling if actual implementation leads to a convenience sample rather than a probability sample. If sampling is implemented, rigorous controls are needed to ensure that a true probability sample is obtained.

ASSESSMENT OF TRACER CONDITIONS VERSUS ASSESSMENT OF ALL DISORDERS

A tracer condition is a single condition that is followed within an organization and is assumed to be generalizable to the systems of care. In a sense, the use of a tracer condition could be considered another form of sampling, although it clearly is not a probability sample as discussed above. The use of a tracer condition facilitates the evaluation of a particular disorder or disease over time. Such an approach reduces the burden of assessment for the organization because assessments of patients, disorders, health status, processes of care, and outcomes of care are intensive and resource-consuming. Studying a tracer condition in health care would be analogous to studying a certain aspect of the automobile assembly line, such as one assembly line within a factory.

It is important that a tracer condition be chosen carefully to reflect or be generalizable to the nature and goals of the organization being assessed. For example, in primary care, asthma, diabetes, or hypertension (or all three) might be chosen as a tracer condition to reflect both the operation of the entire organization as well as a condition frequently under treatment. In a general psychiatric setting, major depression could be the tracer condition. Because many of the findings concerning processes and outcomes of care have implications for the health care organization, the findings are assumed to relate to the entire system of care. For example, if the outcomes for patients with diabetes are found to be associated with inappropriate medication management, it may be assumed that similar patterns occur with other conditions as well. Furthermore, in a TQM framework (Juran, 1988), improvement of medication management for one disorder, particularly a high-volume disorder such as diabetes, may improve the operation of the entire organization.

The disadvantage of choosing a tracer condition is loss of information about disorders that are not studied. For example, if diabetes is chosen as the tracer condition in primary care, then knowledge regarding the treatment and outcomes for hypertension will not be obtained. On the other hand, if every condition is measured, depth of information about any one person or disorder cannot be obtained, and the organization may fail to understand the relationship between specific treatments and outcomes.

BRIEF ASSESSMENTS VERSUS MULTIDIMENSIONAL STUDIES

Brief assessments of patient outcomes have the advantage of increased feasibility and decreased cost. However, most institutions will benefit from the increased precision and information yield of more comprehensive assessments. These trade-offs must be considered when outcomes assessment projects are designed. Such decisions are particularly difficult for health services researchers who are accustomed to lengthy, detailed measures. For reasons of generalizability and statistical power, it is frequently a major advantage to collect brief, well-validated measures on a large number of people compared with longer assessments of just a few individuals.

ASSESSMENT LOGISTICS

There are a multitude of options for collecting data but no data to suggest which method is the best, although health services researchers frequently have strong opinions about differing methods. For example, there are no data indicating differences between traditional keyboard data entry at a remote site versus data entered into a portable computer on site by an interviewer or client. On the other hand, studies have shown that many instruments demonstrate adequate reliability and validity when administered over the phone rather than in person. Some methods, such as centralized optical scanning computerized outcomes measurement packages, may have significant cost advantages in the long run but involve considerable start-up costs. Clinicians need to know more about the advantages and disadvantages of these data collection methods.

Areas of Challenge in Outcomes Assessment

STAKEHOLDERS AND CONSUMER PREFERENCES

Knowledge of consumer preferences for particular outcomes domains is vital to consumer stakeholders but frequently omitted when designing outcomes assessment programs. Health professionals, payers, and researchers have identified the critical outcomes domains, but the perspective of consumers or clients must be understood. Consumers need to identify what domains are important to them. For example, individuals with severe mental illness and their families may find housing at least as important an outcomes domain as reduction in psychotic symptoms.

One way that consumer preferences are currently viewed is in terms of economic utility theory and contingent valuation. Utility theory provides ways to measure satisfaction with goods or services. Valuation approaches are methods for eliciting the utility of goods or services to consumers. In economic theory, all action (both passive and active) is viewed as a decision or a preference. For example, a patient with diabetes who ignores dietary guidelines is understood to have made an informed decision as to the consequences of such a decision. The health care system must understand the multiple trade-offs, including the patient's reason for ignoring the diet, the potentially higher financial cost of conforming to the diet, the likely extended suffering that may occur as a result of ignoring the diet, and the risk of earlier death from complications of uncontrolled diabetes.

It is extremely important that these multiple perspectives and preferences of the various stakeholders be integrated into patient outcomes assessment. These stakeholders include the consumer or client, family members, third-party payers, clinicians and providers, and even regulators. For example, a person with hypertension may prefer to discontinue hypertension medication because of the side effects and risk the complications of hypertension, whereas the clinician may have a strong preference in favor of medication continuation. Frequently health care providers are unaware of patient preferences for their health care.

INTERPRETATION AND MANAGEMENT OF OUTCOMES ASSESSMENTS

The interpretation and management of the results from outcomes assessments are as important as defining the domains, choosing measurement tools, and obtaining valid methods of data collection. Outside the research environment, many users of outcomes data are new to this type of endeavor and may not be sure how to use the data. Users of outcomes data often need and benefit from external assistance to understand the assessment results and, in particular, to facilitate the translation of results to the decision-making process. They may not have had training in statistics and, as a consequence, may rely on overly small sample sizes or be unable to go beyond descriptive analyses. Careful interpretation of outcomes assessment data is critical because these data are observational rather than experimental. In particular, users of outcomes data may not be aware of the various threats to validity that are familiar to researchers. Therefore, outcomes data should be viewed as generating rather than confirming hypotheses.

INTEGRATION OF OUTCOMES INTO INFORMATION SYSTEMS

For outcomes assessments to be successful, it may be necessary to restructure the clinical information system to integrate outcomes assessment and the clinical information system. For example, a clinical quality improvement system designed to improve the process of care can use the same data as the patient outcomes system instead of maintaining two independent systems. Such process engineering is particularly important for transferring the outcomes assessment technology from the research arena into the routine setting.

With advances in clinical decision-making theory, treatment guidelines, and medical informatics, it is feasible and appropriate to integrate clinical systems with outcomes systems. In research settings, computerized medical records have made major advances in these kinds of integration. As electronic medical records become more frequent in general health care settings, it will be critical to immerse outcomes assessment into such systems.

Advances in electronic medical records also make possible enhanced graphic displays of data describing treatment options, guidelines, and outcomes. Using such information systems may enable providers to understand their treatment options and may allow patients to fully understand their choices. Enhanced graphic displays also enable managers to view summary data over time in order to understand treatment processes and patient outcomes. For example, using this technology could lead to an evaluation of the implementation of treatment guidelines into a health care system.

FEASIBILITY

There is little knowledge about how to make outcomes assessment more feasible (and acceptable) to implement. Although scientifically sound assessment systems have been developed, they may be awkward to implement, may meet considerable resistance, and may appear to be overly burdensome to the clinical teams. More must be known about the mechanics of successful implementation of outcomes assessment programs. Research must focus on how to make outcomes assessment programs acceptable to providers and staff, how to reduce the burden of data collection, and how to estimate the costs of outcomes assessment to health care systems.

VULNERABLE POPULATIONS

New technology is also required for vulnerable populations such as children and adolescents and older people with cognitive impairments. Difficult and troublesome scientific questions are raised when considering such populations. For example, how accurately will children report their symptoms? How valid are parents' reports of children's symptoms? How can clinicians measure quality of life in individuals with dementia?

INITIAL DISSIMILARITIES

Another critical issue is case-mix adjustment, or the ability to compare the outcomes of groups of patients who may not be initially similar. Case-mix adjustment helps to compare patients with and without comorbid conditions (for example, patients who have diabetes with and without hypertension). The ability to conduct case-mix adjustment is important for the development of national, state, or local benchmarks or report cards to which clinical programs can aspire. However, the science of case-mix adjustment is still in progress and may be difficult to translate to routine clinical programs with ongoing outcomes assessment programs.

CLASSIFICATION

More progress is needed in nosological research (the science of classifying disorders and diseases). Outcomes researchers frequently have to follow the work of nosologists if they are interested in disease-specific outcomes assessment because disease-specific outcomes domains are so closely tied to disease specification. If nosologists cannot define the disease or disorder, then valid measurement of the outcomes for that disorder cannot begin. Outcomes researchers depend on the work of nosologists in defining homogeneous diagnostic groups to perform diagnosis-specific outcomes measures.

INDICATORS

In clinical care, precise laboratory measures are helpful to assess patient prognosis, disease progress, and health status. However, for many diagnoses, including those in mental health and substance abuse, there is no equivalent of a hemoglobin or blood pressure measurement. More subjective measures of outcomes, such as patient self-reports of symptomatology, have to be substituted with associated concerns regarding the reliability and validity of these measures. Furthermore, when patient self-reports must be relied on for outcomes assessment, the increased cost of obtaining self-reports may be of greater concern to the health care system than the ease of retrieving laboratory values from the clinical information system.

STATISTICS

Improved and accessible statistical approaches to analysis of outcomes data that do not require the services of a doctoral-level statistician and can remain valid when follow-up rates are less than optimal are needed in outcomes assessment. In current outcomes research, a follow-up rate of at least 80 percent is generally considered essential for generalizability to the original population. A follow-up rate of 80 percent is difficult to achieve, especially in certain clinical populations such as substance abusers and people with serious mental illness. Also needed are statistical techniques for case-mix adjustment (statistical control for known prognostic factors) and analysis of longitudinal data that are within the reach of general health care organizations as opposed to research organizations with substantial external funding for analysis of outcomes.

OUTCOME OF OUTCOMES ASSESSMENT

A final unknown factor is whether the technology of outcomes assessment improves outcomes and quality of care. It is assumed, based on TQM and other theories of quality improvement, that the feedback of outcomes information can move services along the road to optimal care (Deming, 1982; Juran, 1988), but scientific studies are lacking.

Conclusion

There already is a strong theoretical foundation for rapid advancement of outcomes assessment (Ellwood, 1988). The implementation field is already mushrooming. Numerous conferences exist in behavioral health care alone. However, it is premature for consensus on a single approach or system of outcomes assessment. More experience with outcomes assessment and innovative research and development projects is necessary. It is also critical to develop new technology to make outcomes assessment feasible in routine human service settings.

Outcomes assessments must be conducted even without final answers to the questions posed here. Any of the approaches discussed, done well and carefully, will yield important information for various stakeholders. It is, however, not cost-effective to conduct outcomes studies hastily and without significant preparation. Research is needed to demonstrate the effectiveness of outcomes assessment systems and to show that these systems are feasible, and technical assistance should be made available to health care and other human service organizations to implement outcomes assessment systems. Well-developed, nonproprietary outcomes assessment systems also must be made readily available for public use.

References

Deming, W. E. (1982). *Out of the crisis*. Cambridge: MIT Press.

Ellwood, P. M. (1988). Outcomes management: A technology of patient experience. *New England Journal of Medicine, 318* (23), 1549–1556.

Hollenberg, J., Rost, K., Humphrey, J., Owen, R. R., & Smith, G. R. (1997). Validation of the panic outcomes module. *Evaluation and the Health Professions, 20* (1), 81–95.

Juran, J. M. (Ed.-in-Chief). (1988). *Juran's quality control handbook* (4th ed). New York: McGraw-Hill.

Lohr, K. N. (1988). Outcome measurement: Concepts and questions. *Inquiry, 25* (1), 37–50.

Rost, K. M., Ross, R. L., Humphrey, J., Frank, S., Smith, J., & Smith, G. R. (1996). Does this treatment work? Validation of an outcomes module for alcohol dependence. *Medical Care, 34*, 283–294.

Ware, J. E., Jr., & Sherbourne, C. D. (1992). The MOS 36-item short-form health survey (SF-36): I. Conceptual framework and item selection. *Medical Care, 30*, 473–483.

CHAPTER 4

Health Care Outcomes from the Patient's Point of View

JOHN E. WARE, JR.

I cannot imagine a topic that I would be more interested in addressing than outcomes from the point of view of the public in health care settings—specifically outcomes from the point of view of the patient. I was originally trained in the theory and methods of measurement. However, my work on the science of patient-based assessment and the experiences that I have had with various databases have focused my interests on the questions that these data are being used to address. I have become an advocate for adding information about the public's experience of social interventions as part of the database in addition to the traditional economic information that is used in decision making.

Health care in the United States is being restructured in a rather dramatic way. This restructuring includes the organization, financing, and delivery of health care and is being done to control rising costs in medical care services. In the absence of any information to the contrary, restructuring decisions will continue to be made on the basis of economic data, and the success of health care reform will be based largely on its success in reducing the medical expenditures in the absence of evidence to the contrary. Because of this, reliable information must be added to the database on which health care decisions are based for purposes of understanding in much broader terms what health care systems are doing to people in their everyday lives. Although I became interested in this as a measurement problem while I was in graduate school, I am now much more interested in outcomes as an important source of information that can play a role in a number of different applications, as I describe in this chapter.

Health Care Decision Making

How are health care decisions currently being made? Essentially, the three elements in a health care database are death, disease, and dollars. Yet, there is more to life than how long one lives, there is more to health than the absence or the seriousness of disease, and there is more to health care than how much it costs. There are two additional concepts about which researchers can get useful information directly from the public: (1) the patient's experience of the burden of disease and the benefit of treatment, that is, functional health and well-being, and (2) the patient's experience with and acceptance of the delivery of health care services or patient satisfaction. According to one physician epidemiologist, "The best measure of quality is not how well or how frequently a medical service is given, but how closely the result approaches the fundamental objectives of prolonging life, relieving distress, restoring function, and preventing disability"(Lembcke, 1967). This comment argues that it really does not matter how often or how well a service is provided; the issue is the results.

Competition among health care providers has created great interest in functional health and well-being and patient satisfaction. There is an interest in understanding the customer much better. Similarly, the auto industry in the United States dealt with quality for quite some time by advertising it, that is, by marketing quality. That was fine until someone else came along and decided both to advertise it and to design it into their products. The rest of that story is history. In health care the United States is currently going through a phase in which much of the approach to dealing with quality and access in health care is simply a marketing agenda, wherein quality and access are being advertised. Many health care organizations advertise claims about how good they are from the point of view of the public. However, beyond simply marketing, continuous quality improvement, which is a consumer-oriented movement in other industries, is now moving into the health care industry.

As noted in chapter 2 by Rossi, an additional factor promoting an interest in the patient's assessment is that technical advances have made it possible for the health field to go forward with such assessments. It is becoming more practical to monitor services from the point of view of customers because the technology of monitoring customer views is improving.

Health Care Objectives

Health care has two objectives: (1) to restore people to the best level of functioning and well-being that they can possibly achieve and (2) to prevent disability. Preventing a disability is an outcomes orientation. Functioning, what people are able to do and how they feel, directly leads us to the consumer or the patient to assess these variants. As noted by Donabedian (1980), "Achieving and producing health and satisfaction is the ultimate validator of the quality of care." Donabedian is essentially saying that the ultimate validator of health care is the patient or the customer in terms of health and the satisfactions that are produced by those who deliver health care services. The new acronym in health care, patient-based assessments (PBA), illustrates this emphasis. This idea will appear increasingly, as will more general consumer-based assessments. Applications of PBAs are evident in phase II–IV clinical trials, outcomes and effectiveness research, health care monitoring and improvement, and population monitoring. PBAs are being done at a growing rate. There is one company that does more than 100,000 PBAs per week for various health care plans and other employer groups interested in the marketplaces they serve. Millions of PBAs are done per year, if not monthly. These assessments focus on the health care perspective of the consumer and the health status perspective.

Measuring Patient Satisfaction

Measuring patient satisfaction with health care can be problematic. It is well known that the desired results of satisfaction surveys can be achieved by manipulating the measure used. In the 1970s we reported data showing that in the same population five different ways of measuring satisfaction will produce satisfaction rates of 90, 50, or 20 percent, respectively. Typically, when people are asked whether they are satisfied with medical care, as many as 80 percent respond affirmatively. In our research we divided the satisfied group further, asking them whether they thought their medical care could be better. We found that about one-third of the people who were completely satisfied with their care thought it could have been better. We were trying to get a distribution of scores that was better from a psychometric point of view. What we found was that the people who were completely satisfied with their care, but who thought it could have been better, were less likely to comply with treatment regimens and were more likely to change to a new provider. This study was not just a psychometric victory; the resulting measures provided more useful information (Ware, Snyder, Wright, & Davies, 1983).

QUALITY AND ACCESS

Several factors determine consumer views of health care, including features of the health plans and features of the care and services. The most important features of care and services are quality and access, and quality is of greatest importance. Quality is clearly the determining factor in satisfaction with health care services. For the first time, the confidence of the public in the quality of care is declining in several major medical markets in the United States. Accordingly, there is considerable interest in evaluating providers. There are many examples of where health care provider performance is being judged by patients. I am interested in the validity of these kinds of patient-based assessments. As noted in chapter 2, adjustments must be made in the analysis of data to ensure validity when attributing reasons for patient satisfaction assessments to particular provider performance. There must be sound science and standardization behind these assessments if they are going to be used in decision making.

NEED FOR STANDARDIZATION

The current lack of standardization is methodologically troubling. Standardization is necessary for a reproducible enumeration of anything, and that standardization and the pedigree of the measure for respectable validity make interpretation possible. Accordingly, the current practice of publicly advertising patient satisfaction statistics using differing and incomparable standards is a major problem. For example, many hospitals know that a satisfaction survey using a five-choice scale, ranging from "excellent" to "poor" and giving a second choice of "average" will get many more "excellent" ratings than one using the psychometrically preferred five-choice scale that gives "very good" as the second choice. I confronted one of the hospitals on this issue, and it was so impressed with the 90 percent "excellent" rating and the marketing value of that information that it was not at all interested in changing. I prefer the scale that uses "very good" as the second choice. Although I do not have any problem if the world wants to use the scale that uses "average" as the second choice, I do have a problem with providers who use the latter to compare themselves with the former and run full-page ads in various magazines. That is a standardization problem.

THE SF-36 HEALTH SURVEY

We developed a standardized form, the Visit Satisfaction Questionnaire (VSQ), which is one of the most widely used forms to evaluate specific visits with physicians (Davies & Ware, 1992). We first started using it in the Medical Outcomes Study in the mid-1980s (see chapter 18 by Coulter; Berry, 1992; Greenfield et al., 1992; Greenfield, Rogers, Mangotich, Carney, & Tarlov, 1995; Kravitz et al., 1992; Rogers, Wells, Meredith, Sturm, & Burnam, 1993; Safran, Tarlov, & Rogers, 1994; Stewart et al., 1989; Stewart & Ware, 1992; Tarlov et al., 1989; Ware, Bayliss, Rogers, Kosinski, & Tarlov, 1996; Wells et al., 1989). The form has been adopted by a number of organizations such as the American Group Practice Association. This scale was developed from the "excellent" to "poor" rating scale questionnaires that I received every time I flew on an airplane, stayed in a hotel, or rented a car. Those types of scales were rarely used in health care before the early 1980s. The only thing we did was apply them to health care and add a fifth response category, "very good."

These scale types can be used to compare services, as in the Medical Outcomes Study, in which we compared fee-for-service plans with prepaid plans. In that study we observed two things about health care in the late 1980s (Rubin et al., 1993). The system was beginning to be much more stressed with respect to access than it was with respect to quality (that is, people were being asked to go to places that were distant, having difficulty getting through on the telephone, and experiencing long appointment and office waits). These were controversial findings when they were published, in part because the data were old. The Health Institute at New England Medical Center in Boston repeated this survey in 1994, and we again found the same basic pattern.

The message is that a lot of the things that are done in managing care to control costs, which means to control access in many cases, affects the patients and the customers in ways that are not as friendly and convenient as they used to be. Health care providers either have to think of a better way to achieve cost containment than the one they are implementing now, or they have to convince the public that the style of medical care to which they are accustomed is not going to be the one they have anymore—at least not at the same price. Both of those options should be considered.

Interestingly, where medical expenditures are the highest is also where people like their medical care the most: that is, patient satisfaction is highest in the Northeast part of the country. Of course, there is a way to make all of the nation's regions and all of the providers in them look good in terms of patient satisfaction surveys: combine the three most favorable categories into one favorable category. This was what was done in a demonstration project conducted by one of the largest health care accrediting organizations in this country. When the organization published its report on 21 plans, it combined the "excellent," "very good," and "good" ratings so that the percentages for all the plans were in the mid to high 90s. I am critical of this methodology. If you take the latest consumer report magazine that uses this scale and combine the top three categories, no matter what the product is, there will be no variability in the products that are compared because there are no products marketed where all the ratings are "fair" and "poor."

Even with good measures, organizations can "cook" the data by aggregating survey responses to their advantage. When I called this to the attention of the field, I was challenged by those who argued that "very good" and "good" ratings were as good as "excellent." Because we anticipated that reaction, we started publishing about this issue in the mid-1980s (Ware & Hays, 1988). As it turns out, among those individuals who rate their care as "excellent," we looked at a number of important behaviors. For instance, we examined the rates for whether respondents would recommend their physicians. We have also looked at respondent opinions regarding changing the physicians and disenrollments from plans. We found that about 80 percent of respondents would recommend their physician if they rated their physician "excellent." That figure drops to 50 percent if they rated the care as "very good." It drops to less than 10 percent if they rate their care as "good." To put those three categories together and to call the combined rating the same is not valid by any reasonable standard. There are consequences of what people think of their care, whether health care professionals think patients are valid judges of that care or not. The consequences are that people do not see the physician when they need to, do not comply as well with regimens, change physicians more often, disenroll from health care plans, are more likely to complain, are less likely to recommend their care to others, and are more likely to sue when they have less confidence in their physician as measured by a typical satisfaction survey.

Measuring Health Status

The other concept that is focused on a great deal is health status, and the reason these two concepts are in the same section is that there is great efficiency in doing an omnibus short patient- or consumer-completed form that covers both of these conceptual domains in whatever mix of questions the administrator thinks is appropriate. The important development in the assessment of health status from the point of view of the patient is the broadening of the focus from the traditional clinical measures of organ functioning to measures of human functioning, which essentially defined the end point in using the proximal–distal way of thinking. Human functioning certainly is what matters most to people. What people care about is what they are able to do and how they feel. It is fine to use clinical measures of organ functioning, which are the building blocks at the level of human organ systems. However, as a society, people increasingly judge the social value of that investment in achieving the best possible organ functioning in terms of what it means to human life. People are not going to purchase things that are technically better unless those improvements can be linked to length and quality of life. For example, if arterial blood flow can be improved, the question is whether that improvement enhances the length and quality of someone's life.

There are many measures of health status. Table 4-1 illustrates several measures beginning with some developed in the 1970s and extending into the 1990s.

Many reliable standardized measurement tools are available for use, and many of them are in the public domain. There is an emerging consensus regarding the concepts to be measured. For example, as Table 4-1 illustrates, all of these general health survey instruments include measures of physical, social, and role functioning, and almost all of them include mental health concepts. There is agreement as to the minimum standard content that is necessary to make any type of claim or decision on the basis of health assessment. Some of these tools are short, such as the SF-36 (a short form with 36 questions), and there is now a two-minute version of the SF-36, the Short Form-12 (SF-12) (Ware, Kosinski, & Keller, 1996).

Both the SF-36 and the SF-12 yield a profile of eight health dimensions that are important to people of all age groups, regardless of disease or treatment. Therefore, they are called *generic* measures. The two-minute version of the SF-36 was developed largely on the basis of a challenge to reduce a health assessment to a format that could be printed on one or two pages of a scannable form without substantial loss of information.

SPECIFIC VERSUS GENERIC MEASURES

As noted by Booth and Smith in chapter 3, there is a debate about the value of specific versus generic outcomes measures. This debate reflects the issue of proximal versus distal measurement. Figure 4-1 illustrates the relationships between specific and generic health concepts.

This question of specific versus generic measurement is not only an issue in terms of the sequence of outcomes over time but also an issue in terms of conceptualization. Clinicians are most familiar and most comfortable with concepts on the left of the schematic of Figure 4-1 where measurement is focused on a particular cause. If a client registers an abnormal score on measures of these specific concepts, the clinician knows that it is abnormal and knows the cause of that abnormality. The right side of the Figure 4-1 schematic shows much more distal concepts that are not measures of specific causes but of outcomes. These generic concepts are sensitive to everything the physicians are doing and everything else that is going on in a client's life. Accordingly, as noted in chapter 2 by Rossi, it is important when these concepts are used as outcomes measures that good study designs can allow clinicians to make strong inferences about what the process is that is producing the variation and the generic outcome.

Table 4-1

CONTENT OF WIDELY USED GENERAL HEALTH SURVEYS

Concepts	QWB	SIP	HIE	NHP	QLI	COOP	EURO-QOL	DUKE	MOS FWBP	MOS SF-36
Physical functioning	•	•	•	•	•	•	•	•	•	•
Social functioning	•	•	•	•	•	•	•	•	•	•
Role functioning	•	•	•	•	•	•	•	•	•	•
Psychological distress		•	•	•	•	•	•	•	•	•
Health perceptions (general)			•	•	•	•	•	•	•	•
Pain (bodily)		•	•	•		•	•	•	•	•
Energy/fatigue	•		•	•				•	•	•
Psychological well-being			•					•	•	•
Sleep		•		•				•	•	
Cognitive functioning		•						•	•	
Quality of life			•			•			•	
Reported health transition						•			•	•

Note: QWB = Quality of Well-Being Scale; SIP = Sickness Impact Profile; HIE = Health Insurance Experiment patient surveys; NHP = Nottingham Health Profile; QLI = Quality of Life Index; COOP = Dartmouth Function Charts; EUROQOL = Western European Cost-Utility Index; DUKE = Duke Health Profile; MOS FWBP = Medical Outcomes Study Functioning and Well-Being Profile; MOS SF-36 = Medical Outcomes Study 36-Item Short-Form Health Survey.

Source: Adapted with permission from Ware, J. E. (1995). The status of health assessment 1994. *Annual Review of Public Health, 16,* 327–354. Copyright 1995, Annual Reviews, Inc.

Figure 4-1

RELATIONSHIPS AMONG SPECIFIC AND GENERIC HEALTH CONCEPTS

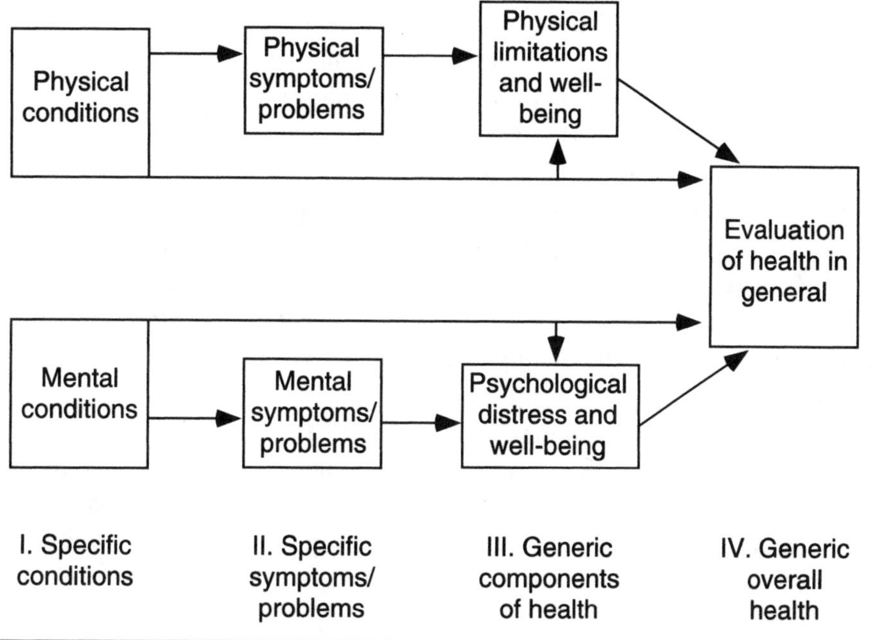

Source: Adapted with permission from Ware, J. E. (1995). The status of health assessment 1994. *Annual Review of Public Health, 16,* 327–354. Copyright 1995, Annual Reviews, Inc.

Patient-Based Measures

Patient-based measures currently are included in traditional clinical trials. Before 1990 it was rare to see a large clinical trial that included a generic health status assessment measure. Now, it is rare to find a clinical trial that does not include such a measure. In fact, some institutes of the National Institutes of Health require an exemption to leave health status or health-related quality of life out of a large trial. In addition to traditional outcomes, these studies focus on outcomes from the point of view of the patient and the consumer. These studies are being used in health care monitoring, and they are being used on a population basis. The increasing use of the same concepts and methods across these applications is allowing a kind of synergy and comparison that was never possible before. For example, some population studies show what the goal of treatment is for a specific patient, Mrs. Smith. Population norms provide an estimate of what Mrs. Smith's functioning should be, given her age and medical condition? With this new information clinicians can establish targets. Now researchers are even accumulating longitudinal data such as a sense of what the rate of physical decline is after age 60 and whether cost-containment procedures are accelerating that rate of decline.

Undesired Effects on Human Functioning and Well-Being

Finally, as noted in chapter 2 by Rossi, because most treatments are interventions, the treatment outcomes models must involve the possibility of both desired and undesired effects. Generic health outcomes models provide a common denominator that allows clinicians to look at the outcomes in a net sense by offsetting the positive desired effects of a treatment with the undesired negative effects. To do this, these generic measures must be comprehensive. The abuse potential of measuring my benefit and your side effect and then showing the Food and Drug Administration that I have a superior product is not an unlikely possibility. For example, the importance of quality-of-life assessments in clinical trials was demonstrated in the mid-1980s by the findings pertaining to effects of antihypertensive agents on quality of life (Croog et al., 1986). Several different antihypertensive medications that all had the same safety and the same efficacy in controlling blood pressure had very different effects on the quality-of-life outcomes. Figure 4-2 illustrates these differences.

As shown, captopril improved quality-of-life outcomes, whereas the other drugs made the condition worse. Probably even more influential than the article reporting these findings was the accompanying editorial, which stated that it is no longer acceptable to evaluate medical treatment only in terms of the specific clinical end point. If products differ in cost and quality-of-life effects, then these effects should be

Figure 4-2

ANTIHYPERTENSIVE AGENTS HAVE DIFFERENT EFFECTS ON QUALITY-OF-LIFE OUTCOMES

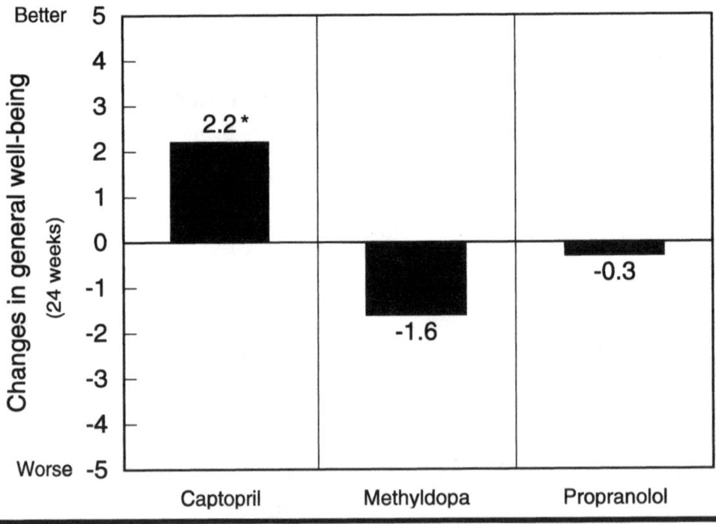

Note: *Captopril > methyldopa, captopril > propranolol, $p < .01$.
Source: Croog, S. H., Levine, S., Testa, M. A., Brown, B., Bulpitt, C. J., Jenkins, C. D., Klerman, G. L., & Williams, G. H. (1986). The effects of antihypertensive therapy on the quality of life. *New England Journal of Medicine, 314,* 1657–1664.

considered in addition to the clinical effects. This example is cited because there are managed care cost-containment organizations that are developing compliance programs to get patients to comply with antihypertensive medications that have negative side effects. Yet, these organizations have determined that it is more cost-effective, as long as quality of life is not in the equation, to spend a little more money to get compliance than to give patients a more expensive drug with fewer side effects. This kind of thinking occurs when dollars are in the equation and when the indirect costs in terms of human functioning and well-being are not. It is frightening to find so many examples of this kind of problem.

A Combined Measurement Strategy

Accordingly, a typical measurement strategy is to include a generic core measure and additional generic measures if there might be effects in those areas. The advantage to these short forms is that there is plenty of room to add other conceptual areas. Table 4-2 illustrates such an approach.

Table 4-2 summarizes the content of the self-report health-related quality-of-life form used in the largest occurring women's trial in the United States. This is a randomized trial of tamoxifen. Because there is concern about side effects, a quality-of-life measure was included (SF-36). Because there is concern about sexual functioning and depression as possible treatment side effects, those areas were measured (MOS Sexual Functioning Scale & CES-D Depression Scale). There also is a symptom/problem checklist that focuses on the specific potential side effects. This questionnaire is filled out four times a year in the first year and twice a year each year for five to seven years.

Table 4-2

SAMPLE QUALITY-OF-LIFE QUESTIONNAIRE USED IN A CLINICAL TRIAL

Category/Measures	Items
Generic core	
SF-36 Health Survey	36
Supplemental generic	
MOS Sexual Functioning Scale	5
Supplemental clinical	
CES-D Depression Scale	20
Specific	
Symptom/Problem Checklist	43

Source: Ganz, P. A., Day, R., Ware, J. E., Redmond, C., & Fisher, B. (1996). Base-line quality-of-life assessment in the National Surgical Adjuvant Breast and Bowel Project Breast Cancer Prevention Trial. *Journal of the National Cancer Institute, 87,* 1372–1382.

Routine Use in Practice

As a result of technology, these tools are being used every day in clinical practice through the use of scannable forms. With the combination of scanning and rapid fax transmission, devices are available whereby a patient can put a self-administered form into a computer and within five seconds all of the items are scored, the scales are scored, and the patient's scores are compared with a normative database that includes previous administrations to that patient or disease or population norms. The results are printed out in five seconds at a cost of less than one dollar per assessment. This technology allows a reproducible measurement core in five seconds, and the cost includes the hardware, the software, and the paper. The physician and the patient can then talk about this profile in addition to the other clinical data.

At the New England Medical Center (NEMC), several services use this procedure routinely. It probably would be fair to say that NEMC nephrologists will never again treat end-stage dialysis patients knowing only the results from traditional clinical measures. They look at SF-36 profiles every three months and talk to the patients regularly. This practice has completely changed patient care (Meyer et al., 1994).

Resources Expended and Benefits Achieved

I would argue that managed care and clinical trials are very much about understanding the relationship between spending money for health care services and health benefits. Whether talking about what is the right dose of health care for the population or what is the right dose for a particular disease, understanding this relationship is central. Figure 4-3 illustrates one answer to the question, "What is the relationship between use of health care resource dollars and health benefits?"

Figure 4-3 illustrates the hypothesis that benefits minus risks in relation to consumption is an increasing function. This is the "more is better" hypothesis. If this hypothesis is correct, cost containment in the United States is going to lead to decrements in the health of the public. Because this linear hypothesis is not correct, it is important to understand the true nature of this relationship.

DISTRIBUTION OF HEALTH BENEFITS

As illustrated in Figure 4-4, outcomes research studies have shown that at every level of investment in health care services there is a distribution of health benefits. It is important to understand this distribution. The variations in outcomes in every disease studied to date appear to be at least as large as the variation in practice styles and utilization.

THE FLAT OF THE CURVE

While at RAND conducting the Health Insurance Experiment, my colleagues and I identified evidence supporting on the so-called flat of the curve in medicine. Figures 4-5 and 4-6 illustrate the concept of the flat of the curve and who we found to be at the flat of the curve (Brook et al., 1983; Ware et al., 1986).

Figure 4-3

WHAT IS THE RELATIONSHIP BETWEEN UTILIZATION AND HEALTH BENEFITS?

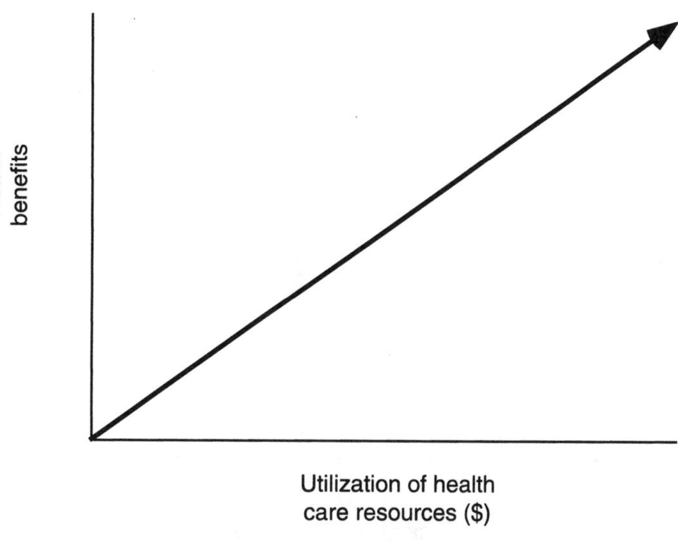

Health Insurance Experiment Findings

The experiment showed that for young, relatively healthy people in the upper two-thirds of income distribution in six regions of the United States whom we randomly assigned to various cost-containment strategies, health care expenditures could be reduced, and they could be moved from the right to the left on these figures. (For discussion of the RAND Health Insurance Experiment, see chapter 18 by Coulter.) Twenty to 40 percent could reduce health care resource expenditures with no measurable change on the vertical axis (health benefits) whether defined clinically, functionally, or in terms of healthy behaviors. Older people (age 65 and older) were not included in this study. Medicare was not included in the Health Insurance Experiment because when that study was done in the 1970s, it was unthinkable to move Medicare into managed care. Accordingly, we excluded from the experiment anyone in Medicare or anyone who would become eligible for Medicare during the course of the five-year follow-up. Not surprisingly, following the publication of these results, there was a tremendous increase in the amount of cost-sharing, copayments, deductibles, and coinsurance in the fee-for-service system in the United States, and the study increased interest in prepaid plans. However, we reported that some subgroups, such as poor people and those with health problems, were hurt. That finding went largely unnoticed. Those at the flat of the curve are clearly those who were financially better off, in better health, and younger. Cost containment tends to work for these groups.

Figure 4-4

THERE IS A DISTRIBUTION OF BENEFITS AT EACH LEVEL OF UTILIZATION

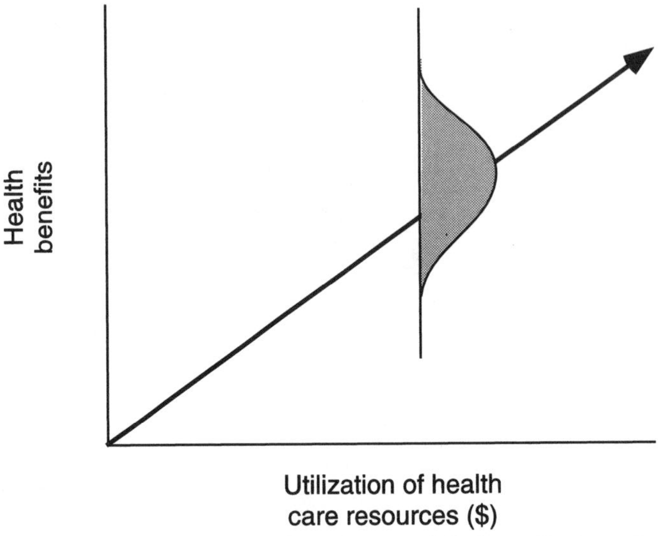

Medical Outcomes Study

Data we have subsequently reported from the Medical Outcomes Study (see chapter 18 by Coulter; Berry, 1992; Greenfield et al., 1992; Greenfield et al., 1995; Kravitz et al., 1992; Rogers et al., 1993; Safran et al., 1994; Stewart et al., 1989; Stewart & Ware, 1992; Tarlov et al., 1989; Ware, Bayliss, et al., 1996; Wells et al., 1989) showed that people who are 65 and older (half of our sample) and those who are within 200 percent of the poverty line (in 1986 dollars) (approximately 22 percent of the sample) who also were chronically ill had significantly worse physical health outcomes in the health maintenance organizations that we studied relative to fee-for-service plans. For the younger patients who were relatively well off financially and for those in better health, we found that cost containment worked well. However, people who did not have those attributes were at significantly greater risk for a poor health outcome. This study examined outcomes in about 400 practices in three cities over a four-year period (1986–1990).

It is naive to think that any social service would have the same effect on every person. Those who plan health care must move away from relatively blunt cost-containment strategies to more discriminating instruments that focus essentially on the unnecessary services. The advantage of generic measures in these kinds of outcomes studies is that they allow us to compare different diseases and different treatments

Figure 4-5

IS THERE A "FLAT OF THE CURVE"?

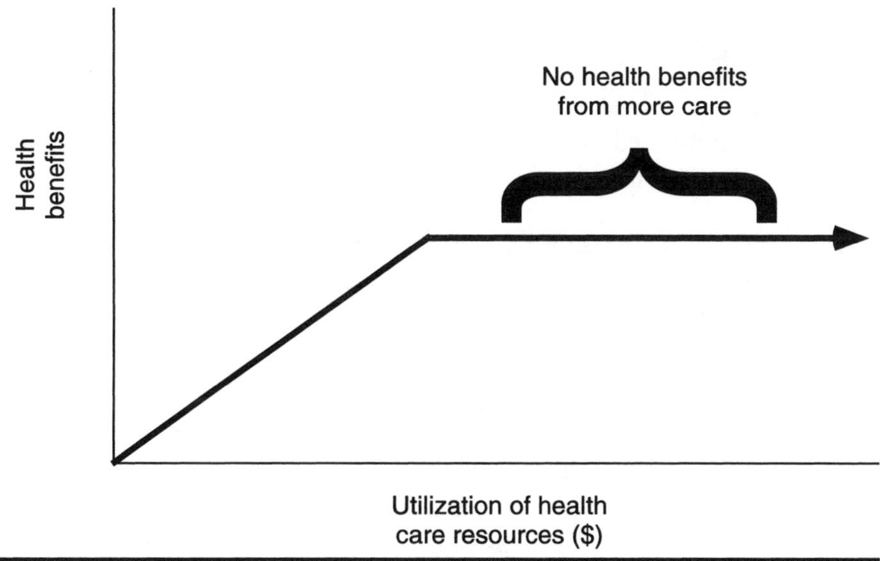

Figure 4-6

WHO IS AT THE "FLAT OF THE CURVE"?

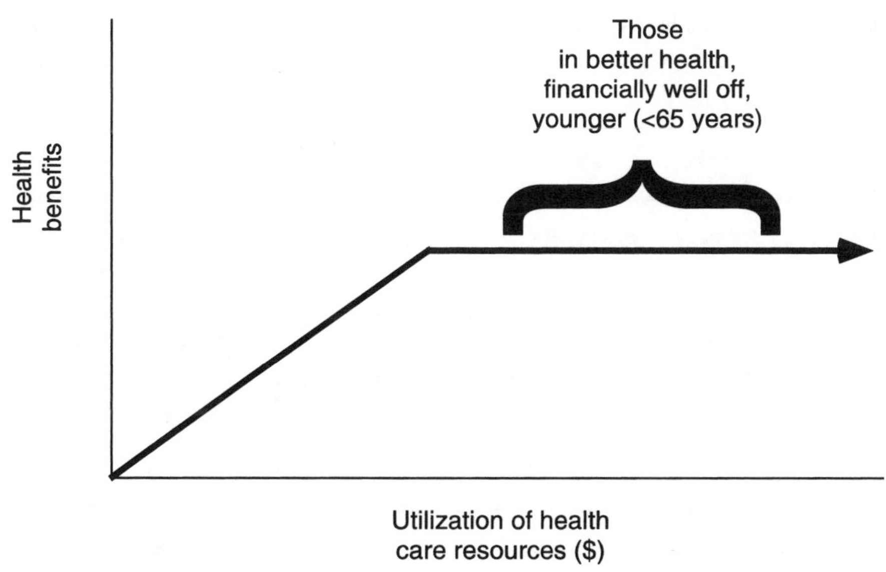

and they improve the comprehensiveness and, therefore, the validity of the measurement. They improve prediction, and they provide a useful common denominator.

Health Status: Causes and Consequences

Generic measures of health outcomes are best understood when viewed in a schematic such as that illustrated in Figure 4-7. This framework illustrates several different sources of information that can be used in interpreting health status data.

FOCUSING ON CAUSES OF HEALTH STATUS

Clinicians have put a great deal of pressure on researchers to develop a measurement system for health status that is responsive to what they do. For example, health outcomes could be defined merely in terms of diagnosis and severity of the "causes" area of Figure 4-7. However, researchers have resisted that pressure and do not define health status in terms of either the current diseases or the current treatments. Health status is a basic human value. Although learning how current medical care and diseases affect different health status concepts is of great interest, clinicians will be served best by a measurement system that includes general health outcomes.

FOCUSING ON CONSEQUENCES OF HEALTH STATUS

An alternative to focusing on the causes of health status is to look at the consequences, as illustrated in Figure 4-7. An important voice in the health care debate, arguably the constituency that will cause health care to be reorganized no matter what the government does, is that of the employers and other payers. This consituency is interested in linking health status to other variables, for example, whether Mrs. Smith goes to work, how satisfied she is with her job, how she gets along with everyone at work, and her productivity. The currency of great importance to this constituency is the effect of health status, disease, and treatment on worker productivity. Some companies are realizing that the indirect costs of disease and health problems are

Figure 4-7

HEALTH STATUS: CAUSES AND CONSEQUENCES

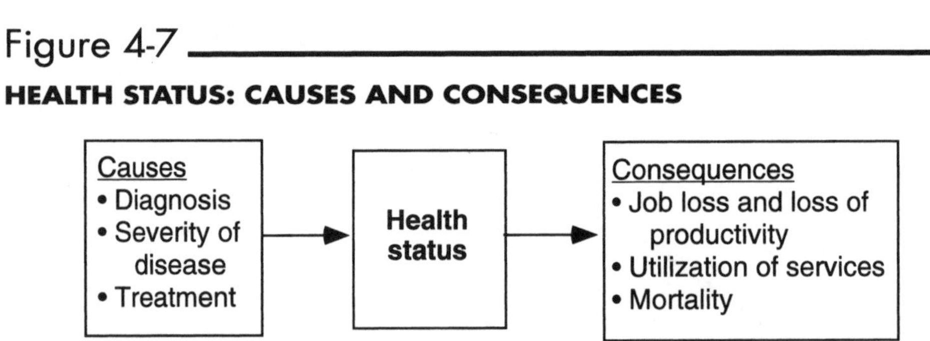

Source: Ware, J. E., & Keller, S. D. (1995). Interpreting general health measures. In B. Spilker (Ed.), *Quality of life and pharmacoeconomics in clinical trials* (2nd ed., pp. 445–460). New York: Raven Press.

probably greater than the direct cost of health care, which is 10 to 12 percent of the domestic economy. Employers care about worker productivity, economists care about use of services, and everyone cares about how long he or she will live. All of these things have been linked to health status.

Effect of Health Status on Hospitalization

As illustrated in Figure 4-8, the hospitalization rate for people who rate their health as poor, the most subjective rating of all, is nearly 10 times greater than if they rate their health as excellent (Kravitz et al., 1992). Similarly, Figure 4-9 shows that the rate of health-related job loss within one year is about 10 times higher for patients in the bottom one-fourth of the physical health scale than for those in the top one-fourth (Ware, Kosinski, & Keller, 1994). This rate has now been confirmed in a two-year follow-up study.

Effect of Health Status on Mortality

Figure 4-10 illustrates five-year mortality rates (from all causes) associated with physical health summary scores. Mortality rates of approximately 17 percent are evident in the bottom one-fourth of the physical health scale: a tenfold difference. When we briefed the RAND board on the findings from the Health Insurance Experiment in which we showed that poor people had lost their confidence in their health insurance plans—both fee-for-service and others that were aggressively managed to control costs—one of the members of the board skeptically asked how we knew that they were not just saying that their health is lower. The response based on mortality rates is that those who rate their health as poor are "at least being true to their word because they are much more likely to die within five years." This kind of validity information can be useful when the results are attacked on the basis of the validity of the measures.

Health Status Indicators and Factors

Researchers have learned a lot about physical and mental health and have learned that there are many different ways of assessing these concepts, including measuring functioning, which has to do with what people are able to do; well-being, which is how people feel; evaluation, which is an expression of people's value system or how people as evaluators rate themselves; and social and role disability, which refers to how health problems affect job performance, schoolwork, housekeeping, and other everyday roles. Rather than choose among these different operational definitions, I would argue that the best measures of each of these concepts provide a good sampling of all these different kinds of indicators. My colleagues and I are now studying indicators to determine factor content and are finding that although our physical functioning scale has a lot of information about physical health, that scale tells us almost nothing about mental health (Ware et al., 1994). Similarly, we have mental health scales that tell us a lot about mental health, but they tell us nothing about physical health. From a measurement perspective, these findings are good because we can use the physical

Figure 4-8

PERSONAL HEALTH EVALUATIONS PREDICT HOSPITALIZATIONS

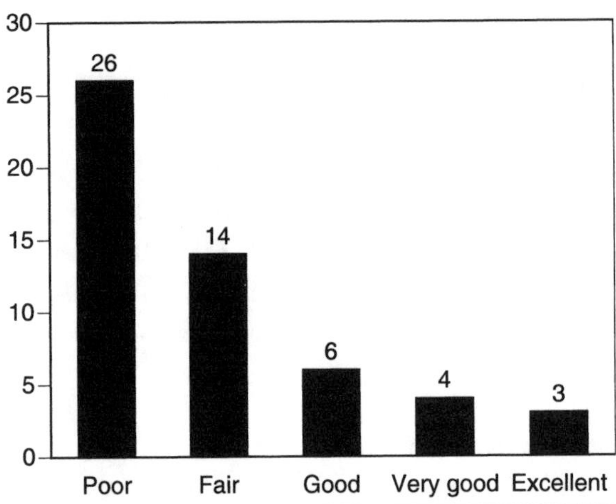

Note: $N = 20{,}158$.

Source: Kravitz, R. L., Greenfield, S., Rogers, W. H., Manning, W. G., Jr., Zubkoff, M., Nelson, E. C., Tarlov, A. R., & Ware, J. E., Jr. (1992). Differences in the mix of patients among medical specialties and systems of care: Results from the Medical Outcomes Study. *Journal of the American Medical Association, 267,* 1617–1623.

Figure 4-9

PHYSICAL HEALTH SCORES PREDICT JOB LOSS ONE YEAR LATER

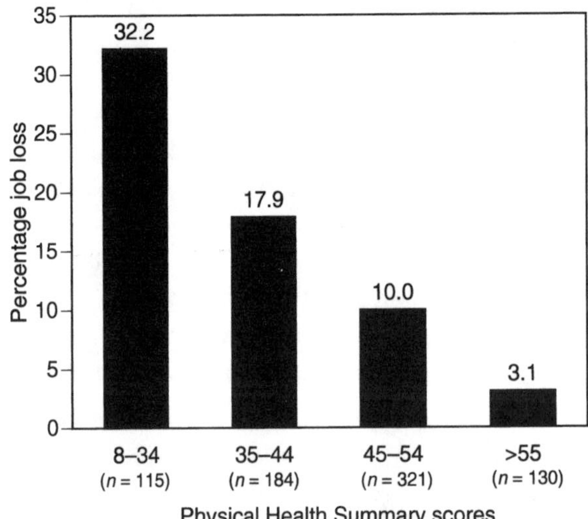

Source: Reprinted with permission from Ware, J. E., Kosinski, M., & Keller, S. D. (1994). *SF-36 physical and mental health summary scales: A user's manual.* Boston: The Health Institute, New England Medical Center. Copyright 1994, John Ware.

Figure 4-10

FIVE-YEAR MORTALITY RATES AT FOUR LEVELS OF PHYSICAL HEALTH

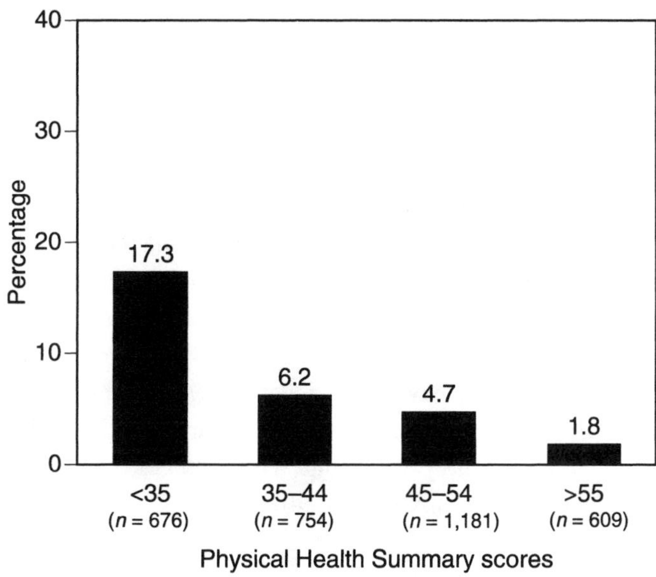

Source: Reprinted with permission from Ware, J. E., Kosinski, M., & Keller, S. D. (1994). *SF-36 physical and mental health summary scales: A user's manual.* Boston: The Health Institute, New England Medical Center. Copyright 1994, John Ware.

health scales to test physical health improvement, and we can use the mental health scales to test mental health improvement.

We have conducted these studies in eight developed countries and have found that the factor content of these scales is consistent across countries (Ware et al., 1995). This multinational research has included 24,000 people across eight developed countries, including the United States, the United Kingdom, Germany, Denmark, the Netherlands, France, Italy, and Norway. This lack of difference across countries suggests that if measures stay close to basic health values and minimize cultural differences, multinational clinical trials can be conducted and the comprehensiveness of population health assessments can be increased. This advance is of more than psychometric importance.

An Example of Clinical Relevance

The best physical scales, psychometrically defined, are the most responsive to medical intervention for physical morbidities. It is encouraging that what researchers know about measures from a psychometric evaluation is directly related to the measures' performance clinically. An example of this is illustrated in Figure 4-11.

Figure 4-11 shows mean SF-36 profiles and summary scales before and after heart valve replacement surgery (Phillips & Lansky, 1992). To take the correlations into account, the researchers summarized this profile into two independent summary measures and a physical health score (see far right of Figure 4-11). There is a difference of about seven points. What does a 7.6-point improvement in physical health mean? What is the value of a new heart valve? Statistically, it is a gain of three-fourths of a standard deviation (*SD* = 10). The statistician would believe that is substantial. To a clinician, a score of seven on that scale is equivalent to a chronic disease. That is like eliminating congestive heart failure or eliminating chronic obstructive pulmonary disease. So the clinician would be happy to call that a substantial benefit. For those who pay for services, the decreased hospitalization rate from 9 percent to 6 percent is a one-third reduction in hospital care over time. For the employer, a patient is one-third more likely to go back to work with a decreased job loss rate of 16 percent than with a rate of 24 percent. Patients' disability is cut in half, from a limitation of 37 percent to 19 percent, and they have a 5 percent increase in the probability of five-year survival (92 percent versus 87 percent). These are the kinds of interpretation guidelines needed for these widely used tools. With such guidelines, researchers can addess the social value of alternative interventions.

Figure 4-11

MEAN SF-36 PROFILE AND SUMMARY SCALES BEFORE AND AFTER HEART VALVE REPLACEMENT SURGERY

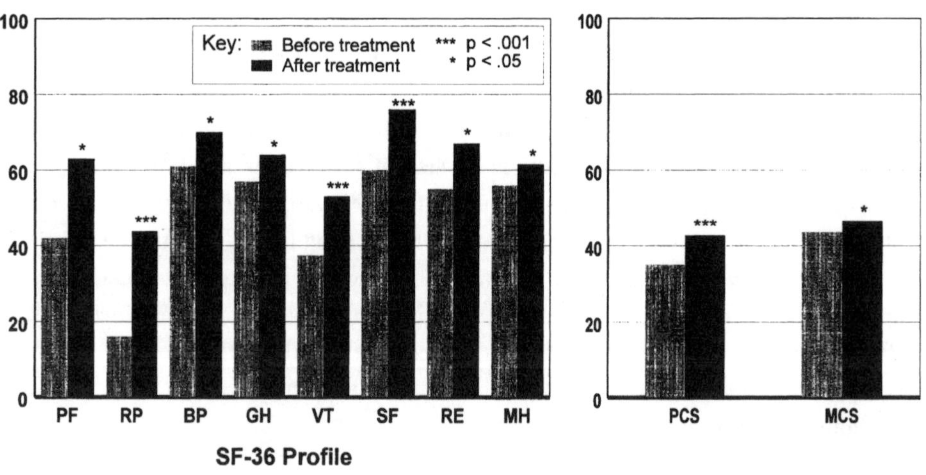

Sources: Phillips, R. C., & Lansky, D. J. (1992). Outcomes management in heart valve replacement surgery: early experience. *Journal of Heart Valve Disease, 1*(1), 42–50; reprinted with permission from Ware, J. E., Kosinski, M., & Keller, S. K. (1994). *SF-36 physical and mental health summary scales: A user's manual.* Boston: The Health Institute, New England Medical Center. Copyright 1994, John Ware.

Figure 4-12

MEASUREMENT MODELS: FOCUS ON STRUCTURE

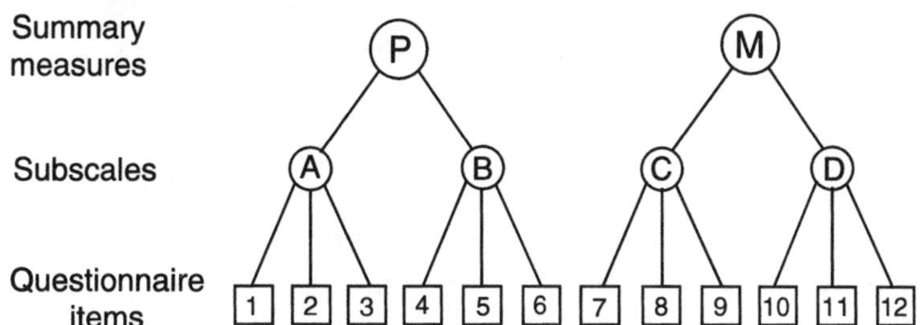

Note: P = physical; M = mental; A, B, C, and D are hypothetical dimensions of health.

Figure 4-13

MEASUREMENT MODELS: FOCUS ON SINGLE INDEX

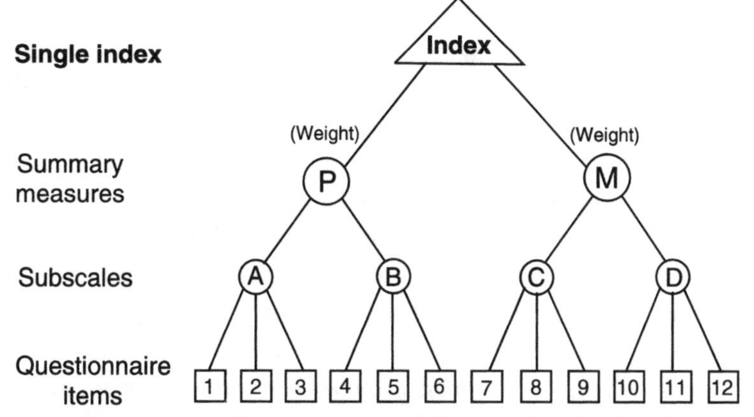

Note: P = physical; M = mental; A, B, C, and D are hypothetical dimensions of health.

Figure 4-14

MEASUREMENT MODELS: UTILITY INDEX APPROACH

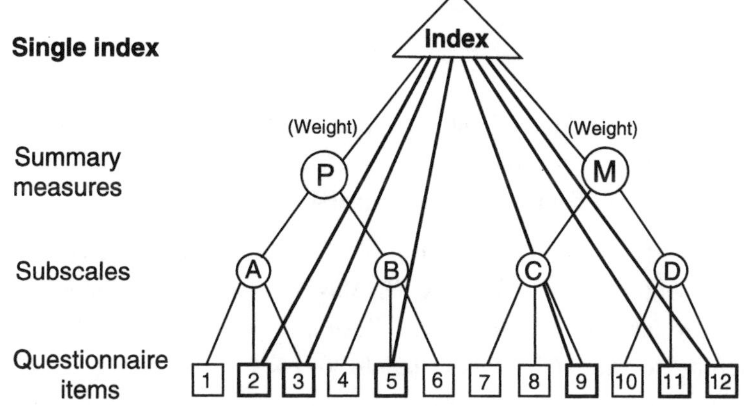

Note: P = physical; M = mental; A, B, C, and D are hypothetical dimensions of health.

Conclusion

Future challenges to patient-based outcomes measurement include more efficient questionnaires (including shorter forms), increased comprehensiveness of normative surveys, greater comparability of concepts and methods across applications, advances in technologies for collecting and processing data, longitudinal monitoring of general and specific populations, and improved systems for linking data sets. (For example, the National Health Interview Survey is being redesigned, and it will include mental health ["Questionnaire Probes," 1992].) New technologies exist, such as scanning and fax systems. Any office that has a fax machine can process a patient-based health assessment and receive results in a matter of seconds using computers on the other end of the phone lines. Longitudinal monitoring is occurring, and databases are being linked. The linking of the clinical, physical, social role, and generic databases with an economic database will revolutionize the evaluation of health care services in the United States.

What will be done with the results? This leads to the last point about aggregation. Figures 4-12, 4-13, and 4-14 illustrate three approaches to measurement modeling. As shown in Figure 14-12, aggregating questionnaire items to make subscales involves carefully studying their internal consistency and their empirical validity. Items that are summarized must be summarized in a way that preserves interpretation and structure. Researchers summarize the measures that are truly redundant, the ones that are likely to give the same results. However, researchers are under a great deal of pressure to go to a single index number as illustrated in Figure 4-13. Imagine a news broadcaster saying, "The market went up yesterday, unemployment is amazingly low, and health is at 82 up from 81." There are people who want to put one number on your whole life or on everything that you do, and this desire should be resisted. As illustrated in Figure 4-14, typically what economists rely on in constructing a utility index is a few items and a few levels of health because they cannot deal with the complete information. They study the resulting permutations and score them into a single index. After going to all of the trouble of getting clinical data, good social and human functioning outcomes data, and good economic data, let's not just add it all up into a single index!

References

Berry, S. (1992). Methods of collecting health data. In A. L. Stewart & J. E. Ware (Eds.), *Measuring functioning and well-being: The Medical Outcomes Study approach* (pp. 48–64). Durham, NC: Duke University Press.

Brook, R. H., Ware, J. E., Jr., Rogers, W. H., Keeler, E. B., Davies, A. R., Donald, C. A., Goldberg, G. A., Lohr, K. N., Masthay, P. C., & Newhouse, J. P. (1983). Does free care improve adults' health? Results from a randomized controlled trial. *New England Journal of Medicine, 309,* 1426–1434.

Croog, S. H., Levine, S., Testa, M. A., Brown, B., Bulpitt, C. J., Jenkins, C. D., Klerman, G. L., & Williams, G. H. (1986). The effects of antihypertensive therapy on the quality of life. *New England Journal of Medicine, 314,* 1657–1664.

Davies, A. R., & Ware, J. E. (1992). *GHAA's consumer satisfaction survey and user's manual.* Washington, DC: Group Health Association of America.

Donabedian, A. (1980). *Explorations in quality assessment and monitoring, Vol. 1: The definition of quality and approaches to its assessment.* Ann Arbor, MI: Health and Administration Press.

Ganz, P. A., Day, R., Ware, J. E., Redmond, C., & Fisher, B. (1996). Base-line quality-of-life assessment in the National Surgical Adjuvant Breast and Bowel Project Breast Cancer Prevention Trial. *Journal of the National Cancer Institute, 87,* 1372–1382.

Greenfield, S., Nelson, E. C., Zubkoff, M., Manning, W., Rogers, W., Kravitz, R. L., Keller, A., Tarlov, A. R., & Ware, J. E., Jr. (1992). Variations in resource utilization among medical specialties and systems of care: Results from the Medical Outcomes Study. *Journal of the American Medical Association, 267,* 1624–1630.

Greenfield, S., Rogers, W., Mangotich, M., Carney, M. F., & Tarlov, A. R. (1995). Outcomes of patients with hypertension and non–insulin-dependent diabetes mellitus treated by different systems and specialties: Results from the Medical Outcomes Study. *Journal of the American Medical Association, 274,* 1436–1474.

Kravitz, R. L., Greenfield, S., Rogers, W. H., Manning, W. G., Jr., Zubkoff, M., Nelson, E. C., Tarlov, A. R., & Ware, J. E., Jr. (1992). Differences in the mix of patients among medical specialties and systems of care: Results from the Medical Outcomes Study. *Journal of the American Medical Association, 267,* 1617–1623.

Lembcke, P. A. (1967). Evolution of the medical audit. *Journal of the American Medical Association, 199,* 111–118.

Meyer, K. B., Espindle, D. M., DeGiacomo, J. M., Jenuleson, C. S., Kurtin, P. S., & Davies, A. R. (1994). Monitoring patients' health status. *American Journal of Kidney Diseases, 24,* 267–279.

Phillips, R. C., & Lansky, D. J. (1992). Outcomes management in heart valve replacement surgery: Early experience. *Journal of Heart Valve Disease, 1*(1), 42–50;

Questionnaire probes patients' quality of life. (1992, July 7). *The Wall Street Journal,* pp. B1–B4.

Rogers, W. H., Wells, K. B., Meredith, L. S., Sturm, R., & Burnam, A. (1993). Outcomes for adult outpatients with depression under prepaid or fee-for-service financing. *Archives of General Psychiatry, 50,* 517–525.

Rubin, H. R., Gandek, B., Rogers, W. H., Kosinski, M., McHorney, C. A., & Ware, J. E., Jr. (1993). Patients' ratings of outpatient visits in different practice settings: Results from the Medical Outcomes Study. *Journal of the American Medical Association, 270,* 835–840.

Safran, D., Tarlov, A. R., & Rogers, W. (1994). Primary care performances in fee-for-service and prepaid health care systems: Results from the Medical Outcomes Study. *Journal of the American Medical Association, 271,* 1579–1586.

Stewart, A. L., Greenfield, S., Hays, R. D., Wells, K., Rogers, W. H., Berry, S. D., McGlynn, E. A., & Ware, J. E., Jr. (1989). Functional status and well-being of patients with chronic conditions: Results from the Medical Outcomes Study. *Journal of the American Medical Association, 262,* 907–913.

Stewart, A. L., & Ware, J. E. (Eds.). (1992). *Measuring functioning and well-being: The Medical Outcomes Study approach.* Durham, NC: Duke University Press.

Tarlov, A. R., Ware, J. E., Greenfield, S., Nelson, E. C., Perrin, E., & Zubkoff, M. (1989). The Medical Outcomes Study: An application of methods for monitoring the results of medical care. *Journal of the American Medical Association, 262,* 925–930.

Ware, J. E. (1995). The status of health assessment 1994. *Annual Review of Public Health, 16,* 327–354.

Ware, J. E., Bayliss, M. S., Rogers, W. H., Kosinski, M., & Tarlov, A. (1996). Differences in 4-year health outcomes for elderly and poor, chronically ill patients treated in HMO and fee-for-service systems. *Journal of the American Medical Association, 276,* 1039–1047.

Ware, J. E., Brook, R. H., Rogers, W. H., Keeler, E. B., Davies, A. R., Sherbourne, C. D., Goldberg, G. A., Camp, P., & Newhouse, J. P. (1986). Comparison of health outcomes at a health maintenance organization with those of fee-for-service care. *Lancet, 1,* 1017–1022.

Ware, J. E., & Hays, R. D. (1988). Methods for measuring patient satisfaction with specific medical encounters. *Medical Care, 26,* 393–402.

Ware, J. E., & Keller, S. D. (1995). Interpreting general health meausres. In B. Spilker (Ed.), *Quality of life and pharmacoeconomics in clinical trials* (2nd ed., pp. 445–460). New York: Raven Press.

Ware, J. E., Keller, S. D., Gandek, B., Brazier, J. E., Sullivan, M., & IQOLA Project Group. (1995). Evaluating translations of health status questionnaires: Methods from the IQOLA project. *International Journal of Technology Assessment in Health Care, 11,* 525–551.

Ware, J. E., Kosinski, M., & Keller, S. D. (1994). *SF-36 physical and mental health summary scales: A user's manual.* Boston: The Health Institute, New England Medical Center.

Ware, J. E., Kosinski, M., & Keller, S. D. (1996). A 12-item short-form health survey (SF-12): Construction of scales and preliminary tests of reliability and validity. *Medical Care, 32,* 220–233.

Ware, J. E., Snyder, M. K., Wright, W. R., & Davies, A. R. (1983). Defining and measuring patient satisfaction with medical care. *Evaluation and Program Planning, 6,* 247–263.

Wells, K. B., Hays, R. D., Burnam, M. A., Rogers, W., Greenfield, S., & Ware, J. E. (1989). Detection of depressive disorder for patients receiving prepaid or fee-for-service care: Results from the Medical Outcomes Study. *Journal of the American Medical Association, 262,* 3298–3302.

CHAPTER 5

Assessment Tools as Outcomes Measures in Social Work

WALTER W. HUDSON

Applied measurement theory was virtually unknown in social work practice before the early 1970s. Its development and use were stimulated by summaries of evaluation research (Fischer, 1973; Mullen & Dumpson, 1972) and the subsequent heated debate about the effectiveness of social work practice at both macro- and microlevels.

In response to the storm of accountability that arose during the early 1970s, a beginning effort was made (Giuli & Hudson, 1977; Hudson, 1982b; Hudson & Glisson, 1976; Hudson & Proctor, 1977) to develop short-form assessment scales that could be used in single-system research designs by practitioners who wished to have improved assessments of specific client problems and a means for monitoring progress over time. Soon after their appearance, they were dubbed *rapid assessment instruments* by Levitt and Reid (1981), and the development and use of such tools gained considerable support. By the end of the decade the idea of applied measurement theory had become an arguably legitimate social work method in research and practice (Bloom & Fischer, 1982; Hudson, 1978, 1982a). Currently, social work has a rich array of short-form assessment scales (for example, Bloom, Fischer, & Orme, 1994; Fischer & Corcoran, 1994; Hudson, 1982a, 1990a; Nurius & Hudson, 1993) and a sound beginning on the development and validation of multidimensional assessment scales for use in practice and research (Gabor, Thomlison, & Hudson, 1994; Hudson, 1990b, 1996b, 1997a, 1997b, 1997c; Hudson & McMurtry, 1997). There is reason to believe that the years ahead will provide many new measurement tools for use by social work practitioners, administrators, and program evaluators.

Measures, Assessments, Outcomes, and Effectiveness

Despite the enormous progress that has been made in the development and acquisition of practice-related measurement tools, social workers still struggle over the same core issues that emerged in the early 1970s. First among them is the question, "Are we effective?" Important corollary questions include "How can we determine whether we are effective?" and "How can we demonstrate effectiveness?"

Does asking the same questions now that were asked a quarter of a century ago mean that little has been learned and therefore little or no progress has been made? The current relevance of these questions could mean just that. However, they could also mean that what has been learned has not been applied, the demonstrations have not been made, and the evaluations that our improved technologies have made possible have not been conducted. It also could be that the technology is not fully understood, improvements in it are needed, and social work providers do not yet have the knowledge or means for using it on a regular basis. It is possible that the important distinctions between measures, assessments, outcomes, and effectiveness are sometimes confused. These are distinctions about which we must first be clear.

MEASUREMENT TOOLS

A measurement tool can be used for assessment as well as to examine outcomes, but first and most important a measurement tool is little more than a device that captures (hopefully accurately) information about some attribute that is used to describe something (for example, a client). A measurement tool must not be confused with an assessment tool, an outcomes measure, or a measure of effectiveness.

It is important to remember that a measurement tool has no value orientation whatsoever: It just measures. For example, a high or low temperature means virtually nothing to a thermometer. The only thing that matters in measurement is that a measurement tool captures information in a reliable manner. If a paper-and-pencil scale accurately measures a client's level of depression, the magnitude of the score is unimportant. A large score is as meaningless as a small one from a measurement perspective. All that is required is that the instrument be accurate.

ASSESSMENT SCALES

An assessment scale is a measurement tool that is used for a purpose and with a value orientation. If a physician uses a thermometer to measure a client's temperature, he or she may characterize a high temperature as abnormal (a value orientation) and then attempt to lower the temperature. If a social worker uses a paper-and-pencil self-report scale to describe a client's level of depression, he or she may regard a high score as abnormal and then attempt to cause the depression to diminish. A measurement tool merely describes. If that measurement tool is used to plan and judge, it is an assessment tool. Because measurement tools can be used for planning purposes within the context of making judgments that are driven by a societally and professionally approved value system, they can be of enormous benefit to clients, practitioners, and those who fund the delivery of services to clients.

Although these observations about measurement tools and assessment scales appear to be obvious or trivial, the point is that assessment scales can be useful to clients, practitioners, supervisors, administrators, and funding organizations, and their usefulness is diminished in proportion to the number of these actors whose information needs are ignored.

OUTCOMES MEASURES

There often is enormous confusion in discussions of outcomes because there are two basic kinds of outcomes. One represents an outcome with respect to the problem for which the client seeks help (for example, to help reduce the client's level of depression). The other represents an outcome with respect to professional behavior; what actually is done to alleviate the problem (for example, providing 20 sessions of psychotherapy). Assessment scales can be used to evaluate outcomes with respect to the problem to be treated, but they are virtually useless in evaluating what was done to solve the problem (Hudson, 1996c; Hudson & Faul, in press). The confusion that arises in discussions about outcomes often centers on the fact that one group of discussants speaks ambiguously about outcomes (as interventive behaviors or as treatment and service protocols), whereas a second group uses the same term, with an equal lack of specificity, to denote changes or the lack thereof in the problem to be treated. One group speaks of outcomes in relation to client well-being, and the other group speaks of outcomes in terms of the treatment protocols and their quality.

EFFECTIVENESS

There can be no effectiveness unless there is change (Hudson, 1996c; Nurius & Hudson, 1993; Patti, 1985). Clients seek help because they want something to improve. They never seek help because they want things to remain the same or to get worse. Improvement cannot occur without change in something. Moreover, *change*, as it is used in the various human service disciplines and professions, means change over time. Issues of efficiency and efficacy discussed elsewhere in this book do not matter unless the importance of measuring change as the key ingredient of effectiveness is understood. Once the concept of change is adequately defined and measured, issues concerning efficiency and efficacy become important.

Measures of Effectiveness

It seems apparent that a measure of effectiveness is a measure of change. Unfortunately, there are no reliable and valid direct measures of change. Measurement tools that can be completed by a client and then scored to show how much the client's condition has improved or deteriorated do not exist. It is surprisingly easy to devise category partition scales such as "Please circle the number that represents your best estimate of change in your marital problem" (–2 = very much worse, –1 = worse, 0 = no change, +1 = improved, +2 = very much improved). Such attempts at direct measures of change have nearly always been disappointing and are virtually useless if one takes seriously their generally unacceptable reliabilities and poor validities. Fortunately, an alternative is available.

This chapter focuses on the notion of outcomes as representing a change in the status of the client's problem (Hudson, 1996c). Thus, to measure change in a client problem (CP), the concept of a CP must be defined and measured at some point in time, t_1. The measure of the client's problem at t_1 can be denoted as CP_1. In an effort to improve the client's quality of life by helping the client solve the problem, a service or intervention will be provided, and then the same CP will be measured at a second point in time, t_2. When the two CP measures are compared, hopefully some improvement from t_1 to t_2 can be perceived. That is, hopefully CP_2 is much improved from CP_1. This provides the simple definition of desired change, where "Δ" means change and

$$\Delta CP = CP_2 - CP_1 \qquad \textit{Eq. 1}$$

(For example, a client receives an initial depression score of 80 and six weeks later scores 30 on the same depression scale, gaining 50 points. Thus, $\Delta CP = CP_2 - CP_1 = 30 - 80 = -50$ [a 50-point decrease in depression is noted by the negative change value].)

This equation is a crisp, mathematical definition of effectiveness. If the value of equation 1 is zero (or close to it), the client has not been helped. If the value of equation 1 is positive and large, the client's condition has deteriorated, and the social worker should wonder whether he or she has harmed the client. Finally, if the value of equation 1 is large and negative in value, then the client's condition has improved, and the desired change has been achieved.

Evidence of Effectiveness

A large negative value for equation 1 does not mean that the treatments, services, or interventions provided have actually caused the observed positive change. The improvement could be attributed to a positive event, such as winning the lottery. To show that the service, treatment, or intervention protocol was responsible for the positive gain, those behaviors that constitute the service or intervention must be defined. If those behaviors are denoted as $X_1, X_2, \ldots X_n$ to signify that there are potentially many different service behaviors to engage in helping a client, an accountability model (or equation) can then be written by expressing desired change as a function of caregiving behavior. That is, the model is fully specified by writing

$$\Delta CP = CP_2 - CP_1 = f(X_1, X_2, \ldots X_n) \qquad \textit{Eq. 2}$$

or the even more succinct form as

$$\Delta CP = f(X_i),_{\ i=1,n} \qquad \textit{Eq. 3}$$

It is important to recognize that equation 3 is expressed as a mathematical function and that real-world observations in the social and behavioral sciences rarely conform to strict mathematical functions. Thus, an error term (e) must be added to the model. The model can be expressed in general terms as

$$\Delta CP = f(X_i),_{\ i=1,n} + e \qquad \textit{Eq. 4}$$

and treated as a probabilistic model. In this form, the model does little more than assert that positive change in clients' problems should be at least in part a result of what is done to help them. Stated differently, the model asserts that the best that can be done, behaviorally, is to increase the likelihood of a more positive outcome for the client.

The beauty of equation 4 is its elegant simplicity and the fact that it serves two purposes. First, it is a model for research that addresses the question of whether the engaged caregiving services (behaviors) actually produce desired change. Second, it becomes the managed care accountability mandate of the next century. Or does it?

Managed Care

Managed care often is perceived as an 800-pound gorilla that has already sat down on workers in other disciplines with its enormous weight, and social work providers are concerned with how and where it will affect them. At core, the issue comes down to the question of how social work providers will respond to the managed care mandates of the late 1990s and the next decade. Should social work providers be held responsible for equation 1 or equation 4?

It is my conviction that social work providers should not be held responsible for equation 4 because it is the domain and responsibility of social work researchers and academics. However, social work providers will likely become increasingly responsible for equation 1, and they should view this responsibility as a normal course of professional behavior. Unfortunately, the profession has not uniformly done a good job of demonstrating even the minimal accountability implied by implementing equation 1. If social workers adopt equation 1 quickly, responsibly, and uniformly as a professional standard of practice accountability, managed care may be content with that. If they do not, they may be held accountable for equation 4.

Computers in the Service of Practice or Accountability

Many would like to believe that computers will increasingly become available to help practitioners respond more easily to the onrushing managed care mandates and to assist practitioners with the actual conduct of practice. This belief is a fantasy given almost the entire history of all human service organizational uses of computers since the mid-1950s. The history of computer use is indelibly clear and must be faced squarely to change the future or have any influence on it.

The overwhelming evidence of the past 40 years is that big agency computers have been governed by a mainframe mentality that has never cared for the practitioner or the client as an end-user or consumer of computers or information-processing services. On the contrary, the behavior almost universally demonstrated by managers of computer services (and administrators who manage the computer managers) is often little more than a thinly disguised contempt for the practitioner and his or her information-processing needs or wishes. This behavior will not change unless practitioners take a forceful, proactive approach in pursuit of their own interests and those of their clients. Instead, what will happen (and is already under development) is that practitioners once more will be treated as data entry clerks for those who control the computer system. The role of measurement in this situation must be understood.

For example, it is easy to develop a five-item self-report scale to measure depression that can be completed rapidly, has a reliability of about .65, and will do a passable job on validity when used to address equation 1 if such a measure is used only for aggregation over 1,000 or so cases to address the question of whether clients' conditions improved. Unfortunately, such a scale is worthless in helping the practitioner or the client to better do the job of bringing about the desired change that is to be reflected through the use of equation 1. Yet, the history of human service computing and the work currently under way in several centers indicate that this is the future use of measurement in managed care and quality assurance monitoring.

Stated differently, there is a high likelihood that practitioners will once more be filling out forms that are of almost no use to them or their clients. The only difference is that they may be using computers to do it, and such an application of computer technology once again asserts that practitioners and clients will not be served as end users or consumers of information-processing technology. This scenario (representative of a 40-year history) is one of computer technology used in service of accountability at its most primitive level. It is not computer technology in service of the day-to-day conduct of human service practice. If practitioners are content with that scenario, they need do nothing but wait. Simply do nothing, be uninvolved, and it will happen.

Earlier in this chapter, in the section titled "Assessment Scales," it was noted that the utility of strong assessment tools is diminished in proportion to the number of organizational actors whose information needs are ignored. It is in this sense that previous and current movements in computer-based effectiveness monitoring can and should be regarded as primitive in nature. They are primitive because the information-processing needs of too many organizational actors are ignored. The consequences for the organization are large, as evidenced by the mound of deceased information systems that lie buried in an enormous database cemetery. If human service agencies do not need professionally trained people who will be vigorous and thoughtful in their efforts to provide services, it would be much more cost effective to hire data entry clerks whose jobs are defined as such. If professionally trained people are needed for service delivery, treatment, and intervention planning and implementation, then it makes sense either to give them no computers at all or to give them information systems that help them do their work.

There is an alternative that will benefit everyone and achieve the long-range goals that are important to managed care: begin working on accountability systems specifically designed to help line-level service providers better do their jobs. In this alternative, the line-level practitioner's information-processing needs and wishes represent the highest priority of the entire system. In short, information-processing needs must be met from the bottom up and not from the top down because if computers can help practitioners get their job done, the act of doing their job will produce data that the top level of the organization can use to address the mandates of both equations 1 and 4. The five essential steps are quite simple:

1. Use client self-report measurement tools that are psychometrically sound for work with individuals.
2. Do not rely on improvement rating scales that are completed by practitioners.
3. Create computer systems that are responsive to workers and clients who will use those measurement scales.
4. Cause computers to use measurement in the service of doing practice, rather than just evaluating it.
5. Let the computer system evaluate the effectiveness of practice as a background activity and not as the its raison d'être.

The future of human service computing is not mainframe computers, although they will play an important role. The future of agency computing is networks (Hudson, 1993), and agencies are working hard to acquire network hardware and personal computers for use by service delivery personnel. Unfortunately, a local area network can also be managed with the same mainframe mentality as has been demonstrated for the past 40 years with mainframe computers. It is not likely that human service workers will behave differently or better, but modern computing technology at least makes it possible and feasible to consider remarkably improved alternatives.

Future Agendas in Outcomes Measurement Research

Applied measurement theory is becoming increasingly important and useful in many different ways for micro- and macrolevel human service professionals (Fischer & Corcoran, 1994). Although work continues in basic psychometric research, the psychometric science currently is solid and will not be the major focus of applied measurement research. More assessment and evaluation tools are needed that will provide broader coverage of the measurement constructs that are useful to clients and service delivery personnel. It should be noted in this regard that there are many good measures for use with adults, but there is an enormous dirth of reliable and valid measurement scales that deal with personal and social functioning and are appropriate for use with children younger than age 12.

Although more work is needed to develop measurement tools for use in practice, attention must also be given to developing computer support systems that will address the day-to-day realities of actually doing practice and will also accommodate the measurement and assessment needs of all actors within the organization: clients, practitioners, supervisors, managers, administrators, and program evaluators.

It is not difficult to have a client complete a short-form assessment scale. It also is not difficult for a practitioner to administer, score, and interpret it. It also is not difficult for a practitioner to prepare a simple time-series graph and plot the score results on the graph to monitor progress over repeated administrations of the same assessment scale. However, although all of these tasks are simple to do and require minimal training, the challenge of engaging these activities on a routine basis with every client is large. It may not be feasible unless special tools are provided to assist with scale administration, scoring, graphing, and large-scale data management using modern database management technology. A beginning effort in this direction is the Microsoft Windows version of the Computer-Assisted Social Services (CASS) (Hudson, 1996a) system. (The CASS software requires an IBM or compatible computer, Windows 3.11 or Windows 95, and a VGA color board and monitor. The software can be obtained by writing to the WALMYR Publishing Company, P.O. Box 24779, Tempe, AZ 85285-4779. The software may be downloaded without fee from the World Wide Web via http://www.syspac.com/~walmyr/.) CASS is a new system that has not yet been fully tested and may require time to mature as new features are added. The development and enhancement of such systems will become a major area of research and development during the coming years.

Despite the improved availability of measurement scales, practitioners often confront an important barrier in using those that are available. Consider the problems recently faced by a child welfare agency in the southeastern United States. The development team reviewed a large group of unidimensional and multidimensional assessment scales and finally located three that contained all of the intake assessment scales they wished to use. Unfortunately, they wanted to use some of the subscales from each but did not want to use all subscales from all three instruments. Aside from the fact that there are important copyright issues involved in using parts of three different commercial assessment scales, the agency confronted large logistical problems in identifying needed subscales, putting them together as a usable instrument, and developing a means of administering, scoring, interpreting, and graphing results while also managing the data for many different clients. The problems faced by that child welfare agency represent a major difficulty for many different service delivery organizations, and measurement-oriented computer systems may help to solve these kinds of problems. A recent development called multidimensional assessment groups (MAG) (Hudson & Faul, 1996) enables a computer-based designer assessment system, but it also is new and has not been widely tested. (The MAG technology has been implemented for the first time within the CASS system.) In short, more work is needed in developing and testing the kinds of measurement-oriented tools and support systems that will deliver improved technologies to practitioners while also making it easy to use them.

A great deal of evaluation research conducted in the 1960s (and much that followed over the past 35 years) was driven by the fundamental question of whether proffered services actually help the client solve meaningful problems or provide useful services. Does social work work? It is a legitimate question that must be addressed. However, the equally important questions of whether quality assurance monitoring works and whether the 800-pound gorilla is going to sit properly and in the right place also must be addressed. That is, we thus far have no evidence to show that managed care produces better results. More research is needed to determine whether methods, devices, policies, and procedures that are used to construct a quality assurance monitoring system, such as managed care, actually produce a useful outcome or whether they misguide social work providers and perhaps even prevent the opportunity of providing clients with useful assistance.

Although the major thrust of this chapter is the future of measurement research and development, it also is important to identify an important need for measurement education. Because the 800-pound gorilla is looking for a place to sit, many will be eager to offer him a seat and pacify the brute. In other words, there may be a rush to measurement never before seen, and at least two cautions are in order. The proper use of applied measurement theory in the field is not difficult. However, it requires some training, and work must be done to determine how best to provide it. Most of what is needed in the way of practical training can be provided in a single day-long workshop, but much work must first be done to organize such workshops and train personnel who can conduct them.

A second caution in any rush to measurement concerns the development and use of measurement tools. It is extremely easy to write some items on a sheet of paper, type them up, and call them a scale. If that is done by people who have no training or experience in basic psychometric theory, the results could be devastating at worst or simply useless. In short, the psychometric performance of measurement tools used in practice must be taken seriously. It is surprising that a large number of people believe they can develop a useful measurement tool when they cannot define, interpret, or calculate a reliability coefficient. Such beliefs must not be encouraged.

In many situations, it is useful to use client rating scales in place of client self-report measures. More research is needed on the strengths of these two approaches. A general guideline should be followed, but its merits must be examined through systematic research. When the construct to be measured is a private event, affect, perception, or judgment, it is always wisest to use a client self-report measure. Observers who complete client rating scales simply cannot get inside the client's head to observe private events, thoughts, perceptions, affects, or judgments. However, when the measured construct is based largely on client behavior, client rating scales that are completed by trained observers can be useful. More research is needed to investigate the relative merits of these two approaches to measurement.

Implications of Using Outcomes Measures for Quality Assurance Monitoring and Accountability

Management information systems have been a popular topic of discussion since the birth of computer technology. The database cemetery is heaped with management information systems (MISs) that either never saw the light of day or were abandoned after they were imposed on unwitting practitioners and other users. This abandonment surely will happen repeatedly because most systems are designed from the top down without any of the developers ever consulting with, or even considering the needs of, those who must enter the data. The wonderfully descriptive term for such a system is "data in, nothing out" (DINO).

In a southwestern state there is an expensive but worthless behavioral health information system that will eventually go to the database cemetery. However, it will survive until taken over by a political regime whose members will not be embarrassed to admit that millions of dollars were wasted. Service personnel spend enormous amounts of time entering data by completing multipage paper-and-pencil forms that are of virtually no use to practitioners or clients. Moreover, this particular DINO information system does not produce a single scrap of feedback information that is used by service delivery personnel to help them do their work.

As yet another example, the insurance industry in the United States has bought into and continues to maintain and rely on a DINO system that is fraudulent at every level. Many such companies insist on having a *Diagnostic and Statistical Manual of Mental Disorders, 4th edition* (DSM-IV) (American Psychiatric Association, 1994) diagnosis before they will pay for services. Moreover, they often are strict about which diagnoses will be reimbursed. It has in such instances become a widespread open secret that human service administrators and practitioners do not write the diagnosis that best describes the client's problem. Rather, they write the one that will produce reimbursement. This practice does not harm clients because a DSM-IV diagnosis provides no new information about the client and is therefore not useful in helping practitioners help their clients. Such a diagnosis is nothing more than a mechanism for reporting what the practitioner already knows about the client. The consequence of maintaining this kind of DINO system is that the diagnostic database that might be used to describe the nature and incidence of mental disorders is so completely flawed as to be utterly worthless. To give it any credence whatsoever would be to deceive oneself about the status of mental health in this country.

Information management systems ultimately are judged in terms of their outputs rather than their inputs. If the outputs are not useful, the inputs do not matter. Yet, it is easy to conceive an MIS that will contain much potentially useful data if one does not have to confront the question of who will use the information and how it will help them do their work. An improvement over a strict DINO system is a "data in, some useful data out" (DISUDO) system. However, the question arises: To whom are the data useful?

The 800-pound gorilla we call "managed care" will have his DISUDO system. About that, we can be certain. At a minimum, such a system might produce information that is useful to top management in an aggregated form for making risky and, in some cases, misguided decisions about what to pay for and what to exclude. The downside of what appears to be coming down the pike is that measurements adequate for such purposes are being developed, but such measures are not adequate to help service providers do their work. Worse yet, systems are being designed with virtually no thought given to the most important actors in the entire organization—clients and practitioners.

On the top rung of the ladder of abstraction is the lofty ambition of producing good service at minimal cost and at maximum profit. Let's face it—managed care is sometimes a euphemism for managed profits. On the bottom rung of the ladder of abstraction are real workers, real clients, and no information management tools to help them do their jobs. One widespread analogy that is not without merit is that practitioners are expected to have all the duties of a marriage but none of the privileges when it comes to information management services, computer supports, and quality assurance management.

The implications for using measurement tools in computerized quality assurance and outcomes effectiveness evaluation systems are urgent and extremely important. If measurement tools are developed, selected, and used because they help clients and practitioners on a day-to-day, case-by-case basis, their potential benefits are enormous. If social work practitioners use measurement tools that ignore the needs of clients and practitioners and wield them through use of various DINO or DISUDO systems, the outcome is going to be disappointing at best and harmful to many of the clients for whom managed care argues its best case.

Conclusion

Managed care and quality assurance management often are euphemisms for back office conversation, crudely expressed as "Let's make sure these workers are doing their jobs or we'll fire them." Whether expressed in this form or not, the meaning often excludes management, administration, and resource allocation authorities as having any culpability for poor service outcomes. It will be a long time before I forget the outrage expressed by a nun who was given $10,000 to care for a large group of children while her central office administrators were given $100,000 to manage the work (the actual figures are likely wrong but the gap is not misleading). The point of this is that responsibility for providing effective services is not the sole province of practitioners. It is a responsibility that must be equally distributed across the entire organization and beyond it.

If we can develop and maintain a sense of perspective about the intensely shared nature of accountability and responsibility for providing useful services to clients, then measurement tools, computers, and information management software systems can be useful and important aids that will help us do a better job at every level of the organization. If such tools are used by one group of actors to control, blame, or hold accountable another group of actors (for example, practitioners), they will likely fail in their promise and they will no doubt result in great harm to many. Clearly the largest issues are the state of the art not with respect to measurement or computer technology but with respect to how we shall use this technology.

References

American Psychiatric Association. (1994). *Diagnostic and statistical manual of mental disorders* (4th ed.). Washington, DC: Author.

Bloom, M., & Fischer, J. (1982). *Evaluating practice: Guidelines for the accountable professional* (1st ed.). New York: Prentice Hall.

Bloom, M., Fischer, J., & Orme, J. (1994). *Evaluating practice: Guidelines for the accountable professional* (2nd ed.). Boston: Allyn & Bacon.

Fischer, J. (1973). Is casework effective? A review. *Social Work, 18,* 5–20.

Fischer, J., & Corcoran, K. (1994). *Measures for clinical practice.* New York: The Free Press.

Gabor, P., Thomlison, B., & Hudson, W. W. (1994). *Family Assessment Screening Inventory (FASI).* Tempe, AZ: WALMYR Publishing.

Giuli, C., & Hudson, W. W. (1977). Assessing parent–child relationship disorders in clinical practice: The child's point of view. *Journal of Social Service Research, 1*(1), 77–92.

Hudson, W. W. (1978). First axioms of treatment. *Social Work, 23,* 65–66.

Hudson, W. W. (1982a). *The clinical measurement package: A field manual.* Homewood, IL: Dorsey Press.

Hudson, W. W. (1982b). A measurement package for clinical workers. *Journal of Applied Behavioral Science, 17,* 229–238.

Hudson, W. W. (1990a). *Multi-Problem Screening Inventory (MPSI).* Tempe, AZ: WALMYR Publishing.

Hudson, W. W. (1990b). *WALMYR Assessment Scale scoring manual.* Tempe, AZ: WALMYR Publishing.

Hudson, W. W. (1993). Guest editorial: The future of social service computing. *Computers in Human Services, 10*(2), 1–7.

Hudson, W. W. (1996a). *Computer-Assisted Social Services (CASS).* Tempe, Arizona: WALMYR Publishing.

Hudson, W. W. (1996b). *Multidimensional Adolescent Assessment Scale (MAAS).* Tempe, AZ: WALMYR Publishing.

Hudson, W. W. (1996c). Professional practice for the 21st century: Information implications. In J. Steyaert (Ed.), *Information technology and human services, More than computers?* Utrecht, Netherlands: Netherlands Institute for Care and Welfare/ NIZW.

Hudson, W. W. (1997a). *Brief Adult Assessment Scale (BAAS).* Tempe, AZ: WALMYR Publishing.

Hudson, W. W (1997b). *Brief Family Assessment Scale (BFAS).* Tempe, AZ: WALMYR Publishing.

Hudson, W. W. (1997c). *Multi-Problem Screening Questionnaire (MPSQ).* Tempe, AZ: WALMYR Publishing.

Hudson, W. W., & Faul, A. C. (1996). *Designer assessment tools using multidimensional assessment groups* (mimeo). Tempe, AZ: WALMYR Publishing.

Hudson, W. W., & Faul, A. C. (in press). *Quality assurance: A system for practice and program evaluation using outcome measures.* Tempe, AZ: WALMYR Publishing.

Hudson, W. W., & Glisson, D. F. (1976). Assessment of marital discord in social work practice. *Social Service Review, 50*, 293–311.

Hudson, W. W., & McMurtry (1997). Comprehensive assessment in social work practice: The Multi-Problem Screening Inventory. *Research on Social Work Practice, 7*, 79–98.

Hudson, W. W., & Proctor, E. K. (1977). The assessment of depressive affect in clinical practice: A brief report. *Journal of Consulting and Clinical Psychology, 45*, 1206–1207.

Levitt, J. L., & Reid, W. J. (1981). Rapid assessment instruments for practice. *Social Work Research & Abstracts, 17* (1), 13–19.

Mullen, E., & Dumpson, J. (1972). *The evaluation of social intervention.* New York: Jossey-Bass.

Nurius, P., & Hudson, W. W. (1993). *Human services practice, evaluation & computers: A practical guide for today and beyond.* Pacific Grove, CA: Brooks/Cole Publishing.

Patti, R. J. (1985). In search of purpose for social welfare administration *Administration in Social Work, 9*, 1–14.

CHAPTER 6

Developing Clinical Outcomes Systems: Conceptual and Practical Issues

WILLIAM H. BERMAN

STEPHEN W. HURT

Changes in financing and accountability in health care have shifted the role of patient-based assessment and outcomes from nonessential research to an essential component of quality evaluation. Evaluating patient care through the eyes of the patient has become crucial to the management of the care delivery process as managed care has become the dominant model of payment and service delivery (Ellwood, 1988). Patient-based outcomes measurement provides a check on both quality and access to care, aspects that are at risk in utilization managment systems. Recent changes toward prepaid payment systems shift the burden to the provider group, which agrees to provide all services needed based on a fixed amount for each person seen (that is, case rate) or for all potential patients (that is, capitation). These payment approaches place the clinician in potential conflict between income and delivery of needed services. Patient-based outcomes encourage high-quality care by providing feedback on clinical change, functioning, and satisfaction that can help identify strong and weak points in the care delivery process, including providers or groups with better results.

The primary purposes of outcomes systems are to measure patient status and change over time on dimensions such as satisfaction with process and outcome; change in clinical and functional status; and change in quality of life, health, and services. Data can be obtained from various sources, measured in a variety of ways, and examined both in aggregate and in detail to address a wide range of questions relevant to purchasers, payers, managers, clinicians, and consumers.

Outcomes systems are tools for measuring and improving service delivery, whether in the mental health sector, the home care sector, or the social services sector. Used as a part of an effort to enhance delivery of patient care known as continuous quality improvement (CQI) (Berwick, Godfrey, & Roessner, 1990), these data can help facilitate triage, simplify referrals, enhance administrative procedures and clinical protocols, eliminate redundancy, and assist in treatment matching and treatment redesign. The measurement of outcomes serves as a means to an end. Unfortunately, outcomes are frequently used as an end, in comparisons of individuals or groups within an organization or in comparisons of one organization with another. These "horse races" are methodologically flawed, and they create tensions among those being profiled. The result is usually the failure of the outcomes measurement process to improve the system (Deming, 1986).

In this chapter, we describe the steps needed to develop an effective outcomes system and describe a software system that has been developed to address these issues. The implementation of outcomes is highlighted because the steps to creating a functioning outcomes system are opportunities for instilling a quality improvement perspective within the health care delivery system.

Outcomes and Improvement

There are four components to outcomes evaluation: services, costs, satisfaction, and clinical outcomes. All of these components are interrelated, but they have typically been studied separately.

SERVICES OUTCOMES

The first area of outcomes is services. In the quality assurance literature, service outcomes have beeen described as the structures and processes of health care (Donabedian, 1968). In health services research, service outcomes refer to concepts such as access, continuity, and comprehensiveness (Safran, Tarlov, & Rogers, 1994). These areas include how easily the patient can access care, the amount of care a patient has recieved, the procedures taken to deliver those services, and the context in which those services have been delivered. Examples in behavioral health would include the timeliness of getting an appointment, how many steps are needed to make that appointment, how the treatment plan is developed, and the number of times a patient is seen in each type of treatment. Service outcomes have been common for many years in behavioral health care, and a number of specific service delivery outcomes have been operationalized by Trabin and his associates in their effort to develop industrywide performance indicators (Trabin & Freeman, 1995). Service outcomes provide essential data on the way in which care is delivered and on the intentions of service providers but tell nothing of the effectiveness of those procedures and intentions.

COST OUTCOMES

The second area of outcomes is cost. The purchasers and payers of health care have focused first and foremost on the cost of care for good reason. The growth in the cost of health care in the United States has been astronomical (Freudenheim, 1995), with little detectable change in outcomes. The driving force in changes in health care delivery has been corporations, which pay for more than 50 percent of total health care costs (Darling, 1995). State and local governments are becoming more attentive to these issues because they are responsible for the specific costs of health care to Medicare and Medicaid recipients. As a result, the emphasis for cost outcomes has been on cost containment rather than quality. Recently, organizations have begun to turn their attention to quality, as cost containment becomes an emerging reality (Noble, 1995), whereas researchers are examining the impact of costs on services (Manning, Wells, Duan, Newhouse, & Ware, 1986). Although cost itself is an important variable, more complex analyses such as cost–benefit and cost-effectiveness will eventually prove most valuable (Sturm & Wells, 1995).

SATISFACTION OUTCOMES

The third area of outcomes is satisfaction. One of the strongest measures of success in both service-oriented and product-oriented business is satisfaction. As customer satisfaction grows, the acquisition of new customers and the retention of old customers grows. This has recently become extremely important in health care (Davies & Ware, 1988). Satisfaction ratings are virtually a requirement for health care delivery systems as a result of mandates from the National Committee on Quality Assurance (NCQA) and many large health care purchasers (Winslow, 1995). Satisfaction has been reported to be correlated with retention in a health care plan, compliance with treatment regimens, and some measures of clinical change (Eisen, 1996). Most health insurance, health management, and health maintenance companies include some form of satisfaction measurement in their standard practices.

CLINICAL OUTCOMES

The fourth area of outcomes is clinical change or effectiveness. Clinical outcomes are the most talked about, least developed, and least conceptualized dimension of outcomes. Clinical outcomes provide information from the provider and from the patient about the changes that have taken place during an episode of care (Mirin & Namerow, 1991). Equally important, clinical outcomes can be used to explain why certain outcomes are achieved and how those outcomes might be improved.

Each of the four outcomes components can be used as a tool for quality improvement. As service delivery systems begin to design and implement procedures for measuring all four components of outcomes in an ongoing process, they will identify those aspects of their system that either help or hinder good outcomes for individuals and groups. Experts in quality management have repeatedly demonstrated that variability in use, services, and procedures within a given clinical setting are frequently a source of poor clinical outcomes (Berwick et al., 1990). In its simplest form, as procedures vary, the probability of getting a high-quality result diminishes. When procedures are more consistent within a given context, the results tend to be more consistent and to meet expectations. Sterile surgical procedures are an excellent example of this. The clinical outcomes data, combined with service, cost, and satisfaction outcomes, can help reduce these variations, standardizing practices and operationalizing procedures to ensure that patients receive optimal care. The types of questions that can be addressed by outcomes systems include

- Which entities are doing the best job?
- What treatment processes are most effective, and which need improvement?
- Which patients need more/different attention?
- How well do providers conform to guidelines?
- What is the cost-effectiveness of care procedures?

Designing an Outcomes System

Designing an outcomes system requires planning, organization, and integration of data collection and data analysis procedures into the existing clinical setting. Outcomes data require cooperation among clinicians, patients, and management, along with the sharing of information among individuals who work in disparate areas of a health care organization. To design a fully functional outcomes information system (OIS), facilities should explore and answer the following questions as part of a continuous process of quality improvement.

CUSTOMERS

Who are the customers? Various groups want information about how individuals, employees, or covered lives are faring in the health care system. Which groups want information and what each group wants to know are crucial to designing an OIS. In the world of quality improvement, customers can be internal (within the organization) or external. Internal customers in behavioral health care include clinicians, administrators, reception staff, and medical records staff. External customers include patients, families, employer-purchasers, and payers. Each customer has different interests in outcomes, and each one will focus on service, cost, satisfaction, and clinical outcomes to different degrees. For example, patients and families will attend primarily to clinical improvement and service availability (Business & Health, 1995), with the other two areas relevant only to the extent that they affect improvement and access. Purchasers of health care services tend to be interested most in service outcomes and have become extremely interested in cost outcomes as health care costs have skyrocketed. Health care administrators are concerned first with satisfaction because it predicts retention in a health plan. Finally, clinicians are interested in clinical outcomes, although satisfaction with the treatment is a close second. Knowing who the customers are and what they want to know is the first step in designing an OIS.

DOMAINS

What domains are to be evaluated? Within the area of clinical outcomes, clinical symptoms have been the primary outcomes domain evaluated. Occasionally, the ability to perform social and occupational roles has also been evaluated (Stewart & Ware, 1992). In the broadest sense, however, outcomes include a wide range of domains. For example, therapeutic alliance is arguably one of the most important domains as a predictor of psychotherapy outcomes. Family functioning, academic performance, and social interactions are important domains especially for children. For patients with substance abuse disorders, physical health, impulse control, legal and financial situation, and living situation may be important. For patients with severe mental illness, grooming, hygiene, ability to obtain and maintain social services, and living situation may be more important than symptom relief. The organization developing an OIS needs to select those outcomes domains that are most relevant to its setting and its customers and focus on those outcomes that it reasonably believes it can change or enhance. In large, multiservice settings, different outcomes may be relevant for different treatment populations or programs. The OIS should be flexible enough to allow different measures and domains for different populations.

DATA TYPES

What types of data will be used, and from where will they come? Recently, outcomes measurement has focused on patient self-reports of symptoms and satisfaction. This is a reasonable approach for people receiving outpatient psychotherapy for nonpsychotic disorders. It is important to remember, however, that outcomes should apply to all behavioral health populations, ranging from children to older people, from adjustment disorders to severe mental illness, and from acute care in an emergency room to chronic care in nursing homes. As such, the OIS needs to access different types of data for different populations and for different customers. In an acute care facility, for example, it may be necessary to use only clinician data and to draw those data from standardized chart records. When working with children, the data should come from a guardian or parent or from a school or residential facility. If the customer is interested in issues of access and follow-through, or issues of work performance, the data can be obtained from existing databases, such as billing or personnel records, and do not have to be drawn from either charts or self-reports. A wide range of data types (for example, self-report, clinical interview, chart review) and data sources (for example, the patient, family, personnel records) are possible. The clinical organization should focus on those types and sources of data that will address its questions, meet the needs of customers, and minimize the burden on patient and staff. Standardized measures with established reliability and validity are invaluable, particularly for the outcomes measures such as symptoms, role performance, and satisfaction.

TIME FRAME

What time frames should be considered? Outcomes are the assessment of a person's status on a set of domains over set time periods. Not all time frames are relevant for all patients or for all facilities. For example, most acute care psychiatric units would not have time to examine change during treatment and would not judge their performance on the one-year follow-up of patients treated in their facility. Rather, assessments at admission and discharge and a one-month follow-up would be as much as could be reasonably evaluated. Patients treated in an outpatient clinic would be much more reasonably evaluated at several points during treatment (depending on duration) and at several months after treatment because the goals of the treatment are expected to be longer lasting. Baseline assessments are essential for a basis of comparison and for case-mix adjustment. Concurrent assessments during and at the end of treatment allow the clinical facility to examine stages in the process of change. Finally, follow-up assessments help to examine the endurance of treatment effects. The OIS needs to be flexible enough to identify different time frames for different populations and settings while at the same time providing valid and reliable predictive measures.

PREDICTORS

Which predictors are to be studied? Outcomes systems are of little value if they do not include measures of outcome predictors and treatment processes. Predictors of outcomes include the patient and setting factors that may account for differences in outcomes independent of the administrative and treatment processes themselves. For example, the presence of a personality disorder has been found to explain variations in use, complications, and outcomes in both medical (Fulop, Strain, Fahs, Hammer, & Lyons, 1989) and psychiatric (Reich & Green, 1991) settings. Sociodemographic, comorbid, and historical factors have also been reported to be valuable predictors of treatment response (Garfield, 1986). These data are essential for risk-adjustment methods (Daley & Schwartz, 1994), which help to equate diverse patient populations. Changes in procedures or programs may follow from the identification of these predictors, generally by the development of novel treatment programs or by facilitating patient–therapist matching for populations or subgroups.

PROCESSES

Which processes should be examined? Three important quality improvement procedures in health care include (1) benchmarking, (2) process improvement, and (3) disease management. These procedures involve the modification of internal processes to improve the results of care. Process measures are essential to the development of quality improvement initiatives. Process measures can include administrative processes (for example, use of a gatekeeper), service-based processes (for example, time to a scheduled appointment or percentage of completed intake reports), financial processes (for example, payment at the time versus monthly billing), or clinical processes (for example, separating versus integrating evaluation and treatment or referrals for medication consultation). Treatment processes can also be included, ranging from the type of treatment (for example, individual versus group treatment) to the process of care (for example, number of contacts or mean treatment alliance).

SUMMARY

Once these questions have been asked and the answers reviewed for the given settings and populations, the shape of the OIS becomes clearer. Domains of data collection can be more readily identified, measures can be selected, and the types of analyses are established by the questions asked. This process increases the likelihood that customers will value the answers given and that involvement and support for the outcomes process will be forthcoming.

Implementing Outcomes

The next step in the process is operationalizing the concepts and implementing the system. The specifics of implementation of an OIS have been described elsewhere (Berman & Hurt, 1996). There are three basic aspects to implementation: (1) guiding principles, (2) basic tasks, and (3) essential characteristics.

GUIDING PRINCIPLES

The guiding principles of an outcomes system are straightforward. First, a facility should minimize the burden of the system on patients, clinicians, and staff. Everyone we have worked with has noted that their work burden is already excessive. The simplest rule is to measure only what you will use. Controlled clinical trials and funded research often collect data on a broad range of topics or measure one domain in several ways. In an outcomes system, this dramatically increases the burden imposed on clients and providers, which in turn decreases compliance with an ongoing outcomes system. New data can be added when their value is clear. Second, the time and costs associated with an outcomes system should be anticipated. Like any information system, an OIS takes time, personnel, and resources. The system is more likely to contribute valuable information if it is developed with adequate resources and trained staff. Third, data completion rates should be emphasized. The value of an outcomes system is directly related to the completeness of data. Missing data at any point threatens the validity of the data. If the resources are not available to develop a complete outcomes system, targeting and collecting data on 90 percent of a single setting or population will produce more useful information than collecting data on 20 percent of the whole clinic population. The former would allow process improvement for that sample; the latter would likely provide distorted or incomplete information that would produce confusing or unreliable change. Finally, the data should be used for change. There is no greater burden than the collection of information that is not used. Plan ahead to use these data.

BASIC TASKS

Effective implementation of an OIS is crucial to its success. An individual clinician can implement these basic tasks by hand or with simple scoring systems. For most groups and organizations, the tasks require the availability of computer hardware and software capable of managing and analyzing the data or the funds to purchase an outcomes service. Regardless of which is used, four basic tasks should be mastered in implementating an outcomes system:

1. The data should be captured in a simple and flexible manner.
2. The data should be entered into the information system in a way that minimizes staff time and maximizes accuracy and throughput.
3. The data should be managed with checks and reminders to ensure the completeness, accuracy, and timeliness of concurrent and follow-up data.
4. The data must be accessible to those gathering and using the data through real-time reporting and should be stored in a manner that allows easy access for aggregate calculations.

ESSENTIAL CHARACTERISTICS

An OIS must meet several conditions to guarantee full functionality in a complex health care setting. It must be simple enough for any member of a health care organization to use without unwarranted time demands; high levels of expertise are costly, and complex decision making tends to result in errors of various kinds. It must be flexible enough to cover a full range of treatment services, from acute to long-term care, and to cover a full range of patient populations. The OIS should allow easy customization for different clinical populations, sites, and service goals; as we have noted above, the populations and the settings vary widely even within a given health care organization. It must allow customization of measures used in the system and reports produced by the system; without such customizability, the data will not be used easily and will not produce the change and fluidity needed in such a system. The OIS must provide a common core of assessments, using industry-standard instruments that allow comparisons across multiple levels of evaluation. It must be able to interface with other information systems. In an ideal system, outcomes, clinical services, and financial data would be stored in a fully integrated information system. In many cases, however, this is not immediately feasible because sizable financial investments may have been made in legacy systems that support core processes. New databases must meet standards for compatibility (for example, Open Database Conductivity standards), allowing data to be transferred across systems and merged for reports and analyses.

Case Example

Human service organizations wishing to implement outcomes measurement often retain for-profit firms specializing in development and implementation of outcomes systems. This section describes one such firm, Behavioral Health Outcomes Systems (BHOS), Inc., in White Plains, NY, which focuses on the development and integration of PC-based software tools that meet the consistency, flexibility, and customizability requirements described above. The original tool was developed to manage data from the Xerox Behavioral Health Outcomes Study, a project commissioned by Helen Darling at the Xerox Corporation (Berman, Hurt, Darling, & Hunkeler, 1994). Xerox was interested in evaluating the quality of care provided by the organizations that offered mental health and substance abuse services to Xerox employees and their dependents. On the basis of experience in this study, and several other projects, a fully functional software system (the BHOSManager™) was developed that includes standard data recording forms, automated data entry and verification, data management and process-design tools, and customizable reporting and output methods. The components of this system are described in the next sections.

FORMS

The BHOSManager system is a forms-driven system. In other words, the system allows data to be recorded on specially designed paper forms and then transferred via software to PC-based databases. Form templates are fully customizable and provide a method of standardizing data collection and automating data entry through coordination of the BHOSManager with PC-based optical scanning software. Through intelligent character recognition (ICR) technology, forms can be completed with handwriting, machine print, Optical Mark Recognition (OMR), or filled bubbles. These forms are scanned or faxed to a computer, and the data are retained in databases where they become available to the BHOSManager. The user can build as many forms as are needed and can use the same forms across different settings or populations.

A forms-based approach was chosen for several reasons:

- It makes outcomes systems easily available to those who cannot invest several thousands of dollars for touch-screen applications or other forms of direct computer data entry.
- It allows quick and relatively inexpensive customization of the system because minimal programming is required.
- It minimizes the potential for error and maximizes the use of people's time by having them fill out standard forms at each point.
- It is a method of data collection that clients and providers find easy to accommodate and familiar from other settings.

MEASURES

The BHOSManager system provides for both standard and customized measures of outcomes, processes, and predictors. Standard measures provide data on both patient-centered and clinician-centered outcomes. These data allow the evaluation of the person receiving services from multiple perspectives, including their own and that of their provider. At the same time, the system allows full customization of outcomes measures for special needs.

Health Status Questionnaire

All health care modules can include the Health Status Questionnaire (also known as the SF-36) (see chapter 4 by Ware, chapter 3 by Booth & Smith, and chapter 19 by Berkman; Ware, 1995). The SF-36 is a 36-item scale that measures eight dimensions of health and mental health status, including health perceptions, physical health, role functioning due to physical factors, mental health, role functioning due to emotional factors, vitality, social functioning, and bodily pain. The scale has been validated extensively in both the Health Insurance Experiment and the Medical Outcomes Study (Manning et al., 1986; Safran et al., 1994). The SF-12, a short form of the SF-36, has recently been added as well.

Behavioral Health

For behavioral health, the system provides coordinated forms for the measurement of symptoms and role functioning (see the BHOS scales of Table 6-1). The Personal Problems Scale (PPS) and Clinician Problems Scale (CPS) are designed to measure the same symptom clusters in all patients. Subscales of the PPS include depression–suicidality, anxiety–trauma, cognitive difficulties, impulsive–substance abuse behavior, and psychosis. The CPS provides measures of depression–suicidality, anxiety–trauma, cognitive difficulties, impulsive–substance abuse behavior, eating disorder symptoms, and psychotic symptoms.

Table 6-1

DATA ON THE BHOS SCALES' RELIABILITY AND VALIDITY

Scale	Internal Consistency	Convergent Validity: SF-36 MH	Convergent Validity: with OQ-45	Discriminant Validity: MD versus AD (>, <, or =)	Discriminant Validity: SA versus No SA (>, <, or =)
PPS–anxiety–trauma	.90	–.74	.55–.71	=	<
Cognitive difference	.81	.61	.68–.82	>	<
Depression–suicide	.83	–.74	.65–.85	>	>
Impulse/substance abuse	.70	–.36	.52–.70	>	>[a]
Positive affect	.83	.76	.65–.77	<	>
Psychosis[b]	—	—	—	—	—
CPS–anxiety–trauma	.80	–.28	not tested	>	no difference
Depression	.89	–.43	not tested	>	<
Cognitive difference	.88	–.33	not tested	>	no difference
Impulse/substance abuse	.80	–.10	not tested	>	>
Psychosis	.63[b]	–.08	not tested	>	no difference
Eating disorder	.60[b]	–.10	not tested	>	no difference
CSI–short	.91	not tested	not tested	no difference	no difference
CSI–system	.63[b]	not tested	not tested	no difference	no difference
CSI–bond	.90	not tested	not tested	no difference	no difference
CSI–alliance	.95	not tested	not tested	no difference	no difference
PFI–major role	.80	–.44	.37–.44	>	>
PFI–interpersonal	.74	–.54	.25–.41	>	>
CFI–major role	.87			>	no difference
CFI–interpersonal	.80			>	<

Note: MD versus AD = major depression versus adjustment disorder; SA versus no SA = substance abuse diagnosis versus no substance abuse diagnosis; PPS = Personal Problems Scale; CPS = Clinician Problems Scale; CSI = Consumer Satisfaction Inventory; PFI = Personal Functioning Index; CFI = Clinician Functioning Index.

[a]Substance abuse scale only. [b]This scale is under development, and data are not yet available.

Role Functioning

The measures of role functioning integrated in the BHOSManager include the Personal Functioning Index (PFI) and the Clinician Functioning Index (CFI). Each scale assesses the three major domains of role performance: (1) major role functioning (work and school care), (2) interpersonal functioning (family and social relations, health, and daily living), and (3) personal care (legal, financial, and home care concerns).

Satisfaction

Satisfaction is measured with the Consumer Satisfaction Inventory (CSI), also a part of the BHOSManager system. This scale comes in two versions: a 13-item scale and a 26-item scale. The 13-item scale provides a global satisfaction measure, whereas the 26-item scale measures a patient's perspectives on the context of treatment (system satisfaction), the person providing the treatment (treatment bond), and the practical components of treatment such as goal-setting, change, and outcomes (called therapeutic alliance).

A user wishing to measure a specific aspect of symptoms or role functioning can have custom measures installed in this system. For example, a clinic specializing in eating disorders might choose to have a specific measure of anorexia or bulimia added. This requires a special order from BHOS, Inc., and the necessary copyright permissions from the copyright holder or publisher. For example, BHOS, Inc., has agreements with the Psychological Corporation to use the Beck Depression Inventory (Beck, 1978) and the Devereux Scales of Mental Disorders (Naglier, LeBuffe, & Pfeiffer, 1994) in the BHOSManager System. In addition, each customer can either use standard BHOS forms to collect data on processes or predictors or select or design its own data collection instruments. Facilities must pay close attention to using measures with established reliability and validity to get useful information. Any of the administrative or treatment process data can be recorded on custom-designed forms and saved as part of the outcomes system database. Data can also be output from a clinical or utilization database to BHOS databases.

DATA ENTRY

The data entry software allows entry of data by flatbed scanner or by fax. In a centralized facility, it is most efficient to attach a scanner to a PC and scan data in. Most scanners have multipage document feeders, so the data can be entered in batches. This process is simple and can be managed with relatively little intervention. It is usually helpful to review the forms to ensure that the identifier marks are not damaged and the forms have been completed correctly (for example, dots have been filled in rather than checked or circled). Scanning then requires little assistance from the operator. In a decentralized system, such as a loose network or group without walls, a central computer connected to a phone line can be used for facsimile transmission. Each clinician can fax the data to the central office via a standard fax machine. The ICR software then reads the data just as it would from a scanner.

The accuracy and correctness of the data must be verified. In punch-card and spreadsheet systems, data are verified by double-punching or proofreading data. In the BHOSManager system, the accuracy of the ICR engine is checked on-line. The ICR software identifies potentially incorrect entries and asks the system operator for verification, particularly on the fields used to identify the patient, facility, and time point. Data verification is facilitated by dictionary look-ups for the individual fields or by numerical checks to make sure the number range is correct. Data are verified and then automatically entered into the system databases for management.

DATA MANAGEMENT

The BHOSManager identifies and records the arrival of new data. Additional verification steps are provided to ensure that the data are correctly identified and associated with the correct case. The program then either associates the data with an existing case or creates a new case if no other data exist for that case. The data are then sent to the correct time point, tagged with the time-based information, and stored for reporting and analysis.

Several administrative reports are provided. First, a list of cases checked in is provided to ensure a printed record of what data have been entered. Second, a report of the number of cases per clinician at each time point allows managers to determine completion rates for each clinician. Third, a report indicating which new cases have incomplete data allows the data manager to give immediate feedback to the person responsible for obtaining data. If there are data missing for a given case, the responsible person can try to obtain that data quickly. Fourth, a tickler file is available to provide timely reminders of when new data are to be collected for a given case. Depending on the case flow, these reports can be designed for daily, weekly, or biweekly printing and can provide a total listing either of all missing or future data or of only those data that are missing since the last report or planned for collection after the last report. These administrative reports allow for simple, timely data management designed to ensure complete data capture and compliance with the policies and procedures of the facility. Data management is also provided on-line, allowing the user to examine cases on the screen, report individual data, and inform those responsible that data are missing or new data need to be collected. Data or case information can be hand-edited, and a log is kept that provides a record of all data editing actions.

REPORTING DATA

The final step in the data management process is reporting the clinical data in a readily usable form. The BHOSManager OIS provides several different types of reports. Individual case reports can be generated to provide real-time feedback regarding symptoms, role performance, and any other outcomes domain. These reports include risk flags for high-risk symptoms such as suicidal ideation; substance abuse; or legal, financial, or self-control problems (Figure 6-1). Aggregate data reports are also included in the clinical report set. Scale scores averaged across clinicians or across clinical sites (usually cost centers or treatment units) can provide an easy preliminary examination of the data. In addition, aggregate scores by diagnostic grouping can

Figure 6-1

SAMPLE INDIVIDUAL CASE REPORT OF PATIENT DATA FROM BHOSMANAGER

BHOSManager ™ Outcomes Data Report

Individual Patient-Rated Symptom Scores

Scores represent the individual's scale score at each time point. All scale scores range from 1 - 5 with higher scores indicating increasing pathology/dysfunction. Risk scores are printed only when risk is substantial. The absense of a risk score does not indicate the absense of risk, only the absense of scores indicating a risk. Norms from an outpatient psychiatric population are given at the bottom of the page. These norms are not adjusted for any diagnostic or risk factors. For disorder-specific norms, or more information about these scales, please examine the scale manuals or contact BHOS, Inc. at 800-494-2467. These data are sensitive and confidential. Use and application of these scales and reports are the sole responsibility of the licensee.

Case #: 81742 **Name:** C, A **Date of Report:** 01/15/1997

Site #: 42 **Primary Diagnoses:** 309.40

Episode #: 1 **Secondary Diagnoses:** 799.90

Date	Event	Clinician	Anxiety & Trauma	Depression & Suicide	Cognitive Difficulties	Impulsive & Substances	Positive Affect	Major Role	Social Role
09/10/96	Admission	COL	1.64	1.29	1.75	1.57	3.00	1.00	2.00
09/17/96	Discharge	COL	1.55	1.29	1.75	1.14	2.57	1.60	1.80

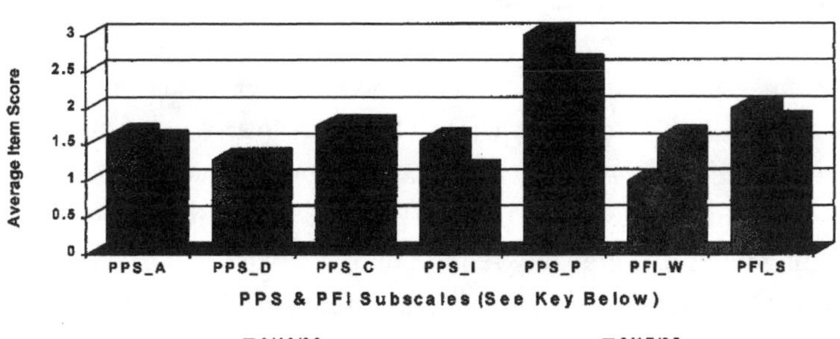

KEY:
PPS_A = Anxiety & Trauma PPS_D = Depression PPS_C = Cognitive Difficulties
PPS_I = Impulsivity & Substance Abuse PPS_P = Positive Affect
PFI_W = Major (Work) Role PFI_S = Social Role

	Anxiety & Trauma	Depression & Suicide	Cognitive Difficulties	Impulsive & Substances	Positive Affect	Major Role	Social Role
Scale Mean	*2.51*	*2.30*	*2.50*	*1.88*	*2.47*	*1.78*	*1.92*
Scale S.D.	*.84*	*.79*	*.92*	*.63*	*.80*	*.69*	*.66*
Scale Range	*1-5*	*1-5*	*1-5*	*1-5*	*1-5*	*1-5*	*1-5*

Scale norms are based on a sample of 660 cases rated at the beginning of a course of outpatient treatment for general mental health or substance abuse treatment. For more information, please contact BHOS, Inc. at 800-494-BHOS or consult your manual.

Source: Reprinted with permission of BHOS, Inc., White Plains, NY. Copyright 1995–97, BHOS, Inc.

provide comparative data controlling for patient diagnosis (for example, depression, subtance abuse, or psychotic disorders).

Finally, with a single menu command, these data can all be output to standard, delimited files, which can then be analyzed using a wide range of data analysis programs. BHOS, Inc., provides input statements for the standard forms and works with clients on both the formatting and analysis of data. Types of descriptive data analyses include sample description, completeness of data elements, and change over time. Inferential statistical procedures include risk adjustment, provider profiling, program profiling, life table analyses, disease management prediction, and disorder-specific treatment response.

Implications for Clinical Practice

The advent of clinical outcomes data poses several challenges and opportunities for clinical practice. Some of these innovations include the use of psychometric data in treatment, the impact of quality improvement initiatives on treatment techniques, and the distinction between mental health care as medical care versus emotional care.

Mental health, unlike most specialties in health care, does not use laboratory data as part of the diagnostic and treatment process. Although current clinical assessment tools lack the psychometric properties of bioassays and radiologic procedures, many current assessment instruments can be used to augment the clinical assessment process. It is a challenge to clinicians to use psychometric data about patients in determining the course and continuation of treatment.

At the same time, these data will be used to identify areas for quality improvement, which will probably require clinicians to learn new techniques and to respect data that suggest that old or familiar approaches are not as valuable. More generally, a quality improvement approach to mental health care will move clinicians away from an intuitive, individualized approach to a more consensual approach based on the best information and techniques available. This approach should help to improve outcomes and reduce the variability in the results of behavioral health services. Accepting these changes without losing the human bond that is essential to mental health care will pose a particular challenge to practitioners.

Finally, it is possible that some mental health care will not meet the suggested criteria for demonstrable disability and improvement implicit in outcomes systems. Not all emotional disorders are measurable or are considered to be of sufficient import to be included in the measurement set. This does not necessarily mean that the disorder or disability is absent, that it is undeserving of services, or that the treatment is not meaningful to the individual. Clinicians will have to struggle with the ethical implications of defining treatable disorders by their ability to be measured or their responsiveness to treatment. Treatment of some disorders outside the health care system or accepting some cases for which change will be immeasurable will be an ethical issue for practitioners.

Future Research Agendas in Mental and Behavioral Health Outcomes Measurement Research

The agenda for outcomes measurement research in the context of mental and behavioral health services is daunting. There is remarkably little information on the assessment, explanation, and prediction of clinical change in mental health and substance abuse. Although a great deal is known about the efficacy of mental health care, much more can and must be known. More important for outcomes measurement in human service settings, little is known about the treatment of these disorders in the real world.

The first item on the agenda is the development of highly valid measurement tools. The SF-36 is one instrument that has the needed psychometric qualities. A large number of measures have been developed in behavioral health care that include a full range of psychiatric and substance abuse problems. Given the multiplicity of symptoms in behavioral health care and the concern with multiple domains, the contrasting demands of psychometric strength and simplicity of use may limit the progress that can be made in this area. Nevertheless, the development of measurement tools with reliability, validity, sensitivity, and specificity that are acceptable on an individual level is an essential research goal.

Mental health has been less than successful in explaining clinical change and in accounting for resource allocation. An important aspect of the outcomes research agenda will be to identify the patient, treatment, and system factors that account for patient improvement. Application of outcomes data to rational decision making is another aspect of outcomes systems that is essential to proving the value of this approach. BHOS, Inc., and several other vendors provide data on these factors.

Finally, the statistical methods by which outcomes data are analyzed will require significant development. Analysis of variance and covariance cannot easily account for the varying time frames, case dropout, and multiple outcomes found in behavioral health populations. People with behavioral health problems often have comorbidities, experience recurrent episodes of illness, receive multiple treatments, improve at different rates in different domains of outcome, and end treatment for multiple reasons. The use and interpretation of sophisticated time series methodologies will be increasingly necessary as efforts to intervene in the most efficient ways increase.

Conclusion

The management and application of information regarding the service delivery process and the resulting outcomes is the key to future improvements in service delivery and redesign. Critical components of any outcomes information system include procedures and processes to ensure the timely acquisition of data, simple tools to enhance the ease of data entry and management, and flexible tools that meet the needs of the clinical organization, rather than the reverse. Data that are valuable to individuals, clinicians, and administrators and can be fed back to the organization to facilitate and streamline clinical and organizational procedures will constitute the most valuable application of outcomes information systems.

References

Beck, A. T. (1978). *Depression Inventory.* Philadelphia: Philadelphia Center for Cognitive Therapy.

Berman, W. H., & Hurt, S. W. (1996). Talking the talk, walking the walk: Implementation of an outcomes information system. *Behavioral Healthcare Tomorrow, 5,* 39–43.

Berman, W. H., Hurt, S. W., Darling, H., & Hunkeler, E. (1994). Academic-managed care—Corporate alliances in outcomes management: Culture shock or synergy. *Behavioral Healthcare Tommorow, 3,* 23–29.

Berwick, D. M., Godfrey, A. B., & Roessner, J. (1990). *Using health care: New strategies for quality improvement.* San Francisco: Jossey-Bass.

Business & Health. (1995). *The quest for accountability.* Montvale, NJ: Medical Economics.

Daley, J., & Schwartz, M. (1994). Developing risk-adjustment methods. In L. Iezzoni (Ed.), *Risk adjustment for measuring health care outcomes* (pp. 199–238). Ann Arbor, MI: Health Administration Press.

Darling, H. (1995). Health reform from the employer perspective. *Health Affairs, 10,* 21–23.

Davies, A. R., & Ware, J. E. (1988). Involving consumers in the quality of care assessment. *Health Affairs, 7,* 33–48.

Deming, W. E. (1986). *Out of the crisis.* Cambridge: Massachusetts Institute of Technology.

Donabedian, A. (1968). The evaluation of medical care programs. *Bulletin of the New York Academy of Medicine, 44,* 117–124.

Eisen, S. V. (1996). Client satisfaction and clinical outcomes: Do we need to meausre both? *Behavioral Healthcare Tomorrow, 5,* 71–73.

Ellwood, P. (1988). Outcomes management: A technology of patient experience. *New England Journal of Medicine, 318,* 1549–1556.

Freudenheim, M. (1995, February 14). Health costs paid by employers drop for first time in a decade. *The New York Times,* p. A1.

Fulop, G., Strain, J. J., Fahs, M. C., Hammer, J. S., & Lyons, J. S. (1989). Mental disorders associated with psychiatric comorbidity and prolonged hospital stay. *Hospital and Community Psychiatry, 40,* 80–82.

Garfield, S. L. (1986). Research on client variables in psychotherapy. In S. L. Garfield & A. E. Bergin (Eds.), *Handbook of psychotherapy and behavior change* (3rd ed., pp. 213–256). New York: John Wiley & Sons.

Manning, W. G., Wells, K. B., Duan, H., Newhouse, J. P., & Ware, J. E. (1986). How cost sharing affects the use of ambulatory mental health serivces. *Journal of the American Medical Association, 256,* 1930–1934.

Mirin, S. M., & Namerow, M. J. (1991). Why study treatment outcome? *Hospital and Community Psychiatry, 42,* 1007–1013.

Naglieri, J. A., LeBuffe, P. A., & Pfeiffer, S. L. (1994). *Devereux Scales of Mental Disorders.* San Antonio, TX: Psychological Corporation.

Noble, H. B. (1995, July 3). Quality is focus for health plans. *The New York Times,* p. A1.

Reich, J. H., & Green, A. I. (1991). Effect of personality disorders on outcome of treatment. *Journal of Nervous and Mental Disease, 79,* 74–82.

Safran, D. G., Tarlov, A. R., & Rogers, W. H. (1994). Primary care performance in fee for service and prepaid health care systems. *Journal of the American Medical Association, 271,* 1579–1586.

Stewart, A. L., & Ware, J. E. (Eds.). (1992). *Measuring functioning and well-being: The Medical Outcomes Study approach.* Durham, NC: Duke University Press.

Sturm, R., & Wells, K. B. (1995). How can care for depression become more cost-effective? *Journal of the American Medical Association, 273,* 51–58.

Trabin, T., & Freeman, M. (1995). *Quality and accountability in managed behavioral care: Report of the National Leadership Council Task Force.* Tiburon, CA: Institute for Behavioral Healthcare.

Ware, J. E. (1995). *The SF-36 manual.* Boston: Health Institute.

Winslow, R. (1995, September 25). Care at HMOs to be rated by new system. *The Wall Street Journal,* p. B12.

PART II

Outcomes Measurement in Mental and Behavioral Health

CHAPTER 7

System Changes and Accountability for Behavioral Health Care Services: Lessons from the Private and Public Sectors

DAVID L. SHERN

TOM TRABIN

Rapid changes are occurring in the financing and oversight of behavioral health care in both the public and private sectors (Trabin & Freeman, 1995). These changes are motivated by the explosive growth of health care expenditures (Starr, 1992) as well as by those associated with behavioral health. Purchasers of health care, including industry and government, use a wide variety of strategies in response to these concerns. Some purchasers have sought to eliminate coverage for behavioral health care from their health care plans (Berlant, Trabin, & Anderson, 1994). Others have controlled the provision of services and their cost through improved management of the care process, with the goal of providing the appropriate level of effective care at a prespecified cost.

Underlying these cost control strategies is a belief that the increases in behavioral health care costs are primarily, if not entirely, attributable to increases in factors other than the morbidity of the population. Similar assertions can be made with regard to general health care where increases in cost are not explainable in terms of changes in the covered population's health status. Because cost increases cannot be attributed to an overall change in health or mental health status, cost containment through managed care is thought to be a reasonable response. Without a standardized comparative measure of the value of services purchased, cost considerations become paramount.

Measuring the Value of Behavioral Health Care Interventions

The belief that factors other than the morbidity of the population may increase costs highlights the need to better understand the value of health and behavioral health care purchases. Ironically, although a corporate purchaser would not consider a business investment without estimating its return, until the past several years health care was routinely purchased without a sense of its value. Because mental health and substance abuse problems are stigmatized and because the symptoms of mental illness are often subjective experiences, the effectiveness of treatment for these problems has been particularly suspect. This skepticism and prejudice exist despite compelling evidence of treatment effectiveness (Berlant et al., 1994; Chambless, 1993; National Advisory Mental Health Council, 1993) and of findings confirming the high personal and social costs of untreated behavioral health problems (Rice, Kelman, Miller, & Dunmeyer, 1990) as well as the dramatic reductions achieved in medical utilization and costs by treating behavioral health problems effectively (Mumford, Schlesinger, Glass, Patrick, & Cuerdon, 1984; Pallak, Cummings, Dorken, & Henke, 1994). The difficulties arising from these prevailing negative biases toward behavioral health problems are compounded by the challenges in determining when behavioral health care interventions are "medically necessary" as opposed to helpful only for personal growth and development. Although the elimination of subjective discomfort might be extremely valuable to an individual's sense of well-being and overall quality of life, it has been challenging for corporate and government purchasers of health care benefits to determine whether they should include coverage for such services in their health care benefits packages. These decisions are particularly troublesome for purchasers when their criteria for value requires linkages between personal benefits and increased productivity—both a business and a social benefit. The challenges of valuing behavioral health care are, therefore, abundant. They range from defining the problems or disorders that are appropriate for treatment through measuring improvement to determining linkages between improvement and a corporate or social good.

These concerns with value lead both public and private purchasers to develop accountability mechanisms through which they can begin to measure the value of behavioral health treatment. As with general medical services, most of the measures relate to the processes of care rather than the outcomes of treatment. They typically include measures of access to and utilization of care, quality and appropriateness of treatment, costs of providing services, and service recipients' satisfaction with services. Access is measured by abandonment rates for telephone inquiries, waiting times for appointments, and so forth. Utilization is closely related to access and is measured by the rates at which covered populations are served with different levels of treatment. Quality and appropriateness are generally assessed after the fact by retrospective review of clinical records, incident reports, complaints, and so forth to determine how closely care management and treatment decisions correspond to established criteria and guidelines. Cost measures reflect the efficiency of a health plan or delivery system;

they usually focus on the proportion of expenses dedicated to overhead compared with direct expenditures on treatment and the costs associated with differing patterns of treatment. Outcomes may include overall health or mental health status but more frequently focus on satisfaction with treatment or other indicators thought to relate to positive outcomes (for example, reduced hospitalization rates, suicide rates, and so forth). As discussed below, the development of treatment guidelines by several national organizations is another attempt to ensure appropriate treatment for specific disorders.

Concerns from the Public and Private Sectors

Although they overlap in many areas, public and private concerns with the estimation of value differ. Public and private systems vary in the types of individuals for whom they must provide treatment and in the range of treatment services they must provide. Private purchasers have circumscribed responsibility for identified populations. Their accountability concerns are restricted to the populations they cover for a specified range of health and behavioral health services. Their costs relate only to this population, and they are likely to be concerned with treatment effectiveness primarily as it pertains to employee productivity and satisfaction.

However, public purchasers have much more poorly delimited populations for whom they are responsible. They have direct responsibility for some covered populations such as government employees, Medicaid and Medicare enrollees, and military personnel and veterans, but public purchasers are also charged with maintaining the general public welfare. The broad range of interconnected human needs in this public responsibility include health, behavioral health, welfare, education, and public safety among others. Public purchasers therefore focus not only on services for defined populations but also on the development and maintenance of service capacity to serve the entire population of particular geographic areas. Their concerns with costs include broad social costs that go well beyond the focus of private purchasers. They also must contend with cost shifts from the private sector and from among areas of the public sector. As with private purchasers, public entities have not focused effectively on the outcomes of health or behavioral health services in evaluations, relying instead on the process measures enforced through licensure or regulatory mechanisms.

This chapter highlights some of the strategies that have been or should be considered by the public and private sectors in designing their accountability structures. From both the public and private perspectives, we identify areas that are of particular relevance to social work practice and research, especially with regard to improving the functioning and efficiency of our behavioral health care system.

Private Sector Reform Efforts and Accountability Issues

Corporations continue to be major purchasers of health care benefits for their employees and their employees' families. Consistent with the overall changes in the health care system, the role of these corporate purchasers has changed dramatically during the past 10 to 15 years. Corporations no longer passively purchase insurance coverage from major carriers or serve as self-insured entities who simply pay fee-for-service claims. They have entered actively into the management of care either directly or, more frequently, through the purchase of services from fiscal intermediaries who are the managers of care.

Corporations and coalitions of multiple corporations continue to provide behavioral health care benefits for employees and their families. As in general health care, the mechanisms used to ensure that these benefits are effective and competitively priced has changed dramatically. No longer is the insurance function restricted to claims payments. In the 1980s it evolved into management of care, involving methods such as preauthorization of care based on codified medical necessity criteria. Most insurance companies either developed these functions for managing behavioral health care internally or acquired specialty managed behavioral health care companies that were already functioning successfully.

In the early 1990s, the behavioral health care industry moved increasingly to consolidate as organizations acquired or developed the capability both to manage and to deliver care. Provider organizations, such as behavioral group practices and hospitals, formed alliances with one another to create regional health care systems, each offering a complete continuum of care and internally developed and operated managed care systems. In competing strategic initiatives, insurers acquired delivery systems and assumed responsibility for treating patients and managing care as well as their traditional function of paying claims. The era of solo private practitioners within a cottage industry is waning, and organized treatment delivery systems are increasing in size as well as in the range of functions for which they assume responsibilities. This movement mirrors trends in the larger, general health care field, in which medical group practices and hospitals are joining forces to accept fully capitated contracts and to be responsible for managing as well as delivering care for defined populations.

CURRENT HEALTH CARE SYSTEM APPROACHES TO CARE MANAGEMENT AND TREATMENT DELIVERY

The emergence of managed care and consequent restructuring of the behavioral health care market were driven by purchaser requirements to contain costs and demonstrate value. Failure to do so would have resulted in the end of most private sector financing of behavioral health care benefits. Instead, behavioral health care benefits were preserved by containing costs through contracted savings targets; capitated, at-risk financing; and other managed care methods.

Capitation is a financing strategy in which a provider is paid a single premium per enrolled member at regular intervals (for example, monthly or quarterly) to provide a specified range of medically necessary care to identified individuals covered by its plan. Successfully managing capitated contracts usually requires integration of the management and delivery of care. The fixed revenue stream can be an important financial security to some organizations. However, if the demand for services exceeds the resources financed through capitation, then the organization runs the risk of bankruptcy. Therefore, the provider must find ways to reduce the demand for services and manage treatment services carefully so resources are not expended unnecessarily, while at the same time maintaining a high level of customer satisfaction and loyalty.

Managed care methods (for example, prior authorization and provider profiling) and capitated financing create incentives that can promote undertreatment. This danger increases as competitive bidding for contracts intensifies the emphasis on lowest-bidder-price criteria and further squeezes the operating margins of managed behavioral health care companies. Both consumers and providers have expressed serious concerns regarding these dilemmas. Because cost-containment pressures are unlikely to abate, managed care will continue to evolve in its form and approach, but it is not likely to go away.

For managed behavioral health care services to avoid becoming a price-based commodity, both government and market forces must take action. The government can set minimum standards in a few areas of quality to protect and preserve the public trust, but their effect will be limited. In the current political climate, extensive mandates and a significantly expanded government role are not likely. Instead, market forces must be galvanized to generate self-correcting mechanisms so that selections of health plans and providers are made on the basis of actual value rather than on price alone. To make this happen, consumers and purchasers need objective data on quality of services that they can use for decision making. Market forces can then more effectively provide checks and balances on overly aggressive cost-containment methods that might otherwise compromise quality.

QUALITY AND ACCOUNTABILITY INITIATIVES

Quality and accountability initiatives are countervailing forces against excessive cost-containment measures in the behavioral health care industry. These initiatives include establishment of performance standards for managed care and provider organizations by public and private sector purchasers and by national accrediting organizations. Other initiatives include developing and implementing outcomes management and practice guideline programs.

Purchasing coalitions are developing internal expertise in the types of performance data they require from the managed care companies with which they contract. These coalitions include the Foundation for Accountability, the Minnesota Business Healthcare Action Group, the Washington Business Group on Health, the Midwestern Business Group on Health, the Pacific Business Group on Health, and others.

Accrediting agencies are also developing their expertise in holding organizations accountable for quality. One way in which they approach this challenge is through establishing accreditation standards and auditing organizations to determine how well (or poorly) they meet these standards. Primary accrediting organizations for behavioral health care include the National Committee for Quality Assurance (NCQA), Joint Commission for Accreditation of Healthcare Organizations, Utilization Review Accreditation Council, Commission for Accreditation of Rehabilitation Facilities, Council on Accreditation of Services for Families and Children, and the Accreditation Council.

An approach closely related to but different from accreditation is measuring and then comparing the performance of organizations on indicators across such domains as access, quality, appropriateness, outcomes, and prevention. This emerging approach is commonly referred to as "report cards." It is being undertaken by such wide-ranging organizations as the Center for Mental Health Services, American Managed Behavioral Healthcare Association, NCQA, and Institute for Behavioral Healthcare. These organizations develop performance indicators, identify measures for these indicators, and define methods for data capture. As more organizations participate in a particular report card format, using the same measures and data collection methods, it becomes more feasible to compare results across organizations with respect to these particular indicators. It also becomes possible for participating organizations to compete for new contracts on the basis of their performance on domains such as access and quality, thereby introducing explicit measures of the value of services into the purchasing equation.

Coalitions to promote quality initiatives are also forming among provider organizations. These include group practices such as the Council on Behavioral Group Practices, psychosocial rehabilitation programs such as those in the International Association of Psychosocial Rehabilitation Services, and children's services agencies represented through the Child Welfare League of America. Members of these coalitions use common outcomes measures and methodologies to pool their efforts, aggregate data for analyses, and benchmark standards for treatment outcomes and for their performance on other indicators.

Another rapidly growing method for ensuring greater quality and accountability is the implementation of practice guidelines that prescribe preferred professional practices for the treatment of specific disorders. These guidelines are usually based on a combination of expert opinions and efficacy research and are used in part to reduce variability in treatment approaches and to improve outcomes. Guidelines are also being considered by managed care organizations for management of treatment delivery. If properly developed and implemented, guidelines can improve the efficiency of service systems and consumer outcomes. However, if inappropriate guidelines are developed and implemented, they may lead to patient harm. Additionally, even the best of guidelines, when applied too rigidly, can stultify creative treatment planning that might otherwise produce more effective outcomes.

Guideline development was spearheaded by the federal government's Agency for Health Care Policy and Research, which applies rigorous, science-based standards to the development of its guidelines. Professional associations are also making significant headway in guideline development, especially the American Psychiatric Association and the American Association of Child and Adolescent Psychiatrists. Pharmaceutical companies are approaching this area, renaming it *disease state management* or *integrated disease management*. Several managed care companies and provider networks have also undertaken this work, albeit with a much more pragmatic orientation.

IMPLICATIONS FOR RESEARCH AND PRACTICE

The changes in the private sector markets for behavioral health care present several important opportunities for social work and human service research and practice. Research questions involve targeting outcomes areas at the individual level and at the system or population level, determining their relative importance at each level, constructing measurement approaches for these areas, and developing norms or standards against which specific provider organizations can be compared. Specific questions in this area include

- What do purchasers and consumers of managed behavioral health care services regard as potentially the most useful types of information on organizational performance to aid in their selection of a behavioral health care provider organization or health plan?
- What are the most valid and feasible measures of organizational performance in behavioral health care for dimensions such as access, utilization, appropriateness, quality, and outcomes?
- Which program, organizational, and system processes and characteristics are empirically linked to clinically significant outcomes?
- What practice guidelines should be implemented, and what are the most effective ways to implement them?
- What measures of population health status are most effective for the behavioral health care field, and what methods should be employed to use these measures effectively?
- What do the empirical data suggest should be appropriate performance standards for organizational benchmarking within behavioral health care?

In addition, much more must be known about the relationship of consumer satisfaction with services and their changes in mental health status (functioning, symptoms, qualilty of life, and so forth). Given the ubiquitous measurement of satisfaction, it is important to develop measurement approaches that differentiate providers and that have known relationships to important outcomes.

These questions are fundamental to the reforms that are underway. The pace and scope of these changes suggest tremendous new opportunities for trained health services researchers and program evaluators. Social work and other human service professions should be heavily involved in shaping this new field of health services research.

The implications for practice are profound. Managed care and treatment delivery organizations will have incentives to collect some of the same types of data and to submit them to neutral organizations for aggregated analyses and public dissemination of results in user-friendly reports. If implemented, this process is likely to create an immediate impact on how consumers and purchasers select providers, delivery systems, and health plans as more weight can be given to quality criteria. Organizations within the health care system are likely to become more responsive to consumers and more outcomes oriented. Clinicians will discover an increased need to access modern computer technology to be able to quickly and easily identify the most up-to-date decision support information on practice guidelines for specific disorders. Incentives to be consumer responsive have the potential to direct the health care system toward providing greater ease of initial access to treatment and overall improvements in the quality of care delivered.

Reforms in the Public Sector: The Importance of Accountability

As with the private sector purchasers, public sector entities have also become concerned with growth in their health and mental health care budgets. In many states, Medicaid expenditures were threatening to outpace education as the largest component of the state budget. According to the U.S. General Accounting Office (1995), states spent approximately $61 billion for Medicaid in 1994; this amount exceeded their expenditures for higher education. Like their private sector colleagues, public sector policy staff were not convinced that the increases in cost reflected any important changes in the health care status of the population but believed that the increases, in part, reflected state strategies to expand coverage for populations with disabilities and mirrored the inherent cost inflation that may be endemic in fee-for-service systems.

Ironically, much of the growth in these budgets for behavioral health care can be explained by the policies of the states themselves in expanding the benefits available under Medicaid—the major state health insurance program for the people who are poor or disabled. Throughout the late 1970s and 1980s, state mental health authorities exploited the flexibility of the Medicaid system. As new options were developed in the Medicaid system (for example, rehabilitation, home, and community-based waivers), states increasingly used the system to leverage their dollars. "Medicaiding" a state-funded service could effectively double its availability by using state general funds to match federal dollars. Given these state strategies to leverage their funds, the Medicaid system became more responsive to the needs of people with disabilities. Efforts at cost containment in Medicaid, therefore, may now pose special threats for these vulnerable populations.

COST–CONTAINMENT STRATEGIES

Work to contain costs in these budgets is occurring at both the state and federal levels. During the 1995–1996 federal legislative session, Congress debated but did not pass a Medicaid block grant program. The essential logic of this legislation was to provide greater flexibility to the states in the administration of the Medicaid program by eliminating various federal mandates. Although the specific mandates to be abandoned were the subject of much debate, mandatory breadth of services and population coverage were of paramount concern. The logic of the proposed changes is that block grants to states will allow states to respond to local needs with local strategies and that the greater efficiency from these locally responsive programs will offset the anticipated reduction in federal support. However, these strategies also herald an important change in federal responsibility for the health care of recipients of Aid to Families with Dependent Children and of individuals with disability.

Under the proposed block grant mechanisms, states become a sole locus of responsibility for vulnerable populations that have recently been a joint state–federal obligation. Although states are not yet operating under block grants, many have requested waivers from the Health Care Financing Administration (HCFA) to restructure the delivery of their Medicaid programs for both general and behavioral health services. Freund and Hurley (1995) reported that 40 states were either developing or operating some form of managed care programs for parts of their Medicaid population by 1994. Those that featured mandatory enrollment required a waiver from HCFA. These waivers seek flexibility in designing programs and often involve limited consumers' choice of providers and establishment of capitated reimbursement rates for identified populations. Although they are not technically block grants, these waivers change key features of the fee-for-service program to accomplish cost controls or reductions and ostensibly to improve services. In these waivers states often divest themselves of responsibility by either relinquishing control of the Medicaid program to counties or localities or by contracting for care with managed care firms that assume the obligation to care for identified populations—generally under fixed budgets. Many local governments are also "corporatizing" care by contracting with managed care firms. The general strategy throughout government is to devolve responsibility for the health care of vulnerable populations from federal interests to state, local, or corporate interests. That strategy, combined with global budgeting and increased flexibility in service provision, is intended as a method to control costs and improve our general medical and behavioral health care systems.

ESTABLISHING ACCOUNTABLE ENTITIES AND ACCOUNTABILITY STRATEGIES

From a public health perspective, these changes in the locus of accountability are of concern. In behavioral health care, states have traditionally been responsible for individuals with severe mental illnesses. Our bad experiences with the uncoordinated deinstitutionalization and community mental health center movements attests to the problems of poorly integrated reforms—particularly for these vulnerable populations. The dangers with the current reforms are perhaps even greater than they were with deinstitutionalization because the social welfare systems that enabled deinstitutionalization, such as Social Security, Medicaid, and Medicare, were designed to expand income and health care support systems rather than to control costs and limit access to care. Current reform movements seek to delimit specific populations that are eligible for care and manage their access to care. Profit is maximized by minimizing care—particularly care in expensive settings such as hospitals and emergency rooms. Poorly defined accountability further compounds these incentives. Although private purchasers are accountable entities for their employees, it is essential that government assume responsibility for the general public welfare as well as for the specific needs of individuals who are poor or disabled. Government must explicitly identify which organizations will be accountable for which population groups and clearly define its expectations for system performance and for the mechanisms that it will use to monitor and enforce this responsibility in a manner not unlike that used by private purchasers.

The problem of establishing an accountable entity is twofold. First, a sensible accountability structure must be determined. Given the ill-defined boundaries of government responsibility and the general trend toward devolution in control, an informed community must decide at which levels of government to establish accountable entities and the relationships among these entities. Our suggestion is that all levels must be accountable but must design their accountability strategies so that they promote flexibility and creativity of the systems for which they are responsible. Perhaps the worst outcomes of these system changes would be reduced resources through cost containment and greater regulatory intrusion into the processes of care by multiple levels of government. Each level must therefore define accountability criteria and standards with which it will benchmark the behavior of the entities for which it is responsible. The federal government should hold states accountable, states should hold localities or contractors responsible, and localities should hold contractors or local provider networks responsible for the outcomes of care.

The second problem involves determining the accountability strategy at each level, which involves identifying the measures that are appropriate for each government level, the mechanisms for gauging performance at each level, and the consequences contingent on system performance. Although the ultimate concerns of accountability systems are changes in consumer health status, assessing and establishing norms for this outcomes variable at varying government levels is a difficult task. The ultimate goal is to assess system characteristics that have a known relationship to consumer outcomes and to use these measures in consumer education and provider management strategies. Many of the mechanisms discussed in conjunction with private sector purchasers (report cards, accreditation standards, treatment protocols, and so forth) are also appropriate for government use. In fact, other than the differences in the definition of the populations for whom they are responsible, the problems of measuring value are much the same for public and private sector purchasers. To the highest degree possible, both should seek to increase the effect of market mechanisms on the regulation of quality, access, outcomes, and cost.

A related set of policy issues involves the definition of the boundaries of the managed care system. Since the 1970s, the mental health field has become increasingly aware of the importance of integrating services and supports across a broad range of human service areas, particularly for people with severe mental illness. Many cost-containment approaches involve identifying discrete populations and funds for their care. Because these strategies are likely to use current categorical budget structures, the service areas included are likely to be limited to those traditionally funded in a specific categorical budget. Rather than integrating funding and administrative mechanisms, which is generally thought to be a desirable strategy, these approaches further reify boundaries between categorical budgets. These boundaries will make the design of sensible accountability systems more difficult because it will be challenging to hold a service provider responsible for outcomes that are contingent on an integrated service system, especially when the consumer's access to the needed services may be compromised by the funding system. It is ironic that these reforms represent both a major step forward in what is structurally required to engineer accountability systems (that is, establishing a clear point of accountability for identified individuals) and a further fragmentation of the system that may frustrate these efforts.

IMPLICATIONS FOR SOCIAL WORK AND HUMAN SERVICES RESEARCH AND PRACTICE

Social work and the human service professions have much to contribute to this reform effort, in terms of both practice and research. No discipline more acutely understands the importance of meeting the broad range of human needs than social work. It is important for the discipline to reassert itself as focusing on the whole person and to reinforce the importance of monitoring outcomes that encompass the full range of indicators addressing social, emotional, and physical well-being. It is also important to alert policymakers to the dangers in further fragmenting systems through payment strategies that rely on historical categorical funding. If, as we hope, accountability strategies are developed from the current reforms that emphasize the overall health and mental health status of populations, then social workers, who are prepared in integrative practice models, should be valuable system leaders and providers. Social workers who are prepared only for private practice psychotherapy are unlikely to find these reformed systems hospitable to their training and career ambitions. Given the historical orientation of the discipline, however, social workers are well positioned to provide leadership and direct services in the new era of managed care.

Much research must be completed on how best to define and implement these outcomes-oriented accountability strategies. Methods for monitoring the overall well-being of populations and their use of services across the full range of human service systems, rather than within only one budget category, must be developed. By understanding these comprehensive service utilization patterns, it will be possible both to document cost shifting across human service domains (for example, from behavioral health to corrections) and to develop the necessary cost estimates to establish rates for integrative treatment and support services. When these monitoring methods become available, it will also be possible to examine the impact of varying organizational forms and financing strategies on maximizing the broad social good. As social workers begin to understand the relationships between these varying strategies and outcomes, they can then begin to design systems in a more intelligent way that considers the broad social implications of a system change rather than the more narrow concentration on cost containment within one budget category.

Conclusion

Depending upon its willingness to adapt to the rapid changes that are occurring in the health and behavioral health sectors, social work is well positioned to lead the effort in both research and practice. Through leadership in system design and in forming interdisciplinary research teams of economists, political scientists, anthropologists, public administrators, and other clinical disciplines, social work can have a profound effect on the shape of these reforms and ultimately on the overall public health.

References

Berlant, J., Trabin, T., & Anderson, D. (1994). The value of mental health and chemical dependency benefits: More than meets the eye. In E. Sullivan (Ed.), *Driving down health care costs: Strategies and solutions* (pp. 315–323). New York: Panel Publishers.

Chambless, D. L. (1993). *Report of the Division 12 Presidential Task Force on Promotion and Dissemination of Psychological Procedures*. Washington, DC: American Psychological Association.

Freund, D., & Hurley, R. (1995). Medicaid managed care: Contributions to issues of health reform. *Annual Review of Public Health, 16,* 473–496.

Mumford, E., Schlesinger, H. J., Glass, G. V., Patrick, C., & Cuerdon, T. (1984). A new look at evidence about reduced cost of medical utilization following mental health treatment. *American Journal of Psychiatry, 141,* 1145–1158.

National Advisory Mental Health Council. (1993). Health care reform for Americans with severe mental illness. *American Journal of Psychiatry, 150,* 1447–1465.

Pallak, M., Cummings, N., Dorken, H., & Henke, C. (1994). Medical costs, Medicaid, and managed mental health treatment: The Hawaii study. *Managed Care Quarterly, 2*(2), 64–70.

Rice, D., Kelman, S., Miller, L., & Dunmeyer, P. (1990). *The economic costs of alcohol and drug abuse and mental illness: 1985* (DHHS Publication No. ADM 90-1694). Washington, DC: U.S. Government Printing Office.

Starr, P. (1992). *The logic of health-care reform.* Knoxville, TN: Whittle Press.

Trabin, T., & Freeman, M. A. (1995). *Managed behavioral healthcare: History, models, strategic challenges and future course.* Tiburon, CA: Centralink Publications.

U.S. General Accounting Office. (1995). *Medicaid: Spending pressures drive states toward managed care* (GAO Publication No. HEHS-95-122). Washington, DC: U.S. Government Printing Office.

CHAPTER 8

Federal and State Legislative and Program Directions for Managed Care

RONALD W. MANDERSCHEID

MARILYN J. HENDERSON

The context for the delivery of mental health and substance abuse care is changing dramatically as advances in managed behavioral health care occur. Approximately 124 million people are currently covered by managed behavioral health care insurance plans (Open Minds, 1996), and 35 states have received federal waivers to implement Medicaid managed behavioral health care programs (The Policy Resource Center and the George Washington Universtiy Center for Health Policy Research, 1996). Both network and health maintenance organization (HMO) arrangements are being set up for managed care, and a range of options are being used to contract with providers.

This chapter describes current and anticipated federal and state legislative and regulatory activities that are relevant to managed care. For the federal level, developments with respect to insurance reform, the Medicaid and Medicare programs, and Performance Partnership Grants (PPGs) are reviewed. For the state level, developments that are designed to protect against the negative effects of managed care are reviewed. These include specification of essential community providers, definition of mandated benefits, development of licensure and accreditation procedures for utilization review firms, community rating of health insurance premiums, and definition of specialty providers as primary care providers. Although most states currently do not have such provisions in legislation or regulation, major efforts are being mounted to effect such changes.

This chapter also explores the implications of current developments in terms of several predictions about the future and examines the steps necessary to foster

---

This chapter was produced while the authors were federal employees and is in the public domain. Part of this material will appear in *Mental Health, United States, 1996,* to be published by the U.S. Department of Health and Human Services.

quality in service delivery using case management as an example from this perspective. Managed care will continue to grow, particularly in the public sector, and many "carve out" programs will become "carve in" programs, except for people with severe problems. Providers will organize networks of care that will compete with managed care organizations for health care and utilization review business, and nontraditional HMOs will become a preferred vehicle for managing care.

Case management is most likely to continue as part of a carve-out program for people with severe problems. Particular attention must be paid to the impact of federal and state developments on payment mechanisms. Case management must be defined operationally, and annual capitation rates must be set for different intensities of service delivery. An opportunity exists to be creative, but action must be taken quickly if case management is to be successful.

Background

Managed care has been practiced since the inception of HMOs during the 1930s and 1940s. However, since the early 1980s, a new form of managed care—the utilization review firm—has grown rapidly in response to dramatic increases in the cost of health care (Freeman & Trabin, 1994). Utilization review firms, frequently called *managed care organizations,* control the expenditure of insurance funds by requiring providers to seek approval to deliver care. Hence, they serve as intermediaries between employers and insurance companies on one hand and providers and consumers on the other.

In the mental health and substance abuse fields, managed care organizations have generally taken the form of carve-out firms that provide utilization review only for mental health and substance abuse problems. Since 1990, these firms have expanded their operations beyond managed care functions to include provision of services through directly owned or contracted networks of providers for mental health and substance abuse services. Collectively, these activities are called *behavioral health care.* Freeman and Trabin (1994) provided a detailed overview of the private sector managed behavioral health care field.

President Clinton's proposed Health Security Act stimulated considerable momentum in the states to engage in health care reform activities (Arons & Buck, 1994). The demise of the national effort has constricted these state initiatives so that, in most states, reform will center on a Medicaid waiver to permit managed care of this population. Medicaid waivers are described later in this chapter. States are interested in Medicaid managed care because they wish to control the rapid growth in state expenditures for the Medicaid program while extending health care to uninsured people.

Without the national service and financing reforms proposed under the Health Security Act (1993), managed behavioral health care has been growing rapidly in an undirected way. In the private sector, approximately 124 million people are currently covered by some type of managed behavioral health care plan (Open Minds, 1996). State interest in managed care has led to the awarding by the U.S. Health Care Financing Administration (HCFA) of 35 Medicaid waivers that involve mental health and substance abuse (The Policy Resource Center and the George Washington

University Center for Health Policy Research, 1996). Many more state waivers are still anticipated.

Within this context, it is important to examine managed behavioral health care and the Medicaid waivers in more detail. These brief analyses will provide a framework for discussion of current developments and expectations for the future.

Managed behavioral health care can be provided through an HMO or through a network as outlined in Table 8-1. HMOs generally integrate health and behavioral health services and are paid through a capitated annual premium. In contrast, networks generally provide behavioral health services in a carve-out arrangement and are paid through some form of reduced fee for service.

The traditional HMO is one in which providers work for the organization, that is, a staff model HMO. Newer types of HMOs include those in which contracted independent providers compose the staff (an independent practice arrangement HMO) and those in which the staff consists of contracted groups of providers (a group practice arrangement HMO). In any of these HMO models, behavioral health care can be provided directly by the HMO or contracted to a managed care organization.

Behavioral health care networks can also be staff, independent practice, or group practice models. Most frequently, they are contracted independent or group practice arrangements that are referred to as *preferred provider organizations*. Generally, members of the network contract with a managed care organization for referrals under a reduced fee-for-service arrangement. Some managed care organizations are currently beginning to use capitation payment arrangements that put providers at financial risk for consumer care using contractual agreements with preset prospective funding for enrollees for an agreed-on set of services and a given period. Providers have some flexibility in determining the nature of services delivered as long as negotiated outcomes are achieved, and they are financially liable for these services regardless of their extent.

Within the past several years, some HMOs and networks have added a point-of-service option to their basic behavioral health care plans. This option allows consumers to go outside the HMO or network to see other providers. However, when consumers do this, they are required to pay part of the cost for the care received through additional copayments and deductibles.

Table 8-1

EIGHT TYPES OF MANAGED CARE ENTITIES

Type of provider	Network Model (generally carve out)	HMO Model (generally carve in)
Staff	X	X
Independent practice	X	X
Mixed	X	X
Group practice	X	X

Note: For each of the eight configurations, a plan may or may not offer a point-of-service option under which participants can go outside the network or HMO to receive care from other providers.

Medicaid is a health care entitlement program for Aid to Families with Dependent Children recipients; Supplemental Security Income recipients; poor people, people with disabilities, and older people; infants, children, and pregnant women who are poor; and medically needy recipients. The states and the federal government share program costs through a formula based on per capita income. Although all states are required to provide a basic set of services, other services can be included or excluded at the preference of the state.

Mandatory Medicaid services important for mental health and substance abuse care include inpatient and outpatient hospital service; home health care services; nursing facility services; physician services; and early and periodic screening, diagnosis, and treatment services for children. Relevant optional Medicaid services include targeted case management, rehabilitation services, clinic services, personal care in the home, and prescription drugs.

Medicaid waivers are granted to the states to change how services are delivered, to change the particular services that can be provided, or to change the population included in the program. Two types of waivers are available: (1) the 1915B waiver, which is specific to the Medicaid program, and (2) the 1115 waiver, which is generic across the Social Security Act.

The 1915B waiver can be used to modify the requirement that Medicaid services be available on a statewide basis; that the amount, duration, or scope of services be the same for all recipients; or that recipients have freedom of choice of providers. In the latter case, a waiver can be used to extend the lock-in for up to six months. Thus, states can use such a waiver to implement Medicaid managed care in a portion of a state or for a particular Medicaid population, using either an HMO or network model.

The 1115 waiver permits everything included in the 1915B waiver plus expansion of program eligibility to other populations, addition of other services, relaxation of the requirement that 25 percent of HMO participants be non-Medicaid consumers, extension of consumer lock-in beyond six months, and reallocation of disproportionate share payments to the Medicaid managed care program. States can use such a waiver to expand the Medicaid population pool to cover uninsured people while containing costs through implementation of HMO or network model programs. Clearly, the 1115 waiver permits more flexibility than does the 1915B waiver.

Description of Current Status

Although the description of the current situation will be divided between federal and state governments for ease of presentation, the reader should remember that these sectors interact with each other and thus mutually influence developments in each.

FEDERAL DEVELOPMENTS

Federal developments pertinent to managed care occur principally in Congress. With the historic congressional change in 1994, the approach to health care reform has become an incremental rather than an integrated one. Several proposals are currently being considered:

- Minor insurance reforms, potentially including elimination of preexisting condition exclusions and adding a requirement of insurance portability from job to job. Although these changes are considered relatively minor by the industry, they could be major for mental health and substance abuse and could represent significant gains for these fields. Senators Nancy Landon Kassebaum (R-Kans.) and Edward M. Kennedy (D-Mass.) introduced a bill that incorporates these changes. It was almost unanimously supported by Congress and was signed into law by President Clinton August 21, 1996, as the Health Insurance Portability and Accountability Act of 1996.
- Reform of the Medicaid program, potentially including program caps on expenditures (analogous to the "global budget" concept discussed in conjunction with the president's Task Force on Health Care Reform) and conversion of the program to a state block grant (Arons & Buck, 1994). Depending on the degree of flexibility permitted, states may find a Medicaid block grant appealing; however, a financial cap could diminish the capacity of states to engage in reform activities aimed at expanding population coverage. For mental health and substance abuse services, a Medicaid block grant might decrease the resources available because governors would likely have additional flexibility to direct program funds elsewhere. Moreover, because many people with mental health or substance abuse problems are not currently covered by Medicaid, a financial cap could prevent needed population expansions.
- Reform of the Medicare program, potentially including limitations on the growth of the program and conversion from fee for service to either managed care service delivery or a voucher system. In this program, beneficiaries may identify a trade-off between limitations on program growth and managed care. If this occurs, then managed care could be perceived as an appropriate vehicle for permitting expansion of the beneficiary population or the benefit package under a reduced financial growth plan. Vouchers would represent an alternative to managed care designed to increase consumer choice while controlling resource expenditures. Because mental health and substance abuse care are not as heavily invested in Medicare as in Medicaid, the effect on these fields could be relatively small. However, the anticipated dramatic growth of the elderly population in the United States in both numerical and percentage terms could lead to unanticipated growth in the demand for mental health and substance abuse services from the Medicare population.

The Clinton administration supports variations on the congressional proposals outlined above, principally with a view toward federal cost containment. The administration is also active in several other areas that require comment:

- Development of PPGs to replace the current array of federal block and categorical grants to the states operated by the U.S. Department of Health and Human Services. For each type of PPG, the Secretary of Health and Human Services would define a menu of objectives and measures, and individual states would negotiate with the department about which objectives to choose for the three- to five-year period of the grants, including unique objectives not in the menu. States would also negotiate about the measures and standards to be used to define success. In addition, a small number of national objectives would be defined for each PPG; states would be required to report on these objectives but would not be judged on them unless they were selected by the state for its particular performance contract. The administration's proposal is for separate PPGs for mental health and substance abuse. An issue for these fields is whether Congress will support several PPGs in the Department of Health and Human Services or seek to convert all of them into a single health block grant.

- Encouragement of states to submit Medicaid waivers to expand the scope of managed care systems to contain costs as well as to expand coverage to uninsured populations. Although the number of states with waivers has grown rapidly, questions have begun to arise about whether the waivers actually contain costs. A report by the U.S. General Accounting Office (1995) suggests that federal Medicaid costs will expand dramatically under the waivers. For mental health and substance abuse care, a related issue could be the degree to which Medicaid resources will continue to be directed toward these problems, as opposed to migrating to other health problems. This concern could encourage states to opt for a carve-out approach to mental health and substance abuse.

STATE DEVELOPMENTS

State developments appear to be directed principally at constructing various protective devices to limit what are perceived to be the negative effects of managed care. Thirty-three states have introduced such legislation: In Alabama, Maryland, New York, Oregon, and Wyoming, the legislation has been passed; three states are still considering it; in 24 states it has failed; and in one state, Washington, it has been repealed. Following is a brief description of the different types of relevant legislative and regulatory initiatives being undertaken by states:

- Legal definition of *essential community providers* with whom managed care organizations must contract for care delivery. Although this may seem to represent a victory for particular groups of providers, no assurance exists that such providers will actually receive sufficient referrals from the managed care organization once they are in the contract pool. A variant of this concept is *any willing provider* legislation, which would permit patients to choose their own provider, whether or not that provider is part of a managed care network. This type of legislation generally permits health plans to charge additional copayments for such point-of-service care.
- Definition of mandated benefits for particular types of illnesses or medical conditions. For example, some states are considering mandating benefits regarding length of stay for vaginal births. Although intended to correct quality

problems with inappropriate brevity of care, such mandates can also have the effect of increasing overall costs because mandated benefits will become the norm for all cases, even if such care is not needed.

- Development of separate licensure or accreditation procedures for utilization review firms to begin to regulate the activities of managed care organizations. Such regulation is equivalent to state regulation of health insurance companies, and it is generally implemented by the same state agency.
- Community rating of health insurance premiums rather than rating by the characteristics of particular client pools, which can have the effect of reducing premium differences among clients while penalizing those who would have lower premiums if the population were subdivided into separate risk pools.
- Definition of specialty providers as primary care providers so that they can serve as a point of entry for care rather than rely on referrals from primary care physicians in managed care networks or HMOs. Although such arrangements appear to be clever, it would be difficult to set capitation rates for such providers because the range of care to be provided could vary dramatically from client to client.

The outcome of state legislative and regulatory initiatives will depend on the relative political strength of business and insurance interests on one hand and provider and consumer interests on the other. Careful delineation must be made in each case on the question of cost versus consumer choice, quality of care, and provider role. Needless to say, the mental health and substance abuse fields should foster discussion of these questions to inform state and local managers, public and private providers, and consumers and family members about the advantages and disadvantages of each issue.

FOUR PREDICTIONS

This brief analysis would not be complete without some discussion about likely future events. For simplicity, these future scenarios have been encapsulated into four general predictions anticipated to occur over the next five to seven years:

1. Managed care will continue to grow, particularly for public sector services. States are interested in controlling their health care expenditures while trying to incorporate uninsured people into health care plans. This goal can only be accomplished through managed care or a similar arrangement.
2. The mental health and substance abuse carve out will become a carve in, except for people with severe problems. For more than a decade, research has shown a primary care cost-offset effect: Provision of appropriate specialty care can reduce primary care costs dramatically (Kessler, Steinwachs, & Hankin, 1982; National Advisory Mental Health Council, 1993). These financial benefits can only be achieved efficiently when the managed care organization controls both primary care and specialty care. People with severe problems will probably continue to be served through a carve-out arrangement by providers with the needed skills for such care, although their health insurance premiums may

eventually be linked to those of broader population pools to spread the insurance risk and to encourage providers to serve these populations.

3. Mental health and substance abuse providers will organize specialty networks and will participate in health care networks to compete with managed care organizations for private and public sector contracts. Minnesota has begun to consider incentive arrangements for providers to form networks to deliver care and perform their own utilization review. Murphy (1995) provided a detailed overview of this topic, including an analysis of the legal implications of such networks.
4. Nontraditional HMOs may become a preferred vehicle for managing care, in contrast to the network approach of managed care organizations. This change may occur because of the primary care cost-offset effect described above and the desire of providers to form their own networks. The outcome will depend on the degree to which the HMO industry focuses on behavioral health care issues. Regardless of the outcome, this approach will not, however, clarify the question of how people with severe problems will be served.

What about Case Management?

Case management for adults with serious mental illnesses and children and adolescents with serious emotional disturbances fits into the world of managed care. *Case management,* as used here, refers to a clinical service designated to locate, coordinate, monitor, and advocate for necessary and appropriate mental health and social services in the community for a consumer. In this section, relevant links are drawn and implications for case management are explored as an example of the steps that need to be taken to maintain and improve the quality of service delivery in a changing environment.

It seems clear from the analyses presented that case management for people with severe mental problems is most likely to continue under managed care as part of a carve out for this population. The payment for care is likely to be capitated on an annual basis and to derive from a combination of federal and state Medicaid funds, direct state appropriations, and federal PPG funds. Thus, potential legislative changes in these programs must be watched carefully for their impact on case management services for adults with serious mental illnesses and children and adolescents with serious emotional disturbances. Another area to watch is innovative insurance arrangements that spread the insurance risk for these populations into broader population pools.

The Medicaid waivers being developed by states must also be watched to determine the range of services covered by the waiver, such as what services, including case management, are covered. The field must also pay attention to the question of how *wraparound services*—for example, social services, vocational rehabilitation, and housing—will be coordinated with services covered under the waiver and how entities providing these former services will be reimbursed for care provided. Without attention to these key issues, case management may not have the essential tools to provide quality care to populations with severe problems.

Case management for populations with severe problems must be defined in clear operational terms. In the language of managed behavioral health care, case management must be defined as a clear clinical protocol that is replicable across a broad array of practice settings. Such operational definition is necessary if case management is to have credibility within a managed care arrangement.

Table 8-2 outlines some key factors to consider in developing a clinical protocol for case management. First, the system protocol for the program in which case management is embedded must be developed. For example, work will be required to translate the community support program model into a system protocol (Mulkern, 1995). Second, the clinical protocol for case management within the systems model must be developed. Third, prior work on cost-effectiveness of case management within the system protocol must be reviewed and compiled, and short methods of assessment of cost-effectiveness within the managed care context must be designed. As is also shown in Table 8-2, measurement questions exist at each of these levels of development. These questions are intended to be illustrative rather than definitive. Manderscheid and Henderson (1995) provided an overview of some key data requirements for managed behavioral health care.

Little work is occurring at present to develop the needed system and clinical protocols. However, the Division of Mental Health of the World Health Organization in Geneva has specified detailed checklists of activities required to ensure quality in mental health facilities and systems (Bertolote, 1994) and has identified essential treatments in psychiatry, including social interventions (Bertolote & de Girolamo, 1993). These reports have provided contextual information for the development of systems and clinical protocols.

In contrast, activities in the field reflect considerable variability from state to state in the definition of service systems and case management. These definitions generally have not been converted into protocols. Two interesting exceptions are the work on the Program for Assertive Community Treatment being undertaken by the

Table 8-2

DEVELOPMENT OF MANAGED CARE PROTOCOLS

Key Elements	Key Questions
Development and testing of system protocol	Prior work? Simplicity? Fidelity of implementation?
Development and testing of clinical protocol	Prior work? Simplicity? Training required?
Development and testing of cost-effectiveness analyses	Prior work? Rigor? Ease of use in managed care arrangements?

Texas Department of Mental Health and Mental Retardation (1996), the National Alliance for the Mentally Ill, and the work on case management currently underway by the National Association of Case Management (1996). Also, states have begun to experience problems with their fee structures under Medicaid managed care because services are not clearly operationalized in protocols and populations are not clearly differentiated into risk pools that require different service intensities. Thus, in addition to the development of protocols, a second type of activity is also necessary. Case management must be capitated so that payers can know what costs will be for different client risk pools. The field must be able to arrive at an annual cost for providing different levels of case management intensity. As a starting point, the field may wish to consider the capitated cost for providing several different intensities of case management, with careful specification of the type of population to be served by each.

Conclusion

Case management has been used as an example to show the types of steps needed to adapt clinical protocols to managed care. However, the criteria discussed also apply to other services. Managed care has changed the context of mental health care dramatically and irreversibly. The mental health field can adapt to these changes, but protocols must be defined clearly. Different system configurations must be costed out to develop annual capitation rates for population pools that require different intensities of services. The opportunity exists to be creative, but changes must be implemented quickly.

References

Arons, B. S., & Buck, J. A. (1994). Mental health and substance abuse benefits under National Health Care Reform. In R. W. Manderscheid & M. S. Sonnenschein (Eds.), *Mental health, United States, 1994* (DHHS Publication No. [SMA] 94-3000, pp. 1–7). Washington, DC: Center for Mental Health Services, Substance Abuse and Mental Health Services Administration, U.S. Government Printing Office.

Bertolote, J. M. (Ed.). (1994). *Quality assurance in mental health care: Check-lists & glossaries.* Geneva: World Health Organization, Division of Mental Health.

Bertolote, J. M., & de Girolamo, G. (Eds.). (1993). *Essential treatments in psychiatry.* Geneva, Switzerland: World Health Organization, Division of Mental Health.

Freeman, M. A., & Trabin, T. (1994). *Managed behavioral healthcare: History, models, key issues, and future course.* Rockville, MD: U.S. Center for Mental Health Services.

Health Security Act. (1993). HR 36001H, S 1757, 103d Cong., 1st Sess.

Kessler, L. G., Steinwachs, D. M., & Hankin, J. R. (1982). Episodes of psychiatric care and medical utilization. *Medical Care, 20,* 1209–1221.

Manderscheid, R. W., & Henderson, M. J. (1995). *Speaking with a common language: The past, present, and future of data standards for managed behavioral healthcare.* Rockville, MD: U.S. Department of Health and Human Services.

Mulkern, V. (1995). *The community support program: A model for federal–state partnership*. Washington, DC: Mental Health Policy Resource Center.

Murphy, A. M. (1995). *Formation of networks, corporate affiliations, and joint ventures among mental health and substance abuse treatment organizations.* Rockville, MD: U.S. Department of Health and Human Services, Center for Mental Health Services.

National Advisory Mental Health Council. (1993). *Health care reform for Americans with severe mental illnesses: Report of the National Advisory Mental Health Council.* Rockville, MD: National Institute of Mental Health.

National Association of Case Management. (1996). *Clinical protocols for case management.* Unpublished draft prepared in support of a contract with Center for Mental Health Services, Substance Abuse and Mental Health Services Administration.

Open Minds. (1996). *Managed behavioral health market share in the United States, 1996–1997*. Gettysburg, PA: Author.

The Policy Resource Center and the George Washington University Center for Health Policy Research. (1996, Winter). *Final Report, Winter 1996, for the SAMHSA Managed Care Tracking System Contract.* Unpublished draft, Substance Abuse and Mental Health Services Administration, Rockville, MD.

Texas Department of Mental Health and Mental Retardation. (1996). *States helping states: PACT and managed care.* Unpublished conference proceedings, October 30–November 1, 1996, Fort Worth, TX.

U.S. General Accounting Office. (1995). *Medicaid managed care: More competition and oversight would improve California's expansion plan.* Washington, DC: Author.

CHAPTER 9

Assessing Effectiveness of Mental Health Care in Routine Clinical Practice

G. RICHARD SMITH, JR.

KATHRYN M. ROST

ELLEN P. FISCHER

M. AUDREY BURNAM

BARBARA J. BURNS

The health care delivery system faces continually increasing pressure to be accountable for the historically unparalleled amount of resources it utilizes. This chapter discusses one set of recently developed tools known as outcomes modules which are used to assess how treatment impacts outcomes in patients with a given disorder. These tools are currently being used to inform administrative decisions about how to improve the quality of care, and can potentially influence decisions by patients, providers, and payers of care as well. The critical components of outcomes modules as well as their administration and applications are described, using modules for psychiatric conditions as examples.

Consider the following scenarios:

- The director of a large multisite community mental health care program is concerned that the organization may not be providing high quality care to all its patients. A mechanism is needed to routinely monitor and evaluate the effectiveness of care in the program and to compare effectiveness among sites.
- Budget cuts are forcing the chief of staff and the chief of psychiatry at a major medical center to reduce services. To reach a rational decision about which

This chapter is reprinted with permission from Smith, G. R., Jr., Rost, K. M., Fischer, E. P., Burnam, M. A., & Burns, B. J. (1997). Assessing the effectiveness of mental health care in routine clinical practice. *Evaluation and the Health Professions, 20* (1), 65–80. Copyright 1997, Sage Publications.

services to cut, the administrators need systematic data on the relative effectiveness of individual therapy, group therapy, and day treatment in their organization.

- A large purchaser of care is attempting to decide whether to pay for psychotherapy for many mental health conditions where its efficacy has not been rigorously tested. The purchaser must decide within the next six months which benefits to offer in next year's plans.

The common thread in these vignettes is the need for tools to permit health care professionals to assess the results of services delivered in routine clinical practice (Mirin & Namerow, 1991). Patient outcomes modules are standardized sets of validated instruments designed to facilitate the systematic gathering of data on patient response to treatment for a particular condition. (Since the term *measure* usually refers to the assessment of a single construct, and understanding the outcomes of care requires the measurement of multiple constructs, we refer to these sets of instruments as outcomes modules rather than outcomes measures.) These tools are currently being used by health care administrators to monitor clinical performance. They can also be used to provide critical and previously unavailable information to inform the decisions made by patients, providers, and payers.

Patient outcome modules for physical conditions such as hip replacement, cataracts, and hypertension are being developed and validated under the leadership of the Health Outcomes Institute, formerly InterStudy (Ellwood, 1988). (The modules described in this article are available for unlimited public use from the Health Outcomes Institute, 2001 Killebrew Drive, Suite 122, Bloomington, Minnesota 55425.) The Centers for Mental Healthcare Research (CMHR) at the University of Arkansas for Medical Sciences has taken an active role in the development of outcome modules for psychiatric conditions in collaboration with the Department of Veterans Affairs and the Health Outcomes Institute. Outcomes modules for alcohol dependence, panic disorder, and major depression have been field tested and validated; modules for drug abuse disorders and schizophrenia are currently undergoing validation.

Initially researchers were the primary consumers of outcome modules. Increasingly, numerous organizations providing capitated mental health services have integrated specific modules into routine clinical care to monitor outcomes for a given diagnosis or tracer condition. This chapter describes the components of outcomes modules for mental health disorders that we view as critical and the uses that we envision for such modules.

Critical Components of a Mental Health Care Outcomes Module

The goal of an outcomes module is to measure the impact of treatment on the outcomes of care adjusting for prognostic characteristics in a diagnostically homogeneous patient population. To develop an outcomes module for each of five psychiatric conditions, separate 5- to 9-member multi-institutional expert panels were covened. Each expert panel was charged with advising on the relevant clinical and methodologic issues in creating a module for each condition with the following critical components:

- ability to verify that patients participating in the protocol met diagnostic criteria for the condition under study
- ability to provide valid and reliable data about salient outcomes from both the patient's and provider's perspective
- ability to measure prognostic variables to permit comparisons across groups
- ability to assess the type and extent of treatment the patient received for the target condition across various health care delivery settings.

Following each expert panel meeting, the research team drafted a module reflecting the direction provided by the panel. We incorporated measures, scales, or items tapping the constructs of interest adapted from previously developed measurement work whenever possible, giving credit in the user's manual which accompanies each module to the scale's original developer. Where no appropriate scales existed, we developed new items (Rost, Burnam, & Smith, 1993) or modified existing items. The expert panel then reviewed the prototype and made suggestions on the protocol for field testing. Following its field test, each module was revised to remedy addressable problems. The following sections discuss the four critical components of outcomes modules, and give examples of how the modules we have developed to date address each component.

VERIFICATION OF DIAGNOSTIC CRITERIA

Because of considerable heterogeneity in the diagnosis of mental health conditions in routine clinical settings, each module collects information about diagnostic criteria for the condition of interest from the patient and/or treating clinician in order to establish the appropriateness of the module for the patient in question. The diagnostic component of each module has been designed to provide a brief assessment which provides the highest possible sensitivity and specificity compared to a structured or semi-structured diagnostic research interview in order to identify a diagnostically homogeneous group of patients who are representative of patients in the practice being treated for the condition. In alcohol dependence, patient reports about diagnostic criteria from the modules show better agreement with structured interviews than clinician reports (Dawes, Frank, & Rost, 1993). The patient-derived diagnosis in the Alcohol Outcomes Module has a 100 percent sensitivity in an alcohol-dependent patient population and a 76 percent specificity in a non–alcohol-dependent drug-abusing patient population (both groups included patients who did not have the diagnosis) to the structured interview diagnosis of current alcohol dependence (kappa = .81). In panic disorder, clinician reports about diagnostic criteria show better agreement with structured interviews than patient reports (Hollenberg, Rost, Humphrey, Owen, & Smith, 1997). Clinician assessment of diagnostic criteria has a 79 percent sensitivity and a 92 percent specificity to the structured interview diagnosis of current panic disorder (kappa =

.61). In major depression, combining clinician and/or patient reports about diagnostic criteria shows the best agreement (Rost, Smith, Burnam, & Burns, 1992). This strategy results in 100 percent sensitivity and 77.8 percent specificity to the structured interview diagnosis of major depression (kappa = .84).

RELIABLE AND VALID OUTCOMES MEASURES

Modules monitor how symptoms of the disorder change over time. Outcomes in each of the modules include not only clinical symptoms associated with the condition of interest but indicators of functioning as well. While the former is often of primary concern to the clinician, the latter may be of greatest importance to the patient.

In terms of clinical symptoms, the alcohol-dependence module measures the extent of alcohol consumption in the past month; the panic outcomes module measures the number of panic attacks in the past month; and the major depression module measures the severity of depression symptoms in the last two weeks.

In terms of general functioning, measures of physical, mental, and social functioning are monitored using the SF-36 (also known as the Health Status Questionnaire) (Ware, Snow, Kosinski, & Gandek, 1993), as well as the module itself. The SF-36 with scales assessing physical functioning, role functioning (physical and emotional), bodily pain, general health, vitality, social functioning, mental health, and reported health transitions permits comparisons of outcomes across and within different physical and mental health conditions (Ware et al., 1993). Each outcomes module supplements the SF-36 by measuring particular aspects of functioning that are relevant for the mental health condition of interest. For example, because panic disorder often limits patients from participating in the range of social activities they would otherwise pursue, the panic outcomes module supplements the measure of social functioning in the SF-36 with measures of several distinct types of social impairment often seen in panic disorder.

Validation studies indicate that the relatively short scales included in the outcomes modules provide reliable and valid measures of a range of relevant outcomes. A detailed description of the psychometric performance of the major outcomes constructs in the three modules validated to date appears in Table 9-1. Interested readers are encouraged to contact the authors for copies of more extended descriptions of the methodology and findings of each validation study.

Ideally, the modules could be used to provide data to clinicians on individual patients and about the patients' clinical change over time. Two problems limit this ability. The first is measurement precision, as can be seen in Table 9-1, the reliability of all of the outcomes measured by the modules discussed in this manuscript allows for group rather than individual comparisons. The second involves the heterogeneity of patients where patients with more favorable case-mix/prognostic factors would be expected to make greater gains than those with poorer prognosis irrespective of treatment. Both problems may be solved with better assessment approaches. Because there is a great demand for a "hemoglobin equivalent" in mental health which would provide standardized feedback to clinicians on the mental health of their individual patients, further measurement work in this area would be very welcomed.

Table 9-1

RELIABILITY AND VALIDITY OF KEY OUTCOMES MEASURES

Module/Outcome	Reliability	Validity
Alcohol[a]		
Alcohol consumption in past month	.87[b]	.74[c]
Physical consequences	.88[d]	.55[c]
Emotional consequences	.85[d]	.40[c]
Social consequences	.72[d]	.42[c]
Panic[e]		
Frequency of panic attacks	.96[b]	.71[c]
Anticipatory anxiety	.82[b]	.61[c]
Avoidance/distress	.89[b]	.62[c]
Suicidality	.80[b]	.56[c]
Depression[f]		
Severity of depressive symptoms	.85[b]	.63[c]
Suicidality	.70[b]	.42[b]

Note: New measure of depression severity was developed to keep the module in the public domain.

[a]Data taken from Rost, K. M., Ross, R. L., Humphrey, J., Frank, S., Smith, J., & Smith, G. R. (1996). Does this treatment work? Validation of an outcomes module for alcohol dependence. *Medical Care, 34,* 283–294.

[b]Kappa or intraclass correlation.

[c]Pearson correlation between module measure and gold standard.

[d]Cronbach's alpha.

[e]Data taken from Hollenberg, J., Rost, K. M., Humphrey, J., Owen, R., & Smith, G. R. (1997). Validation of the panic outcomes module. *Evaluation and the Health Professions, 20* (1), 81–95.

[f]Data taken from Rost, K., Wherry, J., Williams, C., & Smith, G. R., Jr. (1995). The process and outcomes of care for major depression in rural family practice settings. *Journal of Rural Health, 11,* 114–121.

In order for outcomes modules to be useful, they must be sensitive to clinically important changes in outcomes over time. With regard to alcohol, patient reports about any drinking at follow-up on the Alcohol Outcomes Module demonstrate good agreement (kappa = .83) with the Structured Clinical Interview for DSM-III-R (SCID) (Spitzer, Williams, Gibbon, & First, 1992). Similarly, patient reports about the change in physical, emotional, and social problems related to drinking within the Alcohol Outcomes Module show strong correlations ($r > .65$) to SCID judgments about change in severity between baseline and follow-up. In panic, there is good agreement between patient reports on the Panic Outcomes Module about change in the frequency of panic attacks between baseline and follow-up and structured interviewers' determinations of the same constructs (r = .47). We also observe good agreement between patient reports on change in anticipatory anxiety and structured interviewers' judgments (r = .59). In depression, studies in both the general medical setting and the specialty care setting have found that patient reports about change in severity of depressive symptoms as measured on early versions of the Depression Outcomes Module significantly differ between patients who receive pharmacologic intervention concordant with recently released guidelines (Depression Guideline Panel, 1993a, 1993b) and patients who do not (Rost et al., 1992, 1995).

PROGNOSTIC VARIABLES TO COMPARE OUTCOMES ACROSS GROUPS

Prognostic characteristics known to be associated with choice and/or success of treatment have also been included in the modules. These variables, sometimes referred to as case-mix variables, allow analysts to more confidently interpret relationships between treatment and observed outcomes in studies where patients are not randomized to the treatment conditions. They are particularly important when comparing outcomes across sites because they potentially allow analysts to adjust for pre-existing differences in prognosis that would otherwise confound the comparisons. Even with the best adjustments, caution should be taken when interpreting differences observed between patient groups in nonexperimental designs.

While the conclusiveness of the literature admittedly varies across conditions, there appears to be sufficient evidence that clinical variables like disease severity, duration, and comorbidity have an important impact on outcomes for the psychiatric conditions of interest. Outcomes modules also measure a second group of demographic and social factors that impact outcomes, such as age, education, and social support.

Our approach to validating this component of the module has been to demonstrate that the clinical prognostic measures we include in each module (severity, duration, and comorbidity) are reliable and show good criterion validity to structured interviews or other widely utilized "gold standard" measures. In alcohol, the module's measures of disease severity, duration, and comorbidity demonstrated acceptable test–retest reliability: the alpha coefficient for the severity scale was .71, the intraclass correlation coefficient for duration was .81, and the kappa coefficients for indicators of three psychiatric comorbidities ranged from .56 to .79. The measure of disease severity and duration in the Alcohol Outcomes Module also showed good criterion validity, correlating .48 and .58, respectively, to structured interview measurements of the same constructs. However, the module's measures of comorbidity showed unacceptable agreement with structured diagnostic interviews and work is currently underway to improve the module's measurement strategy in that area.

In panic, protocol constraints prohibited us from collecting test–retest information on case-mix variables; however, we were able to examine criterion validity. The module's measure of disease severity showed modest agreement with a structured interviewer's judgment of severity (r = .27). In contrast to alcohol, Panic Outcomes

Module measures of psychiatric comorbidity showed good agreement with structured interview diagnoses of agoraphobia, depressive disorders, and alcohol/drug disorders (kappas = .55 or greater). No gold standard measure was available to test the validity of the module's measure of duration. In depression, limited information is available on the reliability or validity of prognostic characteristics included in the module; however, since all prognostic measures in the Depression Outcomes Module were borrowed directly from previously validated instruments, we do not anticipate significant problems with this component of the module.

Considerably more theoretical and empirical work needs to be undertaken to determine how completely the prognostic variables are able to "level the playing field" in analyses comparing outcomes across nonexperimental groups. Until further evidence accumulates demonstrating that statistical adjustment for differences in these measured prognostic variables sufficiently controls for sample heterogeneity, comparisons of outcomes between nonexperimental groups should be made cautiously, understanding that initial differences between groups can lead to outcome differences irrespective of treatment.

MEASUREMENT OF THE TYPE AND EXTENT OF TREATMENT

A careful and comprehensive description and quantification of the services a patient receives is essential to understand how the provision of care influences outcomes. This component of the module has been designed to measure the types of treatment received for the condition of interest (pharmacotherapy, individual therapy, group therapy, electroshock therapy); the extent (dose, frequency, duration, number of sessions) of each treatment received; and the setting in which the treatment is delivered (primary care, specialty care, emergency room, day treatment, hospital). The modules have been explicitly designed to measure both treatment provided by the system (or payer) as recorded in medical records, as well as treatment received outside the system as reported by patients. Our initial work has not focused on establishing the psychometric precision of measuring treatment received within the system largely because the validity of administrative databases will undoubtedly vary across organizations. While there are few alternative sources to collect information about out-of-system use, the precision of patient reports about out-of-system use also needs to be more extensively investigated.

While outcomes modules have been carefully crafted, they are not static instruments. The modules described here are merely first-generation tools, and as such are open to improvement. The modules will need to be modified on an ongoing basis to reflect changes in knowledge and clinical practice. (Because copyright restrictions are forcing us to develop a new measure of depression severity to keep the Depression Outcomes Module in the public domain, further psychometric testing will have to be performed to verify the module's measurement of depressive symptoms.)

Administration of Outcomes Modules

In order to conduct outcomes monitoring, an organization needs to choose a target diagnosis (or "tracer condition") of particular interest. We generally recommend that patients enter the outcomes monitoring protocol when their clinicians diagnose the disorder of interest at the initial visit for the condition or for a new episode of the condition. Patients complete the Patient Baseline Assessment of the relevant outcomes module, the SF-36 and the Personal Characteristics Form when they enter the protocol. (Future modules for schizophrenia and drug disorders may supplement patient reports with information from a family member or other appropriate informant when the patient cannot or will not provide valid data.) Clinicians complete the Clinician Baseline Assessment of the relevant outcomes module when patients enter the protocol. It is critical to recruit as high a proportion as possible (> 90 percent) of patients (or a probability sample of patients) with the diagnosis of interest into the protocol, including patients from clinicians who are less than enthusiastic about outcomes monitoring. Without high participation rates, the findings will not be generalizable to all patients with the tracer condition who received care in the organization.

Information from the Patient Baseline Assessment and Clinician Baseline Assessment is examined to determine whether patients meet diagnostic criteria to continue in the outcomes monitoring protocol. Those patients who do not meet diagnostic and other minimal eligibility criteria detailed in the users' manuals are excluded from outcomes monitoring. (Minimal eligibility criteria—for example, sufficient cognitive functioning in the judgment of the treating clinician to report about life experiences during the past six months—were put in place to assure the validity of self-reported data without crippling the generalizability of the sample recruited into the protocol.)

However, for conditions like major depression or alcohol disorders (Bush, Shaw, Cleary, Delbanco, & Aronson, 1987; Wells et al., 1989) that are highly prevalent and often underdiagnosed, we developed a modified strategy to identify a representative cohort of patients with the condition of interest. Patients who are at high risk for the condition can be identified by administering a brief screener to all patients before their visit or in a yearly mail survey (Rost et al., 1993). Clinicians and patients complete the baseline portion of the module on all patients who screen positive. Patients who do not meet diagnostic criteria or other minimal eligibility criteria in the baseline component of the module do not proceed further with the protocol. This strategy allows users to examine the outcomes of a representative group of patients with a particular tracer condition in their practice, even when clinicians fail to diagnose sizable proportions of patients with the condition of interest.

We recommend that organizations collect outcomes data on each patient eligible for follow-up at either 4- or 6-month intervals from baseline until remission of the episode. Patients complete the Patient Follow-up Assessment and the SF-36 at follow-up. Data collection from the administrative databases using the Medical Record Review is conducted when patients complete follow-up. Follow-up intervals are chosen by the organization to: (1) provide sufficient time for clinical change to occur, (2) be short enough to be responsive to the needs of the organization for information, and (3) not overwhelm the patient or the organization with work. It is critical to follow as high a proportion as possible (> 80 percent) of patients who were recruited into the protocol and remained eligible after completing the baseline assessments to avoid selection bias. It is important to follow those who dropped out of treatment, as well as those who remain in treatment. Information on respondent burden, follow-up rates, and missing data for the three mental health outcomes modules we have field tested are included in Table 9-2. The reader is cautioned that these estimates may vary across organizations. For example, our follow-up rates reflect that patients were paid to complete the outcomes module as part of a four hour battery of validation instruments.

Application of Outcomes Modules

To date, outcomes modules for mental health conditions have been used primarily for evaluating the effectiveness of routine clinical interventions. Administrators who are charged with improving the quality of care have chosen a tracer condition; provided the necessary training to clinical and administrative staff on protocol implementation; identified personnel to conduct recruitment and follow-up; and made arrangements for data entry, management, and analysis. It is not yet possible to draw definitive conclusions about the impact of outcomes monitoring because even the first organizations to undertake this effort are now just completing data collection. However, even at this early stage, outcomes monitoring has had some expected as well as some unexpected consequences for the organizations involved. One expected consequence was the identification of treatment nonadherence and drop-out rates which were higher than administrators expected, although not necessarily higher than the literature suggested. A second expected consequence was the discovery that extended hospitalizations for major depression not explainable by differences in patient severity produced outcomes similar to shorter hospitalizations. Administrators responded to these findings by conducting concerted quality improvement programs to address these problems. Unexpected (yet not undesired) consequences included the (1) departure of a small number of clinicians (< 5 percent) who were not willing to make practice changes necessary to become goal-congruent with the organization, and (2) the discovery that many clinicians in the organization failed to assign even a tentative diagnosis at the first visit which resulted in the nonreimbursement for thousands of dollars worth of services provided.

We expect that organizations that undertake outcomes monitoring will discover substantial levels of unintended variation in clinical practice which consumes enormous resources without improving outcomes. These variations can provide a rational basis for identifying and correcting quality of care problems in even the best run organization.

We also anticipate that outcomes modules have other important applications for patients, providers, and payers in the health care system. For patients, outcomes monitoring can provide graphic displays to inform the decisions they make about treatment and treatment compliance, as is currently being done with patients deciding about hip replacement surgery. In the mental health field, clinicians can show patients with panic disorder how the frequency of panic attacks and social functioning is expected to change over time if they continue behavioral therapy and/or psychotropic medication.

Table 9-2

MISSING DATA AND RESPONSE BURDEN IN OUTCOMES MODULES

Module/Outcome	Percentage Missing Data Mean (SD)	Estimated Time to Completion[a] (minutes)
Alcohol[b]		
Patient baseline assessment	1.2 (1.7)	20
Clinician baseline assessment	1.3 (2.6)	6
Patient follow-up assessment	7.0 (9.7)	14
82.1% follow-up rate		
Panic[c]		
Patient baseline assessment	1.1 (2.9)	18
Clinician baseline assessment	0.7 (2.0)	5
Patient follow-up assessment	4.8 (2.1)	20
95.1% follow-up rate		
Depression[d]		
Patient baseline assessment	2.3 (3.6)	20
Clinician baseline assessment	not available	3
Patient follow-up assessment	2.6 (3.3)	20
81.0% follow-up rate		

[a]These estimates are derived from subtracting subject's recorded stop time from recorded start time and proportionately reducing the difference to reflect items that were discarded from the module after validation.

[b]Data taken from Rost, K. M., Ross, R. L., Humphrey, J., Frank, S., Smith, J., & Smith, G. R. (1996). Does this treatment work? Validation of an outcomes module for alcohol dependence. *Medical Care, 34,* 283–294.

[c]Data taken from Hollenberg, J., Rost, K. M., Humphrey, J., Owen, R., & Smith, G. R. (1997). Validation of the panic outcomes module. *Evaluation and the Health Professions, 20* (1), 81–95.

[d]Data taken from Rost, K., Wherry, J., Williams, C., & Smith, G. R., Jr. (1995). The process and outcomes of care for major depression in rural family practice settings. *Journal of Rural Health, 11,* 114–121.

For individual providers, the use of aggregate-level information to improve clinical decision making such as how to better match patients to alternate treatment protocols may provide substantial help.

For large group providers, merging the results of outcomes monitoring across several practices can provide a sufficiently large cohort to identify treatment modalities that produce consistently good outcomes in the routine care of the patients they treat.

These treatment modalities may then be formally tested in controlled clinical trials. We expect that outcomes monitoring may provide clinicians evidence which supports their clinical conclusions about which treatments "work," to inform decisions about service cutbacks. As measurement precision continues to improve in subsequent generations of outcomes modules, clinicians may be able to rely on outcomes monitoring to monitor progress in individual patients.

For purchasers of mental health services, outcomes monitoring will provide valuable information on differences in outcomes among provider organizations that, complemented by cost data, can help them judge the value of the services they are purchasing.

Discussion

Among the principal advantages of developing outcomes modules is that they provide an approach to outcomes monitoring that is standardized, comprehensive, adaptable, and relatively low burden for patients and clinicians. At present, researchers and program evaluators use a wide assortment of instruments that make it difficult if not impossible to make meaningful comparisons across studies. The time required to complete the extensive existing research batteries often limits their use to specialized research settings with limited generalizability. By consolidating relevant items from the most robust instruments into a single, brief yet comprehensive tool, we hope to encourage adoption of a standardized measurement package that will permit increasingly meaningful and informative comparisons of the results of independently conducted efficacy and effectiveness assessments.

Utilization of outcomes modules in routine care will also facilitate the introduction of continuous quality improvement into clinical practice. Continuous quality improvement is a process employed by industry to enhance the caliber of its product by monitoring production performance, altering procedures to rectify observed problems and evaluating the results of such changes on an ongoing basis. This process of performance, outcomes, or effectiveness management is eminently applicable to health care. Until recently, however, the tools necessary to implement it have been largely lacking. Outcomes modules help to fill this gap and offer an opportunity to test whether rational choices will in fact be made when needed data are available and whether, as a result, the average effectiveness of health services in the organizations using the modules will increase.

The most interesting question, and the greatest challenge for the future, is whether outcomes modules will be used in ways that facilitate and promote more effective care and better patient outcomes. There is a potential for outcomes data to be used to patients' detriment if they are interpreted simplistically or invoked to merely limit coverage or to otherwise reduce access to care for seriously ill and high-risk, high-cost individuals. The potential is also clearly there for clinicians to use outcomes data to optimize treatment and for managers of health care organizations to identify and provide the most effective forms of care to improve the health status of the patients they care for.

References

Bush, B., Shaw, S., Cleary, P., Delbanco, T. L., & Aronson, M. D. (1987). Screening for alcohol abuse using the CAGE Questionnaire. *American Journal of Medicine, 82,* 231–235.

Dawes, M. A., Frank, S., & Rost, K. (1993). Clinician assessment of psychiatric comorbidity and alcoholism severity in adult alcoholic inpatients. *American Journal of Drug and Alcohol Abuse, 19,* 377–386.

Depression Guideline Panel. (1993a). *Depression in primary care. Volume 1: Detection and diagnosis. Clinical practice guideline, Number 5* (AHCPR Publication No. 93-0550). Rockville, MD: U.S. Department of Health and Human Services, Public Health Service, Agency for Health Care Policy and Research.

Depression Guideline Panel. (1993b). *Depression in primary care. Volume 2: Treatment of major depression. Clinical practice guideline, Number 5* (AHCPR Publication No. 93-0551). Rockville, MD: U.S. Department of Health and Human Services, Public Health Service, Agency for Health Care Policy and Research.

Ellwood, P. M. (1988). Outcomes management: A technology of patient experience. *New England Journal of Medicine, 318,* 1549–1556.

Hollenberg, J., Rost, K. M., Humphrey, J., Owen, R., & Smith, G. R. (1997). Validation of the panic outcomes module. *Evaluation and the Health Professions, 20* (1), 81–95.

Mirin, S. M., & Namerow, M. J. (1991). Why study treatment outcome? In S. M. Mirin, J. T. Gossett, & M. C. Grob (Eds.), *Psychiatric treatment: Advances in outcome research* (pp. 1–14). Washington, DC: American Psychiatric Press.

Rost, K., Smith, G. R., Burnam, M. A., & Burns, B. J. (1992). Measuring the outcomes of care for mental health problems: The case of depressive disorders. *Medical Care, 30* (5), MS266–MS273.

Rost, K., Wherry, J., Williams, C., & Smith, G. R., Jr. (1995). The process and outcomes of care for major depression in rural family practice settings. *Journal of Rural Health, 11,* 114–121.

Rost, K. M., Burnam, M. A., & Smith, G. R. (1993). Development of screeners for depressive disorders and substance disorder history. *Medical Care, 31* (3), 189–200.

Rost, K. M., Ross, R. L., Humphrey, J., Frank, S., Smith, J., & Smith, G. R. (1996). Does this treatment work? Validation of an outcomes module for alcohol dependence. *Medical Care, 34,* 283–294.

Spitzer, R. L., Williams, J.B.W., Gibbon, M., & First, M. B. (1992). The structured clinical interview for DSM-III-R (SCID): 1. History, rationale and description. *Archives of General Psychiatry, 49,* 624–629.

Ware, J. E., Jr., Snow, K. K., Kosinski, M., & Gandek, B. (1993). *SF-36 health survey manual and interpretation guide.* Boston: The Health Institute, New England Medical Center.

Wells, K. B., Hays, R. D., Burnam, M. A., Rogers, W., Greenfield, S., & Ware, J. E. (1989). Detection of depressive disorders for patients receiving prepaid or fee-for-service care: Results from the Medical Outcomes Study. *Journal of the American Medical Association, 262,* 3298–3302.

CHAPTER 10

Use of Rapid Assessment Instruments as Outcomes Measures

KEVIN CORCORAN

In the past two decades, nearly exponential growth of psychometrically sound and clinically useful measurement tools has occurred. These instruments are useful for assessment and diagnosis (Derogatis & Melisaratos, 1983; Millon, 1985), monitoring treatment process (Horvath & Greenberg, 1989), and evaluating treatment outcomes (Stewart, Hays, & Ware, 1988; Ware, Kosinski, & Keller, 1994). However, this increase in available instruments has not been matched with routine incorporation by practitioners (Gingerich, 1984; Mutschler, 1984). The typical mental health practitioner in most private and public settings continues to rely on practice wisdom, clinical judgments, and intuition.

This perspective is changing with managed care. Although educators had only marginal success in persuading practitioners to integrate research and practice, managed care may have major success. Although educators stressed the value of research for practice, managed care is requiring that providers systematically measure client problems and goals, monitor treatment, and evaluate its effectiveness. Suddenly, topics covered in research courses are becoming required clinical practice skills. Standardized measurement and use of cutting score guidelines are clinical practice tools for assessment and triage.

As a consequence of managed care requirements, clinicians of all disciplines now seek good measurement tools that enable them to easily fulfill the demands of managed care. This chapter describes how rapid assessment instruments (RAIs) can be used to measure treatment outcomes and to assess the need for treatment.

Measurement and Managed Care

Managed care, nebulously defined as any program or procedure designed to control costs while ensuring that quality is not jeopardized (cost containment and quality assurance), is a recent arrival in the mental health field (Corcoran & Vandiver, 1996). The characteristics of managed care in behavioral health and mental health have been described in previous chapters.

Utilization reviews are important among managed care procedures. These reviews usually include forms completed by the clinician. A small number of practitioners (approximately 3 percent) are beginning to provide required information for utilization review electronically using computer networks (Ridgewood Finance Institute, 1995). Utilization reviews can be prospective, concurrent, or retrospective. These utilization reviews typically mandate that clinicians incorporate measurement in several phases of treatment: assessing service need (that is, medical necessity), operationalization of a time-limited intervention with a specified protocol designed to attain observable goals, and evaluation of service impact. Practitioners in managed care programs will find RAIs to be valuable in providing information for utilization reviews.

Rapid Assessment Instruments in Managed Care

RAIs are standardized measures that reliably and validly assess the intensity, frequency, or duration of a client problem (Levitt & Reid, 1981). An RAI may be a scale, a checklist, an index, or an inventory. RAIs, which are completed by clients as self-observations, are short and can include short subscales. RAIs also are easy to score and to interpret, providing direct measurement of attributes. Minimal training is needed to use RAIs, and clients understand them.

RAIs are useful for assessing treatment process and outcomes, especially for treatment in managed mental health care where the demonstration of observable change and goal attainment are important ways to ensure the quality of care. Costs are contained when ineffective treatments are not reimbursed or when reimbursement is contingent on the degree of treatment effectiveness.

RETROSPECTIVE UTILIZATION REVIEW

RAIs can measure indicators of treatment outcomes for retrospective utilization reviews. Typical questions addressed in retrospective utilization reviews are as follows:

- Can you contrast the client's current function in each of the following areas with his or her functioning at intake: psychological, social, occupation/educational?
- How did you assess the client's problems, symptoms, and functioning?
- How did you determine (that is, assess, evaluate, or monitor) the client's success in reaching this short-term goal?
- How did you determine (that is, assess, evaluate, or monitor) the client's success in reaching this long-term goal?
- Why was treatment necessary?
- For how many sessions are you requesting payment?

Retrospective utilization review questions can be addressed on the basis of information secured through RAIs. Using RAIs in treatment can provide persuasive evidence for use with a utilization reviewer regarding change in intensity, frequency, or duration of the client's problem. In managed care systems, judgment regarding treatment effectiveness often requires information regarding goal attainment. An RAI may provide such information. For example, a client could establish a score range as a goal for the client (which might approximate the mean score of the general population). When the RAI provides information regarding cutting scores, which is a range of scores distinguishing a clinical sample from the general population, the goal may be to stabilize client scores at some point relative to the general population.

CONCURRENT UTILIZATION REVIEW

RAIs are also useful in a concurrent utilization review that monitors client progress during treatment. Such monitoring is especially useful when the condition for which treatment is sought persists over extended periods (for example, persistent and severe mental illness) or when additional sessions are required beyond those authorized in a prospective utilization review. Some typical questions asked in a concurrent utilization review are as follows:

- Can you contrast the client's current function in each of the following areas with his or her functioning at intake: psychological, social, occupational/education?
- How did you assess the client's problems, symptoms, and functioning?
- How do you summarize the presenting problem for which you are requesting a continuation of treatment?
- What was the short-term goal of treatment? That is, objectively define what you hope to achieve if continued treatment is authorized.
- How did you determine (that is, assess, evaluate, or monitor) the client's success in reaching this short-term goal?
- What was the long-term goal of treatment? That is, objectively define what you hope to achieve if treatment is authorized.
- How did you determine (that is, assess, evaluate, or monitor) the client's success in reaching this long-term goal?
- What progress is still required to warrant continuation of services?
- How many sessions are you requesting?

Concurrent utilization reviews emphasize monitoring of the treatment process. Scores on an RAI may evidence some client change and goal attainment at intervals over the course of treatment. Elementary single-system designs help explain this perspective.

PROSPECTIVE UTILIZATION REVIEW

A slightly different view of RAIs as outcomes measures is to consider their potential to provide data regarding service need. Clinicians require data to document treatment necessity in prospective utilization reviews. Typical prospective utilization review questions are as follows:

- Can you identify current symptoms observed for each problem for which you are requesting authorization of services?

- What is the client's current functioning in each of the following areas: psychological, social, occupational/educational?
- How have you assessed the client's problems, symptoms, and functioning?
- What is the short-term goal of treatment? That is, objectively define what you hope to achieve if treatment is authorized.
- Why is treatment necessary at this time?
- How will you determine (that is, assess, evaluate, or monitor) the client's success in reaching this short-term goal?
- What is the long-term goal of treatment? That is, objectively define what you hope to achieve if treatment is authorized.
- How will you determine (that is, assess, evaluate, or monitor) the client's success in reaching this long-term goal?
- How many sessions are you requesting?

RAIs have a role in this aspect of managed care. Although pretreatment scores can provide a comparison for follow-up assessment, the pretreatment scores also can assess the need for clinical services. Severity determines of the need for services. RAIs can provide quantitative data about severity. Many RAIs can compare the client's scores with a sample from the general population or with clinical samples. Scores similar to the clinical sample, yet different from the general population, would indicate treatment need. The principles of these comparisons are illustrated in Figures 10–1 and 10–2.

The use of RAIs in establishment of treatment necessity requires norm-referenced comparisons. Norm-referenced comparisons are facilitated when RAIs have cutting scores. Most managed care organizations accept comparisons based on a cutting score from a respectable instrument as evidence of the need for treatment.

However, RAIs can provide convincing evidence of the need for treatment, even when a cutting score is not available, provided the instrument has a mean and standard deviation based on calculations from a relevant and representative population

Figure 10-1

POTENTIAL CLIENT'S SCORE COMPARED WITH A SAMPLE FROM GENERAL POPULATION

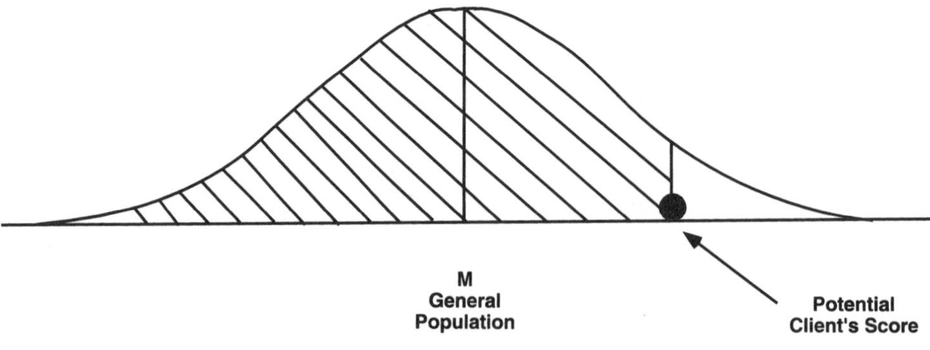

POTENTIAL CLIENT'S SCORE COMPARED WITH A CLINICAL SAMPLE

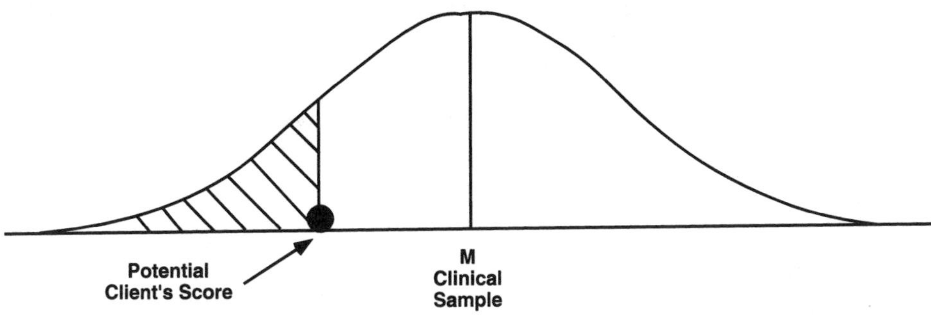

sample. This is accomplished with a *Z* score transformation (Fischer & Corcoran, 1994). The client's *Z* score is easily interpreted relative to a normative sample. An indication of service need can be the percentile ranking of the client's *Z* score. When a comparison is made with a sample from the general population, a score clinically meaningful might be in the 70th percentile or so. Such a score might indicate that the problem is so severe that it warrants treatment. For norm-referenced comparisons with a clinical sample, a score near the mean of a clinical sample may indicate treatment need; the clinical sample is from those already receiving services.

Limitations of Rapid Assessment Instruments

Not only are RAIs useful outcomes measures, but they also help operationalize other aspects of managed mental health care. Scores on an RAI may be used to show the need for treatment or the attainment of goals and indicate changes in a problem as well. However, RAIs have limitations. RAI administration requires time and resources, and their use can be inappropriate with clients who are seen for only a session or two (Corcoran, 1993; Levy, 1981). In some managed mental health care settings, clinicians working two shifts a day conduct 45-minute sessions with four clients per shift. Time is limited in such managed care settings, yet measurement is required, without allocation of more time needed to adequately conduct measurement.

A critical limitation of RAIs is that they produce "a bunch of dumb numbers." These numbers are only meaningful when interpreted by self- or norm-referenced comparisons. However, norms used for interpretation are often not up-to-date or representative. Normative data are difficult and expensive to obtain. Normative data are often not available, especially for people of color, immigrants, children, and people with low income. Norm-referenced comparisons with inappropriate populations lead to invalid conclusions and further confuse already "dumb" numbers.

When time and resources are limited, such as in managed mental health care today, practitioners tend to rely on uninterpreted or uninterpretable numbers. Caution must be used when accepting the veracity of a number as more efficient, such as to foster cost containment. This acceptance occurs when the number supports the clinician's claim that treatment is necessary, that it was implemented correctly, or that reimbursement is warranted. It also is easy to dismiss a number that does not support one's position.

Lack of information about or poor reliability and validity can limit the use of RAIs. Although an increasing number of RAIs are available, the psychometric properties of many RAIs have not been adequately assessed for stability and sensitivity.

Conclusion

Limitations of RAIs can produce inaccurate interpretations and incorrect decisions (Fischer & Corcoran, 1994). Recognition of these limitations, however, can lead to modest claims for the current value of RAIs. The number generated by the scoring of a RAI about an attribute is not that attribute, but a referent of it. A score on the Beck Depression Inventory (Beck, 1978) is not the experience of depression, but simply an indicator of it. Although scores produced by RAIs may be used as guides in clinical decision making, they are neither a supplement nor a substitute for clinical judgment, practice wisdom, and the total human experience found in clinical treatment.

When wisely selected and used, RAIs are valuable outcomes measures, allowing practitioners to monitor treatment and assess its effects. The value of RAIs broadens under managed mental health care. RAIs can assess treatment necessity and the attainment of client goals, and their value is contingent on their interpretability in terms of the representativeness and relevance of contemporary normative data.

References

Beck, A. T. (1978). *Depression Inventory.* Philadelphia: Philadelphia Center for Cognitive Therapy.

Corcoran, K. (1993). Practice evaluation: Problems and promises of single-system designs in clinical practice. *Journal of Social Service Research, 18,* 147–159.

Corcoran, K., & Vandiver, V. (1996). *Maneuvering the maze of managed care: Skills for mental health practitioners.* New York: Free Press.

Derogatis, L. R., & Melisaratos, N. (1983). The Brief Symptom Inventory: An introductory report. *Psychological Medicine, 13,* 595–605.

Fischer, J., & Corcoran, K. (1994). *Measures for clinical practice: Vol. 1. Children, couples and families* (2nd ed.) New York: Free Press.

Gingerich, W. J. (1984). Generalizing single-case evaluation from classroom to practice. *Journal of Education for Social Work, 20,* 74–82.

Horvath, A. O., & Greenberg, L. S. (1989). Development and validation of the Working Alliance Inventory. *Journal of Counseling Psychology, 36,* 223–233.

Levitt, J. L., & Reid, W. J. (1981). Rapid assessment instruments for practice. *Social Work Research and Abstracts, 17,* 13–19.

Levy, R. L. (1981). On the nature of the clinical-research gap: The problems with some solutions. *Behavioral Assessment, 3,* 235–242.

Millon, T. (1985). The MCMI provides a good assessment of DSM-III disorder: The MCMI-II will prove even better. *Journal of Personality Assessment, 49,* 379–391.

Mutschler, E. (1984). Evaluating practice: A study of research utilization by practitioners. *Social Work, 29,* 332–337.

Ridgewood Finance Institute. (1995). Survey report. *Psychotherapy Finances, 21,* 1–4.

Stewart, A. L., Hays, R. D., & Ware, J. E., Jr. (1988). The MOS short-form general health survey: Reliability and validity in a patient population. *Medical Care, 26,* 724–735.

Ware, J. E., Jr., Kosinski, M., & Keller, S. D. (1994). *SF-36 physical and mental health summary scales: A user's manual.* Boston: The Health Institute, New England Medical Center.

CHAPTER 11

Comments and Questions for Outcomes Measurement in Mental Health and Social Work

PAULA S. NURIUS

BETSY S. VOURLEKIS

Our primary interest in outcomes measurement is as a source of information for social work providers and human service programs that can guide efforts to improve the effectiveness of what human service workers do. We also are concerned that outcomes be chosen and defined to encompass the range of mental and behavioral health interventions provided by social workers and measured in the array of settings, in addition to specialty mental health settings, where such interventions take place. Mental health social work interventions range from psychotherapy to social network construction and include intensive case management, psychoeducation, discharge planning, and many other types of interventions. Social workers practicing in hospitals, renal dialysis centers, and home health situations provide behavioral health care. Our outcomes work as social workers in the mental and behavioral health area must be broad and inclusive of a wide array of settings and intervention methods.

Outcomes definition and measurement reflect the values and preferences of different stakeholders. Clearly, from the stakeholder position of social work practitioners and educators, the connection between the interventions and the outcomes (that is, the process–outcomes link) is of the most interest. In chapter 8, Manderscheid and Henderson note that outcomes measurement is meaningful only within a particular principles and protocols context. That is, what is defined and measured as an outcome must be connected conceptually and practically to what is being done and what practitioners believe they are trying to achieve by doing it. Moreover, what is being done must be done with consistency and fidelity to specified intervention models. For example, the Commission on Accreditation of Rehabilitation Facilities in Tuscon, Arizona, has used client movement to a less restrictive environment as an outcomes measure. However, this outcome only makes sense if practitioners also know how the movement occurs—the process and a protocol for discharge planning—and they know something about the circumstances of the new environment. The ultimate adequacy of the match between a person's needs and the new environment is the issue, and meaningful measurement of the outcome must somehow capture that information as well.

In chapter 10 Corcoran presents approaches to outcomes measurement for outpatient psychotherapy services and discusses outcomes measurement with the links between intervention (process) and outcomes clearly in view. Focusing on case-by-case accountability and outcomes monitoring, Corcoran shows that the connection between outcomes measures and the activities of individual practitioners is explicit. In pointing this out we emphaize that the principles, assumptions, and protocols guiding these services, although far from uniform or consistent, are not the same as those that might guide many other components of mental or behavioral health care provided by social workers.

Corcoran goes on to write that managed care may achieve what social work educators never could: getting practitioners, on a case-by-case basis, to clearly specify the case goal, implement an intervention with a specified protocol to achieve the goal, and measure the results. Corcoran argues that the accountability demands of managed care, starting with a demonstration of problem intensity sufficient to justify treatment and ending with a demonstration of outcomes achieved, can be met through the use of rapid assessment instruments. These measurement tools are now rather numerous and cover many aspects of an individual's social, emotional, and behavioral functioning. Short and easy to administer, they can be used on a periodic basis to generate scores that can be compared (in some cases) with normalized reference scores for comparable populations.

The advantages of this approach lie in its flexibility and presumably directly relevant performance feedback to the practitioner as well as the client. Practitioners can individualize goals with outcomes measures and do so, to some extent, on the basis of their own preferred principles and protocols. However, whether the evolving psychotherapy delivery system with its managed care superstructure and increasing market control by large conglomerates will tolerate this practitioner-controlled approach to outcomes measurement is a major question. Social workers cannot call for the acknowledgment of the broader social work intervention repertoire or the importance of a person–environment transactional view without accepting the need for explicit guidelines and protocols that can be linked, conceptually and practically, to relevant and meaningful outcomes. Social work faces an urgent practice and research agenda in this respect. As Dr. Katherine Ell (1995), then director of the Institute for the Advancement of Social Work Research in Washington, DC, wrote in a progress report to the profession,"Among the most underrepresented areas of mental health research of concern to social work is the rigorous testing of treatments and interventions (including preventative) for people and their families with multiple individual and social risk factors" (p. 16). Clearly, social workers as providers must continue to organize, make available, and test models of care as well as remain accountable for what they do currently.

It is ironic that factors such as managed care are seemingly accomplishing nearly overnight what many social work educators and agency leaders have been working toward for years, that is, routine inclusion of measurable outcomes as indicators of case progress and intervention effectiveness. However, the very factors that are driving such shifts and the speed of movement raise "chewy" and potentially worrisome issues as well. The issues go far beyond having many measures available and getting people to use them. It is essential that social workers anticipate the unintended as well as intended consequences, that they maintain a healthy skepticism about the relationship between data and meaningful information, and that they insist that use of outcomes measures be linked to demonstrated enhancement of more effective and appropriate practice. In the framework of this book, we find ourselves thinking about issues related to three questions:

1. What is in the equation (and what is not)?
2. What backs up this formulation (what should be there but is not)?
3. What will it take to harness this accountability and cost-containment engine into a strategic system-changing tool?

What Is in the Equation and What Is Not?

It does not take a long look to discern the person-focused and problem-oriented emphasis within the pool of outcomes measures. Individuals do come for help with problems, so we are not arguing about throwing the baby out with the bath water. Also, strengths and resource-oriented measures are becoming increasingly available. However, the lack of comparable measurement development for other categories of variables is conspicuous. This includes, but is not limited to, social workers' ability to measure change in various aspects of clients' life circumstances and problem conditions; to measure the specific nature, intensity, or integrity of interventions; or to reliably capture intervening variables for inclusion in clinical analysis. To what extent is theory reflected in the equation, that is, in current approaches to outcomes measurement in agencies? For example, in applying measures to explore the relationship of client status to intervention, are researchers examining the various avenues through which intervention would be expected to have indirect versus direct effects? Similarly, are researchers examining the various ways in which outcomes could be influenced by variables that would be expected to exert mediating or moderating influences?

Pursuit of these types of measurement and methods of measurement application, analysis, and interpretation is profoundly complex and difficult, which translates into being costly and intensive. These are issues that several of the chapters address. Social workers must live within realistic constraints. At the same time, social workers must continually be wary of overinterpreting data. Streamlined equations (problem → intervention → outcomes measure) yield streamlined answers that are useful in their own right but give nothing close to the whole picture. Before leaving this topic, we are compelled to comment on one other issue: the fact that prevention intervention and evaluation is nearly absent in the broader discussion of outcomes measurement in the human services. Part of the collective challenge, then, is to keep raising questions about what is in the outcomes measurement equation, what is not, and how social workers can realistically work toward capturing more complete pictures.

What Backs Up This Formulation?

How good is the quality of the social work knowledge base, and does this matter? What do social workers draw on for evidence or assumptions in interpreting outcomes measures? Many measures, perhaps even most, simply do not have sufficient information regarding norms or comparative referents to aid in interpretation. One might even hazard to say that psychometric findings related to validity, reliability, sensitivity, and reactivity are not commonly as solid as they should be, given the degree to which people rely on the measures, the speed with which they are proliferating, and the increased aura of credibility that information technology imbues on computerized measurement. Add to the mix diversity of gender, culture, class, life stage, type of problem, and so forth, and serious deficiencies surface that are related to appropriate interpretation and generalizability of measurement findings (at any stage—assessment, monitoring, outcomes evaluation).

Together these factors underscore the relationship between research and practice. Human services can and should strive toward better use of routinely collected information and actively contribute to the professional knowledge base. However, it is not realistic for agencies to undertake the kind of psychometric work or phenomenon investigation needed to provide the kind of knowledge base necessary to appropriately apply outcomes measures and interpret their findings. This may sound like something of a stranglehold on the obvious. However, social work researchers on the whole have not yet adequately stepped up to this challenge. This gap is further worrisome in that it appears that as accountability pressures rise, federal funding for research, at least the biopsychosocial research that is most informative to the human services, is on the wane. Here, part of the challenge is to keep asking questions regarding what evidence backs up the selection, use, and interpretation of outcomes measures and what is, essentially, a leap of faith or expedience. These questions have a place and are realistically unavoidable, but recognition of such leaps—however necessary they may be—should be an explicit part of outcomes measurement usage.

How Can the Momentum toward Strategic Change Be Harnessed?

As noted in many chapters, evaluation is fundamentally a political process. In addition, much of what is taking place in the current outcomes measurement movement is largely reactive and a scramble. The increasing automation of the human services adds further interesting twists. For example, at present, technology tends to reinforce codifiable, categorizable data and a classification systems approach. Technologic biases and limitations add to methodologic and logistic constraints. Similarly, the challenges and directions raised by attention to multiculturalism as well as the epistemologic discourse vigorously underway in social work and the disciplines hold important implications for outcomes measurement in the human services.

Our point is not that we are in the midst of chaos or that social workers should feel paralyzed by the scale and complexity of the task. To the contrary, as in other chapters of this book, including those in this section, innovation, insight, and coherence are increasingly in evidence. However, many in the human services and in health and mental health services in particular feel far more as if they are responding to powerful external forces than as if they are operating proactively and strategically from within. What will it take to harness this tension and momentum to galvanize a more internally driven vision? What interventions can we as social workers impose on ourselves to get from here to there? What broader system-changing aims and outcomes do we have in mind? What safeguards can and should be built into this process? These are some of the larger questions and targets of change to which our attention must now turn.

Reference

Ell, K. (1995). *Institute for the Advancement of Social Work Research: A progress report* [Mimeograph] (p. 16). Institute for the Advancement of Social Work Research, 750 First Street, NE, Suite 700, Washington, DC 20002-4241. (202) 336-8385.

CHAPTER 12

Outcomes Measurement Systems in Mental Health: A Program Perspective

STEVEN P. SEGAL

In the current environment of cost-cutting and managed care initiatives, mental health programs are being asked to justify their existence with measurable outcomes. Attempts to focus social work programs providing mental health services on outcomes are not new (Fischer, 1973; Mullen & Dumpson, 1972; Segal, 1972). In the past, however, such attempts were unrelated to program financing. Current attempts are being tied to financing and are thus moving forward at a rapid pace.

This chapter focuses on program outcomes as distinct from individual outcomes. Stakeholders evaluate mental health agencies as entities not only by the picture presented by the aggregate of their individual client alumni but also on the grounds of organizational performance. Organizational performance in the areas of governance, accessibility, and human resources development (such as personnel practices, staffing, consumer representation, and training) are some criteria against which agencies are measured by various stakeholders. Agencies must also maintain fiscal stability, community relations, and organizational respect in the community of agencies. The mandate to focus on program outcomes therefore is deceptively simple. Even the focus on aggregated client outcomes is complicated in human service agencies by the difficulty of demonstrating effects, given the diversity in client characteristics (client mix), the lack of specificity in the definition of interventions, the importance of the environmental context (opportunity structures external to the organization) in determining outcomes, and the difficulty of attributing outcomes to actions that are part of a package of program activities. An excellent program may flounder on the

The author thanks Bart Grossman for comments on an earlier draft of this chapter.

political mistakes of one of its components. Finally, and perhaps most important, desired outcomes differ for different stakeholders.

Who Are the Stakeholders, and What Outcomes Do They Desire?

Program stakeholders include clients, employees, administration, payers, and oversight organizations (for example, governments, professional and accrediting bodies, and unions).

CLIENTS

The terms *clients, consumers*, and, in some self-help agencies, *members* denote, respectively, an increasing amount of responsibility accorded the user of services within the agency's structure for the types of care and outcomes they experience than has been inherent in the *patient* role. Clients or consumers have in the past few decades been given a greater say in the determination of the outcomes focus of service agencies. They have obtained positions on governing boards, as volunteers, and as service providers in agencies. Respect, empowerment in service decision making, and responsiveness to the client's perception of the problem are among their desired outcomes (Segal, Silverman, & Temkin, 1993). The term *client* is perhaps most descriptive of the roles of the users of services in most mental health ambulatory care agencies. As clients, users of services have rights and privileges associated with determining the nature of the care they receive, yet limited control of organizational functions (for example, members may actually control agency functions such as budget allocations).

Clients usually have presenting problems and delimited goals in contacting agencies. However, such problems are often only the tip of the iceberg. The child coming to the attention of the mental health agency for disruptive behavior in school is often the same child who is homeless, whose father is in prison, and whose mother is abusing drugs and perhaps sexually abusing the child. The young man who is discharged to the care of the outpatient mental health agency with a diagnosis of schizoaffective disorder is also often living in a shelter, has no work history, has limited educational skills, has tested positive for the human immunodeficiency virus (HIV), and is abusing several street drugs. The outcomes for these individuals are diverse and clearly not independent of one another. The immediate presenting problem of depressed mood may be addressed in each case. The cause of the problem may be a lack of a home. What is the boundary of required service—*medical necessity* in the current jargon of managed care—for these individuals? Is the mental health worker responsible for finding a home for each of these clients? Furthermore, given the complex hostile environment of each case, it would be unusual to find all outcomes moving in the same direction at the same time. Some good and some bad things will result simply from the nature of the environment in which clients are found. Thus, the mental health agency often turns away from *hard* outcomes (for example, the number housed) at the client level to *soft* outcomes (for example, client satisfaction) as a way of handling the complexity of the situations. Whether this is a valid choice or simply a way to diffuse accountability is a function of how the change is implemented within the agency's overall plan for increasing its outcomes focus. As part of a developmental focus leading to specific time-related goals as suggested by Connell, Kubisch, Schorr, and Weiss (1995) in their theory-oriented approach to outcomes specification, the former is more likely true, although the use of such an approach is a time-honored administrative ploy to achieve the latter.

Current changes in the mental health system can create the opportunities to expand or contract the desired boundaries of agency responsibility for program client outcomes. The devolution of responsibility for the provision of care from the federal to the state to the local level leaves the locality with responsibility for the total package of services. It leaves the community with the possibility of greater flexibility for using resources. In the ideal situation, the flexibility in the use of resources allows for the expansion of outcomes objectives to meet client needs in a more efficient way. For example, the objective for the person with chronic schizophrenia is the improvement in his or her quality of life. The outcomes are the hard-core resources of such an improved quality of existence—a job that accommodates a disability, an apartment of his or her own choice, the opportunity for social relations, and the opportunity to exercise decision-making control over his or her care in a constructive manner.

The transfer of responsibility for mental health care to the local level may at once expand and contract desired aggregate client outcomes, placing organizations in a difficult position. Agencies often find themselves with a smaller amount of resources and, in most cases, less expertise for the use of the resources available. Therefore, the specification of the problem to be addressed becomes more varied across communities. Furthermore, communities lacking resources are forced to reach outside for expertise or to rely on the limited expertise available within. Those communities choosing the latter course to some extent have desired aggregate client outcomes determined by the tools (expert training) available. Communities reaching out may find a broader set of desired client outcomes to address. These communities are limited, however, by an increasingly complex picture of financing relying on some form of managed care or capitated arrangement that discourages the use of service through various forms of utilization review. Such reviews can emphasize medical necessity at the expense of social services, which can limit the scope of the desired client outcomes.

EMPLOYEES

Employees are gratified by client success. Stories of successful cases are an important part of their everyday conversations, the exemplars that make the job rewarding. Such stories make it possible to do one's job in the face of what seem to be overwhelming odds favoring client failure. Agency personnel are keenly aware of the fragility and complexity of the client situation. They are therefore skeptical of simple indicators, frustrated by their own inability, often owing to lack of resources, to address issues that are central to the problem. They are particularly concerned with demonstrating the value of their contribution to positive outcomes. In the current service environment, they find themselves caught in a pattern of deprofessionalization in which failure to demonstrate the effect of their work is often taken as a rationale for cutting the program and their jobs. They feel blamed for the inability of the system to provide them with adequate resources to do their jobs. At times this feeling leads to broadening the definition of success too far or ignoring and even attempting to justify dysfunctional and often illegal behavior—actions that may be perceived by some as colluding to "cover up" failure.

ADMINISTRATORS AND PAYERS

Administrators and payers want to maximize efficiency in addition to achieving more client-centered goals. They want the optimum use of resources or the optimum investment of effort in service tasks that will bring about desired outcomes. In current fee-for-service agencies, such efforts often are associated with opportunities to expand service boundaries or target new populations. The incentives are to deliver more services to the least healthy clients, that is, those with the greatest need. In capitated organizations, on the other hand, the incentives are to maintain a healthy target population and to do preventive work to avoid service delivery.

OVERSIGHT ORGANIZATIONS

Oversight organizations, such as community mental health advisory boards, have specific mandates, and they relate their outcomes goals to these mandates. Such mandates may involve ensuring the efficient and quality delivery of particular types of services. They may add reporting effort to already overburdened staffs and may contribute to the dissatisfaction of other stakeholders. On the positive side, oversight organizations may provide needed incentives to ensure quality of care in an increasingly penurious system.

What Are the Best Outcomes Measures Now Available for Program Assessment?

Although the diversity found among those holding a stakeholder perspective does not prohibit consensus on abstract principles such as cost-effective service, difficulties arise in the specification of the measure of the abstract outcomes. The best instrument to assess aggregated client outcomes is the one that measures most precisely the changes the agency is trying to promote in its clientele. There are literally hundreds of measures to choose from. Standard texts offer summaries of available measures including comments on the reliability and validity of specific instruments (Buros 1970, 1974, 1978; Corcoran & Fischer, 1987). Organizations such as the Medical Outcomes Trust (1996) distribute generic measures for health status and functional assessments. However, it is important to choose outcomes measures that reflect the types of changes the organization expects from its clients. Such measures are best selected in consultation between evaluation experts and organization stakeholders. The measure may have wonderful reliability and validity, be a standard part of evaluation protocols in published articles, and be endorsed by established organizations. However, if it fails to capture the organization's change objective, it will put the organization at a disadvantage in detecting measurable outcomes.

With the above caution in mind, standardized measures of aggregated client outcomes—excluding traditional process measures such as recidivism, units of service delivered, number of clients served, and so forth—may be divided into hard and soft measures. A third category of measures, performance outcomes, also must be considered.

HARD MEASURES

Hard measures of aggregate client outcomes are those with concrete, countable referents. Such indicators include number of clients employed, days employed, clients placed in competitive employment, clients placed in sheltered employment, clients housed, clients placed in work training programs, client suicide attempts, client criminal justice system contacts, reductions in client police contacts for situations involving family violence, and, more generally, successful resolution of the presenting problem. Global assessment of functioning scales in which specific behavioral patterns anchor each point of the scale, such as the Global Assessment Scale (Endicott, Spitzer, Fleiss, & Cohen, 1976), have been found to be useful and reliable in measuring change efforts.

SOFT MEASURES

Soft measures of aggregate client outcomes are characterized by the relative status of the response categories (for example, "often," "sometimes," "never," or "very satisfied"; "somewhat satisfied"; "neutral to the experience"; " somewhat dissatisfied"; and "very dissatisfied"). These measures have the benefit of controlling for between-individual variation in ability to change. This benefit is especially important for organizations serving seriously handicapped people whose large achievements are small in comparison to members of the general population. Specific outcomes measures include global assessments of functional status where the response categories are relative (for example, "very often," "often," "sometimes," "rarely," "never") as in the Internal and External Social Integration Scale (Segal & Aviram, 1978); client satisfaction measures (Attkisson & Greenfield, 1995; Segal & Aviram, 1978); quality-of-life assessments (Lehman, Pastado, & Rachuba, 1993); and symptomatology assessments (Beck, Weissman, Lester, & Trexler, 1974; Overall & Gorham, 1962; Santor, Zuroff, Ramsey, Cervantes & Palacios, 1995) .

PERFORMANCE MEASURES

Performance outcomes, or measures of agency performance, constitute outcomes for organization stakeholders. Measures of organizational performance include indicators of governance, accessibility, operations, and human resources development (for example, personnel practices, staffing, consumer representation, and training) as well as cost-effectiveness measures.

Governance

In the area of governance, responsiveness to client and other constituent concerns may be measured with the Intra-Organizational Empowerment Scale (Segal, Silverman,

& Temkin, 1995). The scale is an index of participation of users of services in the governance decisions of the agency. It may further be adapted to measure the participation of other personnel in the agency's governance.

Accessibility

Accessibility measures are particularly important to consumer stakeholders as outcomes in this era of managed care. The shift to capitation strategies in financing services raises concerns about equity of service distribution (Aday & Anderson, 1981) and the need to present indicators that the agency is not skimming or skimping in its casemix. Such measures include indexes of the demographic characteristics of the service population in comparison with that of the host community, measures of the severity of client conditions, and social need indicators such as the number of homeless people.

Operational Performance

Concerns regarding operational performance are a third issue. Measures in this area include indicators such as responsiveness to requests for help. The responsiveness measures include the timeliness and manner in which a client's concerns are addressed, for example, time spent on the telephone by the client waiting to make an appointment, time until scheduled appointment, and follow-up contacts on appointment "no shows." Operational performance measures also may include measures of resource procurement. The resource measures might include insurance coverage and establishment of eligibility for support from Supplemental Security Income (SSI), Section 8, and other programs.

Cost-Effectiveness

Administrative concerns with respect to cost-effectiveness are addressed by indicators of the number of high-cost clients; change in cost per client, taking individual outcomes into account; and number of lives covered. Segal, Eagley, Watson, Miller, and Goldfinger (1995) also present a model for assessing the efficient delivery of services in psychiatric emergency cases. Their model is based on measuring the optimum investment of time in the patient evaluation.

Why Are These Measures Not Being Used More Widely?

HARD MEASURES

There are multiple reasons for the failure to make widespread use of these measures. Agencies are usually aware of the potential of an outcomes measure to demonstrate a positive result. Organization administrators will not use measures they believe will result in the perception of their agency as a failure. Administrators will eliminate some outcomes assessments for structural reasons and others for reasons that are inherent in the environment of the agency. Structural reasons include real or imagined structural blocks to the achievement of such outcomes by agency clients such as a poor job or housing market, lack of client preparation for employment, or lack of education. The opportunity structure of the society may be closed because of discrimination or the failure or inability of educational institutions and work environments to accommodate the disabilities of clients.

Administrators may not use outcomes assessment for reasons that are agency based, such as a lack of familiarity with management information systems or staff resentment of intrusion into professional discretion (for example, the view that improvement is not quantifiable). Some measures may be viewed as inappropriate because of agency specialization or focus. Measures of symptom reduction may be acceptable to a mental health agency, whereas job placement may be viewed as outside the purview of the organization.

Hard outcomes measures have also been found to be minimally influenced by service interventions. Most clinical trials in the mental health field (for example, Bickman, 1996; Passamanick, Scarpitti, & Dinitz, 1967; Solomon, 1992; Stein & Test, 1985) establish differences as a result of the intervention in administrative measures, such as reduced hospital stays and readmissions, but fail to establish differences in hard functioning outcomes. It would seem that the latter outcomes are therefore influenced by external conditions to such an extent that they are not consistently predictable from an intervention effort. As a management information tool, such outcomes are more likely to be subject to chance influences, and relying on them is risky for the organization.

Finally, the extreme difficulties of the clientele may make actually achievable outcomes politically unacceptable. For example, in a recent meeting, an agency fund raiser indicated that his project officer seemed genuinely concerned that he not overstate his objectives or their likely outcomes. The organization saw 256 new cases in the period. The fund raiser suggested that they would be able to work closely with 30 individuals and perhaps help six achieve employment. He sent this modest estimate forward only to discover that this was not a substantial enough statement, although the project officer agreed that the estimate was both reasonable and achievable with the level of disability in the agency's population. The politically astute project officer suggested that the agency "beef up" the figures in its application.

SOFT MEASURES

The use of soft measures of client outcomes, such as client satisfaction, is spreading rapidly through the field. These measures represent a compromise to the complex or overly simplified hard outcomes and do not require the achievement of any hard outcomes. Unfortunately, there is little evidence that client satisfaction is related to any hard outcomes. In a 12-year follow-up study of a population of individuals in California residential care facilities, Segal and Choi (1995) found that no functional outcomes other than residential stability were predictable from client satisfaction. Individuals who were satisfied with their residential care situation at baseline were more likely to be living in the same situation 12 years later. By analogy, would that mean that those who were satisfied with their problematic situation despite being involved in treatment would settle for remaining in that problematic situation? It could also mean that this residential situation was the best option available to these individuals, or it could be taken as an indication of what items are most important to clients. In the latter situation, the finding might suggest that agencies should focus on housing stability as a priority. One of the central strategies of treatment often is to create a disaffection with one's situation to create motivation for change. How might a social worker fare on a treatment satisfaction measure if he or she tried to move a client who was overly dependent on SSI toward independence or if he or she encouraged a client to use antipsychotic medication that prevented the client from experiencing a major relapse, although there were unpleasant side effects?

In the first case, the satisfaction measure might be expected to yield negative outcomes, and in the second example, it is unclear what outcome would be desirable and by whom—absence of side effects or decompensation. At the aggregate level, it is assumed that these issues would wash out, demonstrating the overall value of the measure. It is assumed that a satisfied client is a served client. Yet current debate in the health and mental health fields involves the extent to which such measurement is desirable. A central issue in the field is that of client dependency. A satisfied client may also be a dependent one. Health services consumers may be inadequately informed and therefore ill-equipped to evaluate the effects of complicated treatment interventions. Furthermore, satisfaction scores are usually skewed in a positive direction and are therefore a preordained endorsement with perhaps little relation to functional outcomes.

MEASURES OF AGENCY OUTCOMES

Process measures predominate in the current agency system (Manderscheid & Sonnenschein, 1992, 1994). Some such measures are tied to and rewarded in a fee-for-service system. They include units of service delivered, number of admissions, length of time in treatment, and number of readmissions. As capitation becomes a reality, other performance measures will become a necessary part of fiscal requirements. These other measures, central to capitation financing, reflect equity issues related to casemix (for example, proportion of each racial or ethnic group served). These measures are convenient analogies of service effectiveness in a capitated system. They reflect the current values of political constituencies, are tied to productivity, and by contractual arrangement are often the basis of reimbursement. Furthermore, these measures are achievable in that a program will have something to report that satisfies at least some of its constituents.

The problem involving failure to use such measures is often one of appropriate consultation, an inadequate management information system, and a lack of an effective political process to involve stakeholders in adopting the performance outcomes as their own.

How Can Outcomes Measures Be Made More Useful to Programs?

LINKING THE SERVICE BOUNDARY ISSUE TO A DEFINED MISSION

Organizations with a clear mission from which they can derive a set of specifiable goals should be in the best position to set boundaries on their service delivery and to assess outcomes. Such a mission enables the program to specify where it is going and how it might get there. The development of a mission statement is in itself a political process involving the organization's stakeholders. Bringing together these stakeholders and specifying precisely what they perceive the functions of the organization to be forces the stakeholders to objectify their expectations for the organization. Such expectations include access issues, quantity and quality of service issues, and measurable patient or client outcomes. Involvement in these processes gives the stakeholders ownership of the outcomes proposed, which may contribute to program survival in the face of poor outcomes performance.

LINKING CLIENT OUTCOMES MEASUREMENT SENSITIVITY TO DEVELOPMENT OF INTEGRATED, COMPREHENSIVE CARE PLANS

Organizations should discuss the problem of the sensitivity of proposed measures in relation to the realities of their clients' situations with a consultant so that the problem may be addressed as part of the development of an outcomes assessment package. An appropriate combination of soft and hard outcomes measures can be selected for the assessment package. In practice, this process can be used as a means to redefine practice as more comprehensive and coordinated or as more restricted in its objectives. The process also may be a means of overcoming the lack of sensitivity of integrated service packages by forming alliances with other service agencies to increase the power of the intervention.

EQUITY

In defining outcomes consistent with social work's mission, service to at-risk groups and groups that are poorly served by the system with maximum respect for the client has always been a priority. Performance outcomes, although they do not take the place of client outcomes, should be included in the list of those considered appropriate for agency evaluation. These outcomes include casemix, resource development, and staff responsiveness measures, although in the past such measures have often been considered process issues. The casemix measures must emphasize indicators of skimming and skimping. The resource measures must include insurance coverage, establishment of eligibility for support from SSI, housing vouchers under Section 8, and other resource programs. The responsiveness measures should include the timeliness and manner in which a client's concerns are addressed, for example, time spent on the telephone waiting to make an appointment and the time until a scheduled appointment. Such measures may be considered outcomes.

Conclusion

The development of effective outcomes measurements in mental health services programs is complicated by fiscal, political, and service reality. Outcomes measurement system development is a deceptively simple objective in a complex organizational environment. An outcomes system can be a means to develop and better serve organizational performance objectives for all stakeholders. Outcomes measurement, however, also presents significant risks for participants. Therefore, outcomes measurement will occur to the extent that measurement systems are linked to organizational survival. Such systems can be an impetus for the development of new and more effective service forms. Above all, outcomes measurement systems should be seen as facilitating a process for achieving effective services.

References

Aday, L. A., & Anderson, R. M. (1981). Equity of access to medical care: A conceptual and empirical overview. *Medical Care, 19* (12 Suppl.), 4–27.

Attkisson, C. C., & Greenfield, T. K. (1995). The Client Satisfaction Questionnaire (CSQ) Scales-30 (SSS-30). In L. I. Sederer & B. Dickey (Eds.), *Outcomes assessment in clinical practice* (pp. 120–127). Baltimore: Williams & Wilkins.

Beck, A. T., Weissman, A., Lester, D., & Trexler, L. (1974). The measurement of pessimism: The hopelessness scale. *Journal of Consulting and Clinical Psychology, 42* (6), 861–865.

Bickman, L. (1996). A continuum of care: More is not always better. *American Psychologist, 51* (7), 689–701.

Buros, O. K. (1970). *Personality tests and reviews.* Lincoln: University of Nebraska, Buros Institute of Mental Measurement.

Buros, O. K. (1974). *Tests in print.* Highland Park, NJ: Gryphon.

Buros, O. K. (1978). *Mental measurements yearbook, the eighth.* Highland Park, NJ: Gryphon.

Connell, J. P., Kubisch, A. C., Schorr, L. B., & Weiss, C. H. (1995). *New approaches to evaluating community initiatives.* Washington, DC: Aspen Institute.

Corcoran, K., & Fischer, J. (1987). *Measures for clinical practice: A source book.* New York: Free Press.

Endicott, J., Spitzer, R. L., Fleiss, J. L., & Cohen, J. (1976). The global assessment scale: A procedure for measuring the overall severity of psychiatric disturbance. *Archives of General Psychiatry, 33,* 766–771.

Fischer, J. (1973). Is casework effective? *Social Work, 18,* 5–20.

Lehman, A. F., Pastado, L. T., & Rachuba, L. T. (1993). Convergent validation of quality of life assessments for persons with severe mental illness. *Quality of Life Research, 2,* 327–333.

Manderscheid, R. W., & Sonnenschein, M. A. (1992). *Mental health, United States 1992.* Rockville, MD: U.S. Department of Health and Human Services, Center for Mental Health Services.

Manderscheid, R. W., & Sonnenschein, M. A. (1994). *Mental health, United States 1994.* Rockville, MD: U.S. Department of Health and Human Services, Center for Mental Health Services.

Medical Outcomes Trust. (1996). *Medical Outcomes Trust Bulletin, 4,* 1–4.

Mullen, E. J., & Dumpson, J. R. (1972). *Evaluation of social intervention.* San Francisco: Jossey-Bass.

Overall, J. E., & Gorham, D. R. (1962). The Brief Psychiatric Rating Scale. *Psychological Reports, 10,* 799–812.

Passamanick, B., Scarpitti, F. R., & Dinitz, S. (1967). *Schizophrenics in the community.* New York: Appleton-Century-Crofts.

Santor, D. A., Zuroff, D. C., Ramsey, J. O., Cervantes, P., & Palacios, J. (1995). Examining scale discriminability in the BDI and CES-D as a function of depressive severity. *Psychological Assessment, 7,* 131–139.

Segal, S. P. (1972). Research on the outcome of social work therapeutic interventions: A review of the literature. *Journal of Health and Social Behavior, 13,* 3–17.

Segal, S. P., & Aviram, U. (1978). *The mentally ill in community-based sheltered care.* New York: John Wiley & Sons.

Segal, S. P., & Choi, J. (1995). *Consumer satisfaction of sheltered care residents.* Unpublished manuscript, University of California, Berkeley, School of Social Welfare, Mental Health and Social Welfare Research Group.

Segal, S. P., Eagley, L., Watson, M., Miller, L., & Goldfinger, S. (1995). Factors in the quality of patient evaluations in general hospital psychiatric emergency services. *Psychiatric Services, 46,* 1144–1149.

Segal, S. P., Silverman, C., & Temkin, T. (1993). Empowerment and self-help agency practice for people with mental disabilities. *Social Work, 38,* 705–712.

Segal, S. P., Silverman, C., & Temkin, T. (1995). Measuring empowerment in client-run self-help agencies. *Community Mental Health Journal, 31,* 215–227.

Solomon, P. (1992). The efficacy of case management services for severely mentally ill clients. *Community Mental Health Journal, 28,* 163–180.

Stein, L. I., & Test, M. A. (1985).The evolution of the training in community living model: A decade of experience. In *New Directions in Mental Health Services* (Social and Behavioral Sciences Series, Vol. 26, pp. 7–16). San Francisco: Jossey-Bass.

CHAPTER 13

Outcomes Measurement and the Mental Health Consumer Advocacy Movement

MONA WASOW

This chapter discusses some of the recent developments in the mental health consumer advocacy movement, some of the changes that are taking place between professionals and consumers, and some of the core values that underlie the movement. Although outcomes measurement is not addressed directly, this chapter assumes that outcomes measurement must incorporate consumers as key stakeholders. Consumer interests have played a major role in determining important aspects of outcomes measurement as discussed in other chapters (for example, chapters 7, 9, 11, and 15). The National Alliance for the Mentally Ill (NAMI) has exerted strong leadership in shaping outcomes measurement thinking in mental health. Also, the Center for Mental Health Services, Substance Abuse and Mental Health Services Administration, U.S. Department of Health and Human Services has sponsored a major effort to develop outcomes measures and guidelines based on consumer perspectives. The contribution of consumers to outcomes measurement has been apparent in mental and behavioral health, and it has been documented (Freeman & Trabin, 1994). Rather than review these contributions, this chapter examines recent developments and values in the consumer movement that provide an important context for thinking about outcomes measurement in mental health. This chapter also examines possible ways of advocating for the success of consumer advocacy, as well as the role of human service professionals, especially social workers.

Recent History

The mental health consumer advocacy movement is exciting, largely positive, and complex. Yet, human service professionals and people in the many different consumer movements have multiple agendas, beliefs, passions, and languages. Inability to hear one another often stands in the way. Some of these ambiguities and complexities are discussed below.

In the 1950s, professionals thought they knew what was best for their clients by virtue of their education. Professionals read it in books, so it must be true! More important, many professionals felt unprepared and unwilling to treat clients such as seriously mentally ill patients after deinstitutionalization efforts began taking shape. During the past 10–15 years, professionals have become a bit more humble regarding their expertise. They are listening to the consumers, and in many cases consumers are wanting things that professionals had not previously considered. For example, in the area of severe mental illness (SMI), professionals had long assumed that families having a member with SMI were in need of psychotherapy, so psychotherapy was offered. In 1979, Dr. Agnes Hatfield, both a professional and a person with a relative with SMI, started asking families what they wanted from professionals. She listed 12 items, ranging from psychotherapy to family support, books, and recreation. At the bottom of the list of what families said they wanted was individual therapy, followed by group therapy. At the top of the list were books and information about SMI (Hatfield, 1979).

In 1989, an estimated 6–15 million people were involved in self-help groups in the United States (Powell, 1990). Some of these groups have tremendous strengths in their organizations, such as Alcoholics Anonymous (AA) and NAMI, each of which counts its members in the hundreds of thousands. The consumer movements march forward. For example, at the University of Michigan, the Center for Self-Help Research and Knowledge Dissemination, which studies how people with SMI can coordinate the use of self-help and professional service systems to enhance their well-being, was established. Its sponsorship by the National Institute of Mental Health (NIMH) demonstrates cooperation between consumers and professionals. One of the shifts that is presently occurring is more cooperation between many consumer groups and professionals. Twenty-five years ago most consumer organizations were seen by professionals as suspect. Now it is routine for professionals to recommend self-help groups in conjunction with whatever work they are doing. In 1976, for example, professionals made 3 percent of the referrals to Parents Anonymous (PA). Just 12 years later 41 percent of referrals to PA groups came from professionals (Powell, 1990). Professionals know less about possible attitudinal changes on the part of consumers toward professionals, which vary enormously among different consumer groups. It is important to keep in mind that only broad generalizations can be made about advocacy movements. Lumping together consumer groups as diverse as victims of battery, racism, poverty, alcohol and drug abuse, and SMI in broad generalizations can be misleading.

Client or consumer advocates are often the most articulate of their group, which is true for anyone who takes on leadership responsibility. When consumer advocates speak out and organize effectively, they are often told, "You are so much higher functioning than the clients in our system that you really can't tell us what kinds of services our clients need" (McCabe & Unzicker, 1995, p. 64). This attitude may have some truth to it, but it puts clients in an impossible double bind: Anyone who can speak out and organize is not representative, and anyone who remains sick or dysfunctional does not count.

Professional helping services in the 1990s are being challenged to acknowledge the power imbalance and authoritarian culture in which services have flourished in the past. The arrogance of some of the unfounded assumptions made in the past and the horrendous harm professionals did with them are painful to contemplate. Familiar examples include old beliefs of "the refrigerator mother" causing autism or "the schizophrenogenic mother" causing SMI. Had rigorous scientific methodologies been used to test such beliefs, they would not have held up, and families could have been spared untold agonies.

Different Perspectives

Researchers, clinicians, and clients make different claims regarding the self-help movement. Many clinicians maintain a cynical attitude toward a client-controlled approach to self-help. Professional prestige, power, and pay are at stake. Some professionals fear peers will do more harm than good and that self-helpers have become addicted to their groups. Clients are most interested in empowerment, client-relevant data, and a reduction in stigma against them. Self-helpers argue that "empowerment in any context cannot be bestowed by those with greater power upon those with less; it must be initiated from the bottom up, by those who seek self-determination" (Segal, Silverman, & Tempkin, 1995, p. 217). Researchers are hopefully reasonably impartial and open-minded, but they have biases too. An example of different perspectives can be seen in the area of grief. Some researchers studying grief identify a time frame for grief "resolution." Yet, many bereaved individuals emphatically believe that grief has no resolution. They say that it becomes part of their lives. This feeling is particularly true when one has a relative with SMI. The grief is ongoing and without closure. This view is a relatively minor difference in perspectives. When issues such as the rights of the individual versus the rights of society, client goals versus professional goals, and so on are examined, differences sharpen. Clients under stress, family members, educators, researchers, clinicians, religious leaders, policymakers, and the corner grocer all have multiple perspectives on a wide range of problems. The wonder is that consensus ever is reached on anything.

However, consumers have a set of core values that they would like to see characterize relationships between professionals and clients. Valued qualities that appeared repeatedly during meetings of the Values Group, a consumer–professional group in Madison, Wisconsin, that met for monthly discussion from 1993 to 1995, included caring, autonomy, dignity, empowerment, genuineness, education about their problems, honesty, mutuality, normalization, privacy, recovery, quality of life, respect, self-determination, and the use of nonpunitive approaches to changing behavior (Values Group, 1993–1995). Many consumers, especially in the SMI field, talk about internalized oppression. Degan (1990) referred to this as "spirit breaking," the cumulative experiences of failure and humiliation in environments in which hopes are shattered. If this happens often, and it does, apathy and indifference become a way of surviving. All people involved in SMI have special concerns and specific information critical to managing SMI.

> Patients are experts on the subject of their symptomatology and need effective treatment of their disorders. . . . Clinicians are experts on the psychopathology, diagnosis, and treatment of mental disorders and must refresh their knowledge and skills as the field advances. Researchers increase our knowledge. . . . Administrators facilitate functioning of the mental health system, or should. . . . The ebb and flow and character of information within individuals and between them determine the quality of the psychiatric service system of which we are all a part. (Greist, 1995, p. 989)

An enormous problem for professionals, consumers, and everyone concerned with social issues is the lack of resources to help people. Coercion often is used when there are no good options available. The corollary to this is that coercion could often be avoided if other resources were available. In the past 25 years, peer support and consumer groups have developed an empowerment orientation that is antibureaucratic, anti-elite, and antiprofessional. Some self-help organizations have become true social movements actively involved in both social policy changes and individual self-improvement. There are not only conflicts of interest between consumer and professional organizations but also conflicts between different consumer interest groups. Everyone wants his or her interests taken into account. For example, a highly articulate, well-functioning person who has an affective disorder well under control with medications is not necessarily speaking in the best interests of a seriously ill person, catatonic man with schizophrenia whose illness does not respond to any known treatment.

Professionals also have to confront their own personal prejudices and insecurities. As Degan (1995), a consumer, stated, "Professionals often view consumers as fundamentally different from other people, more childlike. . . crazy and to be ignored, and unable to take risks or determine their own needs" (p. 443).

Professionals say it is important to support clients' goals. What if those goals happen to be wanting money for cigarettes, drugs, and alcohol? According to McCabe and Unzicker (1995), "When working with real people in the real world, it is frequently hard to see how to make decisions based on these values. Clinicians are often confronted with competing goals and concerns" (p. 70). Then it becomes a bit like working in a circular firing squad! In 1937 Abraham A. Low, a psychiatrist, began formulating Recovery, Inc., a highly effective method of partial recovery for patients with SMI. During the 1940s he refined his methods of teaching patients how to run self-help recovery meetings. "Few, if any other self-help groups, have been as misunderstood by their supporters, as well as their detractors, and as ignored or undiscovered by so many professionals" (Lee, 1995, p. 63). Recovery, Inc., is seldom used by professionals. Professionals complained because Low's method was not graduating or discharging patients with SMI and viewed it as making patients "dependent." Professionals making this complaint did not understand the nature of SMI. No other self-help group sets a time limit on membership and discharges them. Most SMIs are chronic. Why should members be terminated? What is so wrong with dependency? Should a diabetic give up dependency on insulin? Part of this is the prejudice toward patients with SMI on the part of professionals. As recently as 1993, 94 percent of professionals in one study (Lee, 1995, p. 64) referred patients to AA, but only 2 percent referred patients to Recovery, Inc. Consumers, professionals, researchers, policymakers, and others have many different perspectives. "Some people focus on treatment, some on social change or education, advocacy, networking research, or housing" (Wasow, 1995, p. 195). Many professionals approve of consumer-operated services but want them to be supplementary to professionally run services. This attitude feels like a put down to many consumers.

> Some of us are fired by pain, others by rage, political convictions, intellectual curiosity, religious beliefs, status, or a combination of these things. Some are no longer fired up but rather burned out. We need to make a massive effort to understand each other's different perspectives and try to stand in the shoes of the others. Out of diversity could come the possibility for creative compromises and solutions. (Wasow, 1995, p. 195)

Complexities, Ambiguities, and Generalizations

One complexity of the 1990s is that administrators feel political pressure from funding and advocacy groups to hire affirmatively, but at the same time they often are confused and threatened by such pressure. There currently are enormous role ambiguities because boundaries, relationships, and power are shifting. Self-images on both sides are changing. Another complexity is danger to poor people and minority groups, who have the least access to competent medical care and the most exposure to environmental and social hazards. Many advocacy groups come from the middle class. The idea of self-help care as a national policy is based on the ideology that individuals have the ability to pull themselves up by their bootstraps (Powell, 1990). However, for those with no boots, it is difficult, if not impossible, to pull themselves up. All this attention to self-care may direct attention away from recognizing that the root causes of misery are national policies of oppression, economic and educational inequalities, poor health care, racism, and so on. Social workers must not use self-help as a substitute for taking social and political action on behalf of poor people. "Although self-help groups are an obvious example of people taking social responsibility for one another, they also may represent retreats from a large social responsibility" (Powell, 1990, p. 293).

Another complexity is that consumers and self-help groups vary enormously. Some groups interact and cooperate more with the mental health system and less with each other. Some groups have more interaction with each other and want nothing to do with the mental health system. Who exactly represents the self-help and consumer groups? It is easier to identify the consumer minority who speak out than to define the consumer majority who do not. The silent majority of consumers do not speak out. They are unable to do so because of the nature of their disabilities, because of internalized stigma and oppression, because of fear of retaliation and further stigma, and perhaps because that is the passive nature of most people.

Ambiguities abound, particularly in the area of roles. There are at least two types of role stress for professionals: role conflict and role ambiguity. An example of this stress is seen clearly in the SMI field. People with SMI are some of the loneliest people in the world. In community support projects it is now common for professionals to take their clients out for coffee (friendship), during which time they hand out medications (professional). These multiple roles are often without clear expectations for behavior on anyone's part. "We have only scratched the surface of what it means to engage in collaborative efforts with individual clients and advocacy groups such as the NAMI" (Haiman, 1995, p. 444). Professionals need role models as well as literature to help them build these bridges. Unfortunately, the message the literature carries is a bit like the Nike advertisement —"Just do it"—but it does not tell how. It is not clear whether and when self-help groups become habit-forming crutches that foster dependency that keeps people stuck in victim roles. Group cliquishness may divert people from dealing with their problems. Medical misinformation may prove harmful (for example, using laetrile [or amygdalin]; rage against electroconvulsive therapy; an antipsychotropic medication stance). Poorly trained self-help leaders may get overly and negatively involved with peers. Antiprofessional and anti-intellectual stances among group members may stand in the way of getting professional help when it is needed. All of these problems can occur in professionally run agencies and groups as well. However, professional training helps in many situations. The roles of professionals are becoming increasingly multidimensional, public, and ambiguous. Because there is much that is not known about the consumer movements at present, professionals must learn to live with ambiguity. Like public agencies, self-help groups suffer from a lack of funding, high drop-out rates, and sometimes an inability to recruit enough members to get off the ground. Self-help groups without professional leaders may have more trouble dealing with disruptive or dominating members, reaching decisions, or keeping their meetings interesting.

There are at present no "right" answers for the new boundary dilemmas aside from the obvious ones: revisiting the meaning of empathy and the integration of caring, holistic, scientific, and artistic approaches to fellow human beings. Some clients cannot advocate for themselves for a variety of reasons, and professionals must advocate for them. Much has been written and said about the superiority of "pure" self-help groups, meaning that self-help without professional involvement may be the best alternative. This view presumes, perhaps, that self-help and professionalism are antagonistic. I think that both sides gain when they maintain respect for differences and try to learn from and cooperate with each other.

Different Ways of Knowing and Changes in Power Shifts

A major premise of human service professionalism has been the value for professionals of maintaining objectivity or emotional neutrality. Professionals have been encouraged to be aware of and control the degree of emotional involvement with clients and client issues. "This isolation and suppression of emotions, however, may only serve to thwart justifiable anger and frustration at the social inequities that clearly are at the root of many client problems" (Haynes & Mickelson, 1991, p. 24). However, emotional neutrality may help keep professionals from burning out. Accordingly, professionals try to maintain objectivity, and self-help sponsors encourage emotional sharing. Sharing and subjectivity give participants role models who are both human and accessible. If for human service professionals, scientific knowledge is the way of knowing in Western, late 20th-century society, then what place is there for experiential knowledge? What is to be done with the language of the heart and the stories? Perhaps there are multiple realities, and what people see and believe depends on where they stand. There may be a connection between public figures' personal experience and the public policy positions they advocate. Aaron Rosen's (1994) investigation of knowledge used by practitioners demonstrated that "value based assertions were the most frequently used rationale to inform clinical or direct practice" (p. 568).

Having glimpsed some of the negatives in the way personal, subjective approaches can and have influenced policy, let us now look at the other side. New voices are discovered as narratives make it possible for those previously silenced to tell their stories. However, these opportunities can evoke conflicts for professionals. Professional education has fostered a perspective "in which knowledge is considered to be 'objective,' something outside of ourselves, reflecting a reality already there, awaiting discovery by prescribed scientific methods considered universal avenues to truth" (Imre, 1995, p. 64). Techniques from the physical sciences are used in an attempt to minimize or eliminate subjective factors rooted in people involved in research. From this perspective, narrative stories may be suspect because they are considered to be "anecdotal," which often means unimportant. It is time to rescue the story, to restore it to its place in the intertwined narratives of social workers' personal and professional lives. It is not necessary to abandon rationality and all that has been learned. However, perhaps social workers have to recognize that reason may explain the darkness, but it is not always a light.

As the 21st century approaches, health care providers must make a paradigm shift related to the emerging societal emphasis on personal power, autonomy, and self-responsibility. Roles and boundaries are changing. Clients are now being viewed less as "patients" and more as their own change agents. This shift may threaten traditional understanding of practice roles and professional self-image (Haiman, 1995). Professionals must continue to be aware of how self-help and advocacy groups have reduced consumer isolation and stigma and have promoted a sense of community among different client groups. By continuing to encourage participation in organizational tasks, self-help groups facilitate the development of personal networks. Experiential knowledge and "having been there" are given great credence. Professionals currently wend their way through many conflicting expectations coming from consumers, agencies, and society.

Past abuses in the use of power on the part of professionals have changed as has as an emphasis on client weaknesses and pathology rather than on strengths. As a result, human service professionals have begun to rethink how to do assessment, diagnosis, and treatment. Now, the medical model is less frequently used, and psychosocial rehabilitation, education, and the impact of social stigma are being considered. This shift is a good one, but professionals should not throw the baby out with the bath water, because many behavioral and cognitive disabilities have biological roots that need medical attention, such as with SMI, developmental disabilities, and attention deficit disorders. Changes in models of care also have implications for boundaries. More clubhouses (for example, Fountain House in New York City), drop-in centers, and support groups mean more reliance on natural helpers and recreational specialists and less reliance on professional helpers. Self-help, peer support, and self-advocacy are increasingly viewed as components of wellness, treatment, and recovery.

Consumer and advocacy groups report degrading, harmful, and humiliating experiences with coercive, involuntary professional interventions. Professionals, especially in the SMI area, report deterioration, homelessness, and violence when they are prevented from giving treatment by laws against involuntary medications and hospitalization. Many consumers, such as small children, frail older people, and many people with developmental disabilities or SMI, are unable to speak for themselves. Families often advocate in these areas, but they and their mentally ill family members still need the help of professionals. Although McCabe and Unzicker (1995, p. 61) stated that "there is virtually no difference in intelligence, ability and talents between people who have experienced treatment in the mental health system and those who have not," Murdoch (1996) said, "In the author's opinion, writing on social work treatment over the past several decades has perhaps overemphasized interventions that promote client self-determination and has paid too little attention to the protective treatment efforts necessarily undertaken by practitioners for the good of clients" (p. 31). Dincin and Bowman (1995) also described agencies run by people with SMI that dissolved into anarchy, and they advocated that professionalism would have prevented that from happening. They asserted that consumers need a sense of pride, hope, participation, input, and choice, as well as professional leadership and management.

Professionals and the Consumer Movement

One person can start a movement. Mahatma Gandhi did, and so did Rosa Parks. However, masses of people are needed to keep it moving, and the greater the number and diversity of individuals who are united in support of a policy, the greater the likelihood of success. Human service professionals, including social workers, could be involved at four levels: (1) policy-making and planning, (2) service delivery, (3) training and education, and (4) consumer-operated programs.

POLICY MAKING AND PLANNING

Leadership training for consumers is essential, as is training in learning how to be assertive and effective board members. Professionals have a role in such training. Some now suggest that consumers should represent 50 percent of policy-making and planning groups. If so, extensive training is required.

SERVICE DELIVERY

Consumers must be trained and employed as staff. However, human service professionals do not know enough about how this works. Accordingly, evaluation of the effectiveness of consumer staff service delivery is needed.

TRAINING AND EDUCATION

It is essential that students and clinicians hear directly from consumers. What has it been like to live with alcoholism, with SMI, or with a relative who has developmental disabilities? How have social workers been helpful or harmful? Professionals can learn much from consumers. This learning can be accomplished both by bringing consumers into the classroom and by using the literature currently being written by consumers.

CONSUMER-OPERATED PROGRAMS

Consumers can operate human service programs providing peer support, including safe houses, crisis phone lines and drop in centers, outreach teams, and support groups. A barrier to these programs is lack of funding. Perhaps in funding mental health services systems, 10 percent of the funding should be set aside for consumer-operated programs. If so, such programs should be reviewed periodically, just as social services agencies are reviewed, to see whether they are operating effectively.

TWELVE-STEP PROGRAMS

Twelve-step programs are distinctive in that they have a focus on offering "spiritual" guidance to their members. Many researchers and clinicians have trouble with the concept of spirituality, especially because it is difficult to define and measure. Some professionals also object to what they perceive as a cult atmosphere in 12-step programs. Such programs are sometimes viewed as unscientific and as having a middle-class bias. Twelve-step programs hold in common the idea of spiritual growth as an antidote to obsessive efforts to control pain and anxiety. Anxiety is increasingly present in a culture of rapid technologic and cultural change, and people are increasingly trying to deal with that anxiety through alcohol, drugs, food, money, and religion. Perhaps 12-step programs are further examples of attempted remedies for such anxiety.

Conclusion

There is no going back to the "good old" or "bad old" days, when professionals thought they knew a bit more than seems to be known now. This is a good thing. Professionals may make up the menu, but consumers have to eat what is offered. Professionals need to know more from consumers about how the services offered taste. This is a transitional era in the relationship and roles of professionals and consumers, and transitions are hard. Both professionals and consumers need to be patient, to live with ambiguities, to listen carefully to one another, to try and stand in the shoes of the other, and above all, to show kindness and mercy to all concerned.

References

Degan, P. (1990). Spirit breaking: When the helping professions hurt. *Humanistic Psychologist, 18*, 301–313.

Degan, P. (1995). Dilemmas in professional collaboration with consumers. *Psychiatric Services, 46*, 443–445.

Dincin, J., & Bowman, D. (1995). Roots, fundamental ideas, and principles. *New Directions for Mental Health Services, 68*, 3–10.

Freeman, M. A., & Trabin, T. (1994). *Managed behavioral healthcare: History, models, key issues, and future course.* Rockville, MD: U.S. Department of Health and Human Services, Center for Mental Health Services.

Greist, J. H. (1995). Computers and psychiatry. *Psychiatric Services, 46*, 989–991.

Haiman, S. (1995). Dilemmas in professional collaboration with consumers. *Psychiatric Services, 46*, 443–445.

Hatfield, A. (1979). Help-seeking behavior in families of schizophrenics. *American Journal of Community Psychology, 7*, 563–569.

Haynes, X. S., & Mickelson, J. S. (1991). *Affecting change: Social workers in the political arena* (2nd ed.). New York: Longman.

Imre, R. W. (1995). Personal narratives do not come easily to the professionally trained self. *Reflections, 1* (3), 64–69.

Lee, D. T. (1995). Professional underutilization of Recovery, Inc. *Psychiatric Rehabilitation, 19* (1), 63–69.

McCabe, S., & Unzicker, R. E. (1995). Changing roles of consumer/survivors in mature mental health system. *New Directions for Mental Health Services, 66*, 61–73.

Murdoch, A. D. (1996). Beneficence re-examined: Protective intervention in mental health. *Social Work, 41*, 26–32.

Powell, T. J. (Ed.). (1990). *Working with self-help.* Silver Spring, MD: NASW Press.

Rosen, A. (1994). Knowledge use in direct practice. *Social Service Review, 68*, 562–577.

Segal, S. P., Silverman, C., & Tempkin, T. (1995). Measuring empowerment in client-run self-help agencies. *Community Mental Health, 31*, 215–227.

Wasow, M. (1995). *The skipping stone: Ripple effects of mental illness on the family.* Palo Alto, CA: Science & Behavior Books.

PART III

Outcomes Measurement in Child and Family Services

CHAPTER 14

Results-Based Accountability for Child and Family Services

HEATHER B. WEISS

The 1990s have brought significant changes to the public sector. From the Clinton administration's reinvention initiative to "create a government that works better and costs less" to Republican calls for devolving service responsibility to states and localities, many agree that government should change. These changes have implications for child and family services. For example, many argue that public sector child and family services should be more like private sector services—that these programs should have an increased focus on organizational responsibility and should be more accountable for program results.

David Garvin (1993) of Harvard Business School proposed a theory of private sector organizations that has implications for the current discussion of reforming public sector child and family services. Garvin argued that for any organization to engage in continuous improvement, it must be a learning organization. That is, organizations must engage in systematic problem solving, allow experimentation with new approaches, promote learning from their own experience and history, promote learning from the experience and best practices of others, and be able to transfer knowledge quickly and efficiently throughout the organization.

Garvin further argued that learning organizations usually undergo three overlapping stages as they develop: (1) heuristic, (2) behavioral, and (3) performance improvement. In the heuristic stage, members of the organization are exposed to new ideas and begin to think differently. In the behavioral stage, employees begin to internalize new insights and to alter their behavior. The performance improvement stage involves

---

This chapter draws heavily on the work of the Results-Based Accountability Project at the Harvard Family Research Project (see Horsch, 1996; Schilder & Brady, 1996; Schilder, Brady, & Horsch, 1996). The author gratefully acknowledges the Ford Foundation and the Pew Charitable Trusts for supporting the Results-Based Accountability Project. The contents of this article are solely the responsibility of the author and do not necessarily reflect the views of the funders.

changes in behavior leading to measurable improvements. As child and family services are challenged to change and to be more accountable to the public, Garvin's theory provides a useful framework for analyzing the development of these changes.

Why Results-Based Accountability?

In many arenas in child and family services, people are calling for systems change. Specifically, people are now beginning to move from provision of specific services that each address a specific need to building whole systems of services that reflect an understanding of children and families in a social context. Systems reform is more than simply coordinating existing services; it means creating a new and integrative system of comprehensive services. In its most ambitious form, it is an attempt to restructure and integrate the service delivery system for a wide array of user-friendly services for children and families. In this system, caseworkers and services providers would have access to up-to-date information about the range of services that families may need. In its most developed form, this system would be a learning system—that is, a system that promotes the acquisition of knowledge and application of it in new ways (Garvin, 1993).

Although some states have begun to embark on the task of reforming child and family systems, the term *systems change* is still in the process of being implemented. States are defining the process differently, depending on their unique needs. At a minimum, promising systems reform models have been results-oriented. Planning and articulating expected results and measures of whether results are being achieved are key components of these change efforts.

According to the proponents, results-based accountability will shift the focus of these services from separate programs with different sets of regulations to a collaborative service approach. Under the current system, separate programs, each with their own eligibility requirements and regulations, provide services for separate aspects of child and family life. The proponents of results-based accountability argue that by shifting the accountability of these programs to results from a process focus, a more comprehensive set of services could be provided to children and families.

What Is Results-Based Accountability?

Although many have embraced the notion of results-based accountability, no single definition of the term exists. People define *results-based accountability* as a management tool that can leverage collaboration among human service agencies, as a method of decentralizing programs, and as an innovative regulatory process. Currently, this term can mean any of these things. At a minimum, the term implies that expected results are clearly articulated and that data are regularly collected and reported to determine whether results have been achieved.

In developing a results-based accountability system, it is important that the level of results be clearly defined. Expected results can be defined at the child and family level, community level, program level, or agency level. An example of a child and family–level goal is that child and family poverty rates will be reduced to 10 percent by the year 2010. An example of a community-level goal is that poverty rates in a given community will be reduced by 10 percent by 2010. An example of a program-level goal for a job training program is that 80 percent of program participants will be placed in jobs within six months of completing training. An example of an agency-level goal is that client satisfaction with services provided by the agency will improve by 10 percent by January 1998 (Schilder et al., 1996).

The level of the expected results dictates who is responsible for achieving the results. For example, everyone in a community, including lay citizens and public agency managers and providers, is responsible for meeting child and family–level goals, such as reducing teen pregnancy rates. In contrast, program managers and providers are responsible for meeting program-level goals, such as increasing job placements for participants in a job training program. Agency managers are responsible for attaining agency-level goals.

Child and family–level and community-level goals can be used to refocus agencies and programs. For example, the goal of reducing teen pregnancy can be used by agencies to prioritize resources and place additional emphasis on those services related to teen pregnancy. Programs can also use child and family– and community-level goals to focus more on child and family–level results. For example, the child and family–level goal of increased self-sufficiency may translate into a goal for a job program of sustained employment in a job with a living wage. This broader goal implies collaboration with other programs, such as child-care programs and transportation assistance programs, that would ensure sustained employment.

Utility of Results-Based Accountability as a Management Tool

When used to their full advantage, results-based accountability systems offer several opportunities. They can engage stakeholders in building broadly shared visions of the goals that are important and the strategies that are required to achieve them. An important first step in developing a results-based accountability system is to engage families, the community, program administrators, and policymakers in articulating a vision. This broad vision and focus on results can be a valuable management tool for agencies to engage in systems reform with citizen involvement. Articulated goals result from this vision.

Results-based accountability systems can provide the framework for articulating indicators and developing a system of data collection to track progress toward meeting these goals. These data then provide information on whether program results are being achieved. As such they answer three questions:

1. What is the program, community, or state trying to achieve?
2. How is the program, community, or state progressing?
3. Have desired results been achieved?

Results-based accountability systems provide the opportunity to give policymakers, providers, and others valuable data that they can use to make better decisions about the families they serve. However, to be powerful management tools, accountability systems must be linked with program evaluation. Whereas results-based accountability systems monitor program progress, evaluations identify why programs are succeeding or failing and what changes might be necessary. Program evaluation answers important questions that can complement the information provided by the results-based system such as, Why were results achieved or not? What links exist between interventions and results? What unintended effects have resulted? How do programs need to change?

Results-based accountability systems allow increased chances of human service organizations becoming learning organizations. As envisioned, results-based accountability information and evaluation data could, in its most advanced phase, be used to change the thinking of decision makers to focus more on outcomes. These data could also be used to inform decision makers about whether specific services and strategies are achieving desired results. Such data could be used by program managers and providers as an administrative tool to better understand whether programs are working, whether clients are being served well, and whether changes should be made to improve results. Individual- and community-level results could be used by communities to understand how to direct future resources and how to prioritize efforts. Finally, the information provided by the results-based system could be used to transfer knowledge quickly throughout the organization to improve overall performance (Horsch, 1996).

Challenges in Results-Based Accountability Systems

Important challenges currently exist with results-based accountability initiatives for child and family services. Child and family services results-based accountability initiatives are different from the cost-containment and managed care initiatives. For child and family services, the systems are being developed in the hope of improving the services but are not strictly looking at bottom-line results. Nonetheless, questions still exist about how to link results with accountability mechanisms. Also, for a system to be fully operational, quality data are necessary, implying financial, technical, political, and human resources commitments. Thus, technical challenges arise in developing valid and reliable measures. Political challenges exist with regard to sustaining the initiatives.

The question of how to link results with accountability is especially an issue for individual-level outcomes. True accountability implies responsibility on the part of specific individuals, programs, or agencies. How can communities be held accountable for achieving results? It is much easier to hold programs or agencies accountable for program- or agency-level results. A related issue is how to attach stakes to the these systems. If results-based accountability replaces process accountability, sanctions and rewards must be in place to ensure that goals are met. However, attaching high stakes to results-based systems, especially early in their development, may corrupt them. These questions have not yet been resolved.

A second issue is that valid and reliable data that are regularly and publicly reported are an important element of a results-based accountability system. Goals are much more easily agreed on than specific measures and indicators. Identifying quality measures and indicators of progress can be time-consuming and expensive because different services require different levels and types of data and have varying confidentiality requirements. Furthermore, if stakes are attached to the measures, the quality of these measures becomes even more important. Developing the data capacity requires financial, technical, human resource, and political commitments.

The third challenge of sustaining these efforts in differing political climates is an especially important consideration in these times of political change. To become fully successful and operational, results-based accountability initiatives must have the political support to endure over time. If the initiatives do not endure, negative consequences can occur. For example, the initiative could decrease the quality of services by creating a climate of cynicism by having child and family services providers feel they have wasted time and resources on a short-lived effort. The issues of how to develop the accountability mechanisms, how to collect quality data, and how to sustain the initiatives must be carefully considered in the development of results-based systems.

How Is Results-Based Accountability Working in Selected States?

Oregon and Minnesota have developed comprehensive individual-level results-based accountability systems. Both states have attempted to link agency and program goals to individual-level goals. The processes of articulating the goals and implementing the systems could provide valuable lessons for others embarking on creating such systems (Schilder & Brady, 1996).

OREGON

Oregon began its initiative, Oregon Benchmarks, in the late 1980s by articulating its vision of the future and its strategic plan for attaining measurable results. This strategic plan, Oregon Shines, outlined three broad areas for the future in Oregon: (1) to increase jobs and income, (2) to improve the economy, and (3) to protect and enhance the quality of life for every Oregonian. Oregon embarked on a planning effort to build community support around the vision and to define the measures within these three broad categories (Schilder, Horsch, Brady, & Riel, in press).

The Oregon Benchmarks have had the support of three separate governors. Governor Neil Goldschmidt was responsible for the planning and development of the benchmarks, Governor Barbara Roberts was responsible for the implementation of the benchmarks, and current Governor John Kitzhaber has been responsible for sustaining the effort.

The Oregon Benchmarks are individual-level, family-level, and community-level goals. They are not agency specific; however, agencies are using them to develop agency goals. For example, the welfare program has changed its mission from disbursing money to reducing the number of families receiving Aid to Families with Dependent

Children (AFDC). The state is therefore measuring agency performance through AFDC caseload data.

Oregon has used the benchmarks to prioritize spending around specific issues and to refocus public and private efforts. For example, in 1993, Governor Roberts used the benchmarks as one tool to determine budget priorities (Schilder et al., in press). It is important to note, however, that the budget decisions were made on the basis of whether programs were aligned with priority benchmarks. To date, budget decisions have not been made on the basis of whether programs meet benchmarks.

Specific state agencies also have used the benchmarks to redirect work and to rethink the current categorical system of programs. For example, the state legislature created a new state agency called the Commission on Children and Families to coordinate child and family services in the state and to give more control to localities in determining child and family services. This new agency consists of a state commission and 36 local commissions. The state and local commissions are responsible for coordinating child and family services and for making funding decisions for a small portion of social services programs. The local commissions—composed of at least 51 percent lay citizens—are given the liberty to choose local benchmarks from the state-defined list. The local commissions then make decisions to fund programs on the basis of whether they are aligned with the local benchmarks.

To date, Oregon is using a results-based approach to rethink the traditional categorical approach to providing child and family services. As such, the system is a results-based management tool rather than an accountability tool. That is, programs are funded on the basis of whether they are aligned with the selected benchmarks. However, the state is still in the process of determining what types of decisions it will make if benchmarks are not met.

MINNESOTA

The state of Minnesota began its initiative, Minnesota Milestones, in 1991 under Governor Arne Carlson. Statewide goals and performance indicators were established through a consensual process that brought together thousands of Minnesotans. Minnesota Milestones produced 20 goals and 79 milestones based on results-oriented government. As planned, spending will eventually be linked to results. Government agencies were required to submit strategic plans and measures for their programs within the Minnesota Milestones framework.

In a separate but related effort, the state recently created a new state-level agency called the Department of Children, Families, and Learning designed to coordinate child and family services. This agency houses selected programs formerly in the Departments of Education, Economic Security, and Human Services. The goal of this new agency is to encourage systems change at the state level. Although the new agency is not directly an outgrowth of the milestones effort, the agency is in the process of planning its work around the expected results. The agency plans to track some of the milestones to inform decision making. For example, the agency is in the process of defining "drop-out" and developing a better data system of reporting this information to managers so they can use it in daily decision making.

Another effort consists of all state agencies responsible for early childhood services (including health services and other services not in the new Department of Children, Families, and Learning, as well as those housed in the new department) defining expected results in the early childhood arena. People representing programs across state departments meet regularly to develop a framework and to articulate the expected results that they hope will eventually be used by all early childhood programs.

To date, the Minnesota Milestones have been used to change the way agency personnel are thinking about social issues and the strategies used to solve social problems. The discussion now is about how to begin to develop measures that can be tied to changes in behavior (for example, reorganizing state government and reorganizing child- and family-serving agencies). The milestones are at the beginning stage, but they give an infrastructure on which to build the next round.

Implications for Future Research

The movement toward results-based accountability initiatives for child and family services has implications for future research in three areas: (1) benefits and drawbacks, (2) challenges and opportunities, and (3) measures.

BENEFITS AND DRAWBACKS

Research on the specific benefits and drawbacks of results-based accountability initiatives is needed to inform those who are attempting to design and implement these initiatives. Although policymakers and practitioners assume that results-based accountability initiatives will bring about greater efficiency and more effective services, more empirical evidence is needed to support these claims. Research is needed that identifies where this private sector model works in the public sector and which aspects are the most salient. For example, future research should address questions about use of information, links and governance structures, and how the public sector can use results to make decisions about budgeting and program continuation.

CHALLENGES AND OPPORTUNITIES

Research on the challenges and opportunities that states are facing in designing, implementing, and sustaining results-based accountability initiatives in different contexts is needed. For example, information on the political, technical, and resource challenges, especially in differing contexts, could inform those who are planning such efforts. Such research findings could be used by policymakers and practitioners to facilitate the implementation of results-based accountability initiatives and could prove valuable in sustaining them.

MEASURES

Research is needed on appropriate, valid, and reliable measures that can be used in results-based accountability systems. Currently, practitioners and program providers are struggling to find valid and reliable instruments. Research on tools that can be used by practitioners and front-line works would be valuable to those implementing results-based accountability initiatives.

Conclusion

The field of results-based accountability and systems reform is at a turning point. It is clear that the development of good and useful accountability systems takes time and that change will not occur overnight. It is necessary to consider not just the technical issues of measurement but how to build this as part of systems reform efforts.

In assessing the development of results-based accountability for child and family services, the states that are the farthest along are now in the heuristic phase of development identified by Garvin (1993). People in these states are just beginning to change the way they are thinking about services and to focus on outcomes. The challenge is to maintain a political momentum to keep the efforts moving forward so that they actually begin to translate into some behavioral changes and ultimately improve services for children and families.

References

Garvin, D. A. (1993). Building a learning organization. *Harvard Business Review, 71,* 78–91.

Horsch, K. (1996, Winter). Results-based accountability systems: Opportunities and challenges. *The Evaluation Exchange, II,* 2–3.

Schilder, D., & Brady, A. (1996). State results-based accountability initiatives. *The Evaluation Exchange, II,* 2–3, 5.

Schilder, D., Brady, A., & Horsch, K. (1996). *Resource guide of results-based accountability efforts: Profiles of selected states.* Cambridge, MA: Harvard Family Research Project.

Schilder, D., Horsch, K., Brady, A., & Riel, E. (in press). *Case studies of state results-based accountability initiatives.* Cambridge, MA: Harvard Family Research Project.

CHAPTER 15

Methodological Considerations in Outcomes Measurement in Family and Child Welfare

FRED H. WULCZYN

This chapter focuses on emerging technologies and research methods that could have a dramatic impact on outcomes measurement and research if they were to become a more integral part of the collective repertoire. These technologies and methods are established in disciplines as diverse as biomedical research, econometrics, geography, and operations research. However, the rate at which child welfare researchers have adopted these methods has been slow, giving the methods an aura of newness. Nevertheless, that these methods have only slowly found their way into child welfare research gives outcomes research a one-sidedness that limits its capacity to understand how child welfare services delivery actually influences the lives of children and families. This chapter addresses this one-sidedness.

Case Examples of Failure to Contextualize

The following examples capture conversations between service providers that could be taking place in the child welfare system. The first conversation takes place between a county executive and the program director, who is trying to explain the impact of the county's recent preventive services initiative, arguing passionately that preventive services worked. Testimony from direct service workers attests to the value of the intensive services that diverted children from placement; and program statistics indicate that the number of families served, the fraction of those served who actually went into placement, and the services those families received, including the cost–benefit analysis, show a demonstrable impact. Although the data are indeed persuasive, the county executive nevertheless counters that despite all this hard work, the population of children in foster care has grown by 3 percent, and the county now has higher foster care expenditures in addition to increased outlays for preventive services. The results, although confounding, cannot be disputed. The county executive listens once more to an explanation about something the program director calls a targeting problem before slashing the preventive services budget.

In the second story, a caseworker, possibly from the same county, ponders a difficult case involving a sibling group of three children, the youngest member having just come into foster care as an infant. The oldest is five years old and has been in placement for 14 months. The three-year-old middle child entered care at the same time as the oldest sibling. The reasons for admission had to do with substance abuse on the part of the parent, violence in the home, and neglect. The mother, who still sees the father sporadically, is having trouble overcoming her addiction; her employment is unstable; and the housing is inadequate but structurally salvageable. In short, the family is representative of families in the child welfare system throughout the United States. If the family is typical in its presenting problem, the worker wonders in what other ways the family is typical. In an effort to establish reasonable expectations for the family, the worker ponders the simple question: How well is this family doing in our system? The worker sets out to contextualize the experiences of these children. A trip to the library produces books and articles on attachment theory; the history of foster care starting with Brace (1967); Fanshel and Shinn (1978); and the evolving concepts of permanency, family preservation, and family support. After several weeks of reading, the worker concludes that the children are not doing very well. They are in foster care, and there is little in the literature to suggest that this is a good thing, although it is sometimes unavoidable. Interestingly, the worker checks with the supervisor and learns that the agency knows little about how long children remain in the agency's custody. Moreover, no one in the agency knows whether certain "types" of children served by the agency tend to stay in care longer than others. The one potential source of understanding comes from a statistical summary assembled by the Department of Social Services, which states that the average length of time in foster care is 2.4 years, and because these children have been in care for only 14 months, something positive can be found in the collective materials.

The common thread in these examples is the inability to place the experiences of families and children into a context that is meaningful to both administrators and clinicians. In the first example, the county administrator and program director made the assumption that the microlevel experiences of the families would produce outcomes with administrative meaning. They failed to consider the possibility that preventive services may actually reduce admissions while the foster care caseload continues to grow. They compounded the problem, trapped in a microscopic view of the world, by attributing the failure to the inability of social work to deliver promised outcomes. In the second example, the worker sought to place the experiences of these three children in the context of children who had passed through foster care in earlier years. The worker began looking for an actuarial basis on which to make judgments about the likely course these children would take but did not find any such characterizations in the literature because for the most part they simply do not exist. Moreover, where they do exist, the underlying model used to present the data is unlikely to provide a technically accurate guide. (As demonstrated later in this chapter, the one barometer typically available is more likely to overstate the expectations with respect to length of stay and is therefore likely to lead to faulty conclusions about baseline experiences.)

Clinical Motif in Child Welfare

The inability to contextualize the experiences of foster children or children at risk of placement in the ways just described owes itself to what might be described as the *clinical motif* in child welfare research. That is, the repeated design elements in child welfare research tend to focus on microlevel details of individual cases and the adjustment of individuals to the circumstances surrounding particular case events such as placement in foster care. Although outcomes research cannot advance without a highly developed sense of how individual characteristics and interventions relate to development over the life course, the almost singular emphasis on individual level research has at least two weaknesses. First, only a small body of research focuses on aggregate-level dynamics and the impact policies and programs have on population trends, leaving administrators with few empirical resources to draw on when they set out to form expectations about the likely impact a program initiative will have on the service population. In short, for many policy-level discussions, especially those that deal with system-level reform, clinically oriented research offers little in the way of direct, usable feedback. Second, the empirical research that has dealt with the question of outcomes is quite often flawed in ways that may actually mislead all but the most careful clinicians. As long as these problems persist, advancing outcomes research in child welfare will be difficult.

Changes Needed in Outcomes Research

To address these issues and broaden the empirical base of child welfare research, four points are addressed: (1) reductionist conceptualizations, (2) statistical models of change processes, (3) selection bias in cross-sectional research, and (4) epidemiology of child placement. Each is designed to move the field toward a better statistical understanding of child welfare experiences and enrich the field's understanding of outcomes.

REDUCTIONIST CONCEPTUALIZATIONS

The first concern addresses the reductionist tendencies in the conceptualization of child welfare measurement and outcomes. Arthur Eddington (1955), in *The Nature of the Physical World,* proposed that a distinction be made between between primary and secondary laws. Primary laws, according to Eddington, deal with individual microscopic entities in the physical world, whereas secondary laws describe the behavior of groups of these microscopic entities. Furthermore, Eddington argued, the methods one uses to understand these two different types of laws are not the same and the description of elementary behaviors is not sufficient for understanding the system as a whole.

If one purpose behind outcomes research is to identify factors that improve outcomes, then Eddington's writings have a simple message. To the extent that the system of services is an important determinant of what happens to children and the eventual outcome, the clinical orientation of most outcomes research will not yield an understanding of the system as a whole or its place among the factors that influence child welfare outcomes. As described later, the remedy involves expanding the conceptual and empirical aspirations of outcomes research beyond the boundaries of clinical research. This fact should not be taken to mean that less emphasis should be placed on clinically oriented research. Rather, the outcomes research agenda should be broadened to include macrovariables such as the distribution of resources and population trends within the system of services to better understand the patterns of service delivery, including movements of children through the system, and their relationship to outcomes. Without well-integrated, macrolevel research, the likelihood that the child welfare system will develop a strong sense of the relative properties so vital to meaningful outcomes research seems remote. (See chapter 4 by Ware for a better understanding of relative properties.) In short, as long as outcomes research retains its clinical emphasis, administrators will continue to search for outcomes data with relevance to the world as they see it.

STATISTICAL MODELS OF CHANGE PROCESSES

The second methodological change has to do with statistical models of change processes. Although everyone readily acknowledges the complexity of family life, child welfare research does not rely on statistical models that extract this complexity from empirical data. There are two ways to address this issue. First, wider use of event history models for analyzing child welfare experiences must be developed. Event history models offer an array of solutions to problems that have confounded child welfare research for some time. Length of stay, the probabilities that children will go home or will be moved to some other place in the child welfare system, and the effect of services on these probabilities cannot be analyzed completely without at least some reference to survival techniques. The second type of statistical model speaks more directly to the reductionist tendencies in child welfare. These models are similar to those used by biologists to study why populations rise and fall over time. Their relevance to child welfare research is fairly clear. For example, poverty is related to the number of children in foster care, but no research specifically addresses the question of how changes in the number of poor children are related to changes in the number of foster children. The threefold increase in the number of foster children in New York City during the late 1980s was not preceded by a threefold increase in the number of poor children. Thus, understanding how poverty relates to changes in the number of foster children depends on a conceptual framework and a data collection/analysis plan that speaks directly to the underlying phenomenon.

The emphasis on population-level models has another advantage in that it focuses researchers on the process of population growth and decline. Although researchers and practitioners readily acknowledge that population growth and decline depend on the balance of admissions and discharges, surprisingly little outcomes research isolates the delivery of services within that larger context. Most research on the efficacy of treatment with respect to child welfare outcomes focuses on placement prevention as if that were the only point along a child's service history when those services might be applied. The same services delivered as part of an aftercare program may have a different impact on the child and the family, but the detection of those effects depends in part on a conceptualization of service delivery that recognizes the distinction between the admission and the discharge process. Although this clearly is not the only way to introduce these ideas into the research agenda, the explict treatment of admission (birth) and discharge (death) processes found in population dynamics brings immediate clarity to the underlying problem.

SELECTION BIAS IN CROSS-SECTIONAL RESEARCH

The third change has to do with developing a deeper appreciation for the problems of selection biases embedded in cross-sectional samples on which much child welfare research has been based. Specifically, most foster care research is based on children who are in care, a sample of children that can influence the perceptions formed about the typical experience of children and the programs developed to respond to percieved problems. To illustrate this point, consider statistics presented in Table 15-1 and Table 15-2, dating back to the late 1970s and early 1980s, when Public Law 96-272 was emerging as the centerpiece of federal child welfare reform (Adoption Assistance and Child Welfare Act of 1980).

Table 15-1 presents reconstructed data from a statistical report that used social indicators to provide baseline data about how long children were staying in the foster care system. At that time, the overwhelming perception from within the child welfare

Table 15-1

CHILDREN IN FOSTER CARE FOR FIVE OR MORE YEARS

Current Living Arrangement	1974	1975	1976	1977	1978
All living arrangements[a]	26.1	26.5	25.9	25.0	26.0
Foster family home	33.2	35.1	33.2	34.1	39.0
Independent living	44.6	53.8	57.4	58.0	60.0
Group care	25.3	28.4	27.6	28.7	28.6

Note: Data are percentage of all children in placement who were in placement for five or more years as of June 30.

Source: Reprinted with permission from Testa, M., & Wulczyn, F. (1980). *State of the child* (p. 45). Chicago: Children's Policy Research Project, Chapin Hall Center for Children.

[a]This category includes types of living arrangements not listed separately.

Table 15-2

NUMBER OF CHILDREN PLACED FOR THE FIRST TIME BY YEAR AND TIME UNTIL DISCHARGE: 1977–1981

Status	1977	1978	1979	1980	1981[a]
Illinois, total children placed	5,774	5,666	6,016	6,327	6,332
Still in care[b] (%)	6.2	7.7	9.8	13.0	17.5
Time until discharge					
Before 3 months (%)	36.4	37.5	34.7	33.9	35.4
Before 12 months (%)	64.5	62.2	59.8	60.7	60.1
Before 36 months (%)	80.9	79.9	80.3	81.1	80.4
After 36 months (%)	93.8	92.3	90.2	87.0	82.5

Note: Time until discharge is the cumulative proportion discharged within the specified time.

Source: Reprinted with permission from Wulczyn, F., Goerge, R., Hartnett, M. A., & Testa, M. (1985). Children in substitute care. In M. Testa & E. Lawlor (Eds.), *The state of the child: 1985* (p. 50). Chicago: Chapin Hall Center for Children.

[a]Discharge data for 1981 may not be complete. [b]As of May 31, 1984.

community was that children in foster care spent too much time in temporary placement. In reponse to the research that demonstrated these tendencies, policymakers at the federal and state levels promoted legislation with an array of fiscal, administrative, and programmatic strategies designed to facilitate early reunification of children with families.

The data in Table 15-1 clearly show why these perceptions were so common. The table displays children in foster care for five or more years as a percentage of all children in foster care. The data for all living arrangements indicate that about one in four children had been in foster care for five or more years. The data also show that duration varies by type of placement. For example, among the children in independent living during 1978, 60 percent had been in care for five or more years. Given the values and policy objectives of the child welfare system even before the 1980 reforms, 60 percent was simply out of step with the prevailing sense of appropriate outcomes. In large part the concern over extended placements, otherwise known as *foster care drift*, was responsible for the Adoption Assistance and Child Welfare Act of 1980.

Although the data in Table 15-1 are compelling, they do not fairly represent what might be called the typical foster care experience. The question addresed is, Of all the children in care today, how long have they been in care? The answer to the question depends on a standard point-in-time or cross-sectional sample of children, the most common approach to sampling applied in child welfare research.

The deficiencies associated with point-in-time samples are best illustrated by comparing the data in Table 15-1 with data drawn from approximately the same time period, but from an altogether different perspective, such as the data presented in Table 15-2. Constructed from the entry cohorts served by the foster care system between

1977 and 1981, these data reveal how much time passed before children who entered foster care left placement for the first time. These data make it clear that perceptions with respect to length of stay in the late 1970s and early 1980s may have been exaggerated to a considerable degree. For example, more than 60 percent of the children placed in 1978 were discharged within one year. After three years, 80 percent of the children had been discharged from foster care. If 80 percent of the children admitted in 1978 were discharged within three years, 26 percent could not have survived for more than five years, as the data in Table 15-1 suggest. In other words, the commonplace understanding of how long children remain in foster care was exaggerated to a large degree, with the consequence that the structure of policy and practice that evolved from those perceptions was similarly distorted.

EPIDEMIOLOGY OF CHILD PLACEMENT

The fourth recommendation is that the field develop a detailed epidemiology of child placement. What is going on in the neighborhoods? How exactly does the structure of urban neighborhoods or rural counties affect the rate of placement? How do those contextual variables influence the likelihood that the children will return to their families? How does the availability of services in communities affect placement rates? These questions have been asked as part of the basic research conducted in other human service sectors, but they have not made their way into the child welfare system. Until they do in a more routine and systematic way, the field is not going to be able to answer the questions pertaining to service effectiveness over time.

Conclusion

This chapter proposes that child welfare outcomes research would be improved by pursuing a combination of strategies including contextualizing child and family services by changing the reductionist conceptualization in current outcomes research, using statistical models that reveal the structure and pattern in the experiences of children, avoiding selection bias in cross-sectional research, and creating geographic sensitivity. As this book clearly suggests, the emphasis on outcomes has intensified, a trend that can only continue. Moreover, as public agencies turn increasingly to managed care as the way to both organize and finance services, the ability to articulate the clinical and programmatic effects of services will be a determinant in program survival. Although the child welfare system undoubtedly can meet these challenges, a critical examination of the empirical foundations of outcomes research can only facilitate the process.

References

Adoption Assistance and Child Welfare Act of 1980, P.L. 96-272, 94 Stat. 500.

Brace, C. L. (1967). *The dangerous classes of New York and twenty years' work among them.* Montclair, NJ: P. Smith.

Eddington, A. S. (1955). *The nature of the physical world.* London: Dent.

Fanshel, D., & Shinn, E. B. (1978). *Children in foster care: A longitudinal investigation.* New York: Columbia University Press.

Testa, M., & Wulczyn, F. (1980). *State of the child.*Chicago: Children's Policy Research Project.

Wulczyn, F., Goerge, R., Hartnett, M. A., & Testa, M. (1985). Children in substitute care. In M. Testa & E. Lawlor (Eds.), *The state of the child: 1985* (pp. 45–56). Chicago: Chapin Hall Center for Children.

CHAPTER 16

Outcomes Measurement for Family and Children's Services: Incremental Steps on Multiple Levels

JACQUELYN McCROSKEY

This chapter draws from 10 years of experience with outcomes measurement in Los Angeles County, California. These experiences have included developing consensus about appropriate outcomes for public child welfare services, defining outcomes measures for a countywide children's scorecard, co-convening a statewide conference on outcomes for families and children, working with practitioners to develop a new measurement instrument to assess changes in family functioning, evaluating child and family services programs, and teaching graduate students about outcomes measurement and evaluation. Yet, even with that range of experiences at different levels, discussion of outcomes for child and family services can be confusing, complicated, and frustrating. Part of the complexity is inherent in the scope of the topic, which spans establishing accountability and creating change across many different child and family programs and systems. Part is a result of the different values and perceptions that a variety of players bring to the task based on their family lives, professional training, and experiences. In addition, there is still little agreement about the definitions of common terms or the principles that should guide development of outcomes measures for family and children's services.

Variation in Perspective and Purpose

People who come to the topic of outcomes measurement from different services systems (for example, health, mental health, and child and family services), perspectives (for example, policy, program, or client perspectives), and disciplines (such as social work, nursing, education, medicine, or psychology) do not necessarily share assumptions or speak a common language. Such differences are amply demonstrated throughout the chapters in this book. Assumptions about the reasons for measuring outcomes influence both processes and results. Such reasons can include measuring outcomes to respond to the market, to justify public expenditures, to lay the groundwork for extending or rationing care, and to understand and be better able to plan work. Differences in professional language, values, and references also can obscure meaning and make communication about complex topics even more difficult.

The geographic, cultural, and service contexts from which stakeholders come also matter because they influence assumptions, attitudes, language, and perceptions. In fact, they frame and color perception so much that it may not be useful to try to divorce the conceptual discussion of outcomes from their specific service, cultural, and geographic contexts. For example, in national deliberations regarding outcomes measurement in family and children's services in the United States, East Coast stakeholders may assume a specific form of public and private agency roles and responsibilities or priorities (for example, managing care for reunification cases), assumptions that would not necessarily be made in similar discussions by stakeholders from the Midwest or West Coast.

Lessons Learned from Implementing Outcomes Measurement

There is considerable discussion about the potential of outcomes measures for improving practice, for informing and rationalizing decision making, and for convincing a reluctant public that education, health, and human service interventions make a difference. Yet, there has been little actual experience with the development and use of such measures. The field is at the beginning of a complex and fascinating enterprise that will undoubtedly require successive approximations, requiring tentative and incremental steps in many different contexts. My colleagues and I played a significant role in both of the applications of outcomes measurement system development that are described next, and the discussion draws from our perspective on those experiences. Both are based on recent experiences in Los Angeles County with measuring outcomes for families and children. The first is development of a countywide children's scorecard to support planning for systemwide services integration. The second is development of a family assessment form to support practitioner-based program-level research and evaluation.

THE CHILDREN'S SCORE CARD

The Los Angeles County Children's Planning Council was established in 1991 to develop a strategic plan to help coordinate and leverage government, nonprofit, business, and community resources for children and families. It now includes representatives of county government, cities, schools, businesses, nonprofit organizations, and various ethnic and geographic communities in the county. Developing common goals for children has been viewed as a critical aspect of a shared strategic plan for families and children that could help cut across the many organizational and community boundaries that currently separate multiple efforts. In addition to agreeing on a shared mission and operational principles, council members began early on to try to develop agreement about shared goals and desired outcomes by developing a children's scorecard. This development has been a fruitful, although often frustrating, process. It forced participants to search for consensus on what is wanted for all county children. It also required discussion and agreement regarding how the county could get from where it is to where it wants to be. (Copies of the Children's Score Card and other recent planning documents including Profiles of Los Angeles County, Service Planning Area Resources for Children, Youth and Families are available from the Los Angeles County Children's Planning Council, Room B-26, Hahn Hall Administration, 500 West Temple Street, Los Angeles, CA 90012.)

Participants have tried to decrease frustration and confusion by using terms more or less consistently and by defining principles to guide the use of outcomes for planning purposes.

- *Outcomes* assess the conditions of children, families, and communities, including the results or impacts of programs, services, supports, or systems.
- *Performance measures* track how well agencies and programs provide services and supports to children, families, and communities.
- *Indicators* are measurable elements that suggest progress toward achievement of broad outcomes. Outcomes are generally better measured by using multiple indicators, none of which give full information on all aspects of achievement. For example, if the outcome desired is good health, indicators might include measures of infant mortality, birthweight, immunization, and sexually transmitted diseases.

The following key principles are among those that have guided the development of outcomes for family and children's services in Los Angeles County.

- Outcomes are useful at multiple levels but should be designed differently to fit different levels. Outcomes can measure the results of service programs for individuals, families, groups, agencies, or communities. Outcomes can be used to track changes in the conditions of children and families in communities, regions, counties, or the state. Outcomes also can be used to plan or track the impact of policy and programmatic changes.
- At any level, outcomes and indicators should be practical, results-oriented, important to the well-being of children and families, and stated in understandable terms.
- Desired outcomes should be stated as positive expressions of well-being rather than as absence of negative conditions whenever possible. Attempts to focus on desired conditions are not only worthwhile in themselves; they emphasize the extent to which current data collection focuses professional and public attention on negative conditions such as problems, illnesses, crimes, and deaths.
- Because no single indicator captures the full dimensions of desired outcomes, outcomes should be measured by a set of indicators chosen from the most valid

and reliable data available. Multiple measures and multiple perspectives are especially important when the outcomes sought are complex and multifaceted. This complexity is the rule rather than the exception in family and children's services.

- Whenever possible, outcomes should reflect the well-being of children, families, and communities rather than the state of the service delivery system. Performance measures are also necessary to track the state of the service delivery system. However, a well-functioning delivery system is a means to an end and not the end in itself.
- Initial efforts should focus on a strategic set of outcomes and indicators that reflect concerns shared by multiple stakeholder communities, including policymakers, service providers, and families. A more inclusive set of outcomes can be built incrementally over time on the basis of initial experiences. The process of developing appropriate, practical, and accurate outcomes measures will be an evolutionary one from which much can be learned.
- One of the most important steps in developing outcomes is clarification of the cultural and value foundations that underlie the process. The process used may be as important as the outcomes selected, in terms both of ensuring understanding and buy-in and of providing opportunities for informed discussion of underlying values and assumptions. Depending on community values, needs, and resources, outcomes and indicators may vary across communities.
- Standards for success and expectations for progress should be set at levels that challenge and encourage improvement without discouraging and burning out participants who are trying to make large-scale changes in complex and multifaceted systems.
- Analysts should not assume that averages tell the whole story but try to disaggregate data for specific cultural, linguistic, geographic, or age groups.

The 1994 Los Angeles County Children's Score Card reflected an initial effort by the Los Angeles County Children's Planning Council to develop countywide consensus on what the county leadership wanted for children; the 1996 version was revised based on experience (United Way, 1996, 1997). Table 16-1 illustrates outcomes data for the 1990–1994 scorecard report. This scorecard was seen as a tool to guide joint planning rather than as an advocacy tool used primarily by outsiders to point out the shortcomings of government programs. The purpose gives the scorecard a somewhat different focus than that sought in other efforts such as the KIDS COUNT scorecards, which provide comparable data in state-by-state profiles of child well-being. KIDS COUNT efforts in each state have been supported by the Annie E. Casey Foundation (Center for the Study of Social Policy, 1993). The primary question for Los Angeles was whether annual countywide expenditures of more than $12 billion on a broad range of educational, health, and social services programs for families and children were producing acceptable outcomes. This question is connected to, but not exactly the same as, how well each of the current programs works. For example, there are some indicators on the list for which no program

Table 16-1

LOS ANGELES COUNTY CHILDREN'S SCORE CARD—1996 (A JOINT EFFORT OF THE LOS ANGELES COUNTY CHILDREN'S PLANNING COUNCIL AND UNITED WAY)

Data Measures for Children		1990	1991	1992	1993	1994	Change since 1990
Population							
1. Total youth population		2,346,634	2,397,524	2,478,073	2,532,461	2,577,819	+10%
Age: 0–4 years		32.4%	34.0%	34.9%	35.9%	36.7%	+13%
5–9 years		27.4%	27.1%	27.1%	26.8%	26.6%	–3%
10–14 years		24.9%	24.7%	24.4%	24.3%	24.0%	–4%
15–17 years		15.4%	14.2%	13.5%	13.0%	12.8%	–17%
2. Births		204,124	202,737	197,415	189,706	180,394	–12%
Good Health							
3. Children with health insurance		77.0%	—	81.0%	—	71.0%	–8%
4. Tuberculosis cases—children		200	246	237	189	146	–27%
5. Pediatric HIV+/AIDS cases, age 0–12		92	114	135	146	184	+100%
6. Teen AIDS cases, age 13–19		21	31	40	69	80	+281%
7. Adequate birthweight (over 2,500 grams)		93.9%	93.9%	93.9%	93.8%	93.6%	0%
8. Drug exposed births		2,347	2,551	2,937	2,678	2,589	+10%
9. Infant death rate per 1,000 births		8.0	7.8	7.2	7.2	7.3	–9%
10. Births to teens age 15 and under		1,845	1,908	1,843	1,933	1,963	+6%
11. Births to teens age 16–17		7,446	7,749	7,469	7,246	7,157	–4%
12. Teen birth rate, age 15–17 per 1,000		25.7	26.8	26.3	26.2	26.0	+1%
13. Children fully immunized at age 2		42.6%	40.2%	39.1%	58.4%	52.1%	+22%
14. Substance use, 11th grade,	Alcohol	—	—	—	43.2%	47.0%	+9%
self-reported in last 30 days	Tobacco	—	—	—	26.2%	27.5%	+5%
(1993/94, 1995/96)	Illicit drugs	—	—	—	28.0%	29.8%	+6%
Safety and Survival							
15. Child abuse cases opened		108,088	120,358	139,106	171,922	169,638	+57%
16. Victimization rate (violent crime) age 12–19, U. S.		71.6	68.6	76.8	118.7	118.2	65%
17. Juveniles incarcerated: Juvenile Hall and CYA		—	—	23,259	22,727	22,317	–4%
18. Juvenile probation: petitions filed		31,543	31,010	30,646	29,565	29,347	–7%

Table 16-1 *(continued)*

Data Measures for Children		1990	1991	1992	1993	1994	Change since 1990
Safety and survival (continued)							
19. Gang crimes		36,136	39,129	39,214	39,125	36,160	0%
Gang vs. gang incidents		1,766	3,698	5,350	3,655	2,372	+34%
Gang related deaths		690	771	800	719	779	+13%
20. Violent deaths age 0–19	Homicide	422	520	446	434	423	0%
	Suicide	61	52	54	83	47	–23%
	Accidents	381	351	256	313	283	–26%
Economic Well-Being							
21. Children below poverty level		21.2%	23.7%	27.1%	27.7%	28.0%	+32%
22. Children receiving AFDC		435,360	501,076	552,075	542,078	619,104	+42%
23. Homeless children & youth		46,000	52,000	54,000	47,604	46,515	+1%
24. School lunch program enrollment		48.6%	51.1%	53.5%	56.1%	57.1%	+17%
25. Child support enforcement: collections (millions)		—	$128.2	$160.1	$174.1	$195.2	+52%
Social and Emotional Well-Being							
26. Children living with at least one parent		85.5%	—	—	—	—	0%
27. Children in foster care rate per 1,000 age 0–17		—	13.0	13.2	13.9	14.7	+13%
Family Reunification—temporary placement		—	10,200	11,298	12,155	11,637	+14%
Permanent Placement		—	22,429	23,348	24,463	26,189	+17%
Probation: camp, foster home, group home		—	—	—	5,584	5,877	+5%
28. Children placed in adoptive homes		824	1,000	985	1,049	1,027	+25%
Achievement/Work Force Readiness							
29. High school graduation rate		58.5%	59.0%	60.0%	58.9%	59.6%	+2%
30. Enrollment in college—all ages		534,353	527,808	541,743	496,176	519,468	–3%
31. Students fluent in English/bilingual		78%	76%	73%	70%	68%	–13%
32. Registered to vote, age 18–24 (1995)		—	—	—	—	36%	0%
33. SAT scores		861	852	852	853	850	–1%
34. Graduates completed courses for U.C. admission		33.0%	36.0%	35.0%	35.0%	36.0%	+9%
35. 16–19 yr.olds, in school or working (80/90)		89.8%	—	—	—	90.5%	+1

Note: — = No data available.

Source: Reprinted with permission from United Way of Greater Los Angeles. (1996). *State of the county report: Los Angeles 1996.* Los Angeles: Author.

would claim sole responsibility or want to be evaluated on but are nevertheless important for the well-being of children.

The 1996 Children's Score Card for Los Angeles County uses the same overall format, but indicators in many sections have been modified. The second scorecard was released with a parallel form, the Community Conditions for Children Score Card, which measures the well-being of the communities in which children and families live. Regional scorecards have also been published that reflect trends in the state of children in each of the county's eight service planning regions. The county also has experimented with scorecards for children from different ethnic groups with limited success because such scorecards depend on disaggregated data, which often are not available. (Many departments or reporters still are either prohibited from asking about race or ethnicity or do not give high priority to such information.) Each of these variations has not only helped focus on the dismal state of what is but also revealed some surprising positive trends. In the context of the planning council, outcomes measurement helps determine the practical steps needed to improve the lives of children and families by building on those strengths.

THE FAMILY ASSESSMENT FORM

In addition to the systems-level planning work illustrated by the county scorecard, focus has also been placed on practice-based measurement strategies that help practitioners assess the impact of their work at the program level. The family assessment form (FAF) has been developed during the past 10 years through an interactive process involving direct service practitioners, administrators, and researchers at the Children's Bureau of Southern California (McCroskey & Nelson, 1989; McCroskey, Nishimoto, & Subramanian, 1991; Pecora, Fraser, Nelson, McCroskey, & Meezan, 1995). The FAF was originally designed to help practitioners in home-based child abuse prevention and treatment programs assess the strengths and problems of families, prioritize family needs, develop targeted service plans, and assess the effectiveness of services. Since its development, the FAF has also been used by practitioners in agencies providing a broad range of other services. These other services include preventive maternal and child health care, child care, substance abuse treatment, parent education, and foster care and adoption services. Accordingly, the FAF has been used to assess the strengths and problems of many different kinds of families. (The FAF is available from the Children's Bureau of Southern California, 3910 Oakwood Avenue, Los Angeles, CA 90004.)

FAF qualities found to be valuable by users include practice relevance and ecological orientation to the functioning of whole families within their environments. Few family functioning instruments serve the immediate needs of practitioners, program evaluators, and administrators (Pecora et al., 1995). When the FAF was first developed, it was thought that participation of practitioners in instrument development would ensure buy-in of workers and practice relevance. The first set of workers felt ownership of this tool in a way that they would not have felt with any form suggested by an outside researcher, especially one designed for research purposes. Yet, staff members who came to the agency after the FAF was developed and those who have used it in other agency contexts have also felt positive about the FAF. It appears that the FAF's usefulness in defining the information needed about families in a logical structure and order is more important than participation in the development process. It is important to note, however, that the FAF has worked least well in agencies that have imposed or required its use without consulting staff members. It has worked best when staff have been given the opportunity to adjust and refine the form to fit their own purposes and context. The Children's Bureau of Southern California suggests that agencies involve staff members in discussing the form and that the FAF be adapted to fit different agency purposes.

Reports from agencies and practitioners who have reviewed and used the form have provided a cross-section of perspectives beyond the child abuse and neglect prevention perspective that informed instrument development. Not surprisingly, people with these different perspectives have also suggested areas in which the FAF could use further development, clarification, or augmentation.

Also, the FAF was used as one of the primary instruments in a recent study of the effects of family preservation programs on family functioning for abusive and neglectful families (McCroskey & Meezan, in press; Meezan & McCroskey, 1996; Pecora et al., 1995). The research included a factor analysis that helped identify the six major conceptual underpinnings of the form: (1) living conditions of the family, (2) financial conditions of the family, (3) social support available to the family, (4) relationships between caregivers, (5) interactions between caregivers and children, and (6) developmental stimulation for children. This research also identified a subset of 34 items of more than 100 included in the FAF that are most important to measure for purposes of tracking outcomes.

Conclusion

On the basis of these results, as well as reactions of many different agency users over time, the Children's Bureau is currently revising the instrument for publication by the Child Welfare League of America. (A revised form will soon be available through the Child Welfare League of America. The Children's Bureau will readily grant permission to use the form but would like to keep track of its use in multiple versions and settings.) With help from the Stuart Foundations, a group of experienced FAF users were convened to assist in this revision and to ensure the relevance of the form across different kinds of practice settings. If the FAF is to remain relevant to practitioners facing a host of changes in communities and families, it will require periodic updating and revision. The desire to ensure practice relevance, rather than a focus on standardization or psychometric properties, is one of the qualities that differentiate the FAF from many of the research-oriented instruments currently available. In the context of the FAF, outcomes measurement helps practitioners understand the complexities of family functioning, plan services, and evaluate their effectiveness. It can also help agencies better train and supervise workers and demonstrate the results of different kinds of programs used to help families build on their own strengths to improve the lives of their children.

References

Center for the Study of Social Policy. (1993). *KIDS COUNT data book: State profiles of child well-being*. Washington, DC: Author.

McCroskey, J., & Meezan, W. (in press). *Family preservation and family functioning.* Washington, DC: Child Welfare League of America.

McCroskey, J., & Nelson, J. (1989). Practice-based research in a family support program: The family connection project example. *Child Welfare, 67,* 574–589.

McCroskey, J., Nishimoto, R., & Subramanian, K. (1991). Assessment in family support programs: Initial reliability and validity testing of the family assessment form. *Child Welfare, 70,* 19–34.

Meezan, W., & McCroskey, J. (1996, Winter). Improving family functioning through family preservation services: Results of the Los Angeles experiment. *Family Preservation Journal*, 9–29.

Pecora, P., Fraser, M., Nelson, K., McCroskey, J., & Meezan, W. (1995). *Evaluating family-based services*. Hawthorne, NY: Aldine de Gruyter.

United Way of Greater Los Angeles. (1996). *State of the county report: Los Angeles 1996.* Los Angeles: Author.

United Way of Greater Los Angeles. (1997). *State of the county report: Los Angeles 1997.* Los Angeles: Author.

CHAPTER 17

Outcomes in the Context of Empirical Practice

RAMI BENBENISHTY

Managed care initiatives have increased interest in the outcomes of social work interventions. Such interest is not new. For many years questions regarding social work intervention effectiveness resulted in a growing focus on studying and evaluating outcomes. However, managed care has contributed to a move toward focusing attention on a narrow set of outcomes issues. As is evident in this book, much of the interest is technical in nature, focusing on a search for valid measures and methods. The search for valid outcomes information is carried out as a distinct effort, separate from other efforts to improve practice. Much of this activity is motivated by an effort to prove and document effectiveness rather than to learn how to become more effective.

Empirical Practice as Context

This chapter examines outcomes measurement within the context of the information foundation needed in empirical and accountable human service practice. This context provides a basis for addressing outcomes issues. Without this broader practice context the field may simply continue to react to outside pressures that may reflect an agenda quite different from what should guide the helping professions.

Empirical practice is "continuously informed and guided by empirical evidence that is systematically gathered and processed" (Benbenishty, 1996). Thus, in empirical forms of practice, practitioner information needs include data regarding outcomes but extend far beyond outcomes measurement. Instead of asking, "How effective are we?" an empirical practice orientation requires practitioners to ask a series of questions to help them become more effective. Therefore, a major task of proponents of empirical practice is to identify what types of information are needed to improve practice and what are the most effective methods to gather, process, and interpret this information.

This chapter focuses on both program-level and practitioner-level outcomes. At the program level, large evaluation and outcomes studies are evident. Program-level evaluations attempt to gather information regarding program or treatment outcomes. Recent evaluations of family preservation programs and their merits are an example of program evaluations (Schuerman, Rzepnicki, & Littell, 1994). At the practitioner level, single-subject evaluations are frequently used and are often conducted by practitioners studying a small number of clients.

This chapter suggests that social work and the allied human services move to a position between the program and the practitioner, a middle ground that focuses on practitioners within organizations (Benbenishty, 1989, 1996). This is a move to local generalization. Such local generalization creates a need to support empirical practice on the agency level and requires the gathering, processing, and interpretation of information by all practitioners within an agency. In this approach, the information needs of all agency personnel involved in shaping services are coordinated and aggregated: Practitioners, supervisors, administrators, managers, and policymakers all combine to create a learning environment that moves toward more effective practice. Given the task and the context, a new strategy should be formulated. Several principles to guide this formulation of effective empirical practice are proposed next.

Principles of Effective Empirical Practice

GATHER INFORMATION ON CLIENTS AND INTERVENTIONS

The current focus on outcomes measurement diverts attention from the need for an understanding of clients and of interventions that shape outcomes. Thus, before child welfare agency staff can deal with the complex question of family preservation intervention effectiveness, they need basic information about family characteristics and the details of the services provided to these families. Such information is needed to interpret outcomes data.

INTEGRATE SYSTEMATIC MONITORING INTO EVERYDAY PRACTICE

Large-scale, one-shot evaluation studies should be given low priority because resources are limited. Such studies have little generalizability across service contexts, and their findings are rarely disseminated in service delivery. Instead, systematic gathering and processing of information should be prioritized as an integral part of everyday practice. Monitoring efforts should be carried out by each practitioner with coordination and integration of these data conducted at the agency level (Benbenishty, 1989, 1996). This strategy will have a more direct and widespread impact on the quality of care provided to clients. Practitioners' ability to assess, plan, execute, monitor, adjust, and evaluate will be greatly enhanced as they become better informed about clients, interventions, and outcomes. Agencies can better adjust and improve as they become more informed and knowledgeable about their clients, practice, and outcomes.

INFORM PRACTITIONERS CONTINUOUSLY

An essential element of integrating systematic monitoring into practice is to inform practitioners of what is being learned as a regular part of practice. The responsibility for learning from experience shifts to the agency level. The feedback loop that consists of information gathering, processing, learning, and planning becomes shorter because it is contained in-house. The agency becomes an autonomous learning organization, which is a shift from two current models: (1) the practitioner–researcher model, which focuses on the individual worker learning from his or her experience, and (2) the research dissemination model, which counts on academic research filtering to individual practitioners.

BUILD ON LOCAL GENERALIZATIONS

The previous principle implies that the ability to generalize from what is learned in each agency will be limited. Rather than seeking to establish general practice principles and methods, much more limited and local generalizations are pursued. Several learning organizations may form a learning community. Sharing and comparing local generalizations may prove an effective way to assess differential impact in varying service contexts.

INTEGRATE INFORMATION TECHNOLOGY INTO PRACTICE

The only practical way to follow the above principles is to make computers an integral part of practice. Computer-enriched environments are required to address the information needs of each practitioner, the agency as a whole, and interagency systems. Many agencies currently are increasing their use of computers. However, provision of computers alone will not result in full use without a plan for such use. Under such circumstances computers will have a limited impact on improvement of services to clients. Agencies should assess how information can improve their practice and then design and implement computerized systems. Computers can become an integral part of the learning organization, and their use can facilitate the creation of the learning community.

A Child Welfare Agency Case Example

If these principles were implemented, what might happen in practice? How will outcomes be affected? In an imaginary child welfare agency that provides foster care, practitioners gather information about children and families in systematic and consistent ways. All practitioners use a core set of forms and tools, including scales that were published in the professional literature, were shown to be valid, and have established standards as to "normal" and "clinical" scores. Other information-gathering tools are "homegrown" instruments that reflect the specific needs of the agency. Also, several assessment tools are being used only in certain cases. For instance, when there is an indication that the child or adolescent may be endangering himself or herself, a suicide risk assessment is performed.

Information is gathered on a continuous basis rather than just when reports to outside agencies are due. Practitioners gather information on child and family characteristics; monitor changes in key issues regarding the children, families, and the interaction among them; report on services and interventions provided; document resources allocated to families; and provide assessments regarding status, progress, and outcomes. Given the competing demands on practitioners' attention, time devoted to information gathering and documenting is being kept to the necessary minimum. Coordination among all partners in the agency ensures that each is gathering the information most relevant to his or her tasks, and duplication is avoided.

An information system is designed for the particular needs of this agency. All information gathering is done with computers. Software guides the practitioner as to what information is required. As information is entered into the computer, the information system provides guidance and advice. Some of this guidance is more technical in nature and can be seen as low-level supervising and quality assurance. Other elements of this immediate feedback can be seen as expert advice.

Suggestions, references, and alerts are based on the expertise of agency personnel, on the professional literature, and on lessons learned from the cumulative experience of the agency. For example, a worker entering the description of a two-year-old girl who lost her parents in an accident may be advised to consider adoption. A worker entering information about an adolescent who has run away from the foster home for the third time may encounter a short note indicating that the experience of this agency with adolescents who ran away more than once has been negative, and a team meeting may be advised.

The continuous stream of information provided by practitioners at all levels creates the reliable agency database. Each item of information entered into the system has been inspected several times, and practitioners and supervisors have discussed its accuracy. Reports have been submitted to state authorities, and testimonies to courts have been based on this information. Most of the information has also been presented to biological and foster families and, when appropriate, to the child in question.

This database provides the kinds of answers that empirical practice requires. It provides descriptive information about the children, their life circumstances, strengths and difficulties, family background and current status, experience in care, and the outcomes of their stay. This information is most useful for treatment planning. Thus, in this imaginary agency, a caseload in one site consists mainly of African American children, four years old and younger, whereas the other site primarily handles white adolescents. This information has clear implications for planning services and interventions.

Descriptive information is also provided on the services rendered by this agency. The aggregation of the information provided by all practitioners tells the story of the agency as a whole. This descriptive information may provide important insights as to what is being emphasized and what is being neglected as well as what proportion of efforts are spent in each of the tasks that face the agency. This picture may serve as corrective feedback to each practitioner and to the agency as a whole.

Furthermore, the juxtaposition of information on the clients and the services provided can have a major impact on the provision of care in the future. In this agency the analysis may indicate that children in a certain neighborhood receive twice the amount of individual therapy as children in another area. This finding may be explained on the basis of the differential needs of these children, and this differential allocation of resources can be justified. If no clear reason for this difference in treatment can be discerned, the agency may need to make some changes in resource allocation. This corrective action, and the ensuing possible improvement in fairness and effectiveness, is possible because information was gathered on clients and services.

The agency can consider outcomes on the basis of a solid understanding of clients and services. The database has information on child and family status at several points in time during stay in care. It is possible to assess degree of change and to identify whether changes are more evident on some indicators than others. The final outcomes of care, such as the child's disposition and other outcomes indicators, can be described in detail. Statistics such as average stay in care are computed accurately and effortlessly.

Given the components of client characteristics, intervention, and outcomes, the agency can examine questions such as the relationship between them. The complexities involved in such examinations are formidable, and it is unlikely that clear answers will emerge immediately. Only tentative conclusions relevant to this specific agency are offered and discussed with staff. Some of the lessons learned from the analysis are clear enough to be folded back as advice and conclusions for future practice, whereas other conclusions are offered as working hypotheses. Some changes are introduced into the information-gathering process so that future analysis can be more accurate.

The process is continuous. The agency is on a continuous loop of self-learning. This imaginary agency provides a semiannual report to all practitioners. This detailed but nontechnical report outlines what has been learned, what changes are evident when compared with previous reports, and some tentative conclusions and implications for practice. Given the major differences between sites unearthed by this process, a site-specific report may be generated.

Another agency may become interested in the process. It is clear that lessons learned in one agency cannot be generalized "as is" to another one. The experience of major differences among sites is a clear warning against unwarranted generalizations. Therefore, the learning site is duplicated. Thus, after a while, these two agencies can share their findings and identify what is similar and what is not. Together it is easier to sort out circumstances and interventions that affect outcomes. This learning community can expand as the advantages of information for empirical practice become clearer.

Conclusion

This is a realistic vision of the future. It does not require more resources than are currently spent to improve practice; it requires a different focus. In fact, it requires the breaking up of the current focus. Instead of a narrow emphasis on outcomes and on broad generalization, a much wider information base and a much lower level of generalization regarding practice and practice outcomes are necessary.

An agency that is able to create this type of information environment is better prepared than others to face the challenge of accountable practice. Such an agency will have a better chance to provide quality service and will stand a better chance of surviving the challenges facing human services in an era of shrinking political and financial support.

References

Benbenishty, R. (1989). Combining single-system and group comparison aproaches to evaluate treatment effectiveness on the agency level. *Journal of Social Service Research, 12,* 31–48.

Benbenishty, R. (1996). Integrating reserach and practice: Time for a new agenda. *Research on Social Work Practice, 6,* 77–82.

Schuerman, J. R., Rzepnicki, T. L., & Littell, J. H. (1994). *Putting families first: An experiment in family preservation.* New York: Aldine de Gruyter.

PART IV

Outcomes Measurement in Health

PART IVA

Conceptual and Methodolgical Dimensions

CHAPTER 18

The Development of Health-Related Quality-of-Life Measures at RAND

IAN D. COULTER

This chapter traces the historical development of Health-Related Quality-of-Life Measures (HRQL) with respect to patient-reported outcomes at RAND, discusses current work, and focuses on patient satisfaction as an exemplar of the process of development and evolution of specific instruments. The chapter examines the major psychometric demands made for reliable and valid instruments. The work on HRQL at RAND can be construed as evolving attempts to answer two broad questions left unanswered by two landmark studies (the Medical Outcomes Study and the Health Insurance Experiment): (1) whether the instruments developed were reliable and valid for other populations and (2) whether shorter, more efficient scales, could be developed with similar psychometric properties.

RAND

RAND is a nonprofit institution dedicated to furthering and promoting scientific, educational, and charitable purposes for the public welfare and security of the United States. Its mission is to improve public policy through research and analysis. RAND operates in terms of independent public interest research, policy orientation coupled with research depth, multidisciplinary approach to policy problems, nonpartisan and nonproprietary research, rigorous peer reviews, self-initiated research, and broad-based dissemination of research findings. The organizational structure of RAND includes a domestic research division incorporating the health sciences, which is the area responsible for the development of HRQL measures.

HRQL Development

HRQL has been defined as how well an individual functions in daily life and the individual's perceived well-being (Hays, Anderson, & Revicki, 1995). At RAND the development of HRQL arose from four interrelated key issues of health research of the 1970s: (1) the increasing demand to measure clinical effectiveness and clinical outcomes, (2) the problem of measuring quality of care, (3) acceptance of the value of the patient's perspective in assessing quality of care, and (4) the increasing demand for psychometrically acceptable instruments in terms of reliability and validity.

Each of these issues confronted the researchers at RAND with significant challenges whose solutions were largely reached in two pivotal studies that stand as exemplars for RAND research: (1) the Health Insurance Experiment (HIE), begun in 1975, and (2) the Medical Outcomes Study (MOS), begun in 1986.

THE HEALTH INSURANCE EXPERIMENT

The HIE was a five-year controlled experiment investigating the impact of variations in health insurance on utilization patterns and health outcomes. The HIE enrolled a total of 2,750 families who were randomly assigned to a variety of health plans with differing payment and copayment formulas. The experiment included a variety of cost-sharing coverage plans that could then be correlated with outcomes. A key issue was whether the variance in coverage led to systematic differences in health outcomes. The HIE provided a unique opportunity to develop HRQL measures. Ware (1992) noted that the HIE was "one of the most extensive applications of psychometric theory and methods to the development and refinement of health status surveys" (p. 5). Both the extent of the project and the amount of funding ($80 million) allowed RAND to assemble a team of methodologists to focus on measurement issues. The study was notable in at least three major ways: (1) the extensive use of psychometric methods for measuring health status, (2) the use of a broad range of instruments to measure well-being, and (3) the use of self-administered surveys that were shown to be reliable and valid. These features established in the HIE characterize the RAND work on HRQL.

The HIE measures included physical, mental, and social functioning and general health perceptions. However, the HIE left two questions unanswered (Stewart & Ware, 1992). Would the same instruments and scales work on sicker and older populations? Could more efficient scales be constructed? HRQL work at RAND since the HIE can be construed as continuing attempts to answer both questions over a broad range of patients, illnesses, and health care settings. Ware (1992) noted that the MOS provided the next large-scale opportunity to test the use of self-administered questionnaires and generic health scales for chronic illnesses and older patients.

THE MEDICAL OUTCOMES STUDY

Although the MOS continued the objective of developing psychometrically sound instruments, it also took into account patient burden and collection costs. Both the funding and the patient type (older and chronically ill) demanded that the instruments be feasible and practical (Stewart & Ware, 1992), which meant, in large part, that the instruments should be shorter. Furthermore, the MOS tested both long and short forms of the instruments to enable the calculation of return in relation to costs and effort. Because it also used self-administered questionnaires, the MOS was a pivotal demonstration of techniques that have been widely used by RAND since the MOS.

The MOS was a quasi-experimental study focusing on variations in physician practice style and patient outcomes in different health care delivery systems (Tarlov, 1992; Tarlov et al., 1989). An essential feature of the MOS was that patients with different medical and psychiatric conditions completed the same instruments. Furthermore, the measures were done both cross-sectionally and longitudinally and controlled for disease severity and other aspects of clinical status.

The MOS was also characterized by use of a multidimensional model of health, standardized measures, self-administered questionnaires, and functioning and well-being measures; by involvement of generic measures and testing across new populations; by description of chronic disease; and by development of new items and new scales.

The size of the effort in the MOS was also unique, spanning the 1980s and 1990s. At least 36 scales were developed for the project. Approximately 22,000 patients were sampled from 523 medical practices. At the time of the visit with the physician, approximately 2,500 patients were followed up longitudinally for four years.

The MOS increased understanding of existing measures, improved measures, constructed new measures, and attempted to measure new health concepts. The measures were generic—that is, they were not specific for any one age, disease, or treatment group. They assessed basic human values and HRQL outcomes. The categories measured included clinical status, physical functioning and well-being, mental functioning, social and role functioning, and general health perceptions. New measures were developed for health distress, social activity limitations, family and sexual functioning, role functioning, pain, physical and psychophysiologic symptoms, and sleep. Other measures were revised. Work is still continuing on the MOS, and the Patient Satisfaction Questionnaire (PSQ) (Marshall & Hays, 1994) and the MOS Short Form General Health Surveys (SF-36, SF-20) (Hays, Sherbourne, & Mazel, 1993) have been used extensively.

Current Work at RAND

The current work at RAND differs in some significant ways from the HIE and the MOS. Although both projects were responsible for establishing "psychometric teams" with the specific objective of developing instruments, current HRQL work tends to be an inherent part of most projects and is project specific. No team exists at RAND specifically for the purpose of developing such instruments. Much work has been done at RAND and at other institutions since the development of HIE and MOS, and many more instruments are now available. The work of expanding their use over differing patient groups continues. Two current projects illustrate some of the features of the approach used in the HIE and the MOS and at the same time demonstrate the differences.

The Exploratory Center for Research on Health Promotion in Older Minority Populations (RAND/Drew University, Martin Luther King Junior Hospital) has used a centralized team to evaluate and select the psychometric instruments to be used over a wide range of projects in the center. (This project is funded by the National Institute for Aging [NIA]; the principal investigator is Walter Allen.) However, this project extends previous work by validating the instruments in minority populations. The HIV Cost Services Utilization Study similarly has a group of methodologists developing a core set of instruments for the interviews using previously developed instruments such as the SF-36 and instruments developed specifically for this study. Here the extension of the instruments is to a specfic illness type, the human immunodeficiency virus (HIV).

The Evolution of Patient Satisfaction Instruments

Perhaps the best concept for describing the development of HRQL instruments is *evolution,* which can be illustrated by examining the development of patient satisfaction measures at RAND. Patient satisfaction has become an integral part of outcome measures. As Ware (1992) noted, "A medical outcome has come to mean the extent to which a change in a patient's functioning or well-being meets the patient's needs or expectations" (p. 3). In chapter 4 of this book, Ware elaborates on these measures and in chapter 19, Berkman discusses applications in social work. Donabedian (1980) suggested that patient satisfaction is a fundamental measure of the quality of care.

PATIENT SATISFACTION QUESTIONNAIRE

A generic measure asks the patient for an evaluation in a given time frame, such as six months, whereas the visit-specific measure collects data during a single visit to the provider (Ware & Hays, 1988). The Patient Satisfaction Questionnaire (PSQ) was a periodic measure initially developed at Southern Illinois University by Ware and Karmos (1976). Figure 18-1 diagrams the evolution of this instrument through several RAND studies.

The PSQ was reduced in size and used in the HIE and in the MOS as a periodic instrument. It was used again in the CHAMPUS Study (Sloss & Hosek, 1993) but had been further reduced to 18 items from the initial 68 items. The MOS also developed a derivative from the PSQ, which was not a periodic instrument but was visit specific (VSQ) and contained only nine items.

The original PSQ has several major features. Its item stems refer to specific features of care in general. The response scale is a Likert scale ranging from "strongly agree" to "strongly disagree." It can be either self-administered or administered through an oral interview. It has multi-item subscales that measure distinct dimensions. The original PSQ measures seven dimensions of care (which have become almost standard dimension of such instruments): (1) interpersonal manner of the provider, (2) technical quality, (3) accessibility and convenience, (4) finances, (5) efficacy and outcomes, (6) continuity of care, and (7) overall satisfaction.

The psychometric properties of the PSQ have been documented extensively (Marshall, Hays, Sherbourne, & Wells, 1993; Ware, Snyder, Wright, & Davies, 1983).

Figure 18-1

EVOLUTION OF THE PATIENT SATISFACTION QUESTIONNAIRE

Southern Illinois University
PSQ I (68 items), generic

↓

HIE RAND
PSQ II (43 items)

↓

MOS RAND → MOS RAND
PSQ III (50 items) | VSQ (9 items) Visit specific

MOS RAND	→ MOS RAND
PSQ III (50 items)	VSQ (9 items) Visit specific
↓	↓
CHAMPUS Study RAND	Chiropractic Satisfaction
PSQ IV (18 items)	Questionnaire (14 items)
	Visit specific

Note: HIE = Health Insurance Experiment; MOS = Medical Outcomes Study; PSQ = Patient Satisfaction Questionnaire; VSQ = Visit-specific Questionnaire.

In the MOS the PSQ was extensively tested before it was used. It was initially tested during a four-year period in 12 separate studies and replicated in four field tests. The constructs were based on an extensive review of the literature, and the items were generated by the use of group sessions. The 2,300 items were reduced to 500 in this process. The items are based on the vernacular of the patients. Independent judges were used to sort the items into content categories.

The extent of testing done on the PSQ is unique. Response format categories, number of response categories, personal versus general experiences, oral versus self-administered forms, placement of items within the PSQ in both interviews and questionnaires, time needed to complete the PSQ, and response set effects (for example, acquiescence and socially desirable responses) were among the categories tested.

Two methods were used to test the reliability of the PSQ: (1) internal consistency and (2) test–retest measures. In the initial 18 subscales, 60 of 72 internal consistency estimates exceeded .50 (Cronbach's alpha) (Cronbach, 1951), and on the test–retest of 17 subscales, 28 of 34 test–retest estimates exceeded .50 (at six weeks).

The PSQ is multidimensional and has replicated consistently over independent field tests. Four higher-order factors were identified with the original PSQ: (1) quality of care, (2) access to care, (3) availability of resources, and (4) continuity of care.

In comparison of scale scores to open-ended questions, the PSQ has shown good convergent and discriminant validity with the exception of interpersonal manner. However, three issues remained regarding the PSQ after the MOS: (1) whether the PSQ detects satisfaction by different systems of care, (2) whether the PSQ provides useful information about the source of satisfaction and dissatisfaction, and (3) whether the subscales measure different dimensions. The first two concerns led to the development of a hybrid instrument, the Outpatient Satisfaction Questionnaire (OSQ-37) (Hays, 1995).

OUTPATIENT SATISFACTION QUESTIONNAIRE

The Outpatient Satisfaction Questionnaire is an ambulatory care instrument developed by RAND researchers in collaboration with Value Health Sciences, Santa Monica, California (Hays, 1995). The OSQ-37 has 37 items and takes approximately seven minutes to complete. The instrument includes six dimensions: (1) interpersonal quality of care, (2) technical quality, (3) understanding of health problems, (4) financial aspects, (5) access and convenience, and (6) overall satisfaction.

The item stems consist of statements about different aspects of care with seven response categories ranging from "very poor" to "the best." It is self-administered. All items are used in scoring. Each item appears in only one subscale, and higher scores indicate higher satisfaction. The OSQ-37 has been tested in three independent studies with 400 patients. Estimates for reliability exceed .90 for interpersonal quality, technical quality, and access and convenience; .89 for financial matters; and .87 for overall satisfaction. Correlations between satisfaction and specific aspects of medical care ranged from .69 to .87, and interpersonal and technical quality were most strongly related to overall satisfaction. The six dimensions correlated well with alternative measures of satisfaction that dealt with possible improvements in medical care. They also correlated with willingness to recommend the provider to others, getting care elsewhere, and telling others about the care. Patient satisfaction was significantly correlated with allegiance, gender, age, education level, better health, complaints about care received, and rating of care relative to other care. In summary, the OSQ-37 has been shown to have good internal consistency, good item discrimination across the subscales, supportive validity coefficients, and distinguishes successfully between patients' perception of interpersonal and technical quality of care (Hays, 1995).

THE CHIROPRACTIC SATISFACTION QUESTIONNAIRE: AN EXAMPLE OF OSQ–37 ADAPTATION

This instrument is a derivative of the OSQ-37 but has been designed specifically for ambulatory care in a chiropractic clinic. It consists of 14 items, 13 of which deal with specific features of care and one of which deals with general satisfaction. The dimensions covered include interpersonal quality of care (eight items), technical quality (three items), time spent with the chiropractor (one item), cost of care (one item), and overall satisfaction (one item).

The rating scale is a Likert scale ranging from "very poor" to "the best." The instrument has been tested on 486 patients and has been shown to have internal consistency of .95 (Coulter, Hays, & Danielson, 1994). Its items are unidimensional. The CSQ-14 also correlated significantly with patient confidence that treatment would be successful and with how much the patient thought he or she was helped by the care. Patients who rated their chiropractor in the top 20 percent were three times more likely to report that they were helped by the care than patients who rated their chiropractor in the bottom 20 percent. The CSQ-14 also correlated significantly with a three-item allegiance score. Patients rating their chiropractor in the top 20 percent are more likely to report they would return for care than those in the bottom 20 percent. The CSQ-14 is currently being tested on 2,300 patients in managed care in the state of Washington and on 1,000 patients in a national survey of chiropractic offices.

Conclusion

This discussion illustrates that, as the frequent references to these measures throughout this book show, HRQL measures have become an integral and standard part of research at RAND. As new projects arise, the present instruments are adapted and tested, and new ones are created. Each project offers an opportunity to continue the psychometric testing of the instruments and to expand the database on their reliability and validity. Instruments initially developed on acutely ill institutionalized patients are expanded to chronically ill ambulatory patients, instruments developed for medical patients are expanded to include chiropractic patients, and so on. The instruments become more efficient in the process. There is therefore a constant evolution of the instruments, and the original instruments have produced several progeny.

Some of the remaining challenges are the same as those that existed at the conclusion of the HIE, such as whether the instruments are reliable and valid across varying populations and whether they can be made more efficient without drastic loss of information.

However, some new challenges are being confronted. There is increasing attention being applied to the use of cross-cultural measures in countries around the world. "Performance of HRQL across different cultural groups has rarely been studied" (Hays et al., 1995, p. 109). Such studies raise several major issues including item-translational equivalence, operational equivalence, scale equivalence, and order equivalence (Hui & Triandis, 1985).

Equally significant is the work being done on the development of culturally sensitive instruments within the United States. In studies of patient satisfaction, variables such as ethnicity and race have been shown to be minor predictors of satisfaction. However, few studies are designed to collect culturally relevant information, and most do not report ethnic-specific results. To date, "variables, such as race, can relate directly to satisfaction in one study, inversely in another and be unrelated in a third" (Fox & Storms, 1981, p. 557). Therefore, it is not clear whether the results are an artifact of the instruments or whether such things as race are truly not significant predictors of satisfaction. Given the significance of demographic variables generally, the latter result raises some important sociological questions. Therefore, the goal of current work is to develop reliable and valid instruments but also to develop instruments that are culturally sensitive and that are tested over a wide spectrum not only of patient categories but also of social categories such as race, ethnicity, gender, and social class.

References

Coulter, I. D., Hays, R. D., & Danielson, C. D. (1994). The Chiropractic Satisfaction Questionnaire. *Topics in Clinical Chiropractice, 1* (4), 40–43.

Cronbach, L. J. (1951). Coefficient alpha and the internal structure of tests. *Psychometrika, 16,* 297–334.

Donabedian, A. (1980). *The definition of quality and approaches to its assessment.* Ann Arbor, MI: Health Administration Press.

Fox, G., & Storms, D. H. (1981). A different approach to sociodemographic predictors of satisfaction with health care. *Social Science and Medicine, 154,* 557–564.

Hays, R. D. (1995). *The Outpatient Satisfaction Questionnaire (OSQ-37)* (P-7885). Santa Monica, CA: RAND.

Hays, R. D., Anderson, R., & Revicki, D. A. (1995). Psychometric evaluation and interpretation of health-related quality of life data. In S. Shumaker & R. Berzon (Eds.), *The international assessment of health-related quality of life: Theory, translation, measurement and analysis* (pp. 103–114). Oxford, England: Rapid Communications.

Hays R. D., Sherbourne, C. D., & Mazel, R. M. (1993). The RAND-36 Item Health Survey 1.0. *Health Economics, 2,* 217–227.

Hui, C., & Triandis, H. C. (1985). Measurement in cross-cultural psychology: A review and comparison of strategies. *Cross Cultural Psychology, 16,* 131–152.

Marshall, G. N., & Hays, R. D. (1994). *The Patient Satisfaction Questionnaire Short-Form (PSQ-18)* (P-7865). Santa Monica, CA: RAND.

Marshall, G. N., Hays, R. D., Sherbourne, C. D., & Wells, K. B. (1993). The structure of patient satisfaction with outpatient medical care. *Psychological Assessment, 5,* 477–483.

Sloss, E. M., & Hosek, S. D. (1993). *Evaluation of the CHAMPUS Reform Inititative. Beneficiary Access and Satisfaction, Vol. 2* (R-4244/2-HAQ). Santa Monica, CA: RAND.

Stewart, A. L., & Ware, J. E. (Eds.). (1992). *Measuring functioning and well-being.* Durham, NC: Duke University Press.

Tarlov, A. R. (1992). Foreword. In A. L. Stewart & J. E. Ware (Eds.), *Measuring functioning and well-being* (pp. xv–xvi). Durham, NC: Duke University Press.

Tarlov, A. R., Ware, J. E., Greenfield, S., Nelson, E. C., Perrin, E., & Zubkoff, M. (1989). *The Medical Outcomes Study: An application of methods for monitoring the results of medical care* (N-3038-RWJ/HJK/PMT). Santa Monica, CA: RAND.

Ware, J. E. (1992). Measures for a new era of health asessment. In A. L. Stewart & J. E. Ware (Eds.), *Measuring functioning and well-being* (pp. 3–11). Durham, NC: Duke University Press.

Ware, J. E., & Hays, R. D. (1988). Methods for measuring patient satisfaction with specific medical encounters. *Medical Care, 26*, 393–402.

Ware J. E., & Karmos, A. H. (1976). Scales for measuring general health perceptions. *Health Services Research, 11*, 396–415.

Ware, J. E., Snyder, M. K., Wright, W. R., & Davies, A. R. (1983). Defining and measuring patient satisfaction with medical care. *Evaluation and Program Planning, 6*, 247–263.

CHAPTER 19

Outcomes Measurement for Social Work Research and Practice in Health Care

BARBARA BERKMAN

The importance of outcomes-focused research is not new to social workers and other human service professionals. However, only recently has outcomes research received priority over studies of program process and structure. The health-related quality of life (HRQL) standardized outcomes measures and studies have been the primary force in this refocusing. Standardization is critical for reproducibility and for comparisons between patient groups. This new capability to assess outcomes through standardized measures allows uniform screening, consistency in treatment decision making, consistent client progress monitoring, and monitoring of quality while freeing practitioners to experiment with varying structures and processes toward identification of better outcomes.

The current focus on outcomes measurement means that attention is given to quality-of-life outcomes that are important to clients. Why has the role of the client become the focus? It is now accepted that clients must participate in treatment choices and that their perceptions may differ from those of their health care providers. Understanding and responding to client perceptions is believed to promote compliance with health care recommendations, and evaluating care from a client perspective tells whether the care provided had the desired result or effect on the client. For example, does a particular combination of services provided at a certain level of cost produce optimal client perception of outcomes? If the cost of optimal care is too high, to what extent does quality in outcomes suffer from the client's point of view if services are cut? In the current era of critically and chronically ill patients cared for by health organizations that are experiencing staff shortages as well as cost controls, measuring the effect on the health care consumer of the industry's doing "more with less" is important. Analyzing client perception of outcomes allows such measurement.

Outcomes represent the effect of one or more processes on a patient at a defined point in time. Such measures can be taken during in-hospital treatment, at hospital discharge, or at some follow-up point during or after outpatient care. HRQL outcomes measurements are positively perceived by social workers primarily because measures are made of social work as practiced rather than under controlled clinical trials and because HRQL questions focus on the effects of interventions on HRQL dimensions of importance to clients such as social functioning and mental health status.

This chapter focuses on measurement of social work client outcomes in health care. It is impossible at present to determine the specific effects of most social work services on clients because outcomes research has not been widely conducted. Outcomes research should use standardized HRQL measures. By using standardized conceptual definitions and measurements and by focusing on the effects of intervention on health-related components of quality of life that are important to clients, social workers then can look at those dimensions most relevant to practice. Too frequently health outcomes have been defined narrowly, focusing on biological dimensions. HRQL measures extend the physiological to the functional and some psychosocial components of importance to social work. It is hoped that these measures will be extended further in the psychosocial arena. Such measures are a first step in multidimensional, multistage diagnostic screening (Chen, Broadhead, Doe, & Broyles, 1993). HRQL measures can identify possible functional or emotional deficits in patients. Such identification permits clinicians to direct needed services to individual patients. For example, breast cancer patients considering radical mastectomy will have varying degrees of anxiety and fear. An assessment of functional impairment associated with such anxiety could lead to selective use of preoperative interventions to alleviate fears and improve functioning.

Selecting Measures of HRQL

There are conceptual and methodological questions to be answered when evaluating measures for appropriateness to social work, such as conceptual linkage to the intervention, validity, reliability, sensitivity, and practicality of administration. A number of HRQL outcomes measures are suited for social work clinical practice and research (Nelson & Berwick, 1989). This chapter focuses on the Health Status Questionnaire (SF-36) (Ware & Sherbourne, 1992), a widely used HRQL measure that is of considerable relevance to social work practice in health settings. By presenting applications of the SF-36 in social work health settings, this chapter complements discussions of the SF-36 and general discussion of HRQL measures presented in previous chapters.

The SF-36

As noted in chapters 4 and 18, the SF-36 was developed at RAND as part of the Medical Outcomes Study (Ware & Sherbourne, 1992) and New England Medical Center in Boston, where Ware is now based. The SF-36 was designed for use in clinical practice and research, health policy evaluations, and general population surveys. It is based on the assumption that health care should be evaluated for its impact not just on morbidity and mortality but also on the client's view of its effect on quality of life.

The SF-36 was constructed for self-administration by people 14 years of age and older or for administration by a trained interviewer in person or by telephone. It can be completed in less than 10 minutes, can be administered in a waiting room or mailed to the respondent, and can be scored with optical scanning or by hand. For each scale, responses are summed and scored on a scale ranging from 0 to 100, with a score of 100 indicating best functioning or well-being. The SF-36 is brief yet comprehensive, composed of short multi-item scales. Preliminary results support the use of SF-36 scales in studies based on group-level analyses. As described in chapters 4 and 18, studies are being conducted to extend the questionnaire's generalizability to additional client groups, and research is underway to assess its relevance for monitoring the outcomes of individual clients. Monitoring outcomes through a standardized HRQL measure such as the SF-36 has several potential benefits: Clients could describe their health more fully, health care practitioners could learn of their interventive limitations and strengths, change could be tracked, and screening for deterioration could be done.

Although there are shorter versions (for example, SF-20 [Ware, Sherbourne, & Davies, 1992]), the most widely used version (SF-36) has 36 questions assessing eight dimensions: (1) limitations in physical activities because of health problems, (2) limitations in social activities because of physical or emotional problems, (3) limitations in usual role activities because of physical health problems, (4) bodily pain, (5) general mental health (psychological distress and well-being), (6) limitations in usual role activities because of emotional problems, (7) vitality (energy and fatigue), and (8) general health perceptions.

SF–36 AND SOCIAL WORK HEALTH SETTINGS

Although the SF-36 includes seven distinct health status concepts and one item measuring self-reported health, some concepts important in social work are not measured. In the study reported here of elderly patients in primary care at Massachusetts General Hospital, questions were added to assess additional areas relevant to social work such as recent hospitalizations, use of the emergency department, death of significant others, and instrumental activities related to daily living.

STUDY QUESTIONS

Can the SF-36 be used as a screen for psychosocial needs?

This question raises other questions, such as whether SF-36 subscales correlate with additional social work items and, if so, is anything to be gained or lost by inclusion or deletion of the additional items? Preliminary analysis indicated that although many of the social work items were correlated with SF-36 scale scores, many were not. (The items not correlated included following dietary restrictions, using the telephone, problems with sleeping, memory, concentration, alcohol or drug abuse, hearing, vision, sexual functioning, urinary incontinence, ability to pay for medications, or caring for someone else.) Final analysis may show that items needed for screening purposes may be left in the questionnaire, but the questions that correlate with SF-36 scales may be deleted.

Can SF-36 cutoff scores that are predictive of need for social work assessment be identified?

Preliminary data on use of the SF-36 scores as a screen of need for assessment showed that there was a significant relationship between the care coordinator's decision to assess and SF-36 scale scores. Consistently, across all eight scales, the patients who received a telephone assessment had significantly lower mean scores on every SF-36 scale. In addition, there was a greater chance of intervention if the patient scored below 50 on three or more scales. There also was a significantly greater chance of the care coordinator intervening if there was a "yes" answer on three or more of the social work–specific questions. There was a significantly greater chance of assessment being necessary if the patient had been in the emergency department during the past six months, had experienced a death in the family, was divorced or separated, or was an older adult. For each of these factors, the patients who received interventions had significantly lower SF-36 scale scores on almost every scale.

Can SF-36 cutoff scores that are predictive of need for social work care management be identified?

Preliminary data showed a significant relationship between social work care coordination and the number of SF-36 scales on which a patient scores lower than 50. Of those for whom the care coordinator believed assessment plus follow-up care coordination was indicated, 73 percent were below the 50th percentile on three or more SF-36 scales. The general health scale was found to be particularly important. Patients for whom the social worker gave care coordination had significantly lower mean scores than those for whom coordination was not indicated ($p > .04$). Preliminary analysis found that the social worker gave care coordination significantly more to women than to men, 86 percent to 14 percent ($p > .002$, phi = .33). However, women scored significantly lower than men in physical functioning, physical role, emotional role, bodily pain, vitality, mental status, social role, and general health. Finally, the social worker gave significantly more coordination to those patients who lived alone, 60 percent to 40 percent ($p > .006$, phi = .30).

Analyzing Outcomes Data

Measures taken at initial assessment establish a baseline for periodic posttreatment measures that can be used to assess change. However, both baseline and change scores require comparison with appropriate sample statistics. Such comparisons may be done among samples drawn from one institution's population or against external populations. Normative and comparative data for social work outcomes still must be developed and disseminated. Until comparison data become available, analyses must depend on comparisons of health status scores among patient groups served at one location. A health status measurement project in the health care setting will not succeed unless it can provide useful and timely reporting to key users such as practitioners and administrators. Before initiating measurement projects and collecting data, basic analysis methods and reporting formats should be developed. This preparation will ensure that all necessary data items are collected and will permit participants to receive useful feedback as quickly as possible. Typical steps in analyzing outcomes data include

- describing the population in terms of demographics and clinical measures;
- describing HRQL status at baseline both for all patients and for clinically meaningful subsets such as cardiac patients, oncology patients, or patients in different stages of disease;
- evaluating appropriateness of treatment course (is it as expected?) and identifying process variations that may be associated with outcomes;
- describing outcomes, such as physiological outcomes, health status changes, and functional changes, for all patients and key subsets at posttest;
- comparing outcomes among key subsets at posttest; and
- identifying process variations associated with outcomes.

Four broad comparisons in outcomes analyses can be made: (1) outcomes of alternative treatments provided to similar patients, (2) outcomes of a specific treatment given to different types of patients, (3) providers performing the same treatment on similar patient groups, and (4) treatment effects over time.

Conclusion

Despite advances in measuring outcomes and the early favorable experiences with their use in research studies, HRQL instruments are not widely used in clinical practice. Properties of measurement tools must continue to evolve toward higher levels of convenience and acceptability to the practitioner. Brevity, ease of administration, ease of scoring, and simplicity of interpretation all will be requirements for any instrument with a chance of achieving widespread use in stressed practice situations. Furthermore, acceptable tools must be comfortable for patients, meaning that they should be visually well-designed for comprehensibility and convenience of response. Early experience in using the SF-36 indicates that it may serve as a screen of need for social work services in primary care and may become a useful outcomes measure of social work intervention.

References

Chen, A.L.T., Broadhead, W. E., Doe, E. A., & Broyles, W. K. (1993, September). Patient acceptance of two health status measures: The Medical Outcomes Study Short-Form General Health Survey and the Duke Health Profile. *Family Medicine, 25*, 536–539.

Nelson, E. C., & Berwick, D. M. (1989). The measurement of health status in clinical practice. *Medical Care, 27* (3 suppl.), S77–S90.

Ware, J. E., & Sherbourne, C. D. (1992). The MOS 36-item short-form health survey (SF-36), I: Conceptual framework and item selection. *Medical Care, 30*, 473–483.

Ware, J. E., Sherbourne, C. D., & Davies, A. R. (1992). Developing and testing the MOS 20-Item Short-Form Health Survey: A general population application. In A. L. Stewart & J. E. Ware (Eds.), *Measuring functioning and well-being: The Nedical Outcomes Study approach* (pp. 277–290). Durham, NC: Duke University Press.

CHAPTER 20

Using Available Information in Practice-Based Outcomes Research: A Case Study of Psychosocial Risk Factors and Liver Transplant Outcomes

IRWIN EPSTEIN

FELICE ZILBERFEIN

STEPHEN L. SNYDER

This chapter examines the merits of using available health information for outcomes measurement in effectiveness studies and reviews recent literature comparing outcomes studies based on available data with those based on randomized, controlled trials (RCT) in medical effectiveness research. A methodological debate within social work research is examined, and it is suggested that rather than being obsessed with failures to achieve the "gold standard" of RCT social work research, more practice-based research should be conducted with available health information (Epstein, 1995). A study that uses routinely available information is described as an example.

Human service professionals in health care settings routinely record many types of psychosocial information including intake information, patient progress notes,

The authors wish to acknowledge the assistance of Martin Drooker, MD, Andrea Gannon, CSW, Carolyn Hutson, CSW, Joanne Lindbom, CSW, and Sandi Zelniker, CSW, in developing and testing the research instruments described in this chapter.

treatment objectives and intervention plans, and patient satisfaction surveys. This information is gathered for many purposes such as quality assurance, clinical supervision, accountability, accreditation, and billing and is rarely aggregated, integrated, and analyzed to systematically evaluate patient interventions and outcomes, to support patient care decisions, or to minimize patient care costs. Moreover, its usefulness for improving treatment effectiveness and efficiency is rarely explored and even more rarely exploited. Also, although problems of validity, reliability, and missing data are associated with available information, measures can be taken to minimize these problems. The possible savings associated with the conduct of effectiveness studies using routinely available data require serious consideration. Thus, in comparison with studies based on original data generation, available information studies are likely to raise fewer ethical problems, are faster and less costly to complete, are less disruptive to existing staff and patient care routines, and make use of compliance and outcomes indicators that are likely to be more agency and practice relevant. Hospital networks, health maintenance organizations, and drug companies have recently recognized the potential of available health information and have begun purchasing medical records and accumulating them in commercial databanks for research and marketing purposes (Kolata, 1995b).

Use of Available Data in Medical Effectiveness Research

In the words of Lawler and Raube (1995), a "medical outcomes movement" is currently underway, exemplified by "a national program of research" that "is radically reshaping the way health services are understood, justified, and delivered" (p. 383). Although the policy impetus for this movement is linked to managed care and cost control, much of the financial support for the conduct and dissemination of medical effectiveness research has come from the Agency for Health Care Policy and Research. Since 1989, through its Medical Treatment Effectiveness Program, this agency has sponsored several Patient Outcomes Research Team (PORT) projects to empirically assess the effectiveness of medical interventions for a wide range of conditions. In 1994, the Agency for Health Care Policy and Research (1995) sponsored a conference on measuring the effects of medical treatments.

Large, randomized, controlled experiments using standardized outcomes measures represent the gold standard within medical effectiveness research (Agency for Health Care Policy and Research, 1995). However, medical researchers have begun to question the wisdom of always going for the gold. In a review of published studies of the effectiveness of drugs to reduce excess cholesterol, Andrade, Walker, and Gottlieb (1995) questioned the generalizability of findings from RCTs to nonexperimental populations. They found that drop-out rates and other forms of patient noncompliance in natural settings far exceed those of patients in controlled experiments. Consequently, the authors suggested that inferences about the effectiveness of interventions drawn from RCTs may not apply to nonexperimental contexts. Likewise, in a comparison of the quality of life of cohorts of individuals infected with the human immunodeficiency virus (HIV), Cunningham, Bozzette, Hays, Kanouse, and Shapiro (1995) found significant social class and ethnic differences between those who were included in RCT research studies and those who were not. Both of these studies raise serious questions about the external validity or generalizability of inferences about the effects of medical interventions extrapolated from RCTs and applied to nonexperimental practice contexts and patient populations.

Another problem associated with the implementation of RCTs is the reluctance of physicians and other health providers to refer patients to RCT studies (Kolata, 1995a). Physicians and other health services providers often are not comfortable with random assignment of patients to treatment and control groups. Patients frequently refuse to participate in experimental studies for fear that they will receive a placebo.

Despite their methodological preferences, medical researchers are recognizing the ethical, practical, and epistemological limitations of RCTs and the advantages of naturalistic designs. In the proceedings of the 1994 conference on measuring the effects of medical treatments, Neuhauser (1995) remarked:

> However ideal the advantages of the classic experiment, we do not always want to study outcomes in controlled settings. We may wish to learn about causal relationships in the everyday world of health care and medical practice. The results of carefully designed trials of efficacy may not generalize to causal relationships in practice. Randomization in field studies may not be feasible, or ethical problems may arise from withholding or giving experimental treatments. Furthermore, many important opportunities for learning about causation would be lost if researchers relied only on randomized designs. (p. 6)

In the same volume, Moses (1995) considered methodological alternatives to RCTs, most notably nonrandomized studies using databases constructed from available management information systems. When RCT is not feasible, Moses offers some useful principles for conducting available database studies:

- "Let the undertaking be carefully planned, with participation of those who produce the data and also from future users of the results." (p. 8)
- "Let the planning result in a protocol, and in provisions for a quality assurance program." (p. 8)

According to Moses (1995), the "idea of information routinely generated in the course of health care delivery for assessing the effectiveness of alternative therapies has an undeniable attraction," and he concludes that research based on available information calls for "imaginative thinking, experimentation, and patience, but it is an idea deserving much effort" (p. 8).

Use of Available Data in Social Work Effectiveness Research

RCTs are treated as the gold standard in social work research as well as in medical effectiveness research. Clearly, in principle, no design surpasses the classic experiment for the purpose of establishing definitive, cause–effect relationships between intervention and outcomes. However, in the context of social work practice with seriously at-risk patients, classic experiments are rarely successfully implemented. Here, threats to design integrity are perhaps more problematic than the threats to measurement validity predicted by Campbell and Stanley (1963). The continuing emphasis placed on RCT research may also contribute to the gulf between researchers and practitioners (Hess & Mullen, 1995).

Assuming that practitioner–researcher partnerships remain an important objective in outcomes research, this chapter proposes a collaborative alternative to RCTs for studying patient outcomes in health settings. It begins with a systematic exploration of available information and the practice knowledge that emerges from it. Epstein (1995) referred to this as practice-based research. Like physicians, social workers in health agencies routinely generate enormous quantities of practice-relevant information for clinical, supervisory, administrative, and accountability purposes. Although not originally intended for research, these information sources can be converted into databases for practice-based outcomes research. Although using available information for outcomes measurement purposes presents challenges, such use can promote practice–research integration and practitioner–researcher collaboration.

Recent experience with practice-based research using routinely available information suggests that in addition to generating useful findings, such studies have many secondary benefits (Ben Shahar, Auslander, & Cohen, 1995; Epstein & Grasso, 1990). Such studies often lead to new problem identification, greater practitioner clarity and consensus about intended interventions and outcomes, explication of previously tacit practice theories, team building, professional recognition, pride, and satisfaction.

A Retrospective, Quasi-Experimental Outcomes Study of Psychosocial Selection of Applicants for Liver Transplant Based on Routinely Available Information

This chapter describes a retrospective, practice outcomes research study using routinely available information. Conducted in a collaboration between the Hunter College School of Social Work and the Mt. Sinai Medical Center in New York City, the study considers the medical outcomes and psychosocial risk factors of liver transplant recipients. Although it is too early to report the findings of this ambitious study, the secondary benefits for the liver transplant team and the social workers involved are examined. (In recent decades, organ transplantation has provided an impressive technology for saving lives. The technology had its origins in identical twin kidney transplants in the

1950s. Heart and liver programs were developed in the 1960s but were hampered by serious problems of rejection of the donor organ. With the development of antirejection drugs during the past two decades, there has been a resurgence in organ transplantation. Transplant centers now routinely perform liver, heart, lung, kidney, pancreas, bone marrow, and cornea transplants. Mt. Sinai Medical Center in New York City began its liver transplant program in 1988 and now has the third largest liver transplant program in the world, receiving an average of 800 referrals per year.) The collaboration began when Irwin Epstein was asked to design a prospective, psychosocial risk study for the liver transplant unit. The study began with the seemingly innocuous question, "What information do you currently have about transplant recipients?" The answer led away from a prospective study and to a decision to address the research questions through a retrospective study using available data.

PRIOR RESEARCH

There has been little systematic research on the subject of psychosocial predictors of outcomes of liver transplants. If such studies were available, they would help liver transplant teams deal more objectively with these difficult situations. The literature on psychosocial selection in liver transplantation focuses primarily on the issue of whether and when to transplant livers for patients with alcohol problems (Kumar et al., 1990; Lucey et al., 1992; Snyder, Drooker, & Strain, 1996; Starzl et al., 1988). (Two of these studies [Kumar et al., 1990; Lucey et al., 1992] have demonstrated that selected alcoholic patients may do quite well up to two years posttransplant. It remains unclear how impaired an alcoholic patient would have to be before it would be predicted that he or she would do poorly.) Numerous other conditions such as drug dependence, severe mental disorders, noncompliance, or unstable home environments or family supports may conceivably lead to excess morbidity and mortality after liver transplant. However, virtually no outcomes studies are available that might guide selection decisions in these circumstances.

MAKING DECISIONS WHEN OUTCOMES DATA ARE LACKING

Lacking research-based outcomes data, liver transplant teams commonly make selection decisions on the basis of a priori criteria concerning psychosocial suitability for transplantation. In practice, a medical team composed of physicians, nurses, social workers, psychiatrists, ethicists, and others who have interviewed the patient reviews a patient's history and then works to frame a coherent and fair response to each patient situation. Team members articulate reasons for inclusion or exclusion of patients for transplantation candidacy. Because of the complexity of the decision-making issues involved and the absence of empirically based outcomes data, team members expect ongoing discussion and disagreements concerning what is fair. Psychosocial factors such as a severe substance abuse history or a history of noncompliance with medical treatments are likely to raise questions of whether the patient will care for the organ properly after transplant. In such cases, transplant teams may either reject the applicant on psychosocial grounds or require that the patient obtain treatment for his or her psychosocial problem. Despite their poor prognoses, certain high-risk patients do well, whereas others do poorly.

STUDY DESIGN AND METHODS

This project presents an opportunity to articulate and empirically test the "practice wisdom" developed over time by the team (Klein & Bloom, 1995). (The team of investigators on the research study currently being conducted at Mt. Sinai Medical Center is composed of four liver transplant social workers, one supervisor, two psychiatrists, two hepatologists, a transplant nurse coordinator, and a research consultant. Team members have been working closely as a group for several years and know both the patients and the subtleties of transplant social work and psychiatry.) More generally, the study examines whether any psychosocial characteristics, individual or composite, predict long-term outcomes after transplant. The study itself is based on a retrospective review of the Mount Sinai Liver Transplant team's available medical and psychosocial data on patients evaluated by the team's staff of social workers and psychiatrists who then received transplants between July 1, 1992, and December 31, 1994 (approximately 275 patients). Psychosocial intake, intervention, and follow-up data on patients who received transplants for a 2½-year period are correlated with medical and psychosocial outcomes data for a 1–3½-year period after transplant. Available information can be used to address questions such as: How many patients died or became ill again? In how many cases did behavioral factors appear to contribute to poor outcomes? How many patients returned to substance abuse? Additional associations among initial psychosocial variables, psychosocial interventions, and final medical and psychosocial outcomes will be sought in examining such questions. In addition, the initial psychosocial records will be compared with those of a similarly evaluated group who did not receive transplants to study psychosocial differences between those who were selected for transplant and those who were not (approximately 350 patients). The study is designed to provide a detailed profile of psychosocial selection at Mount Sinai Medical Center and to be of use in designing future prospective evaluation studies to determine what psychosocial characteristics may predict adverse long-term outcomes after transplant. Ultimately, the study is intended to inform practice decision making with regard to selection for liver transplantation.

The core research group developed an instrument for retrieving and recording routinely available data from psychosocial and medical staff records. The instrument was piloted twice with several patient records to ensure its usefulness in organizing available data. Multiple consensus meetings were conducted in an attempt to ensure validity and reliability of its application. Special attention was given to those variables about which there was disagreement.

Independent Variables

The instrument assesses *independent variables*, which are measures obtained from available data enumerating patient characteristics before transplant. The instrument includes four modules: (1) a general module that includes demographics, support system, life stresses, and functional status; (2) a mental health module that includes mental symptoms and diagnosed disorders both past and present, cognitive deficits, mental health treatment both past and present, and suicidality; (3) a substance use module that includes substance use symptoms and diagnosed disorders, intravenous drug use, various prognostic measures from the substance abuse literature, and history of substance use disorder treatment both past and present; and (4) a medical module that includes such items as medical diagnosis, history of noncompliance to treatment, and acuity of need for transplant.

Intervening Variables

The instrument assesses intervening variables for all of the patients who received transplants and for some of the patients who did not. These are actions performed or recommended by the staff to address psychosocial problems noted either before or after transplant. For both groups the intervening variables include concrete services, counseling and psychotherapy, and psychiatric interventions.

Outcomes Variables

The instrument assesses medical and psychosocial posttransplant outcomes measures that are broken up into the same categories as the independent variables and contain comparable information:

- The general outcomes module includes the actuarial survival data, social difficulties, disposition, stability of adjustment after transplant, return to work, insurance data, and functional status.
- The mental health outcomes module includes whether the patient was seen by a psychiatrist or social worker after transplant, and if so, it includes mental symptoms, noted psychiatric problems and diagnoses, cognitive deficits, and treatment interventions after transplant.
- The substance use outcomes module includes whether the patient (if prior substance use history was noted) relapsed to the same or a different substance, whether family or staff have identified substance use as a problem, and other factors after transplant.
- The medical outcomes module includes related medical information post-transplant such as survival, liver disease, rejection, readmission, retransplantation, pathology on biopsy, possible contribution of behavioral factors to death, and pathology results.

On completion, this research project has the potential to have a significant impact on social work practice with liver transplant patients at Mount Sinai Medical Center as well as to contribute to general knowledge about psychosocial risk factors and liver transplantation. With this knowledge, current criteria for patient selection can be evaluated, and new program protocols can be designed. It also will be possible to determine the efficacy of psychosocial programs currently in place to help patients prepare for and cope with the rigors of transplantation.

SECONDARY BENEFITS

The idea for this practice-based research project emerged out of a practice decision-making need experienced by both social workers and psychiatrists working with liver transplant patients. Both groups believed that they were making profoundly important decisions about patients and scarce resources without a systematic theoretical framework or an empirical basis on which to make them. After conceptualizing the project and succeeding in obtaining a small, intramural grant for data entry and analysis, work became real, and the dedication of the group became apparent. The grant was viewed as an acknowledgement of both respect and professional recognition for the research group and helped to motivate the group to work diligently, most of the time outside of working hours. In addition, the project has had an enormous impact on interdisciplinary working relationships as well as on relationships among the social work colleagues and their supervisor. There have been times along the way when the core group would dismantle and the cohesiveness would diminish because of varying work styles; professional differences; and, naturally, personalities. At times, questions of equal distribution of workload and shared contribution to meetings arose. The members decided that periodic "group therapy" sessions helped in the team-building process and facilitated the continuation of the project.

In the process of developing and piloting the research instrument and thinking about the ways in which staff approached their work, greater clarity about desired outcomes and decisional criteria emerged, as did greater standardization in practice methods among the major disciplines. As a result, psychiatrists and social workers currently see themselves more cohesively as a psychosocial team.

This project has the potential to improve liver transplant program outcomes in two ways: (1) by developing valid outcomes data concerning the results of selection and management practice and (2) by providing a disciplined forum in which the team can confront and evaluate its own personal and professional decision-making practices.

Conclusion

This chapter offers an alternative to RCT designs for studying social work effectiveness and psychosocial risk in health care settings. The alternative is retrospective designs based on routinely available information. In such studies, Neuhauser (1995) pointed out that "we must rely more heavily on the logic of inquiry than on any 'gold standard' for inferring cause and effect" (p. 7). In his article on measuring treatment effects when RCTs cannot be used, Moses (1995) suggested, "Before accepting that very difficult, if not forlorn task" of using available data "make certain that an RCT cannot be used" (p. 12). In contrast, our enthusiastic advice is that starting with what is available may still yield gold.

References

Agency for Health Care Policy and Research. (1995). Drugs to control high cholesterol may be less successful than clinical trials suggest. *Research Activities, 187,* 4.

Andrade, S. E., Walker, A. M., & Gottlieb, L. K. (1995). Discontinuation of antihyperlipidemic drugs: Do rates reported in clinical trials reflect rates in primary care settings? *New England Journal of Medicine, 332,* 1125–1131.

Ben Shahar, I., Auslander, G., & Cohen, H. (1995). Utilizing data to improve practice in hospital social work: A case study. *Social Work in Health Care, 20,* 99–111.

Campbell, D., & Stanley, J. (1963). *Experimental and quasi-experimental designs for research.* Boston: Houghton Mifflin.

Cunningham, W. E., Bozzette, S. A., Hays, R. D., Kanouse, D. E., & Shapiro, M. F. (1995). Comparison of health-related quality of life in clinical trial and nonclinical trial human immunodeficiency virus–infected cohorts. *Medical Care, 33,* 15–25.

Epstein, I. (1995). Promoting reflective social work practice: Research strategies and consulting principles. In P. M. Hess & E. J. Mullen (Eds.), *Practitioner–researcher partnerships: Building knowledge from, in, and for practice* (pp. 83–102). Washington, DC: NASW Press.

Epstein, I., & Grasso, A. J. (1990). Using agency-based available information to further practice innovation. In H. Weissman (Ed.), *Serious play: Creativity and innovation in social work* (pp. 29–36). Silver Spring, MD: NASW Press.

Hess, P. M., & Mullen, E. J. (Eds.). (1995). *Practitioner–researcher partnerships: Building knowledge from, in, and for practice.* Washington, DC: NASW Press.

Klein, W., & Bloom, M. (1995). Practice wisdom. *Social Work, 40,* 799–808.

Kolata, G. (1995a, February 15). Women resist trials to test marrow transplants. *The New York Times,* C-8.

Kolata, G. (1995b, November 15). When patients' records are commodities for sale. *The New York Times,* A-1, C-14.

Kumar, S., Stauber, R. E., Gavaler, J. S., Basistan, M. H., Dindzans, V. I., Schade, R. R., Rabinovitz, M., Tarter, R. E., Gordon, R., Starzl, T. E., & Van Thiel, D. H. (1990). Orthotopic liver transplantation for alcoholic liver disease. *Hepatology, 11,* 159–164.

Lawler, E. F., & Raube, K. (1995). Social interventions and outcomes in medical effectiveness research. *Social Service Review, 69,* 383–403.

Lucey, M. R., Merion, R. M., Henley, K. S., Campbell, D. A., Turcotte, J. G., Nostrant, T. T., Blow, F. C., & Beresford, T. P. (1992). Selection for and outcome of liver transplantation in alcoholic liver disease. *Gastroenterology, 102,* 1736–1741.

Moses, L. E. (1995). Measuring effects without randomized trials? Options, problems, challenges. *Medical Care, 33* (1), 8–14.

Neuhauser, D. (Ed.). (1995). Study designs: Introduction. *Medical Care, 33* (1), 6–7.

Snyder, S. L., Drooker, M. A., & Strain, J. J. (1996). A survey estimate of academic liver transplant teams' selection practices for alcoholic applicants. *Psychosomatics, 32,* 432–437.

Starzl, T. E., Van Thiel, D., Tzakis, A. G., Iwatsuki, S., Todo, S., Marsh, J. W., Koneru, B., Staschak, S., Stieber, A., & Gordon, R. D. (1988). Orthotopic liver transplantation for alcoholic cirrhosis. *Journal of the American Medical Association, 260,* 2542–2544.

CHAPTER 21

Prospective Psychosocial Interventions: A Merger of Clinical and Research Techniques

JAMES R. ZABORA

Research methods are rarely considered to be important as social workers seek to enhance their clinical effectiveness. The enhancement of clinical skills often directly depends on continuing education programs that lack any emphasis on outcomes measurement. Clinical effectiveness can no longer be divorced from research methods that apply scientific measurement principles and evaluation designs. For clinical interventions to be effective in health care settings, high-risk patients and families must be identified as early as possible. In conjunction with early identification, prospective interventions can be offered as a replacement for reactive referral systems. As a profession, social work can no longer wait for other disciplines to identify patients and families in need of clinical services. The amount of distress associated with adaptation to any chronic illness can be conceptualized on a continuum from low to high. Given that each patient varies in the amount of distress, patients may benefit most from a range of services. Through techniques such as psychosocial screening, social workers can prospectively identify vulnerable patients and families and offer psychosocial interventions early in the disease process. Research methods can aid the development of screening practices, selection of a screening instrument, and development of a framework for outcomes measurement. In essence, use of a standardized measure as a screening tool provides two significant opportunities for social work. First, the standardized measure will identify cases and their level of risk, which will enable social workers to offer appropriate interventions. Second, this initial measurement point—defined as screening—serves as a preintervention measurement point. Whether the intervention is education, support groups, or psychotherapy, a postintervention assessment point can be compared with the screening data to determine the effectiveness of any intervention.

Background

Cancer and its related treatments disrupt every aspect of daily living and challenge patients' and families' psychological, social, spiritual, and financial resources. Most patients derive critical support from significant others to develop a buffer against multiple sources of stress and to facilitate problem-solving strategies to make effective decisions. Cancer creates fear, anxiety, anger, sadness, and depression as patients and families struggle to define and resolve the decisions that confront them (Mishel, Hostetter, King, & Graham, 1984). To comprehend the plight of cancer patients and their families, health care providers must understand the dynamic nature of coping to design and implement effective psychosocial interventions. (*Coping* can be defined as cognitive–behavioral or social strategies that patients and families use to solve problems in relation to a perceived threat or a demand such as cancer and to restore equilibrium as a result of disruptions associated with a chronic illness [Singer, 1984].) Cancer is not only a threat; the demands associated with the diagnosis and treatments may be insurmountable for some patients and families. Clinical observations and research studies confirm that the majority of patients effectively cope with the disease and treatments. In other words, most learn to live with cancer and incorporate it into their lives. However, it is also clear that a significant portion of patients will not adequately adapt to the diagnosis and treatments. Patients and families who cannot adapt are a loss to the health care team as an ally and a resource. Evidence suggests that patients with elevated levels of psychological distress may experience poorer treatment outcomes, possess greater levels of dissatisfaction with health care, and experience increased health care costs (Allison et al., 1995; Greenley, Young, & Schoenherr, 1982; Richardson, Marks, & Levine, 1988). State-of-the-art psychosocial programs offer interventions including education, support groups, cognitive–behavioral interventions, and psychotherapy to address the psychosocial needs and concerns of cancer patients and their families (Zabora & Loscalzo, 1996). If services are organized on theoretical principles and research methods, programs can be structured to demonstrate the effectiveness of interventions through outcomes research. In other words, research methods can be incorporated into service delivery to enhance and demonstrate clinical effectiveness.

Effective Adaptation

Patients can exhibit coping as verbal statements or actual behaviors in their efforts to resolve problems and decrease distress. Table 21-1 details the 15 primary coping strategies as defined by Weisman (1979). Some strategies are more effective than others. Although anger or hostility may be appropriate emotions, they do not provide relief from the distress associated with the disease because emotions are ineffective

Table 21-1

COPING STRATEGIES AND THEIR LEVEL OF EFFECTIVENESS

Most effective	Intermediate Effective	Least Effective
Confrontation	Seek information	Suppression
Redefinition	Share concern	Stoic submission
Compliance with authority	Humor	Acting out
	Distraction	Repetition compulsion
		Tension reduction
		Withdrawal
		Blame others
		Self-blame

Source: Weisman, A. D. (1979). *Coping with cancer.* New York: McGraw-Hill.

when used to solve problems. Patients who manifest ineffective problem-solving techniques can benefit from psychosocial interventions that teach and promote intermediate or effective strategies and problem solving. However, some critical psychosocial variables may promote or inhibit a patient's or family's attempt to respond to the challenges associated with cancer and its related treatments.

Evidence suggests that a patient's initial adaptation to a cancer diagnosis is significantly influenced by preexisting psychosocial factors that patients bring with them into their cancer experience. Table 21-2 defines these factors under the general headings of past history of functioning, social support, current concerns, and key demographic variables (Weisman, Worden, & Sobel, 1980). Psychosocial providers can use these variables to form patient profiles that are predictive of which patients will effectively adapt to their diagnosis and treatment as well as those patients who will experience difficulty in their adjustment. Techniques such as psychosocial screening can be used to identify patients who may experience a higher level of distress. Many standardized instruments are available for use in a psychosocial screening program for cancer patients and families (Fobair & Zabora, 1995; Zabora, in press).

Two brief patient profiles may help illustrate the diversity of patients' responses. In the first example, a 60-year-old woman recently diagnosed with lung cancer reports that she is married, lives with her family, and has some other family members in the vicinity. Although she reports periodic episodes of depression, her mood is positive and she has never required mental health services. She is generally optimistic concerning the outcomes of treatment and possesses minimal regrets about how she has lived her life. Current concerns are minimal as she anticipates beginning treatments. In the second example, the same 60-year-old newly diagnosed cancer patient may be a widow who lives alone and has only three other family members who live nearby. A history of depression has resulted in a prior psychiatric hospitalization and she continues to receive care for recurrent changes in her mood. As a result of these factors, she is generally pessimistic about the outcome of her treatment and is

Table 21-2

VARIABLES ASSOCIATED WITH PSYCHOSOCIAL ADAPTATION

Social Support	Past History	Current Concerns	Other
Marital status	Substance abuse	Health	Education
Living arrangements	Depression	Religion	Employment
Number of family members and relatives in vicinity	Mental health	Work and finance	Physical symptoms
Church attendance	Major illness	Family	Anatomical staging
	Past regrets	Friends	
	Optimism versus pessimism	Existential	
		Self-appraisal	

Source: Weisman, A. D., Worden, J. W., & Sobel, J. (1980). *Psychosocial screening and intervention with cancer patients: Research report* (p. 17). Boston: Harvard Medical School and Massachusetts General Hospital.

rather indecisive about the alternatives presented to her. Despite three discussions with her physician and additional written information, the health care team awaits her decision about beginning radiotherapy after surgery.

These clinical examples describe some preexisting psychosocial factors that patients possess as they enter their cancer experience. These two cases will require different levels of resources and staff; such information is not often apparent early in the treatment process. The first patient may be best served by an early interaction with a lung cancer survivor who can provide useful information as the patient approaches chemotherapy. Patients who are similar to the second profile will experience a gradual increase in their level of psychological distress and consequently require short-term psychotherapy. Patients often conceal their distress from their health care providers so that physicians and nurses maintain their focus on the treatment of their cancer (Weisman & Worden, 1976). However, the distress in these patients will increase and can result in a sense of crisis events that can affect the course of cancer treatments. This reactive approach to the psychological and social needs of patients is characteristic of most cancer centers and community hospitals where a referral to social work or psychiatry occurs only if the problem has become severe and unmanageable for the team and the patient's level of distress is readily apparent (Rainey, Wellisch, & Tawny, 1983). Relationships exist among these psychosocial variables and problems such as noncompliance with drug regimens, appointment breaking, and indecisiveness about treatment alternatives (Cramer, Scheyer, & Mattson, 1990; Lebovits et al., 1990). Estimates of noncompliance with chemotherapy regimens range from 20 percent to 80 percent; noncompliance can lower quality of life and affect survival outcomes (Geddes et al., 1990). The potential role of each psychosocial variable (for example, depression, lack of social support, history of addictions, and so forth) in relation to noncompliance is not understood. A defined theoretical approach that provides direction to the development and implementation of clinical intervention also creates a sound framework for outcomes measurement.

The Disease and Distress Continua

Two salient continua must also be simultaneously considered in relation to patient and family adaptation to cancer and related treatments. The first continuum is the disease time line. Patients' needs vary and fluctuate significantly as they move from the point of diagnosis, through treatment, and into remission (Zabora, Smith, & Loscalzo, 1995). For some patients, the disease continuum includes recurrent disease and entry into terminal care. For families, the continuum includes bereavement for an indefinite period of time. The second continuum relates to the previously discussed level of psychological distress that each patient experiences as he or she moves along the previously defined disease time line. Prevalence studies of psychological distress indicate that 25 percent to 30 percent of all newly diagnosed and recurrent patients experience significantly elevated levels of emotional distress, and as many as 47 percent have a psychiatric diagnosis (Derogatis, Morrow, & Fetting, 1983; Farber, Weinerman, & Kuypers, 1984; Stefanek, Derogatis, & Shaw, 1987). In all probability, these patients enter their cancer experience with significant distress that is related to preexisting psychosocial problems. The diagnosis of cancer generates significant distress for all patients; however, most learn to live with cancer, address the consequences, and solve the multiple problems that confront them. Overall, the psychosocial needs of patients and families vary significantly on the basis of the patients' level of psychological distress and their exact point on the disease continuum. The provision of services as early as possible on the disease continuum may be less stigmatizing to the patient and more easily incorporated into the comprehensive medical care of the patient (Fawzy, Fawzy, Arndt, & Pasnau, 1995). The alternative is to allow these patients to suffer needlessly through treatment as their distress increases. Unfortunately, the intensity of their distress results in a crisis event manifested by symptoms such as severe depression or suicidal thoughts that triggers a referral for immediate psychosocial intervention. This reactive model of psychosocial care forces patients to medicalize their emotional concerns and to manifest distress as a crisis to receive assistance. This reactive system will inevitably consume more resources and therefore generate higher costs. Furthermore, reactive referral systems consolidate patients into a uniform and homogeneous group of cancer patients. Outcomes measurement must consider the significant variation in the level of psychological distress as well as the diverse needs across the disease continuum.

The Family—A Critical Source of Social Support

Families simultaneously struggle to adapt and cope with the many challenges associated with cancer and its treatments. The family often serves as the primary source of support for the patient and as a buffer against stress as well as a facilitator for effective decision making. However, families also exhibit a significant variation in their ability to adapt and respond to cancer (Zabora, Smith-Wilson, Fetting, & Enterline, 1990). If families do not adapt, the health care team loses a significant resource in the overall care of the patient, and the patient loses a primary source of emotional support. Again, early intervention can address family concerns on behalf of the patient to reduce resource use and overall costs.

For conceptualizing and understanding family dynamics, Olson's Circumplex Model of Family Functioning (Olson et al., 1983) provides a framework in which to examine family behavior. The two critical constructs of adaptability and cohesion emerge to explain families' ability to adjust to the stressors associated with cancer and their capability to provide the necessary level of support to the patient. Adaptability describes the family's ability to reorganize processes such as decision making, financial management, and role assignments under the threat of a significant stressor such as cancer. Cohesion quantifies the degree of emotional bonding within each family. Each family construct also falls on the continua that are detailed in Figure 21-1. Families that fall on the extreme end of either continuum may present unique behaviors that the health care team defines as difficult or problematic. A brief example may be helpful. A family may experience a high level of cohesion, or emotional bonding, and may act as though each family member is equally affected by the diagnosis. As a result, boundaries among family members are minimal. Consequently, this family may be overprotective of the patient, speak for the patient, and demand excessive amounts of staff time regarding concerns about the patient. This family may find it difficult to follow inpatient unit guidelines or may encourage the patient to not follow medical directives. These behaviors can be intensified by the patient's psychological distress level as well as any emotional reactions in family members (Zabora & Smith, 1992).

Family difficulties and problems often emerge as the patient proceeds through treatment and into remission. As with the patient, a family that may be extreme in adaptability or cohesion (or both) may reach a crisis event. A family crisis can

Figure 21-1

CRITICAL VARIABLES RELATED TO FAMILY ADJUSTMENT

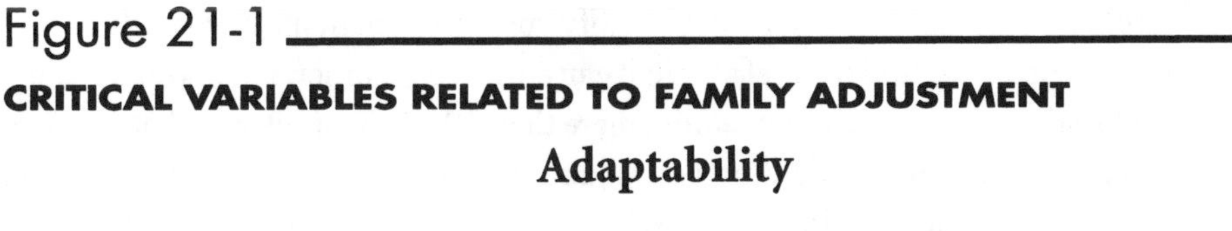

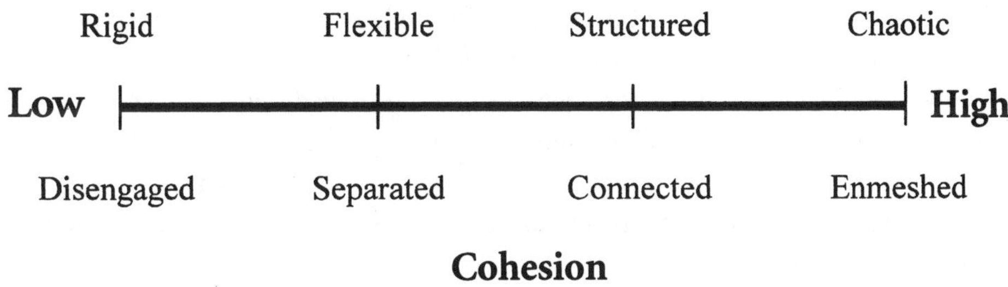

occur in the middle of outpatient care or as plans are finalized for the patient's discharge from the hospital. Given dramatic decreases in lengths of stay, expectations of families as caregivers have increased. The expectations of families held by the health care team often do not carefully consider the family's actual capability to perform the complex role of caregiver. In addition, all families experience difficulty as the role of caregiving is prolonged (Zabora, Smith, Baker, Wingard, & Curbow, 1992). For example, families should be reassessed at six months after bone marrow transplantation to examine their physical and psychological fatigue. As for the patient, the same premises of early identification and intervention for families who will experience significant or prolonged distress can facilitate the delivery of care for the patient by the health care team (Zabora, Smith-Wilson, Fetting, & Enterline, 1990). Early identification of families with brief measures of functioning who may experience significant problems is critical as the health care team increases its reliance on family members as caregivers.

Psychosocial Screening

Screening for psychological distress among patients or difficulties among families offers the opportunity to identify vulnerable patients and families early in the diagnostic or treatment phases. Although some clinicians and investigators have described screening questionnaires, words of caution are necessary. First, the term "screening" is frequently used interchangeably with "assessments." *Screening* is a method to quickly identify which patients or families may be vulnerable to the cancer experience through the use of a standardized measure (Mausner & Kramer, 1985); *assessment* is an ongoing process in which a comprehensive examination of key variables is undertaken in an effort to to understand them (Hepworth & Larsen, 1993). These two concepts cannot be equated. Many screening questionnaires have not been psychometrically tested for their reliability and validity. If a screening instrument is attempting to identify and measure psychological distress or family functioning, adherence to psychometric principles is critical. Measures must be reliable and valid to screen and identify vulnerable patients and families. Any screening instrument should be brief so that it can easily be incorporated into ambulatory settings. Questionnaires should not require more than 10 or 15 minutes so that they can be completed in waiting or examination rooms. Although specific instruments and methods have been identified (Barg, Cooley, Pasacreta, Senay, & McCorkle, 1994; Pruitt, Waligora-Serafin, McMahon, & Davenport, 1991; Radloff, 1977), more work is necessary in this area. A brief screening instrument should be available that can be easily and rapidly scored so that patients and families can be triaged and prospective services obtained as early as possible after completing the diagnostic phase. Use of one or more standardized instruments at the time of initial diagnosis or entry into treatment generates a preintervention measurement point that can serve as a baseline for future outcomes. Potential variables to be measured as part of a psychosocial screening program include psychological distress, family functioning, and physiological symptoms such as fatigue, shortness of breath, or sexual dysfunction.

Psychosocial Services Needs across the Disease and Distress Continua

Given that screening offers the opportunity to identify vulnerable patients and families, services to meet the needs of patients and families across both continua can be developed and offered prospectively. Figure 21-2 details potential interventions across each continuum. Although it appears that these programs increase costs, alternative sources of funding such as grants, foundations, or gifts may be used to support new program development. Also, a program such as a Cancer Survivors' Program (Zampini & Ostroff, 1993) can be incorporated into existing departments and positions. Fawzy et al. (1995) have clearly defined psychosocial interventions (that is, education, support groups, cognitive–behavioral techniques, and psychotherapy) and described their ability to reduce distress and improve quality of life. In other health care populations, the role of psychological distress and its inherent ability to increase health care costs are being described (Allison et al., 1995). Although psychosocial interventions possess proven efficacy in reducing distress and enhancing quality of life, their ability to reduce overall health care costs has not been demonstrated. Preliminary evidence suggests that a small investment of funds early in treatment to address psychological concerns may actually result in reduction of costs as a result of a decrease in rehospitalization and overall use of health care resources.

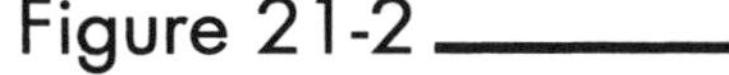

Figure 21-2

CONTINUA OF CARE FOR CANCER PATIENTS AND THEIR FAMILIES

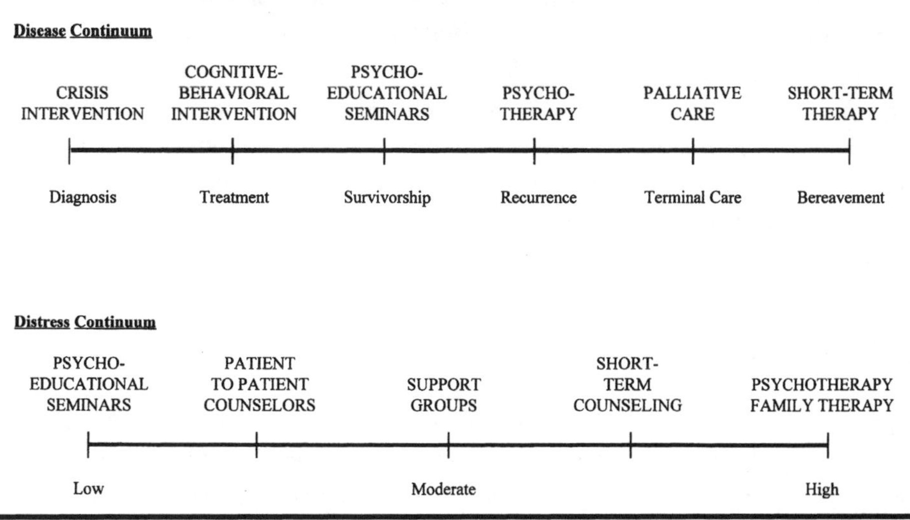

Note: These are potential interventions at specific points on each continuum. For example, patients may benefit from psychotherapy at any point on the continuum.

Conclusion

The managed care environment demands comprehensive services to meet patients' needs. Although survival statistics and overall costs will always be the primary considerations, factors such as patient satisfaction and quality of life play a salient role. Data that demonstrate cost savings would position psychosocial services for inclusion in global contracts. Psychosocial providers possess the skills to provide leadership in the appropriate measurement of outcomes such as patient satisfaction and quality of life. Unless leadership is provided, managed care organizations will define and measure these concepts despite a lack of expertise in instrument development and psychometrics.

Prospective psychosocial interventions provide an unusual opportunity to address the concerns of patients and families as early as possible in the disease process. Early problem identification and resolution enable patients and families to gain control of their lives and become more effective partners with the health care team. In addition, more appropriate matches with specific psychosocial services offer patients and families the greatest benefit in relation to where they fall on the disease and distress continuums. Unresolved psychological distress not only may increase the overall costs of care but also may jeopardize the actual outcomes of cancer therapies. Finally, systematic collection of data at the initial point of contact through activities such as psychosocial screening enables clinicians to establish baseline measures before any intervention. Measurements at this point serve many functions. Primarily, a measure of variables such as anxiety or depression before any intervention can be correlated with data obtained at the completion of cognitive–behavioral training or psychotherapy. In addition, these outcomes can be compared with patients who decline offers for these interventions. Patients and families who refuse a psychosocial intervention can be monitored for their ability to effectively interact with the health care team and for overt symptoms of distress such as extreme anxiety or hostility. If psychological distress is not identified and treated, quality of life diminishes, patient satisfaction decreases, and the overall cost of health care increases. A theoretical framework for service delivery and outcome measurement provides the opportunity to demonstrate social work effectiveness and the capability of clinical interventions to reduce health care costs. Given the dynamic nature of the managed care environment, social workers must implement comprehensive service delivery systems that incorporate evaluation and outcomes measurement as essential components of clinical practice in health care settings.

References

Allison, T. G., Williams, D. E., Miller, T. D., Patten, C. A., Bailey, K. R., Squires, R. W., & Gau, G. T. (1995). Medical and economic costs of psychologic distress in patients with coronary artery disease. *Mayo Clinic Proceedings, 70,* 734–742.

Barg, F. K., Cooley, M., Pasacreta, J., Senay, B., & McCorkle, R. (1994). Development of a self-administered psychosocial cancer screening tool. *Cancer Practice, 2,* 288–296.

Cramer, J. A., Scheyer, R. D., & Mattson, R. H. (1990). Compliance declines between clinic visits. *Archives of Internal Medicine, 150*, 1377–1378.

Derogatis, L. R., Morrow, C. R., & Fetting, I. (1983). The prevalence of psychiatric disorders among cancer patients. *Journal of the American Medical Association, 249*, 751–757.

Farber, J., Weinerman, B. H., & Kuypers, J. A. (1984). Psychosocial distress in oncology outpatients. *Journal of Psychosocial Oncology, 2*, 109–118.

Fawzy, F. I., Fawzy, N. W., Arndt, L. A., & Pasnau, R. O. (1995). Critical review of psychosocial interventions in cancer care. *Archives of General Psychiatry, 52*, 100–113.

Fobair, P., & Zabora, J. (1995). Family functioning as a resource variable. *Journal of Psychosocial Oncology, 13*, 97–114.

Geddes, D. M., Dones, L., Hill, E., Law, K., Harper, P. G., Spiro, S. G., Tobias, J. S., & Souhami, R. L. (1990). Quality of life during chemotherapy for small cell lung cancer: Assessment and use of a validation daily diary card in a randomized trial. *European Journal of Cancer, 26*, 484–492.

Greenley, J. R., Young, T. B., & Schoenherr, R. A. (1982). Psychological distress and patient satisfaction. *Medical Care, 20*, 373–385.

Hepworth, E., & Larsen, J. (1993). *Direct social work practice: Theory and skills.* Pacific Grove, CA: Brooks/Cole.

Lebovits, A. H., Strain, J. J., Schleifer, S. J., Tanaka, J. S., Bhardwaj, S., & Messe, M. R. (1990). Patient non-compliance with self-administered chemotherapy. *Cancer, 65* (1), 17–22.

Mausner, I. S., & Kramer, S. (1985). *Epidemiology: An introductory text.* London: W. B. Saunders.

Mishel, M. H., Hostetter, T., King, B., & Graham, V. (1984). Predictors of psychosocial adjustment in patients newly diagnosed with gynecological cancer. *Cancer Nursing, 7*, 291–299.

Olson, D., McCubbin, H., Barnes, A. L., Barnes, H., Larsen, A., Muxen, M., & Wilson, M. (1983). *Families: What makes them work.* London: Sage.

Pruitt, B., Waligora-Serafin, B., McMahon T., & Davenport, J. (1991). Prediction of distress in the first six months after a cancer diagnosis. *Journal of Psychosocial Oncology, 8*, 91–102.

Radloff, L. S. (1977). The CES-D scale: A self report depression scale for research in the general population. *Applied Psychological Measurement, 1*, 385–401.

Rainey, L. C., Wellisch, D. K., & Tawny, F. T. (1983). Training health professionals in psychosocial aspects of cancer: A continuing education model. *Journal of Psychosocial Oncology, 1*, 41–60.

Richardson, J. L., Marks, G., & Levine, A. (1988). The influence of symptoms of disease and side effects of treatment on compliance with cancer therapy. *Journal of Clinical Oncology, 6,* 1746–1752.

Singer, J. E. (1984). Some issues in the study of coping. *Cancer, 53,* 2303–2315.

Stefanek, M., Derogatis, L., & Shaw, A. (1987). Psychological distress among oncology outpatients. *Psychosomatics, 28,* 530–538.

Weisman, A. D. (1979). *Coping with cancer.* New York: McGraw-Hill.

Weisman, A. D., & Worden J. (1976). The existential plight in cancer: Significance in the first hundred days. *International Journal of Psychiatry in Medicine, 7,* 1–15.

Weisman, A. D., Worden, J. W., & Sobel, J. (1980). *Psychosocial screening and intervention with cancer patients: Research report.* Boston: Harvard Medical School and Massachusetts General Hospital.

Zabora, J. (in press). Pragmatic approaches in the psychosocial screening of cancer patients and their families. In J. Holland, P. Breiburt, & M. Loscalzo (Eds.), *Handbook of psychooncology* (2nd ed.). London: Oxford Press.

Zabora, J. R., Fetting, J. H., Shanley, V. B., Seddon, C. F., & Enterline, J. P. (1989). Predicting conflict with staff among families of cancer patients during prolonged hospitalizations. *Journal of Psychosocial Oncology, 7,* 103–111.

Zabora, J. R., & Loscalzo, M. J. (1996). Comprehensive psychosocial programs: A prospective model of care. *Oncology Issues, 11,* 14–18.

Zabora, J. R., & Smith, E. (1992). Early assessment and intervention with dysfunctional family systems. *Oncology, 5,* 31–35.

Zabora, J. R., Smith, E., Baker, F., Wingard, J. R., & Curbow, B. (1992). The family: The other side of bone marrow transplantation. *Journal of Psychosocial Oncology, 10,* 35–46.

Zabora, J. R., Smith, E., & Loscalzo, J. (1995). Psychosocial rehabilitation. In M. D. Abcloff, J. O. Armitage, A. S. Lichter, & J. E. Neiderhuber. (Eds.), *Clinical oncology* (pp. 2255–2270). New York: Churchill Livingstone.

Zabora, J. R., Smith-Wilson, R., Fetting, J. H., & Enterline, J. P. (1990). An efficient method for the psychosocial screening of cancer patients. *Psychosomatics, 31,* 192–196.

Zampini, K., & Ostroff, J. S. (1993). The post-treatment resource program: Portrait of a program for cancer survivors. *Psycho-oncology, 2* (1), 20–24.

CHAPTER 22

Continuous Quality Improvement and Health Care Outcomes Measurement: Implications for Social Work Services

MARGARET DIMOND

PENNY GOLDBERG ROCA

Traditionally, outcomes measures in hospital departments were used only as a quality assurance mechanism. The diversity of each clinical department mandated different outcomes guidelines. However, the empirical nature of outcomes measures as opposed to structural or process measures has gained popularity with hospital administrators, not only as a beacon of quality but also as a method by which to allocate resources and determine each department's viability and strength. Thus, social work is placed in an awkward position. How are the complex functions of counseling and discharge planning reduced to a formula by which success can be determined? Furthermore, the formal training given to social work directors for outcome-focused care has been on an ad hoc and individual basis. Many directors can network and share information to assess the most proficient manner of documenting outcomes, but given the myriad departmental functions and purposes across the country, it is difficult to reduce the diversity to a common language. This is one reason why more research on outcomes measurement systems needs to be conducted with findings disseminated in social work and the human service professions.

Outcomes Defined

In the field of social work in medical settings, positive outcomes are often indicated by a successful nursing home transfer, a foster home placement, or transportation arrangements being completed. To achieve positive outcomes, several variables are involved. Productivity, work processes, availability of resources, staffing patterns, and leadership are among the input variables (Joint Commission on Accreditation of Healthcare Organizations, 1994b). Many of the aforementioned variables are also monitored as quality indicators and are subject to process improvement planning, which ultimately affects the outcome (Deming, 1986).

Concurrent with planning change that will improve outcomes is the necessity of valid and reliable data collection and analysis. One cannot rely on subjective hunches or secondary information to buoy a department's reputation and credibility. Statistical expertise and knowledge of detailed information systems are essential to health care managers in all settings. Data will become a crucial tool for social work leaders as the future of health care is forged. Thus, credible data must be married to revised outcomes projections to strategically plan for present and future departmental operations.

Types of Outcomes

Key outcomes variables can be broken into the following categories: financial, quality, inpatient, and ambulatory.

FINANCIAL OUTCOMES

In the field of social work, the financial outcomes argument is imperative because many social work departments are an overhead expense to an institution as opposed to a revenue-producing area. Many social work directors argue that social work interventions decrease length of stay and potential lawsuits and increase patient and family satisfaction. However, data to prove the hypothesis are not readily available nor regularly compiled.

Within the broad spectrum of financial outcomes lie subgroups of cost-effectiveness, revenue enhancement, and decreased institutional liability. Social work departments that have been successful in creating a business plan for the institution and gathering useful data have used productivity formulas to gauge outcomes. Some examples of financial measurements that can be broken down into formulas reflect staff activity as follows:

Hourly wage X number of patient contacts per day = Outcome

Number of problems identified ÷ number of problems resolved = Outcome

Number and type of discharge delays ÷ length of stay = Outcome

Number or type of discharge disposition ÷
target number of dispositions or weight (relative value unit) dispositions = Outcome

Number of problems + case acuity ÷ number of hours worked (per staff) = Outcome

Number of patients contacted per day ÷ number of inpatient days = Outcome

Data to substantiate financial outcomes should be available through hospital departments. Thus, the responsibility of the social work department is not only to originate but also to gather data. The social work manager should reduce the broad objective data and use the information to calculate a financial formula measuring such areas as length of stay and discharge disposition. It is good practice to maintain some financial data, whether or not administrators ask for that information. Such data may be useful to the director when doing project planning or future staffing predictions.

QUALITY OUTCOMES

Quality theorists have changed the theory and practice of quality management in health care. For example, W. Edward Deming's influence has permeated not only hospital administrations but also the Joint Commission on Accreditation of Healthcare Organizations (1994a) philosophy. Continuous quality improvement has been imprinted into hospital operations. The crux of quality management means that streamlining and improving processes affects improvement in outcomes. Deming has stressed data collection and employee involvement in the change process (Deming, 1986).

What does the continuous quality improvement (CQI) emphasis in health care mean for social work? Emphasis is on continuous process improvement of both psychosocial and discharge planning activities. Social work managers should be concerned with collecting data on patient and family satisfaction with social services, physician and nurse satisfaction with social work intervention, timeliness and appropriateness of the discharge plan, number of discharge delays as a result of social or family circumstances, and social work staff satisfaction.

Some of these measures can be converted to simple formulas such as the following:

Number of cases closed per month ÷ number of compliments or complaints = Outcome

Average department length of stay ÷ hospital length of stay = Outcome

Number of patient problems identified ÷
number of patient problems resolved = Outcome

Number of high-risk cases evaluated within 24 hours of admission ÷
total number of department cases = Outcome

Number of social admissions avoided ÷
total number of emergency department social work staff cases (or total number of outpatient cases) = Outcome

Total number of social readmissions within 48 hours ÷
total number of social work cases = Outcome

These examples are a fraction of the innovative and diverse quality indicators a department can use. Each social work department must assess what indicators are needed to fulfill regulatory requirements. In addition, each institution may have an emphasis on particular aspects of quality outcomes. The organizational needs should be both known and addressed by department managers. Patient satisfaction, for example, is being closely watched by hospital administrators. Social work managers should have departmental monitors in addition to data the hospital may collect. Careful analysis of the data is imperative.

Two Case Illustrations

To illustrate these ideas, we undertook two studies at our institution. The first is an interdisciplinary outcomes study concerning the timely discharge of patients from inpatient units. The second illustrates an approach to establishing care pathways including costing out of inpatient mental health services.

IMPROVING SERVICES THROUGH DISCHARGE PROCESS MONITORING

The discharge process is a complex one, culminating on the last day of hospitalization with an expectation of the smooth and efficient movement of the patient from the acute setting to home or other care site. Delays on the day of discharge contribute to cost overruns, poor resource use, and patient and family dissatisfaction. There may be differing opinions as to why delays exist. In this study some physicians claimed that the social work discharge planning effort was flawed. To determine reasons for the delays, this study group developed an interdisciplinary team led by the social work discharge planning manager. A flowchart detailing the process and potential obstacles during the 24 hours leading to a patient's discharge was developed. One week's data were collected by surveying all nursing units, and a record was made of causes for discharge delays. Findings indicated that 30 percent of patients were discharged with delays. More than 50 percent of those discharge were delayed as a result of medical reasons: chemotherapy treatments were scheduled for the morning of discharge; discharge prescriptions were written the day of discharge, not the day before; and 24-hour notice of discharge was not being given to the patient and family. Other reasons included families who were unable to pick up the patient (this is in large part dependent on 24-hour notice of discharge) and discharge plans not completed in 12 percent of the cases. The delays were largely attributable to variables under the control of physicians rather than social workers. When the findings were provided to the physician leadership, it was decided that teams should be set up with membership to include physicians, social workers, and nurses. These teams were to monitor movement of patients through the system concentrating on the discharge process. Included in the monitoring were physician behaviors that affected timely discharge. As a result of this process, significant improvement has been seen not only in the social work and physician relationship but also in outcomes. For example, patients are moving more speedily through the system. In a repeat survey it was found that 18.2 percent of the patients were discharged with delays, a significant decrease from the previous finding of 30 percent.

Underlying social work participation in this study are layers of ethical concerns related to faster discharge of patients to their homes where more of the care is being delivered. Care burden is placed increasingly in the hands of the patients and family members. To foster increased care quality and enhance outcomes, social work staff development programs were initiated to rethink and redesign the focus of interventions. This redesign included planning for the preparation of patients and families before admission and development of service delivery models that concentrate resources on ambulatory care areas when the patient is returned home. This case study example illustrates the use of a study process that resulted in improved services. The study process included interdisciplinary team collaboration whereby team members analyzed and changed practice patterns and institutional systems that impeded the discharge process, thus fostering a timely but safe discharge of patients.

ESTABLISHING CARE PATHWAYS: COSTING OUT INPATIENT MENTAL HEALTH SERVICES

The second study illustrates how costing out services can provide a basis for comparison of differential costs of care. In this study social work services on the pediatric oncology program were compared with costs of consultation services in the Department of Psychiatry. The decision to focus on this arena was related to a new institutional initiative whereby clinical pathways were being delineated and costed out by disease. (Clinical pathways are computer-based algorithms that graphically display the patients' progress along disease-specific continuums of care. Narratives describing the care and status of the patient, both medically and psychosocially, accompany the algorithms.) The intent of this disease management model is to cost out services, to provide the groundwork for decision making regarding patient care options, to reduce resource use, and to provide the foundation for negotiating with managed care entities. The facility studied was a tertiary care academic center whose overall care costs are high—beyond what the managed care companies expect to pay. There is tremendous pressure to not only cost out services but also to justify the provision of services altogether. The department of pediatrics was the first to include the psychosocial components of care in their disease management approach. Leadership from social work, psychology, and psychiatry met to look at what services were being provided, the volume and type of service, redundancy or overlapping of services, and charges and costs. Data were collected by the social work staff for one week on direct, individual meetings with patients and families. Included in the database were the following: the reason for which service was provided to the patient and family beyond the assessment, rank order of these reasons, and the time spent during that week. It was found that 30 percent of all the patients in active treatment and 20 percent of patients who continued to be followed took up 60 percent of the social work staff time. This finding was based on a psychosocial severity index that was developed by staff. On average, 67 minutes were spent per patient family per week, with 66 percent of that time devoted to counseling of some type. On average the cost of delivering services by a social worker per patient and family was $24.75 for interventions overall and $16.33 for interventions for emotional or behavioral issues. Social workers had seen 136 patients and families during this one week, whereas for the entire year psychiatry treated 50 patients, averaging two visits, with a total average of 40 minutes per patient and family, at an average fee of $125 to $150 per consultation. Approximately 11 percent of the pediatric population was being seen by psychiatry practitioners. These data validated, among the psychosocial leadership, that social workers were providing the bulk of the mental health services to the pediatric patients and families at a low cost. In addition, the data provide the foundation for costing out of social work interventions per disease category, which is essential for inclusion in the disease management approach and subsequent negotiations with managed care.

These study descriptions provide examples of disciplined work using objective data easily implemented by social work staff. The importance of critically examining one's practice—with data to support the validity of interventions through outcomes measurement—cannot be overemphasized. If social work is to remain a vital part of the service delivery system in health care and is to be included in negotiation with managed care companies, the profession must embrace outcome studies as the vehicle by which our services, costs, functions, and value to patients and families can be measured.

References

Deming, W. E. (1986). *Out of crisis*. Cambridge, MA: MIT Press.

Joint Commission on Accreditation of Healthcare Organizations. (1994a). *Forms, charts, and other tools for performance improvement 1994*. Oakbrook Terrace, IL: Author.

Joint Commission on Accreditation of Healthcare Organizations. (1994b). *A guide to establishing programs for assessing outcomes in clinical settings*. Oakbrook Terrace, IL: Author.

PART IVB

Practice–Research Case Examples

CHAPTER 23

Hospital Discharge Planning: A Comparative Analysis of Two Social Work Models Serving Patients with HIV/AIDS

MARIANNE C. FAHS

KATHLEEN WADE

This chapter examines outcomes measurement and cost-effectiveness comparing two models of hospital care for patients with acquired immunodeficiency syndrome (AIDS): a specialized cluster unit and a scattered general inpatient unit. The outcomes measures examined—cost containment and reduction of length of stay—are mainly of interest to hospital administrators (Weil & Stam, 1990). The study compares discharge planning for patients with AIDS needing placement in a nursing home facility and those discharged to the community by analyzing length-of-stay differences for similar patients in the two settings. This is the first study to examine the relationship among alternative inpatient care models, patient disposition, type of discharge planning, and length of stay. In addition, the broader implications of specialized versus generalized services for discharge planning are addressed.

The development of effective and appropriate models of hospital care for patients with AIDS or, more broadly, human immunodeficiency virus (HIV) is a vital policy issue. As the geographic distribution of people with HIV widens, hospitals are looking for guidance from program models that have been developed in those cities hardest hit by the HIV epidemic (Benjamin, Lee, & Solkowitz, 1988; Weil & Stam, 1990). Yet

---

This chapter is adapted with permission from Fahs, M. C., & Wade, K. (1996). An economic analysis of two models of hospital care for AIDS patients: Implications for hospital discharge planning. *Social Work in Health Care, 22* (4), 21–34. Copyright 1996, Haworth Press.

little data exist on how to organize quality, cost-effective care for patients hospitalized with HIV illness (Fahs et al., 1992; Strain, Fahs, Fulop, & Sacks, 1989). One question to be addressed is whether to cluster patients in units with specialized care management services or to maintain patients in a general inpatient unit. Examining the impact that specialized versus nonspecialized social work staff has on discharge planning is another important and related question.

The following factors must be included if patients are treated in a specialized AIDS unit: presence of a dedicated staff who are knowledgeable about patients with AIDS, provision of continuity of care spanning multiple admissions and the range in care needs, targeted preadmission screenings, and comprehensive service planning. Patient education and patient therapy groups can be provided to ease a patient's adjustment to hospitalization and to assist the patient in coping with AIDS (Taravella, 1989). If patients with AIDS are to be integrated into the general inpatient population, the following factors must be present: preservation of their confidentiality, safeguarding of their human rights, and reduction of opportunities for stigmatization and prejudice (Fahs et al., 1992).

Study Methods

SETTINGS

The study was conducted at Mount Sinai Medical Center in New York City. The hospital provides care to patients with AIDS both in regular beds throughout the hospital (general inpatient units) and in an AIDS cluster unit. The AIDS unit has existed since October 1987 and has 10 beds with a dedicated staff of four registered nurses (two on the day shift and two on the night shift) and one specialized social worker. House staff are assigned to patients in the unit sequentially as part of their medical and surgical rotation. Approximately 40 patients with AIDS are in the hospital on any given day in both models of care.

Patients can be admitted directly to the AIDS unit or transferred there after admission to a general inpatient unit. When the census of clients with AIDS is higher than the number of available beds in the cluster unit, patients are prioritized for admission, with those patients awaiting a bed from the emergency department or infectious diseases clinic given first priority. Those patients who have been in the unit previously also are given priority. Patients with AIDS in general inpatient units are offered the option of transfer to the unit. In addition, they must be aware of their diagnosis and consent to admission to the unit.

SAMPLE AND DATA COLLECTION

Using the computerized hospital information management system, all adults who had been discharged from the Mount Sinai Hospital were selected who met the standards of HIV-related disease as defined by the International Classification of Diseases modification for HIV instituted in January 1, 1988 (Centers for Disease Control, 1987). This case information was merged with computerized hospital billing information. All unique identifiers were deleted from the analysis file.

Information was collected for each patient regarding age, gender, race, diagnoses (up to seven), insurance status, patient origin (direct admission to the unit or intrahospital transfer), emergency department admission, discharge status (long-term care facility or other), use of specific resources such as intensive care units, length of stay, charges (room and board and ancillary), outcome of hospitalization (survival versus death), and disease severity. Severity of illness was coded on the basis of criteria developed by Turner, Kelly, and Ball (1989; Kelly, Ball, & Turner, 1989) using the probability of inpatient mortality for patients with AIDS in New York hospitals in 1985. The criteria allow the classification of patients into one of 20 stages according to their *International Classification of Diseases, 9th Revision, Clinical Modification* (1989) diagnoses reported at discharge. The computerized staging algorithm for this index was developed in cooperation with the Agency for Health Care Policy and Research, Department of Health and Human Services (National Center for Health Services Research and Health Care Technology Assessment/Hospital Studies Program, 1988).

DATA ANALYSIS

The individual patient was the unit of analysis. Differences were assessed between the two settings by comparing the length of stay for patients in both settings. Descriptive comparisons between the two groups were performed using unpaired t tests (two-tailed unless otherwise noted) on continuous outcome variables and Fisher's Exact Test on dichotomous variables. A semilog regression model was estimated with analysis of covariance to test whether the AIDS unit setting had an independent effect on length of stay. The semilog specification normalizes the distribution of the dependent variable: length of stay. In this model we controlled for patient characteristics. The predictors were age; race; gender; and a vector of clinical indicators composed of stage of disease, number of diagnoses, discharge placement, and death. In addition, we added five dummy variables (coded 0 or 1) differentiating each of the attending physicians in charge of the case and included whether the patient was admitted directly to the AIDS unit or transferred from a general inpatient unit. Only the first discharge for each study patient was entered in the logistic regression to avoid statistical bias resulting from dependence in the error term occurring when separate discharges are analyzed for the same patient.

In this multivariate regression model, we maintained a high level of detail in the specification of clinical characteristics. The number of secondary diagnoses and the substage of illness indicating the patient's illness severity are specified in greater detail, that is, without collapsing into broader categories such as Kaposi's sarcoma, *pneumocystis carnii* pneumonia, and other diseases, which has been done in previous studies predicting resource use and outcome (Bennett et al., 1989; Hellinger, 1990). Two social characteristics, race and health insurance, were too highly correlated to both be entered in the analysis; thus, health insurance was omitted.

Results

Thirty thousand patient discharges were screened, and 465 adult discharges associated with an *International Classification of Diseases, 9th Revision* code of 42-44

(HIV-related disease) (n = 345) or 795.8 (HIV seropositive but no disease) (n = 120) diagnoses were identified. The study population consisted of 465 cases with HIV- or AIDS-related disease: 320 discharged from general inpatient units, and 145 discharged from the AIDS unit. Excluded were lengths of stay of one day only, which indicated chemotherapy treatment.

Table 23-1 presents the sociodemographic and clinical characteristics of the sample by service type. This sample is ethnically diverse and primarily male, with patients typically in their late 30s. Approximately 43 percent were privately insured. Most patients (98 percent) were admitted from noninstitutional residential settings, and 90 percent, from the emergency department. Relatively few (9 percent) were discharged to long-term care facilities. Patients in the AIDS cluster unit were significantly more likely to be younger, male, and white. AIDS-unit patients had a higher level of severity than patients with AIDS in general inpatient units as measured by mean stage of disease and by mean number of diagnoses. Parallel with the higher severity ratings, a higher proportion of the unit patients died in the hospital.

Table 23-2 illustrates patient dispositions showing a marked difference in mean length of stay between services. For patients in the AIDS unit, mean length of stay

Table 23-1

CLINICAL AND SOCIODEMOGRAPHIC CHARACTERISTICS OF HIV-RELATED DISCHARGES FROM THE AIDS UNIT AND FROM GENERAL INPATIENT BEDS

Characteristics	AIDS Unit (n = 145)	Inpatient Beds (n = 320)	p
Sociodemographic variable			
Mean age (years)	36.8	39.0	<.05
Gender			
Female (n = 54)	11.3%	20.3%	<.05
Race			
Hispanic (n = 132)	45.1%	33.9%	NS
Black (n = 93)	22.6%	32.8%	<.05
White (n = 100)	30.1%	31.3%	NS
Private insurance (n = 141)	42.9%	43.8%	NS
Clinical variable			
Mean disease stage	2.4	2.2	<.01
Mean number of comorbid conditions	5.2	4.7	<.01
Inpatient death (n = 51)	21.1%	12.0%	<.05
Discharge to a long-term care facility (n = 30)	12.8%	6.8%	NS
Emergency admission (n = 290)	98.1%	97.8%	NS

Note: NS = not significant.

Table 23-2

PATIENT DISPOSITION—DESCRIPTIVE CHARACTERISTICS

Site	Skilled Nursing Facility	Community	Length of Stay (mean ± *SD*)
Scatter site ($n = 320$)	13	307	14.8 ± 13.9
Cluster unit ($n = 145$)	17	128	23.4 ± 17.7
Total ($n = 465$)	30	435	17.5 ± 18.6

was 23.4 days ($SD = 17.7$) compared with 14.8 days ($SD = 13.9$) for patients in general inpatient units.

Table 23-3 shows the independent effect of placement on the AIDS unit on resource use. The model demonstrates a high level of overall significance ($F = 5.5, p < .0001$) and explanatory power ($R^2 = .44$). Eight of the 10 substage groupes were significantly related to an increased length of stay (over the reference group in substages 1.0–1.3). In addition, requiring discharge to a long-term facility significantly increased the length of stay. The only sociodemographic characteristic significantly associated with length of stay was race; white patients had shorter stays. After controlling for age, gender, race, attending physician, admission status to the unit (direct admission or transfer from a general inpatient unit), patient disposition, number of comorbid conditions, and disease stage, patients admitted directly to the unit did not have longer lengths of stay than patients in general inpatient units. Patients transferred to the unit, however, did have significantly longer stays than similar patients remaining in general inpatient units. Moreover, cluster patients requiring discharge to a skilled nursing facility showed a significantly shorter average length of stay. General inpatient unit patients requiring nursing home placement showed an increased average length of stay of 3.7 days compared with similar cluster patients who showed a decrease in average length of stay of 2.1 days. The magnitude of the overall difference is almost six days. This difference in average length of stay for patients requiring nursing home placement is substantial and statistically significant.

Discussion

Although focused on a limited aspect of discharge planning, the magnitude of the effect in reduced average length of stay is of economic significance. Discharge placement from the cluster unit into long-term care decreased average length of stay by almost six days. The trend in discharge placement efficiency may be explained by the presence of a specialized AIDS discharge planning social work staff on the AIDS unit.

The two models of service provision, generalized versus specialized AIDS service, each have advantages and limitations (Cohen & Wills, 1985; Fahs et al., 1992; Koeske & Koeske, 1989; Taravella, 1989). A specialized service provides a continuity of care that bridges the multiple inpatient stays and outpatient care for people with AIDS. The team approach has the advantage of clarifying the complex biological, psychological, and social needs of this patient population and providing ongoing assessments and treatment planning for them, which is particularly important

Table 23-3

REGRESSION RESULTS OF PREDICTOR VARIABLES ON LENGTH OF STAY

Predictor Variable	Length of Stay	*p*
Reference group	+5.1	<.001
AIDS unit		
Direct admission	+1.3	NS
Transfer from scatter bed	+3.8	<.001
Discharge to a facility		
From a scatter bed	+3.7	<.05
From a direct admission unit bed	–2.1	<.05[a]
From a transfer unit bed	+1.6	NS
Race		
Black	+1.1	NS
White	–1.6	<.01
Gender		
Female	–0.7	NS
Age	+0.9	NS
Number of comorbid conditions	+0.4	NS
Stage 1: Substage groups		
1.3 Hematologic disease only, or		
1.4 1 NOI only, or		
1.5 1 non-PCP opportunistic infection only	+3.2	<.05
1.6 Combinations of 1.1-1.3 and/or lymphoma, or		
1.7 1 non-PCP opportunistic infection + NIC, or		
1.8 1 NOI + NIC	+2.5	NS
Stage 2: Substage groups		
2.0 >1 NOI, or		
2.1 PCP + NIC	+4.7	<.05
2.2 PCP only	+6.2	<.001
2.3 1 non-PCP opportunistic infection + NOI	+5.8	<.01
2.4 PCP + NOI	+8.1	<.001
2.5 >1 opportunistic infection	+12.7	<.0001
Stage 3: Substage groups		
3.0 Nonopportunistic central nervous system infection		
3.1 Dementia/encephalopathy	+2.3	NS
3.2 > 1 opportunistic infection + NOI		
3.3 Nonopportunistic septicemia	+7.0	<.05
3.4 Organ failure	+6.1	<.05
$R^2 = .44$	$F = 5.6$	<.0001

Note: Data shown are incremental days of hospitalization relative to the predictor reference group. NS = not significant; PCP = *Pneumocystis carinii* pneumonia; NIC = noninfectious complication; NOI = nonopportunistic infection.

[a]One-tailed *t* test.

in the disease progression of AIDS, where multisystem failure occurring as a result of a severely debilitated immune system creates a clinical challenge for the health care team. Early screening and intervention can maximize efficiencies in the discharge planning process (Fillit et al., 1992). A specialized team can collaborate to maximize the use of existing services, avoiding duplication of services and advocating for patients when there are gaps in service.

The AIDS cluster may also foster other efficiencies. The cluster approach allows an interdisciplinary team to evolve. The team works collaboratively to develop continuous treatment plans necessary for this patient population. The team can help increase efficiencies in patient care and role clarity while creating formal and informal support systems to reduce staff stress and burnout (Cohen & Wills, 1985; Koeske & Koeske, 1989). Thus, a specialty unit incorporates technical advantages and offers a milieu that more efficiently addresses the psychosocial and discharge planning needs of the patients and the staff caring for these patients.

The responsibility of the social worker on the AIDS unit differed from that of social workers on a general medical unit. The AIDS cluster social worker had responsibility for the 10-bed AIDS unit as well as three outpatient clinics. The social workers in the general medical units had responsibility for approximately 38 inpatient medical beds but no outpatient responsibilities. This experience in the continuity of care between outpatients and inpatients may have allowed the AIDS-unit social worker to provide a triaging of discharge needs so that those with difficult discharge placement needs received priority. Familiarity with the patient disease process and with the specialized resources available for patients with AIDS needing nursing home placement may have contributed to the greater efficiency with respect to these patients. The general medical social worker, with multiple complex service demands and without the specialization in AIDS resources and community services, may be at a disadvantage in setting priorities for early planning for a patient with AIDS who requires placement. The complex needs of the patient with AIDS must compete for the social workers' time and attention with the special needs of a diverse medical unit. The medical patient population varies significantly in terms of age, diagnosis, service needs, and discharge resources. The lack of specialization may decrease social workers' ability to keep current on the availability of community agencies and resources for the many different diagnoses and patient care needs on a medical unit, thus decreasing their ability to discharge the patient earlier. Cluster social workers, aware of the limited facilities and beds, would prioritize this patient, thereby expediting discharge. These issues are pertinent to social workers who have often been responsible for the coordination of care and discharge planning for this population.

However, problems are associated with the specialized unit. The AIDS cluster consists of many ill patients. Because of the multitude of needs, intensity of work, and scarcity of resources for these patients, a high level of staff burnout can occur that may create inefficiencies for staff (Oktay, 1992; Ross, 1993; Stein, Wade, & Smith, 1991). It may be difficult to hire and retain staff on an AIDS unit and to overcome the resistance of those serving on a unit exclusively for patients with

AIDS—problems that may result in inferior care or in higher costs. In terms of the role of social work, the AIDS worker may be split between the cluster and several outpatient clinics. The caseload consists of patients in all stages of HIV infection, from those requiring a total array of services to dying patients needing more intensive services. However, the generalized social worker has responsibility for inpatient services only. The general medical unit has patients with a treatable acute episode of illness with severity levels that are lower on average. Services and counseling sessions on the general unit are typically not as consistently intensive as those on the cluster unit. High-risk criteria on the medical unit enabled the worker to triage patients according to social risk. The AIDS social worker had difficulty triaging patients who had less variation in the severity of illness.

The team concept may also foster some inefficiencies. Role strain can cause health care workers to replicate services and fragment the treatment plan. In addition, team members experience turf issues and feel threatened, thus creating barriers to efficient care. Cost containment may be thwarted as the team strives to maximize the amount and level of care to patients. Economic feasibility is replaced with duplicated or unnecessary services being rendered.

The efficiency of discharge planning for patients with AIDS is one component to the overall management of care. This study indicates that at least one important difference exists in discharge planning—that is, length of stay. Although reducing unnecessary hospital days is an important goal, the need for coordinated quality discharge planning for patients with AIDS is also an important outcome to be sought. This study did not assess specific indicators of quality such as success of the discharge plan, family and caretaker impact, or readmission rate. In a separate report, another outcomes measure, patient satisfaction, was found to be significantly positively associated with the AIDS cluster unit (Cleary et al., 1992).

Another limitation of this study is its retrospective design and lack of randomness. It was not possible to identify whether patients were newly diagnosed with AIDS nor at what point during the admission the diagnosis occurred. Newly diagnosed patients with AIDS were referred for home care services to the local health department's Division of AIDS Services (DAS). Eligibility criteria for most services was a full-blown AIDS diagnosis. Some delays could have been related to waiting for a conclusive AIDS diagnosis. Also, waiting times for home care services through DAS often were two to three months. For patients transferred to the cluster, the initiation of discharge planning services may have been pending a final diagnosis of AIDS. The group of patients transferred to the cluster, with longer lengths of stay, may have been disproportionately composed of newly diagnosed patients. Patients previously diagnosed and currently receiving DAS home care services may have been admitted directly to the unit, thus lowering the apparent length of stay for patients in the AIDS unit requiring long-term care placement.

Conclusion

This outcomes measurement study supports the conclusion that a specialized AIDS service is cost-efficient. The patient with AIDS needing skilled nursing placement on a general medical unit requires 3.7 additional hospital days, controlling for clinical and sociodemographic variables. By contrast, the analysis indicates a decrease in length of stay of 2.1 days for similar specialized unit patients. The results suggest that early inpatient screening and specialized discharge planning on the AIDS unit have a significant impact on decreasing average length of stay. Patients who were transferred to the cluster from general inpatient units and who required community services had a longer length of stay, leading to speculation that "problematic" discharges were among those cases transferred. Patients requiring difficult or complex discharge planning may have been transferred to the cluster to obtain the maximum benefits of the interdisciplinary, specialized team approach.

The changes in health care policy and practice and the lasting effects from downsizing in hospitals throughout the United States make outcomes measurement studies such as this noteworthy. The need for quality, cost-effective, timely discharge planning for patients with AIDS is important because of frequent hospitalizations, limited community resources, increasing health care costs, and limited acute care beds. Inpatient services comprise the largest single component of direct medical expenditures for people with AIDS (Fahs et al., 1994; Fleishman, Hsia, & Hellinger, 1994; Hellinger, Fleishman, & Hsia, 1994; Scitovsky & Rice, 1987). Future outcomes measurement studies should be developed to systematically evaluate the cost-effectiveness of hospital-based social workers, using prospective experimental designs, to establish the net impacts of varying services on patient outcomes and institutional and social costs.

References

Benjamin, A. E., Lee, P. R., & Solkowitz, S. N. (1988). Case management of persons with acquired immunodefiency syndrome in San Francisco. *Health Care Financing Review* (Annual Suppl), 69–74.

Bennett, C. L., Garfinkle, M. S., Greenfield, S., Draper, D., Rogers, W., Mathews, C., & Kanouse, C. E. (1989). The relation between hospital experience and in-hospital mortality for patients with AIDS-related PCP. *Journal of the American Medical Association, 261,* 2975–2979.

Centers for Disease Control. (1987). Human immunodeficiency virus (HIV) infection classification. *Morbidity and Mortality Review, 36* (S-7), 1–20.

Cleary, P. D., Fahs, M. C., McMullen, W., Fulop, G., Strain, J., Sacks, H. S., Muller, C., Foley, M., & Stein, E. (1992). Using patient reports to assess hospital treatment of persons with AIDS: A pilot study. *AIDS Care, 4,* 325–332.

Cohen, S., & Wills, T. A. (1985). Stress, social support and the buffering hypothesis. *Psychological Bulletin, 93,* 310–357.

Fahs, M. C., Fulop, G., Strain, J. J., Sack, H. S., Muller, C., Cleary, P. D., Schmeidler, J., & Turner, B. (1992). The inpatient AIDS unit: A preliminary empirical investigation of access, economic and outcome issues. *American Journal of Public Health, 82,* 576–578.

Fahs, M. C., Waite, D., Sesholtz, M., Muller, C., Hintz, E. A., Malleo, C., Arno, P., & Bennett, C. (1994). Results of the ACSUS for pediatric AIDS patients: Utilization of services, functional status, and social severity. *Health Services Research, 29,* 549–568.

Fillit, H., Howe, J. L., Fulop, G., Sachs, C., Sell, L., Siegel, P., Miller, M., & Butler, R. N. (1992). Studies of hospital social stays in the frail elderly and their relationship to the intensity of social work intervention. *Social Work in Health Care, 18,* 1–21.

Fleishman, J. A., Hsia, D. C., & Hellinger, F. J. (1994). Correlates of medical service utilization among people with HIV infection. *Health Services Research, 29,* 527–548.

Hellinger, F. J. (1990). Updated forecasts of the costs of medical care for persons with AIDS, 1989–93. *Public Health Reports, 105,* 1–12.

Hellinger, F. J., Fleishman, J. A., & Hsia, D. C. (1994). AIDS treatment costs during the last months of life: Evidence from the ACSUS. *Health Services Research, 29,* 569–581.

International Classification of Diseases, 9th Revision, Clinical Modification.(1989). Ann Arbor, MI: Commission on Professional and Hospital Activities.

Kelly, J. V., Ball, J. K., & Turner, B. J. (1989). Duration and costs of AIDS hospitalizations in New York: Variations by severity of illness. *Medical Care, 27,* 1085–1098.

Koeske, G. F., & Koeske, R. D. (1989). Workload and burnout: Can support and perceived accomplishments help? *Social Work, 34,* 243–248.

National Center for Health Services Research and Health Care Technology Assessment/ Hospital Studies Program. (1988). *A severity classification for AIDS hospitalization* (Publication No. PB88-249412:D1-1-D1010). Springfield, VA: National Technical Information Service.

Oktay, J. (1992). Burnout in hospital social workers who work with AIDS patients. *Social Work, 37,* 432–438.

Ross, E. (1993). Preventing burnout among social workers employed in the field of HIV/AIDS. *Social Work in Health Care, 18,* 91–105.

Scitovsky, A. A., & Rice, D. P. (1987). Estimates of the direct and indirect costs of acquired immunodeficiency syndrome in the United States, 1985, 1986, and 1991. *Public Health Reports, 102,* 5–17.

Stein, E., Wade, K., & Smith, D. (1991). Clinical support groups that work. *Journal of AIDS Nursing Care, 2,* 29–36.

Strain, J. J., Fahs, M., Fulop, G., & Sacks, H. (1989). AIDS: Epidemiology and treatment issues. *Mount Sinai Journal of Medicine, 56,* 233–237.

Taravella, S. (1989). Reserving a place to treat AIDS patients in the hospital. *Modern Healthcare, 19,* 33–37.

Turner, B. J., Kelly, J. V., & Ball, J. K. (1989). A severity classification system for AIDS hospitalizations. *Medical Care, 27,* 423–437.

Weil, P. A., & Stam, L. M. (1990). Hospital administrators' response to AIDS: Results of a national survey. *Medical Care, 28,* 468–472.

CHAPTER 24

A Veterans Administration Community-Focused Residential Care Program: Objectives and Outcomes

DAVID GITELSON

ARTHUR RUSSO

LISA CARAISCO

The Intensive Psychiatric Community Care (IPCC) program of the Franklin Delano Roosevelt Department of Veterans Affairs Hospital in Montrose, New York, was established in 1987 under the auspices of the Department of Veterans Affairs Northeast Program Evaluation Center in West Haven, Connecticut. The IPCC program is administered by the hospital's Social Work Service. Its goal is to provide outpatient intensive case-managed services to patients with severe and persistent mental illnesses who have been heavy users of inpatient resources and have been considered by many staff to be undischargeable or incapable of maintaining themselves in the community. "Heavy use" was initially defined as more than six months of continual hospitalization (although most candidate's hospital length of stay exceeded several years) or a minimum of four rehospitalizations in the previous year. Since its inception, 173 patients have been discharged to the program. Currently, between 90 and 95 patients are being followed in six privately owned and operated rural and urban homes in the community that participate in the program.

It is the philosophy of the IPCC program that many patients with severe mental illnesses can leave institutional settings and adjust to community living if they and their nonfamilial caregivers are provided with a network of community supports and appropriate levels of supervision. To this end, case managers provide veterans placed in the program with training in social skills required for community living, intensive casework, continuity of care, group work support, psychoeducation, and assistance in

The thoughts and ideas presented in this chapter are not intended to represent the policies of the Franklin Delano Roosevelt Hospital or the Department of Veterans Affairs.

forming links with community resources. Should readmission be necessary, direct ongoing involvement with in-hospital staff occurs to convey information regarding the patient's stay in the community and to expedite his or her next discharge. This philosophy supports the importance of developing individual relationships and treatment plans; continuity of care; knowledge of and access to hospital- and community-based resources; and a minimum of weekly contact in the community to provide ongoing assessment, treatment, and support. Program staff are available to veterans, their families, and their nonfamilial caregivers 24 hours a day (Russo, 1995).

Outcomes Components

In addition to providing intensive case-managed services to patients selected for the program to prepare them for discharge from the hospital and—once placed—to assist them in maintaining themselves in the community, the IPCC staff, hospital administration, and members of the Northeast Program Evaluation Center (NEPEC) were interested in determining the program's impact on discharge rates and length of stay in the hospital and community. This impact was to be measured by examining the hospital days of a randomly selected experimental and control group. In addition, the cost-effectiveness of the program was to be determined by comparing the costs of treating patients in the hospital with the costs of community-based care (Neale & Rosenheck, 1995; Rosenheck, Neale, Leaf, Milstein, & Frisman, 1995).

To initiate the program, the names of eligible patients in the hospital who met the criteria for admission to IPCC were placed into a hat. An impartial individual randomly drew names and placed them into either an experimental group (59 patients) or a control group (55 patients). Patients in the control group continued to receive standard discharge planning services that consisted of meetings with unit-based social workers and multidisciplinary treatment team staff to explore community options. Because of the severity of the patients' mental illnesses, the chronic nature of their conditions, family and patient resistance to discharge, and ward staff concerns about the patients' abilities to manage in the community with available resources (which did not include intensive case management), patients often remained in the hospital for prolonged lengths of stay. (Additional data collected on participants during the study, but not reported here, included information on school and work activities, community activities, instrumental activities of daily living, family and social relationships, medication use, and data on psychiatric functioning.)

Program

Patients placed in the experimental group were visited on their units before discharge by IPCC program social workers and nurses who were knowledgeable about working with outpatients. Visits focused on discussions of program services. Recognizing that many of the patients feared leaving the facility, excursions were planned to "ride about" the community, go out for ice cream, participate as guests in social activities in IPCC homes, and so forth. These activities allowed patients to familiarize themselves with local communities and with the same staff who would visit them outside of the hospital if they entered the program. Passes for trial visits were issued, and IPCC staff visited as often as necessary to ease patients' anxiety. Program staff also met with in-hospital unit team members to educate them about the program and its model of intensive case management. Most significantly, program staff addressed any anxiety hospital staff members experienced around plans to discharge patients with severe mental illnesses. IPCC staff also assisted unit team members to complete referral packets to expedite the process. These interventions were viewed as further validation of the program's commitment to patients.

The IPCC staff also met with any involved family members to allay their fears. Staff members described the intensity of supervision and case management services the patient would receive in an IPCC home, and they confirmed the patient's right to readmission should it be necessary. These meetings addressed the intensive levels of resistance some families presented to the discharge of their relative from the protective environment of the hospital. In addition, the staff provided education to the private owners of the then five homes participating in the program and made themselves available directly, or by telephone, 24 hours a day. Finally, the IPCC staff became knowledgeable about resources in the local communities in which IPCC homes were located and regularly participated in the evaluation sessions of the IPCC patients conducted by various community-based programs. When "crises" arose between IPCC patients and individuals or groups in the community, the IPCC staff quickly and directly involved themselves outside of the hospital—whenever necessary—to resolve the issue.

Services Provided

Patients served in the program have ranged in age from 30 to 85 years old and have as their primary diagnosis a major psychiatric illness, including schizophrenia, major depression, bipolar disorder, and mental illness and chemical abuse. Many have experienced more than 20 admissions to psychiatric facilities. Concerns raised by participants have included anxiety around leaving the hospital setting, managing finances, dealing with peer relationships, using public transportation, and dealing with minimal stress. To address these issues, IPCC staff members have provided individualized social skills training; accompanied participants while they shopped, banked, or went to restaurants; paired participants with others in the program who were skilled at using resources in the community; allowed participants to make decisions while offering suggestions; provided education regarding medication and symptom management; and, most importantly, offered support and guidance. Caregivers have been provided with ongoing education and guidance in areas related to psychiatric conditions, medications, the social and emotional needs of participants, nursing requirements, dietary issues, and community relations (Tracy, Gitelson, & Sayeedi, 1994).

In addition, staff members learned about community programs outside the Department of Veterans Affairs to which IPCC participants are referred and frequently attended their evaluation conferences as allies in the treatment process. The staff members' ongoing availability to participants' nonfamilial caregivers and family members has served to resolve concerns and reduce anxiety.

All interventions listed previously served to expedite patient discharges and reduce their use of hospital resources as shown by the following outcomes data: Both IPCC and control treatment groups had essentially the same number of inpatient psychiatric hospital days before entry into the IPCC program (302.29 and 300.89, respectively, of a possible 365 days). However, as Table 24-1 shows, from one year to five years after entry, IPCC group participants experienced fewer inpatient psychiatric hospital days than the patients in the control group.

In addition, as shown in Table 24-2, the intensive predischarge interventions of the IPCC staff increased the number of patients with severe mental illness who returned to the community compared with the experimental group.

Finally, a cost analysis indicated that the 59 patients followed by the program during its initial five years spent 656 fewer days in the hospital, per veteran, than those in the control group. On the basis of these data, the cost per day of each hospitalized veteran, and the costs of the program, the Northeast Program Evaluation Center estimated a savings of $8,900,000 during the program's first five years.

What Was Learned

Observers of the process said that the direct interventions of IPCC staff on hospital units as active participants in the discharge planning process and their intensive case-managed services to patients after leaving the facility expedited patient return to the community, reduced patient and staff anxiety, and decreased use of hospital resources in a cost-effective manner. The program began changing the culture of several long-term care units that had perpetuated the belief that patients with serious and persistent mental illnesses could not sustain themselves in the community. With the assistance of the IPCC program, patients with hospital stays as long as 40 years or with as many as 50 readmissions since they first became known to the mental health care system have maintained themselves in the community for several years.

The initiative has reconfirmed the importance of the program's social workers and nurses joining with unit-based social workers, nurses and other staff, patients, and family members in a collaborative discharge planning effort as well as working together when readmission is necessary. Also important was the establishment of strong links by IPCC program staff with community-based agencies and private citizens within the community.

Table 24-1

INPATIENT PSYCHIATRIC HOSPITAL DAYS FOR EXPERIMENTAL VERSUS CONTROL GROUPS

Group	*n*	Year 1 Predischarge	Year after Discharge 1	2	3	4	5
Experimental	59	302.29	125.14	89.98	88.56	80.27	91.71
Control	55	300.89	273.15	222.44	200.36	184.27	156.44

Source: Rosenheck, R. A., & Neale, M. S. (1997). *Intensive Psychiatric Community Care (IPCC): Dissemination of a new approach to care for veterans with serious mental illness in the Department of Veterans Affairs.* Manuscript in preparation.

Table 24-2

NUMBER OF PATIENTS CHOSEN FOR DISCHARGE RANDOMLY VERSUS NUMBER ACTUALLY DISCHARGED FOR EXPERIMENTAL VERSUS CONTROL TREATMENT

Treatment Group	Number Chosen for Discharge by Random Selection	Number Actually Discharged	Percentage
Experimental	59	55	93
Control	55	29	52

Conclusion

The next steps have been identified: Anecdotally, staff believe that the quality of life of many participants has improved. Many patients are currently involved in vocational and community programs not sponsored by the Department of Veterans Affairs, including sheltered workshops, day treatment programs, Mental Health Association socialization programs, and community recreational activities, including multiday excursions away from their IPCC homes. The need to systematically study changes in the individuals' quality of life outside of the hospital, as program participants, is apparent. This effort is currently underway at the Franklin Delano Roosevelt Department of Veterans Affairs Hospital under the direction of the Northeast Program Evaluation Center, although preliminary data have already indicated an improvement in quality of life. Clearly the value of the existing outcomes data has supported and guided the direction of the IPCC program and has demonstrated the compatibility of engaging in outcomes studies while providing effective, direct client care.

References

Neale, M. S., & Rosenheck, R. (1995). Therapeutic alliance and outcome in a VA intensive case management program. *Psychiatric Services, 46,* 719–721.

Rosenheck, R. A., & Neale, M. S. (1997). *Intensive Psychiatric Community Care (IPCC): Dissemination of a new approach to care for veterans with severe mental illness in the Department of Veterans Affairs.* Manuscript in preparation.

Rosenheck, R., Neale, M., Leaf, P., Milstein, R., & Frisman, L. (1995). Multisite experimental cost study of intensive psychiatric community care. *Schizophrenia Bulletin, 21,* 129–140.

Russo, A. (1995). *Mental Health Initiative Program Statement.* Montrose, NY: Franklin Delano Roosevelt Department of Veterans AffairsHospital (Hospital Memorandum).

Tracy, R. A., Gitelson, D. A., & Sayeedi, N. J. (1994, April). *Continuity of care: A psychoeducational program for non-familial caregivers.* Unpublished manuscript, Franklin Delano Roosevelt Department of Veterans Affairs Hospital, Montrose, NY.

CHAPTER 25

An Application of the Use of Outcomes Measures with Multiply Diagnosed, Low-Income, Ethnically Diverse Clients

MARJORIE H. ROYLE

ROSEMARY T. MOYNIHAN

Many social scientific research methods were developed based on the college sophomore, who traditionally has been young, white, middle-class, well-educated, generally motivated, in good health, and a captive audience. These methods must be adapted for people who may be none of the above, such as those in the inner city who are infected with the human immunodeficiency virus (HIV). One such adaptation was done to evaluate a Ryan White Special Project of National Significance in Paterson, New Jersey, that provides mental health services integrated with their primary medical care to such a population.

The Program

St. Joseph's Hospital and Medical Center was established in 1867 to provide health care to poor people working in the silk mills of Paterson. Despite having evolved into a major urban, tertiary care center, it maintains this mission to poor people. Paterson,

Publication of this chapter was made possible by Grant BRH 970165-02-0 from the Health Resources and Services Administration (HRSA). Its contents are solely the responsibility of the authors and do not necessarily represent the official views of HRSA. The authors would like to thank their collaborators at the other institutions in the consortium that developed and implemented this grant: Barbara C. Kwasnik, ACSW, Helen D. Isenberg, MPH, and Ada Hernandez, BA, at St. Joseph's; Mark Winiarski, PhD, at Montefiore Medical Center; and Michael Mulvihill, DrPH, and Brian Taylor, PhD, at Albert Einstein College of Medicine.

with a population of about 140,000, is an ethnically diverse city, settled by successive waves of immigrants. It has—like many other low-income urban areas—inadequate housing and high levels of substance abuse and violence.

St. Joseph's began treating HIV-infected patients in the early 1980s. By 1985 the hospital established the Comprehensive Care Center for HIV Services to provide a broad range of medical services, including adult outpatient clinics; a designated inpatient unit; specialty clinics in dentistry, ophthalmology, dermatology, and gynecology; a pediatric HIV clinic; a pediatric residence; and a Head Start program. In 1991 Ryan White Special Projects of National Significance funds were received to develop a multidisciplinary mental health program to be integrated on-site with primary medical care. As the program evolved, it became clear that "integrated care" meant working and thinking together, however, not just being in the same place. The goal of this program was to make mental health services easily accessible and less threatening for individuals who are HIV-infected, poor, emotionally disturbed, and substance abusing. This was to be accomplished by doing the following:

- integrating mental health services into all primary medical care sites
- developing a service model that is flexible in time, place, frequency, duration, and modality such as by meeting patients where they are most comfortable and providing screening, brief psychotherapy, and outreach contacts in addition to traditional individual, family, and group therapies
- providing continuity of care with the same therapist and psychiatrist from diagnosis to death in both inpatient and outpatient settings and through episodes of service
- establishing a treatment goal of abstinence from drugs, rather than requiring abstinence as a prerequisite for treatment
- providing on-site services at drug treatment programs, parole offices, and schools
- using interdisciplinary rounds and consultations with medical staff as opportunities to model how to manage mental health issues and problems.

About 600 people, including HIV-infected clients of the medical services and their children, partners, and family members, are seen annually for mental health services. Forty-eight percent are African American, 30 percent are Latino, and 20 percent are white. About half are women. Half are substance abusers, and most of the remainder are partners or family members of substance abusers. Approximately 80 percent have had no previous mental health or psychiatric history and have not followed through on traditional mental health referrals from the medical clinics.

Evaluation Methods

OUTCOMES SELECTED

The primary outcome of interest was whether integrating mental health services with primary medical care improves *access* to care. Therefore, the appropriate population for study was those newly diagnosed patients receiving HIV medical care who were not already receiving mental health services. Specific outcomes for these patients include the following:

- Appropriate referrals were made for mental health services. That is, those who were most in need of such services should be more likely to be identified and referred in integrated than in nonintegrated sites.
- The referrals were completed and the patients actually received the services.
- Patients who received such services experienced decreased psychiatric symptoms and improved quality of life.

A second outcome of interest was whether providing integrated mental health care changes the way medical and mental health staff treat patients and interact with each other. Specific outcomes for staff include the following:

- Staff were more comfortable making referrals.
- Medical staff felt more confident in treating emotionally disturbed patients.
- Staff had more positive attitudes about treating patients who were multiply diagnosed with substance abuse and mental illness as well as HIV.
- Staff reported more work group cohesion and less job-related stress.

STUDY DESIGN

Traditional methods were modified to study these outcomes in this population. First, a quasi-experimental design was chosen, rather than an experimental design with a control group and random assignment. This choice was made because assigning individuals randomly to integrated or nonintegrated care would not have been feasible within a single institution. In addition, an increasing body of literature (D'Agostino & Kwan, 1995; Seligman, 1995; also see chapter 20) argues for measuring effectiveness, that is, how a procedure works in practice in the real world—rather than efficacy—or how it works in a carefully controlled, randomized experiment. For this study, the outcomes for St. Joseph's patients and staff with integrated care were compared with those from the Barnert Hospital, also in Paterson, with a similar clientele and an active HIV program. The Barnert Hospital, however, referred people to the traditional mental health clinic for mental health services, rather than having mental health integrated with primary medical care. The two sites had similar demographic variables and initial measures of symptomatology and quality of life.

When randomized designs are not used or are not feasible, experimental designs should use a variety of methods to attempt to balance or cancel out the problems and biases inherent in each. To do so, we gathered data from three different sources: patients, staff, and patient records.

Patients

A repeated-measures design was used in which all new adult patients to the HIV medical clinics who had not received mental health services before and who agreed to participate completed a battery of survey instruments. In the 18-month study period, 192 patients were enrolled: 123 at the integrated site and 69 at the nonintegrated site, with only nine refusals. The lower numbers at the comparison site were a result of fewer new medical patients than expected. Patients completed the battery again at four- and eight-month intervals, so that changes in symptomatology and quality of life could be measured for both integrated and nonintegrated sites. In the integrated site, 79 percent completed the second battery and 63 percent completed the third, whereas in the comparison site, 64 percent completed the second and 29 percent completed the third. The lower retention rates at the comparison site were a result of more patients dropping out of medical treatment and thus being unavailable for follow-up.

Staff

Both medical and mental health staff at both sites completed surveys.

Archival Information

Information on referrals made and kept and the amount of mental health services received was gathered from patient charts and other hospital records.

MEASURES SELECTED

Traditional paper-and-pencil research instruments were adapted for use with this population. In measurement, trade-offs were made between measuring "nothing well and something poorly." Although psychometric theory and practice advocate that multi-item, standardized, validated measures should be used for each construct, such instruments may be too long and complex for use with patients who have little education and a debilitating illness. The bias introduced by using data from only the few patients who complete such measures to generalize to the entire population may be a greater problem than using less rigorously developed instruments.

Instruments were selected for their brevity, simple language, availability in both Spanish and English, and history of successful use cross-culturally with a similar population, as well as for their appropriateness for measuring the outcomes. The two instruments that were chosen were the Brief Symptom Inventory (Derogatis, 1992) and the Medical Outcomes Study SF-36 (Ware & Sherbourne, 1992). The Brief Symptom Inventory was used both to identify those most in need of mental health services and to measure changes in symtomatology over time, whereas the SF-36 measured changes in physical functioning and quality of life. In addition, a brief demographic survey was developed and pretested.

Because reading level and length were less of a concern for the staff surveys, two standardized instruments were used. The Primary Care Physicians and AIDS Survey (Gerbert, Maguire, Bleecker, Coates, & McPhee, 1991) measured staff attitudes toward treating people with HIV and substance abuse, whereas the Work Environment Scales (Insel & Moos, 1994) measured work group cohesion and stress. Of the Work Environment Scales, only the six scales hypothesized to be most affected by integrated care (Involvement, Peer Cohesion, Supervisor Support, Autonomy, Task Orientation, and Innovation) were used, and the four other scales (Work Pressure, Clarity, Control, and Physical Comfort) were dropped, for two reasons. First, not using the full instrument shortened the survey, both to increase staff cooperation and to minimize the use of staff time. Second, omitting the scales not directly related to the hypothesized outcomes decreased the perception that work group leadership and morale, in general, were being measured. To maximize the likelihood of finding differences in areas in which integrated care was hypothesized to have the greatest effect, we supplemented these surveys with specific questions about confidence in diagnosing, treating, or referring for mental health problems.

MEASUREMENT ADMINISTRATION

A research assistant recruited patients for the study and assisted them completing the surveys by reading them in Spanish or English if necessary. Because answering health-related questions can be an additional stressor to someone who has been recently diagnosed with a debilitating, fatal disease, the assistant also provided reassurance and support. She formed a relationship with many patients, which was instrumental in their returning for follow-up surveys. Use of such a person introduced another source of bias, particularly because the study was not blind, although the assistant did not know which patients were receiving mental health services. This bias was minimized by training and by emphasizing the importance of getting complete, accurate data from as many people as possible, rather than the importance of changes over time in their responses.

Incentives were provided to participants. Patients were reimbursed $10 per session for their time and expenses, an amount large enough so that some people sought out the research assistant and asked to participate or to complete follow-up surveys. Staff members who completed surveys were presented with a small chocolate novelty as a token of appreciation. This incentive created goodwill among staff members for the project and may have also increased response rates for the staff survey.

The design took advantage of naturally occurring "captive audiences" where possible. The research assistant identified new patients using hospital records and approached them in the HIV outpatient clinic waiting room while they were waiting to see the physician or other medical staff. She also met patients at subsequent appointments or in their hospital rooms for follow-up surveys. Because they were at the clinic anyway and were being paid to participate, they usually agreed to complete the survey. Most failures to obtain completed surveys were a result of patients not keeping their appointments. However, by being in the clinic offices, the research assistant often enrolled them or administered follow-up surveys when they came to the clinic for an unscheduled visit at another time.

Experience in Implementing the Research Design

Modifications to traditional methods such as those used in this study were successful in collecting outcome measures from enough patients to provide a meaningful test of the effects of integrated care in a hard-to-reach population. Further analysis will determine the results of that test. Several observations can be made based on the implementation process itself.

- Settings that clearly identify eligible patients enhance enrollment. Because both Paterson sites had designated HIV clinics, the research assistant could approach newly diagnosed patients directly. However, at Montefiore Medical Center where a similar integrated mental health model was implemented and evaluated, patients with HIV received services at general medical clinics. They could not be enrolled in the study except through a clinic staff member or by responding to an enrollment notice posted in the clinic. Enrollment of patients at those sites was only about half as successful as at the Paterson sites, despite identical instruments and incentives.
- The research assistant's interpersonal skills, including caring and concern for the patients as people, was an important factor. The relationship that she formed with the patients—keeping in contact when she saw them at the clinics between surveys—made them more likely to complete the follow-up surveys.
- Investment of the medical and mental health clinical team in the success of the outcomes effort made its implementation easier. Several factors increased investment in outcomes measurement: their early involvement in the research planning; their understanding that outcomes measurement was an effort to assess the best way to help this patient population and to test the integrated care model, not the expertise of the staff; the research assistant's integration into the clinical team; and good communication between research and clinical staff.
- Surveying patients on their first clinic visits proved difficult because these visits often took several hours. Even patients who were interested in participating often were exhausted by the time they finished and did not want to stay for another survey, no matter how brief. To compensate for this, patients were enrolled as late as their third visit.
- Many patients, particularly those who were recently diagnosed, found the surveys to be confronting. Not only did the process test their social and reading skills but also the surveys—particularly the SF-36—forced them to consider decrements to their quality of life that they might anticipate in the future. Many of these patients required some emotional coaching to complete the forms.
- The greatest drawback to the methods used is their cost. A full-time research assistant had to be available during clinic hours, both for scheduled appointments and for drop-ins. Not infrequently, she spent an entire day waiting for clients who failed to keep or cancelled their clinic appointments. Although some of this time was used to perform required chart reviews and to assist the clinic staff—which helped her be perceived as part of the team—much of it could not be justified except as part of a special, grant-funded research study. Such intensive use of staff time is not possible in routine outcomes studies.

Conclusion

Traditional research methods and instruments can be adapted successfully to gather outcomes measures from nontraditional populations and settings such as those described in this chapter. Measurement procedures and survey instruments should be brief and simple, written in appropriate languages, distributed to a captive audience, and accompanied by an appropriate incentive whenever possible. The process should be sensitive to the emotional impact it may have on chronically or terminally ill individuals. If the target audience contains people who—because of limited language ability, education, infirmity, or other reasons—have difficulties with written surveys, some provision may be required to make assistance available by using clerical staff or volunteers. Sources of outcome information should include case records and staff ratings as well as client perceptions wherever possible. These extra efforts should produce results that will be useful in measuring and understanding program outcomes for all clients, especially for those who—although vulnerable—have a great deal to contribute.

References

D'Agostino, R. B., & Kwan, H. (1995). Measuring effectiveness: What to expect without a randomized control group. *Medical Care, 33,* AS95–AS105.

Derogatis, L. R. (1992). *BSI: Administration, scoring and procedures manual-II.* Baltimore, MD: Clinical Psychometric Research.

Gerbert, B., Maguire, B. T., Bleecker, T., Coates, T. J., & McPhee, S. J. (1991). Primary care physicians and AIDS. *Journal of the American Medical Association, 266,* 2837–2842.

Insel, P. M., & Moos, R. H. (1994). *Work environment scale manual.* Palo Alto, CA: Consulting Psychologists Press.

Seligman, M. E. (1995). The effectiveness of psychotherapy. *American Psychologist, 50,* 965–974.

Ware, J. E., & Sherbourne, C. D. (1992). The MOS 36-item short-form health survey (SF-36). *Medical Care, 30,* 473–483.

CHAPTER 26

Outcomes of Social Support for Women Survivors of Breast Cancer

SHERRI SHEINFELD GORIN

In the 1990s more than 1.5 million women will be newly diagnosed with breast cancer; nearly 30 percent of these women will ultimately die from the disease (American Cancer Society, 1993). Furthermore, women in the United States and Western Europe have the highest incidence of carcinoma of the breast. Because of the nature and treatment of the illness, breast cancer continues to exact physical and psychological adjustments even in the best of cases (Meyerowitz, 1980).

In general, the strength of the social support system—whether provided by friends, family, or professionals—seems an important factor in the long- versus short-term survival of women with cancer (Wortman, 1984; Wortman & Dunkel-Schetter, 1979). Studies of women with breast cancer have reported the importance of receiving psychological support of varied types and amounts from husbands (Northouse, 1988; Northouse & Swain, 1987), other family members (Jamison, Wellisch, & Pasnau, 1978; Wortman & Dunkel-Schetter, 1979), physicians and nurses (Bard & Sutherland, 1955; Weisman & Worden, 1976–1977), and other patients (Schwartz, 1977; Winick & Robbins, 1977) on quality of life (Nelles, McCaffrey, Blanchard, & Ruckdeschel, 1991) and survival (Funch & Marshall, 1983).

Research over the past 15 years has found that individuals who receive little support from others have lower positive well-being (Schaefer, Coyne, & Lazarus, 1981). Longitudinal research has shown that individuals who occupy few social roles, have little interaction with others, and maintain no close contacts have higher mortality rates than others (Berkman & Syme, 1979; Blazer, 1982). Conversely, social support seems to reliably enrich the prospects for recovery among people who are already ill

The author would like to thank the clients, volunteers, and staff of the New York Statewide Breast Cancer Hotline and Support Program at Adelphi University and Barbara Balaban, ACSW, director, for their participation in and support of this study.

(Chambers & Reiser, 1953; Cobb, 1976; Dimond, 1979; Robertson & Suinn, 1968; reviews in DiMatteo & Hays, 1981; Wallston, Alagna, DeVellis, & DeVellis, 1983).

In a review of social support and its effect on the health of postmastectomy women, Meyerowitz (1980) summarized a series of studies in which social support was either directly measured or found to be a major factor mediating adjustment after breast cancer diagnosis and treatment. Quint (1963) followed 21 women for one year after surgical treatment of breast cancer and found adjustment significantly linked to social support. Woods and Earp (1978) studied 49 women both immediately and four years after mastectomy and directly measured two dimensions of social support: helping and listening. They found that in women with few physical complications and a large amount of "helping" social support, depression was significantly reduced. No other relationship was found between social support and physical symptoms or depression. Ervin (1973) interviewed 12 women who had survived between five and 10 years after surgery with no evidence of disease. He found that emotional morbidity depended on the woman's inner resources, helpful professional guidance, and support of family and friends.

Several studies have systematically evaluated the impact of co-survivor social support groups, a part of many service programs for women diagnosed with breast cancer. The findings concerning the effectiveness of these groups on quality of life and survival have been mixed (Gellert, Maxwell, & Siegel, 1993; Spiegel, Bloom, Kraemer, & Gottheil, 1989; Van den Borne, Pruyn, & Van den Heuvel, 1987).

The present research was designed to examine the contribution of social support to quality of life and recurrence of breast cancer among a sample of women survivors attending a university-based rehabilitation program (the program) and to develop a model to further test these relationships. It seeks to overcome the criticisms leveled at other studies, namely of unreliable measures and the heterogeneity of samples (Gellert et al., 1993).

Method

A survey was administered by mail with repeated follow-ups. All instruments were chosen because they had excellent psychometric properties and were appropriate for administration to this sample.

THE PROGRAM

The program is multiservice and designed to provide information and referral, counseling (by telephone and in person individually or group), and volunteer opportunities to New York State residents concerned about breast cancer. The program receives its funds from the State of New York and a School of Social Work that is part of a small, private university. More than 500 women receive services annually.

Seventy-one percent of the respondents received information and referral from the program; 24 percent, telephone counseling; 14 percent, individual counseling; and 67 percent, group counseling. Fifteen percent of the respondents, who may have received information and counseling, also volunteered at the program. The average number of contacts per subject with the program was fewer than two, with great variation (mean = 1.84, *SD* = 4.66). On average, subjects spoke with a staff person for 50 minutes, although the range was great (*SD* = 47 minutes). When subjects were asked about the amount of support they received from program staff (1 = none at all, 5 = a great deal), the average level of support received was 2.66 (*SD* = 1.58).

SUBJECTS

One hundred seventy-three women with early-stage breast cancer (stage I, T_1, N_0, M_0 or IIA, T_3, N_0, M_0) and no nodal involvement were recruited from the program. Subjects were middle-aged in the main (mean = 53.09 years, *SD* = 10.75). Thirty-eight percent were postmenopausal, and nearly all were white (97 percent). The median family income was $50,000 per annum, with 47 percent of the women working outside the home; 24 percent, homemakers or unemployed; 2 percent, full-time students; and 27 percent having more than one occupational status. Seventy-eight percent of the sample were married or living as married, with more than one-half (64 percent) college educated, from associate's to post-master's degrees. The average household had 2.4 children (*SD* = 1.12).

Twenty-three (13 percent) women in the sample experienced a recurrence of the breast carcinoma. The median number of years between diagnosis and first recurrence was 2.5, with the average number of recurrences about one (mean = 1.29, *SD* = .64; see Table 26-1). The site of the first recurrence was generally on the same or other breast (two subjects each); on the lungs, abdominal cavity, pelvis, skull, spine or sternum, skin, ovaries, and cervix (one subject each); or elsewhere (two subjects). After the first recurrence of the carcinoma, most women had received adjuvant therapies, with 82 percent receiving a mastectomy; 20 percent, a lumpectomy; and 10 percent some subsequent breast reconstruction. More than one-half of the sample (57 percent) received some form of chemotherapy; 27 percent, radiation; and 32 percent received another hormone therapy, such as tamoxifen (Nolvadex) (30 percent), megestrol acetate (Megace) (1 percent), or an unspecified hormonal treatment (2 percent).

INSTRUMENTATION

Quality of life was assessed using the Life Satisfaction Index (Muthny, Koch, & Stump, 1990), a 13-item scale (mean = 3.65, *SD* = .77). Muthny and colleagues (1990) found a similar outcome using the Life Satisfaction Index with 131 healthy male and female subjects recruited through a 15-center study of quality of life across the then–Federal Republic of Germany (mean = 3.57, *SD* = 4.22). The internal reliability coefficient for the Life Satisfaction Index was very high (alpha = .93). A multidimensional scale was used to maximize the economy of interpretation and to increase construct validity.

The Life Satisfaction Index was evaluated relative to the Short Form Health Survey (SF-36), a well-regarded quality-of-life instrument for individuals receiving health care services (McHorney, Ware, & Raczek, 1993; Ware & Sherbourne, 1992), among a sample of 51 female graduate students—88 percent of whom were white and 6 percent each of whom were black and Hispanic. Sixty-one percent of the sample

Table 26-1

DESCRIPTION OF THE SAMPLE

Measure	Mean	Mean Percentage	Median	*SD*
Age	53.09			10.75
Menopausal status				
Pre		62		
Post		38		
Race/ethnicity				
Caucasian		97		
Black		1		
Hispanic		2		
Family income			$50,000	
Employment status				
Working full- or part-time		47		
Homemaker/unemployed		24		
Student		2		
More than one status		27		
Marital status				
Married or living as married		78		
Divorced or separated		8		
Single or widowed		14		
Number of children	2.4			1.12
Educational level				
High school		36		
Associate's degree		11		
Bachelor's degree		12		
Master's degree		22		
Post–master's degree		19		
Recurrences		13		
Time between diagnosis and first recurrence			2.5	
Number of recurrences	1.29			0.64

Note: N = 173. *SD* = standard deviation.

Source: Sheinfeld Gorin, S. (1994b). Social support as a predictor of recurrence and quality of life among female breast cancer survivors. In J. Einhorn, C. E. Nord, and R. Norrby (Eds.). *Recent advances in chemotherapy: Proceedings of the 18th International Congress of Chemotherapy* (p. 1058). Washington, DC: American Society for Microbiology.

were single, 25 percent were married, and 14 percent were divorced. Their average age was 30 (*SD* = 8.89), and their average income was $40,000–$59,999 (*SD* = $20,408). A small yet significant association was uncovered between the Life Satisfaction Index and the SF-36 ($r[47] = .25, p < .05$); similarly, a small significant association was found between the global measure and the SF-36 ($r[47] = .27, p < .05$). The Life Satisfaction Index is more comprehensive (including satisfaction with financial situation and spiritual life, for example) and less detailed in attention to particular health behaviors (such as difficulty walking or bathing and bodily pain) than the SF-36. Thus, the relatively small association among the measures of quality of life may highlight differences of the two scales in defining this multidimensional construct.

Overall, as would be expected, the range in number of recurrences—the measure of survival—was narrow. Thus, recurrence was measured by number of months since first diagnosis using a self-report with physician confirmation (mean = 4.67 years, *SD* = 6.25). Social support was evaluated by three measures—quality, density, and size of the network—that assessed central dimensions of the construct from the woman's perspective. Participants were asked about the quality of support received from others they listed in their networks using the Norbeck Social Support Instrument (Norbeck, Lindsey, & Carrieri, 1981). Quality of support was measured with six items, assessing the aid, affirmation, and affect received from each nominated member of the woman's social network. Affirmation concerned the woman's ability to confide in others and the trust received from others. Aid addressed the instrumental resources the woman shared with others, such as a car ride. Affect described the extent to which others made the woman feel liked or loved. To capture the multidimensional aspects of support, the six items were combined and an average score was computed (mean = 12.32, *SD* = .85). This average score is somewhat higher than that uncovered for 75 first-year graduate students in nursing, 74 of whom were female (mean = 11.02, *SD* = 4.66) (Norbeck, Lindsey, & Carrieri, 1983).

The RAND Corporation Social Support Scale (Donald & Ware, 1982) provided an index of the density of support (in number of contacts) with others (mean = 2.84, *SD* = .54). Women in this study manifested levels of support (mean = 2.84, *SD* = .54) comparable to those uncovered in a 4,603 household survey in three American cities (mean = 2.74, *SD* = 1.3) (Donald & Ware, 1982). The scale is homogeneous, has high internal reliability, and has high factorial stability.

To measure the overall number of individuals in their social support network or size, women were asked to name each member of their social support network within a series of concentric circles indicating their most to least important contacts. The instrument is derived from work by Kahn and Antonucci (1981) on "convoys" of social support. This sample reported about 21 others in the network (*SD* = 12.75). When the number of members of the social support network was compared with the 78-subject subsample from the classic Northern California Community Study, women in this study tended to maintain a somewhat larger and more variable number of network members (mean = 16.83, *SD* = 6.48) (McCallister & Fischer, 1978).

The 31-item Functional Status Measure (FSM) (Selby, Chapman, Etzadi-Amoli, & Boyd, 1984) assessed the physical factors related to the neoplasm multidimensionally, as well as with a global measure. The FSM addressed general health, disease, and treatment-related dimensions (mean = 4.93, *SD* = .54). The global FSM measure is moderately correlated with the highly regarded Karnofsky index ($r > .6$) (Karnofsky, Abelmann, Craver, & Burchenal, 1948).

The Mental Adjustment to Cancer Scale (Watson, Greer, & Bliss, 1989), an instrument with high reliability and factorial independence (Nelson, Friedman, Baer, Lane, & Smith, 1989), captured the subject's varied adaptations to the illness. The scale included four subscales: the Fighting Spirit (mean = 50.7, *SD* = 7.12); Helpless/Hopeless (mean = 8.94, *SD* = 2.75); Anxious Preoccupation (mean = 23.86, *SD* = 3.72); and Fatalism (mean = 16.5, *SD* = 3.64). These findings were comparable with those found by Watson et al. (1989) in their assessment of the instrument with 235 patients from Kings County Hospital and The Royal Marsden Hospital: Fighting Spirit (mean = 51.5, *SD* = 5.8); Anxious Preoccupation (mean = 20.9, *SD* = 4.2); Helpless/Hopeless (mean = 9, *SD* = 2.6); and Fatalism (mean = 17.9, *SD* = 3.7). The internal reliability of the scale is moderate (alpha = .57).

Findings

The Pearson product–moment correlations among the independent and dependent measures are found in Table 26-2. Significant correlations ($p < .05$) were found among two of the three sociodemographic factors: age and function ($r[173] = -.18$, $p < .05$); age and quality of life ($r [172] = -.17$, $p < .05$); and function and quality of life ($r[172] = -.17$, $p < .05$). Marital status was significantly correlated with function ($r[172] = -.18$, $p < .05$) and with quality of life ($r[173]= -.2$, $p < .01$), although not with age ($r[173] = .09$, not significant). Therefore, age and function were controlled in the remaining analyses. Furthermore, given the significant association of marital status and quality of life, as well as the importance of husbands to perceived quality of life of survivors (Northouse, 1988; Northouse & Swain, 1987), marital status too was controlled in subsequent analyses. To test the predictive strength of social support on quality of life and survival, experimenters performed a series of hierarchical multiple regression analyses. An interaction term, composed of social support (predictor) x fighting spirit (moderator) was entered on the last step in each equation to test for a moderator model. To avoid problems of multicollinearity, data were "centered" (Finney, Mitchell, Cronkite, & Moos, 1984) by subtracting subjects' mean scores on the predictor and the moderator variables from their raw scores. When entered on the last step in each multiple linear regression analysis, neither of the interaction terms was statistically significant.

The significant findings of the multiple linear regression analyses are found in Figure 26-1. Looking at social support as a predictor of quality of life, the entire equation was statistically significant, explaining 27 percent of the change in this sample of survivors ($F[7,165] = 8.57$, $p < .000$, $R^2 = .267$). Only one dimension of social support, however—quality of the woman's social support network—assumed a significant positive independent association with quality of life (beta = .17, $p < .01$).

Fighting spirit emerged as a mediator in the relationship between the quality of social support and the quality of life (Baron & Kenny, 1986). Fighting spirit manifested a statistically significant association with quality of life ($r[173] = .39$, $p < .001$), was strongly associated with social support ($r[76] = .33$, $p < .01$), and related

Table 26-2

MEANS, STANDARD DEVIATIONS, AND CORRELATIONS AMONG THE MAJOR MEASURES

Measure	M	*SD*	1	2	3	4
1. Fighting spirit (FS)	50.65	7.07				
2. Norbeck Social Support Questionnaire (NSSQ)	12.28	1.33	0.33**			
3. RAND	2.84	0.55	0.31***	0.25*		
4. Number in support network	20.64	12.75	0.28***	0.22	0.22**	
5. Quality of life	3.65	0.77	0.39***	0.4***	0.22**	0.13
6. Length of survival	4.67	6.25	–0.22	–0.11**	–0.63**	–0.23
7. NSSQ x FS[a]	2.45	7.08	–0.03	0.17	0.11	0.03
8. RAND x FS[a]	1.2	3.88	–0.31***	0.15	–0.15*	0.04
9. Age	54.28	10.2	–0.02	0.11	0.06	–0.06
10. Function	4.94	0.54	–0.01	–0.1	0.02	0.04
11. Marital status[b]	1.21	0.41	–0.06	–0.1	0.18*	–0.05

Measure	5	6	7	8	9	10
1. Fighting spirit (FS)						
2. Norbeck Social Support Questionnaire (NSSQ)						
3. RAND						
4. Number in support network						
5. Quality of life						
6. Length of survival	–0.28					
7. NSSQ x FS[a]	0.01	–0.52				
8. RAND x FS[a]	–0.1	0.32	0.36***			
9. Age	–0.17*	0.52*	0.08	0.22*		
10. Function	–0.17*	–0.07	0.01	0.02	–0.18*	
11. Marital status[b]	–0.2**	–0.16	0	–0.14	0.09	–0.03

[a]These data were centered to reduce multicollinearity (Finney, J. W., Mitchell, R. E., Cronkite, R. C., & Moos, R. H. [1984]. Methodological issues in estimating main and interactive effects: Examples from coping/social support and stress field. *Journal of Health and Social Behavior, 25*, 85–98).

[b]These data are categorical data, with 1 = married, living as married; 2 = single, divorced, widowed.

$*p < .05$; $**p < .01$; $***p < .001$.

SIGNIFICANT PREDICTORS OF QUALITY OF LIFE AND RECURRENCE

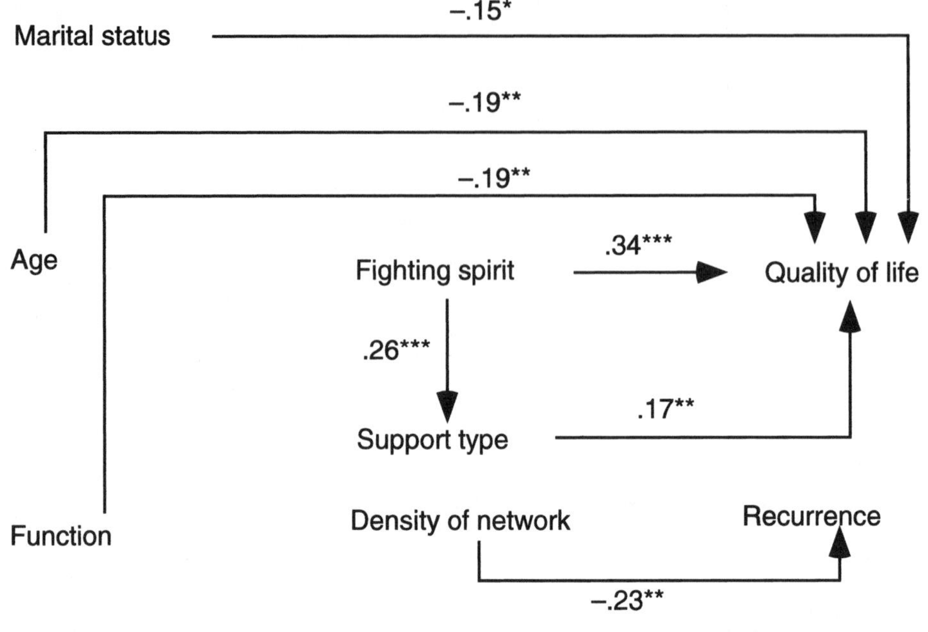

Note: Data are beta weights.
*p < .05; **p < .01; ***p < .001.

to quality of life when social support was controlled (beta = .26, $p < .01$). Furthermore, to meet the fourth criterion for mediation, when fighting spirit was controlled statistically as part of the multiple linear regression analyses, the relation became less strong, although still statistically significant (beta for quality of support with fighting spirit controlled = .18, $p < .01$; beta for social support with fighting spirit in the equation = .17, $p < .01$, R^2 change = .01).

Looking at length of survival, the major independent, dependent, and mediating factors predicted simply 8 percent of the variation in survival, and the equation was statistically insignificant (F[7, 165] = 1.91, not significant, R^2 = .076). Looking at each of the predictors, however, the density of the network emerged in a significant association with survival, with the anomalous negative finding that a less dense network was associated with more time between diagnosis and first recurrence (beta = –.23; $p < .01$). When assessed within the context of recent results supporting a lack of association between social support and survival among early-stage survivors (Gellert et al., 1993), this finding suggests that each of the components of support may manifest different outcomes (that is, linear or curvilinear) over the course of the woman's survival history.

Interestingly, the program showed no significant measurable effects on either participant quality of life or survival. The relationship between program impact on quality of life as measured by times contacted the program (beta = –.10; not significant), amount of time per contact (beta = .06; not significant), and quality of support from center staff (beta = .008; not significant) were small and insignificant. Similarly, no statistically significant influences of the program, in number of contacts (beta = –.08; not significant), time per contact (beta = –.05; not significant), or quality of support (beta = –.02; not significant) were uncovered for recurrences.

Conclusion

Social support, although conceptualized multidimensionally, exerted a unidimensional influence—in quality of the network—on enriched life satisfaction. As the quality of support increased, perceived quality of life was enhanced. The mechanism through which this influence was felt, or the mediator, was fighting spirit, a type of coping style. Women expressing a belief in the importance of a more positive attitude toward their illnesses and in their abilities to "fight" the disease seem better able to mobilize more dense networks and to experience enhanced life satisfaction.

Using the social ecology framework and viewing the reciprocal relations of individuals and their environments over time, one may better understand these relationships (Bronfenbrenner, 1979; Kelly, 1979; Moos & Moos, 1976 in Hirsch, 1981). The early work of Tolsdorf (1976) on "multiplex" relationships or associations with others in the network along a number of content areas—such as aid, affirmation, and affect—was one characteristic of a successful coping ecology during times of life change. Consonant with this approach, women who—after diagnosis—relate to others around them along multiple levels, from asking for transportation to trusting others, create a broad base for further support. Where these women also evidence "fighting spirit," they may be more able to maximize the effectiveness of increased network contacts in enhanced life satisfaction.

Anomalously, recurrence was less likely when the density of the woman's support network was also less, although this sample may have a statistically better chance of less recurrence irrespective of social support or because of it. Or, sample women's networks were maximally rich, and any immunologic effects derived from increasing the density of that support network would not be observed in decreased recurrence.

Alternatively, social relationships do not always convey support. In his study of altruistic suicides, Durkheim (1897/1951) acknowledged that although integration into societies and groups frequently benefited individuals, it sometimes actually increased their risk of death through excessive involvement and control. For example, a member of the network may develop a strong emotional grip on the woman survivor (Vaughn & Leff, 1981), or several network members may delimit the woman's expression of negative feelings, thus diminishing her quality of life and perhaps decreasing her survival chances (Pettingale, Morris, Greer, & Haybittle, 1985). Several studies have suggested these negative effects of social support among network members on survival (Croog, 1970; House, McMichael, Wells, Kaplan, & Landerman, 1979; Pearlin & Lieberman, 1979). Through training members of the social support network in optimal support mechanisms, for example, using a program developed by Sheinfeld Gorin (1994a), network member overinvolvement and control may be diminished.

Of interest to service providers, this program—designed to enhance social support—seemed to manifest little effect on either perceived quality of life or survival. The program, oriented toward brief information exchange, incorporates few central features of successful psychosocial interventions cited by Fawzy, Fawzy, and Arndt (1995), particularly a structured intervention, consisting of health education, behavioral training, coping strategies including problem-solving techniques, and psychosocial group support. As suggested in the finding concerning the negative relationship between social support density and survival, however, increased contact with this low-intensity program evidently did no harm.

Given the varied importance of differing components of social support for both quality of life and recurrence, further research is suggested, using multidimensional measures of both social support and quality of life.

References

American Cancer Society. (1993). *Cancer facts and figures*. Atlanta, GA: Author.

Bard, M., & Sutherland, A. M. (1955). Psychological impact of cancer and treatment IV: Adaptation to radical mastectomy. *Cancer, 8,* 656–672.

Baron, R. M., & Kenny, D. A. (1986). The moderator-mediator variable distinction in social psychological research: Conceptual, strategic, and statistical considerations. *Journal of Personality and Social Psychology, 51,* 1173–1182.

Berkman, L. F., & Syme, S. L. (1979). Social networks, host resistance, and mortality: A nine-year follow-up study of Alameda County residents. *American Journal of Epidemiology, 109,* 186–204.

Blazer, D. G. (1982). Social support and mortality in an elderly community population. *American Journal of Epidemiology, 115,* 684–694.

Bronfenbrenner, U. (1979). *The ecology of human development: Experiments by nature and design.* Cambridge, MA: Harvard University Press.

Chambers, W. N., & Reiser, M. F. (1953). Emotional stress in the perception of congestive heart failure. *Medicine, 15,* 38–60.

Cobb, S. (1976). Social support as a moderator of life stress. *Psychosomatic Medicine, 38,* 300–314.

Croog, S. H. (1970). The family as a source of stress. In S. Levine & N. A. Scotch (Eds.), *Social stress* (pp. 19–53). Chicago: Aldine.

DiMatteo, M. R., & Hays, R. (1981). Social support and serious illness. In B. H. Gottlieb (Ed.), *Social networks and social support in community mental health* (pp. 117–147). Beverly Hills, CA: Sage.

Dimond, M. (1979). Social support and adaptation to chronic illness: The case of maintenance hemodialysis. *Research in Nursing and Health, 2,* 101–108.

Donald, C. A., & Ware, J. E., Jr. (1982). *The quantification of social contacts and resources.* Santa Monica, CA: RAND Corporation.

Durkheim, E. (1897/1951). *Suicide: A study in sociology.* New York: Free Press.

Ervin, C. (1973). Psychologic adjustment to mastectomy. *Medical Aspects of Human Sexuality, 7,* 42–61.

Fawzy, F. I., Fawzy, N. W., & Arndt, L. A. (1995). Critical review of psychosocial interventions in cancer care. *Archives of General Psychiatry, 52,* 100–113.

Finney, J. W., Mitchell, R. E., Cronkite, R. C., & Moos, R. H. (1984). Methodological issues in estimating main and interactive effects: Examples from coping/social support and stress field. *Journal of Health and Social Behavior, 25,* 85–98.

Funch, D. P., & Marshall, J. (1983). The role of stress, social support, and age in survival from breast cancer. *Journal of Psychosomatic Research, 27,* 77–83.

Gellert, G. A., Maxwell, R. M., & Siegel, B. S. (1993). Survival of breast cancer patients receiving adjunctive psychosocial support therapy: A 10-year follow-up study. *Journal of Clinical Oncology, 11,* 66–69.

Hirsch, B. J. (1981). Coping and adaptation in high-risk populations: Toward an integrative model. *Schizophrenia Bulletin, 7,* 164–172.

House, J. S., McMichael, A. J., Wells, J. A., Kaplan, B. N., & Landerman, L. R. (1979). Occupational stress and health among factory workers. *Journal of Health and Social Behavior, 20,* 139–160.

Jamison, K. R., Wellisch, D. K., & Pasnau, R. D. (1978). Psychosocial aspects of mastectomy: I. The woman's perspective. *American Journal of Psychiatry, 135,* 432–436.

Kahn, R. L., & Antonucci, T. C. (1981). Convoys of social support: A life-course approach. In S. B. Kiesler, J. N. Morgan, & V. K. Oppenheimer (Eds.), *Aging: Social change* (pp. 383–405). New York: Academic Press.

Karnofsky, D. A., Abelmann, W. H., Craver, L. F., & Burchenal, J. H. (1948). The use of nitrogen mustards in the palliative treatment of carcinoma. *Cancer, 1,* 634–656.

Kelly, J. G. (1979). Tain't what you do, it's the way you do it. *American Journal of Community Psychology, 7,* 244–261.

McCallister, L., & Fischer, C. S. (1978). A procedure for surveying personal networks. *Sociological Methods and Research, 7,* 131–148.

McHorney, C. A., Ware, J. E., & Raczek, A. E. (1993). The MOS 36-item short-form health survey (SF-36): Psychometric and clinical tests of validity in measuring physical and mental health constructs. *Medical Care, 31,* 247–263.

Meyerowitz, B. E. (1980). Psychosocial correlates of breast cancer and its treatments. *Psychological Bulletin, 87,* 108–131.

Moos, R. H., & Moos, B. S. (1976). A typology of family social environments. *Family Process, 15,* 357–371.

Muthny, F. A., Koch, U., & Stump, S. (1990). Quality of life in oncology patients. *Psychotherapy and Psychosomatics, 54,* 145–160.

Nelles, W., McCaffrey, R. J., Blanchard, C. G., & Ruckdeschel, J. C. (1991). Social supports and breast cancer: A review. *Journal of Psychosocial Oncology, 9,* 21–35.

Nelson, D. V., Friedman, L. C., Baer, P., Lane, M., & Smith, F. (1989). Attitudes to cancer: Psychometric properties of fighting spirit and denial. *Journal of Behavioral Medicine, 12,* 341–355.

Norbeck, J. S., Lindsey, A. M., & Carrieri, V. L. (1981). The development of an instrument to measure social support. *Nursing Research, 30,* 264–269.

Norbeck, J. S., Lindsey, A. M., & Carrieri, V. L. (1983). Further development of the Norbeck Social Support Questionnaire: Normative data and validity testing. *Nursing Research, 32,* 4–9.

Northouse, L. L. (1988). Social support in patients' and husbands' adjustment to breast cancer. *Nursing Research, 37,* 91–95.

Northouse, L. L., & Swain, M. (1987). Adjustment of patients and husbands to the initial impact of breast cancer. *Nursing Research, 36,* 221–225.

Pearlin, L. I., & Lieberman, M. A. (1979). Social sources of emotional stress. In R. Simmons (Ed)., *Research in community and mental health* (Vol. 1, pp. 217–248). Greenwich, CT: JAI Press.

Pettingale, K. W., Morris, T., Greer, S., & Haybittle, J. L. (1985, March 30). Mental adjustments to cancer: An additional prognostic factor. *The Lancet, 1* (8431), 750.

Quint, J. C. (1963). The impact of mastectomy. *American Journal of Nursing, 63,* 88–92.

Robertson, E. K., & Suinn, R. M. (1968). The determination of rate of progress of stroke patients through empathy measures of patient and family. *Journal of Psychosomatic Research, 12,* 189–191.

Schaefer, C., Coyne, J. C., & Lazarus, R. S. (1981). The health-related functions of social support. *Journal of Behavioral Medicine, 4,* 381–406.

Schwartz, M. D. (1977). An information and discussion program for women after a mastectomy. *Archives of Surgery, 112,* 276–281.

Selby, P. J., Chapman, J.A.W., Etzadi-Amoli, J., & Boyd, N. F. (1984). The development of a method for assessing the quality of life of cancer patients. *British Journal of Cancer, 50,* 13–22.

Sheinfeld Gorin, S. (1994a, September). *Relationship enhancement intervention: A model social support program for women at high risk for breast cancer.* Paper presented at the meeting of the First International Conference on Cancer Prevention, New York.

Sheinfeld Gorin, S. (1994b). Social support as a predictor of reccurrence and quality of life among female breast cancer survivors. In J. Einhorn, C. E. Nord, & R. Norrby (Eds.), *Recent advances in chemotherapy: Proceedings of the 18th International Congress of Chemotherapy* (p. 1058). Washington, DC: American Society for Microbiology.

Spiegel, D., Bloom, J. R., Kraemer, H. C., & Gottheil, E. (1989, October 14). Effect of psychosocial treatment on survival of patients with metastatic breast cancer. *Lancet,* 888–891.

Tolsdorf, C. (1976). Social networks, support, coping: An exploratory study. *Family Process, 15,* 407–417.

Van den Borne, H. W., Pruyn, J.F.A., & Van den Heuvel, W.J.A. (1987). Effects of contacts between cancer patients on their psychosocial problems. *Patient Education and Counseling, 9,* 33–51.

Vaughn, C. E., & Leff, J. P. (1981). Patterns of emotional response in relatives of schizophrenic patients. *Schizophrenia Bulletin, 7,* 43–44.

Wallston, B. S., Alagna, S. W., DeVellis, B. M., & DeVellis, R. F. (1983). Social support and physical health. *Health Psychology, 2,* 367–391.

Ware, J. E., & Sherbourne, C. D. (1992). The MOS 36-item short form health survey (SF-36): Conceptual framework and item selection. *Medical Care, 30,* 473–483.

Watson, M., Greer, S., & Bliss, J. M. (1989). *Mental adjustment to cancer (MAC) scale user's manual.* Sutton, Surrey, England: Cancer Research Campaign Psychological Medicine Group (CRCPMG), The Institute of Cancer Research and the Royal Marsden Hospital.

Weisman, A. D., & Worden, J. W. (1976–1977). The existential plight in cancer: Significance of the first 100 days. *International Journal of Psychiatry in Medicine, 7,* 1–15.

Winick, L., & Robbins, G. F. (1977). Physical and psychologic readjustment after mastectomy: An evaluation of Memorial Hospital's PMRG program. *Cancer, 2,* 478–486.

Woods, N. F., & Earp, J. L. (1978). Women with cured breast cancer. *Nursing Research, 27,* 279–285.

Wortman, C. (1984). Social support and the cancer patient: Conceptual and methodological issues. *Cancer, 53* (Suppl), 2339–2362.

Wortman, C., & Dunkel-Schetter, C. (1979). Interpersonal relationships and cancer: A theoretical analysis. *Journal of Social Issues, 35,* 120–155.

PART V

Concluding Observations

CHAPTER 27

Comments on Outcomes Measurement in Mental and Behavioral Health

ROBERT ABRAMOVITZ

ANDRÉ IVANOFF

RAMI MOSSERI

ANNE O'SULLIVAN

This commentary summarizes the measurement and evaluation issues specific to the mental and behavioral health care field according to the part IV authors and the symposium discussions. (The chapters in part III are revisions of papers originally presented at the 1995 Center for the Study of Social Work Practice National Symposium on Outcomes Measurement in the Human Services and chapters prepared specially for this book. Extensive discussion followed the presentations, and this chapter is based on both the papers and those discussions.) The desired outcomes of mental and behavioral health as well as areas of consensus and disagreement also are examined. The current state of the outcomes measurement field, as described by part IV authors, is briefly revisited at the system and policy, program, and client levels. Finally, outcomes measurement in mental and behavioral health future directions are explored.

"Accountability": For What and to Whom?

Outcomes measurement and evaluation issues extend far beyond simply applying methodology at individual client (or client groups) and program and policy system levels; nowhere is this better seen than in mental and behavioral health care. The issues identified in part IV of this book illustrate the breadth and complexity in defining and operationalizing outcomes measurement in mental and behavioral health care.

Public doubts about the value of mental health services plague public and private providers and clients, fueling the demand for accountability independent of value and quality. The highly politicized environment and stigma discussed by Wasow contribute to widespread colloquialism and ignorance about the course of behavioral disorders and treatment. In the absence of empirical data about what constitutes effective treatment or any standards about what constitutes well-established treatments, the development of numerous treatment approaches is encouraged, and each is considered viable. A high degree of interaction exists between clinical status and life circumstances, perhaps even more so than in the physical health care arena. These characteristics of the mental and behavioral health care system are generally acknowledged; however, they are complicated by some obstacles to measurement and evaluation also specific to mental health. One of these obstacles is a lack of resources (that is, people, money, technology, and knowledge). Another obstacle is that the difficulty in defining success prevents standardized, if not all, measurement. Finally, a focus on functional or clinical outcomes determines the level, type, and to some extent, generalizability of measurement.

Part IV examines these issues of accountability from two different perspectives: the public and private mental and behavioral health systems. The public system, serving most patients with severe and persistent mental disorders and substance abuse problems, is characterized by complex social issues including substance abuse and criminal behavior; highly political funding issues; and ongoing conflict among professionals, clients, and their advocates about what constitutes appropriate treatment. In contrast, the private system, serving more middle- and upper-income clients, receives extensive funding through third-party payers and insurance programs that also fund physical health care. Determining the medical necessity of mental and behavioral health treatment is not as easy as in physical health care, but ultimately the same question is posed: What should be paid for, how much should be paid for, and by whom? Although the private payment system tends to stress clinical outcomes, the public payment system tends to stress functional outcomes.

Part IV authors present a consensus regarding the necessity for outcomes measurement stressing cost-containment and cost-effectiveness pressures. However, this consensus extends only to initial agreement. After agreeing that demonstrating the effectiveness of mental and behavioral health outcomes is necessary, defining this task sorely challenges the existing knowledge base.

The demand for outcomes data has outstripped current measurement capacity. The authors in part IV view the mental and behavioral health field as rapidly achieving a respectable level of measurement capacity and the balance is shifting from reactivity to proactivity. Consequently, at each level of the mental and behavioral health system, consensus is emerging concerning important principles and technologies.

Systems Level

At the systems and policy level, diligent efforts are being made to resist expedient approaches to outcomes measurement. The need for reliable and valid measurement instruments has emerged as a core principle that policymakers must require. Another principle that has the strong support of program, client, and advocacy levels concerns the need for equal representation among all stakeholders. This need takes on added significance when one recognizes the depth and extent of the mental health consumer advocacy movement chronicled by Wasow.

At first glance it appears that the fiscal resources needed to ensure ongoing outcomes measurement conflict with cost-containment strategies. Consequently, policymakers must ensure that the fiscal resources necessary to provide competent outcomes measurement are available. Pressure for competitive cost containment among providers threatens the ability of smaller mental health providers to demonstrate the effectiveness of their work. Smaller providers are at a serious disadvantage when reimbursement policies do not include resources for service evaluation.

Controversy exists between the need for uniform standards and measurement instruments and the pressure for immediate measurement with whatever instrument is available. Although such ad hoc outcomes measurements are unintegrated at best and at worst incoherent, their use continues to dominate. Until normative databases are developed and made available, even if the outcomes data generated are capable of being aggregated, findings for such ad hoc measures are difficult to assess. The use of narrow or broad-band outcomes measures fuels related debate. Should the focus be on symptoms and functional status, or should the person's entire context be assessed? The latter would mean that variables such as housing, employment, and social support systems would need to be included in the scope of measurement.

Program Level

At the program level, consensus about outcomes measurement falters. Although most programs are pressed to integrate evaluation measures and demonstrate service effectiveness, few programs actually develop, use, and monitor operational outcomes measurement systems. Program directors and staff share ambivalence toward evaluation and worry about the outcomes of measurement. They often do not share a common vision of urgency or a need for outcomes measurement. Given fiscal and human resource limitations, controversy repeatedly erupts over the amount of resources that should be devoted to direct care and the amount that should be devoted to outcomes measurement. Corcoran and Smith, Rost, Fischer, Burnam, and Burns address this concern by recommending the use of standardized instruments that assist assessment and diagnosis while simultaneously measuring outcomes variables. Although this attention to measure instrument feasibility and user-friendliness is essential, it does not often convince staff of an instrument's clinical use or prevent thinking such as, "OK, but what does this have to do with *my* job?" or—more importantly—"What does this have to do with improving services?" Program directors are under pressure to develop ways to demonstrate to staff that outcomes measurement can support good clinical practice and to provide reassurance that practitioners' jobs are not automatically at risk. Program directors will need sophisticated means to ensure that individual workers have comparable case-mixes so that appropriate comparisons can be made. Case management technology for mental health care is primitive at best because of many of the same definitional problems.

Client Level

At the client level, there is consensus that the existence of valid outcomes data will eventually allow the client to make an informed choice from among treatment approaches. However, clinicians and clients often have different expectations about what constitutes a satisfactory outcome. Mechanisms must be developed to bring consumers and providers together to reach a consensus definition of quality and effectiveness.

Future Directions in Outcomes Measurement

In the past, mental and behavioral health services have not proven the connection between cost and value of services. However, the recent political movement to reduce health care costs has pushed the need to use outcomes as the means by which the value of services is established. The connection between cost and value and its critical examination will continue to be the driving force behind outcomes-oriented accountability strategies in mental and behavioral health. The future of outcomes measures in the public and private sectors will be driven by cost containment.

Nonetheless, standardization of outcomes measures is one of the most important tasks for the future of outcomes in mental and behavioral health care. Current measurement tools represent a "Tower of Babel" approach with no standard language or ability to compare value of services and attached costs.

Future outcomes measures in mental and behavioral health also will have to address the gap between the abundance of new measures and the available technologies. Despite the numerous systems, policy, program, and client measures developed throughout the nation as technology advances, the availability of such technology is tied to costs and therefore poses challenges. Any real investment in new technology will have to be made within both the public and private sectors. Although the private sector has immediate incentives for such investments, the public sector may lag behind because its motivation is not propelled by profit-making efforts. The obvious need for technologically well-supported tracking systems, for example, may be viewed as conflicting with clients' rights to confidentiality.

Shern and Trabin view the public sector's future role as measuring the well-being of populations at large and their use of services across the full range of service systems. The private sector will continue to concentrate on services to individuals on a category-of-service basis. No end appears to a two-tiered system. In principle, however, both public and private sectors will continue to examine the value of services through outcomes measures driven by cost considerations.

We close with a comment made by Hudson in chapter 5 that perhaps summarizes best the future of outcomes measurement, "Attention must. . . be given to developing computer support systems that will address the day-to-day realities of actually doing practice and will also accommodate the measurement and assessment needs of all actors within the organization: clients, practitioners, supervisors, managers, administrators, and program evaluators" (p. 74).

CHAPTER 28

Comments on Outcomes Measurement in Child and Family Services

BRENDA G. McGOWAN

STEVEN D. COHEN

The chapters in part III of this book offer a rich array of approaches to questions of outcomes measurement in family and children's services, and it is tempting to adopt the relatively optimistic stance of the authors and focus solely on the implications of the alternative strategies they propose. To present a broad view of the current status of outcomes measurement in this field, however, we also include as a basis for our comments the workshops and extensive discussions that accompanied the presentation of these papers. (The chapters in part III are revisions of papers presented at the 1995 Center for the Study of Social Work Practice National Symposium on Outcomes Measurement in the Human Services and chapters prepared specially for this book.)

The symposium sessions on child and family services were attended by many of the field's leading scholars and practitioners, most of whom could cite interesting local or state initiatives related to evaluation of service outcomes. Yet there was widespread agreement that the field of outcomes measurement in child and family services as a whole is in sorry shape and that little is known about what should be measured, how it should be measured, or by whom it should be measured. This conclusion led some participants to express jealousy about recent developments in the health and mental and behavioral health sectors compared with the limited progress made in child and family services. Others expressed some relief that this field has been slower to engage in outcomes measurement, pointing out the risks of applying a linear causation model to the complexities of service intervention with high-risk families and children.

This chapter summarizes the key barriers to outcomes measurement identified in the child and family services symposium sessions and examines the ways in which some of the approaches discussed in part III of this book can address some of these barriers. One set of barriers derives from political and value considerations, and the other derives from technical and methodological issues.

Political and Value Considerations

The most obvious barrier to satisfactory outcomes measurement is the lack of consensus about two questions. First, should priority be given to measuring the outcomes of traditional child welfare services, those directed toward helping children whose parents are unable or unwilling to fulfill their traditional role expectations? Or should priority be given to measuring the broad dimensions of family and child welfare that result from the full range of social, economic, educational, and health services provided to families and children in different communities? Second, what are the specific outcomes that should be achieved and whose outcomes are to be measured? The historic debates about family preservation versus child protection still pervade most discussions of outcomes measurement in the traditional child welfare field. The terms of the debate are not even clear in the broader arena of family and child welfare.

Current ambiguity regarding the objectives of child and family services is compounded as a result of different stakeholders in the system having different goals. One of the key obstacles to effective outcomes measurement is the tendency to look for single measures of success and to blur distinctions among what might be desirable at the case, program, and policy or systems levels. These levels are clearly interrelated, but the ethical and political imperatives are different at each level. This difference is illustrated by the emphasis on prevention of placement as the ultimate criterion of success in child welfare services. Although placement prevention may be a desirable cost-saving goal at the systems level and family preservation may be applauded as a public policy objective, placement prevention is not always an appropriate goal at the case level. Programs that have higher rates of foster care placement may simply be handling more difficult cases or have lower rates of subsequent child maltreatment than programs that have lower placement rates. Hence, it seems questionable to use placement prevention as the primary measure of program effectiveness.

According to some symposium participants, another barrier to the development of appropriate outcomes measures is increased emphasis on the need to achieve positive results that could lead to increased blaming of clients and increased efforts to cut public costs by reducing program funding. Unlike the health care field, clients in family and child welfare agencies frequently are blamed for their problems, and service providers in this field are often censured for failing to effect dramatic improvements in family functioning, no matter how severe the personal and social problems confronting these families. Many symposium participants expressed a sense that this service system is currently under siege and that it would be dangerous to give added ammunition to those who would further reduce the limited services and resources now available to low-income families.

Finally, symposium participants noted the dilemmas posed by a historic tendency to dismiss the value of client assessments of service outcomes in child and family services. (There are some notable exceptions such as the research reported by Festinger, 1983.) Unlike other fields in which consumer satisfaction is defined as a key outcomes measure, researchers in child and family services often are reluctant to give credence to this question, perhaps reflecting the social control function inherent in much of child welfare practice.

Technical and Methodological Issues

Several technical and methodological problems constrain measurement of service outcomes and compound the barriers created by political and value considerations. One factor is the high proportion of involuntary clients in child and family services, which makes sample selection and recruitment difficult. Another is the fact that service needs and interventions in this field are less clearly defined and more variable than treatment interventions in some other service arenas. For example, if 100 patients with high blood pressure are given the same medication, the extent of the hypertension problems they were experiencing can be specified, and it can be reliably concluded that they received the same treatment. Yet if 100 families are experiencing parenting problems and given family support services, it cannot be assumed that they had the same difficulties or that they received the same intervention.

A major methodological barrier emphasized in symposium discussions was the enormous impact of different environmental variables on most families in the child welfare system. This means that the range of variance in outcomes accounted for by service interventions is likely to be much smaller in child and family services than in other fields in which client problems are not so directly affected by environmental factors. Moreover, given that researchers in this field of practice have no reliable means of measuring or controlling for the influence of various environmental factors, they are forced to make assessments of service outcomes that may ignore key causal variables. To illustrate this point, the 1996–1997 changes in welfare payments to low-income families influenced the lives of many child welfare clients. Because these changes were implemented on a universal basis, child welfare researchers have no means of separating the effect of these cutbacks from the impact of different service interventions.

Finally, in chapter 15, Wulczyn examines the barriers that derive from what he terms the "clinical motif" in child welfare research that focuses on the details of individual cases rather than aggregate-level trends and the macrovariables that shape patterns of service delivery. He also highlights the failure of most child welfare researchers to use statistical models of change processes that can extract complexity from empirical data.

Potential Approaches to Outcomes Measurement

Despite the many obstacles to outcomes measurement identified by the participants, the symposium workshop sessions on child and family services concluded with a general sense of the importance of meeting these challenges and a recognition that despite some progress, an important process is beginning. Although increased attention to outcomes measurement poses the risks identified earlier, everyone agreed that policymakers and funding organizations are likely to start imposing judgments about service effectiveness from outside if child welfare practitioners and researchers do not take responsibility for developing feasible measures for the field.

Symposium participants struggled with the differences among outcomes measures that examine the effectiveness of specific service programs and those that assess the well-being of families and children in a community. It was agreed that these measures must be clearly distinguished. Perhaps most important was the recognition that the field should use multiple measures and indicators of outcomes that are practical and results oriented and stop pursuing a futile search for a single outcomes criterion such as placement prevention.

Other promising recommendations have been made by authors in part III as well as by symposium participants. There is widespread agreement with Wulczyn's suggestion that case outcomes data be separated from aggregate outcomes data as well as with McCroskey's recommendation to begin with gross, aggregate measures that convey a picture of how the entire system is succeeding. As McCroskey noted, outcomes measures can be useful at all system levels, but they must be differentially designed to be helpful to case practitioners, agency administrators, and community leaders.

One immediate recommendation that derives from the symposium discussions is the importance of implementing regular consumer satisfaction surveys in every child and family services system. Although such measures cannot serve as the sole measure of service effectiveness, they offer a critical perspective on service outcomes. No valid outcomes evaluation can ignore consumer views. Wulczyn's recommendation to make greater use of event history analysis and epidemiological studies rather than continuing to rely on cross-sectional samples was supported by symposium participants.

The strategic planning initiatives in Oregon and Minnesota reported by Weiss and the experiences with the Children's Score Card in Los Angeles County described by McCroskey provide interesting examples of ways that these localities have addressed the challenge of obtaining consensus on service objectives among different stakeholders. What seems clear from these illustrations is the importance of involving all stakeholders in a collaborative process focused on identifying shared individual-, family-, and community-level goals. If this is done, it should then be possible—as these experiences suggest—to link case and aggregate data and to use outcomes measures to establish community priorities and to allocate public resources.

To accomplish this, it is essential for child and family services to adopt what Weiss describes as a "learning organization" model (Garvin, 1993) and engage in a continuous process of problem solving, experimentation, and rapid information dissemination. Such a process seems likely to encourage the type of open exploration and learning required to enable coalitions to reach consensus on the difficult value questions that pervade discussions of outcomes.

Although Benbenishty uses somewhat different terminology, the approach he advocates uses many of the same concepts as Weiss's "learning organization." Benbenishty states that outcomes should be addressed within the context of the requirements for empirical practice. Consequently, practitioners and agencies should emphasize learning how to become more effective rather than just proving and documenting their effectiveness. The principles Benbenishty proposes for supporting empirical practice all build on the idea of creating a learning environment at the agency level. This idea requires that agencies encourage workers to integrate systematic monitoring of their clients, interventions, and outcomes into everyday practice; create feedback loops that encourage learning from experience; make computers and advanced information technology an integral part of front-line practice; and form learning communities composed of agencies willing to share the local generalizations they can derive from the experiences of their own practitioners. A final practical suggestion that builds on Benbenishty's proposals is the development of more comprehensive management information systems in every child and family services agency, which would permit aggregation of case data and examination of outcomes at the program level.

In summary, we believe, with renewed recognition provided by part III authors and many symposium participants, in the importance of giving increased attention to the issues inherent in outcomes measurement. We appreciate the progress. Nonetheless, the many obstacles to effective outcomes measurement must be addressed, and the need to create a learning environment among practitioners and researchers in child and family services must be met if the types of innovation, experimentation, and sharing of ideas required to make substantive progress are to occur.

References

Festinger, T. (1983). *No one ever asked us—A postscript to foster care.* New York: Columbia University Press.

Garvin, D. A. (1993). Building a learning organization. *Harvard Business Review, 71,* 78–91.

CHAPTER 29

Comments on Outcomes Measurement in Health

GRACE H. CHRIST

RITA BECK BLACK

The chapters in part IV document advances that have taken place in social work research in health care and in the health care field in general during the past several years. Therefore, we highlight some of the critical issues addressed by the research presented and identify the questions and concerns raised by the studies. We draw on our assessments of the studies and comments made by participants in the health workshops at the 1995 Center for the Study of Social Work Practice National Symposium in Outcomes Measurement in the Human Services.

At the 1995 symposium Helen Rehr observed that a different interaction exists between practitioners and researchers than was evident at the Center for the Study of Social Work Practice's 1993 conference, which focused on resolving conflicts in relationships in practitioner and researcher partnerships (see Hess & Mullen, 1995). In contrast, the 1995 symposium focused on research measurement. This change in focus suggests an evolution in the focus of research in clinical health care settings. In addition, the studies presented at the outcomes measurement symposium and included in part IV either were practice based or were implemented through collaborative relationships among services program providers, administrators, and researchers. Feedback systems were described not only in terms of defining the outcomes and measures but also in terms of evaluating service implications once results were obtained. Research results often were quickly used for redesigning.

Advances in the development and sophistication of studies in health care are driven in large part by the demand for cost reductions in the health care system. Downsizing, re-engineering, and other forms of institutional restructuring have made it necessary for human service providers to define roles, goals, and functions in precise and economically advantageous ways. Cost reductions can be achieved through at least three strategies: (1) decreases in use of services, (2) more appropriate and timely use of services, and (3) personnel reduction or use of less costly personnel. The studies presented in part IV were designed to achieve at least one of these outcomes.

Developing and Using Standardized Measures

The development and use of effective, valid, and reliable measures of quality of life and of patient satisfaction is a theme that runs throughout part IV. Both Berkman and Coulter highlight the positive underlying value system established in health care that supports the development of quality-of-life and patient satisfaction measures. This value system includes the acceptance of the value of the patient's perspective in assessing quality of care. As Berkman states, "It is now accepted that clients must participate in treatment choices and that their perceptions may differ from those of their health care providers" (p. 218). This is different from the tradition in child and family services that tends, at best, to distrust the perspectives of the client.

Zabora joins Berkman and Coulter in emphasizing the importance of using measures that have established validity and reliability so that comparisons can be made across populations rather than confining measures to individual hospitals or health care services. When standardized measures are used, individual scores take on greater meaning. Only with the use of such measures can social workers address the long-range goal of documenting how social work interventions help reduce overall health care costs. Zabora also reiterates that the positive impact on cost reduction has not been demonstrated. Although it is clear from the presentations that progress has been made in developing standardized measures of patients' quality of life after illness episodes as well as patient satisfaction, these measures are not widely used in clinical practice.

The purposes for which valid and reliable measures of quality of life and patient satisfaction can be used in health care social work include screening for psychosocial needs, identifying patients who need a psychosocial assessment, predicting needs for social work care management after assessment, and measuring outcomes that demonstrate the effects of social work services. What then are some of the barriers that exist to the use of these measures in health care?

Barriers to the Use of Standardized Measures

Barriers to the use of standardized outcomes measures in health care settings are identified in part IV, and some were identified by symposium participants. Part IV authors note that some current measures are impractical for administration in health care settings and that more work should be done to develop appropriate measures. Zabora suggests that such measures should not require more than 10 or 15 minutes to complete in settings such as waiting rooms or examination rooms. Clearly the cost of using these measures is a vital consideration if they are to be routinely used or used with large numbers of patients who are in various stages of medical illness.

Another barrier is that social workers are not adequately trained in research methods; they lack knowledge and expertise in the appropriate use of existing measures. Continuing education programs used by social workers to update their skills rarely include a focus on outcomes measures.

An additional barrier pertains to a negative attitude among social workers and other human service workers, such as mental health professionals, regarding the use of standardized measures. Such professionals are inclined to believe that these measures are reductionistic and inhibit the system from relating to patients in a holistic way. These attitudinal barriers should be addressed in educational efforts if outcomes measurement is to become a reality.

Another barrier is the insufficient focus of social work research efforts on developing new measures or modifying existing ones that are more relevant for the complex social work situations faced in most health care settings. Berkman describes her excellent efforts to modify an existing measure to make it more relevant to a specific patient population that social work serves. Without such tailoring, measures may not be used properly to evaluate the kinds of outcomes social work interventions they are designed to achieve.

A final barrier all part IV authors identify is that most standardized measures have not been tested with culturally and socioeconomically diverse populations. The ability of these measures to be effective with such patient populations is largely unknown.

An Approach to Overcoming Barriers to Studying Culturally Diverse Populations

The study described by Royle and Moynihan demonstrates an innovative effort to explore this important area, that is, the application of standardized quality-of-life and patient satisfaction measures with culturally diverse individuals. These researchers describe a model of community-based services that aims to make services accessible and less threatening to vulnerable, multiply diagnosed patients (that is, individuals diagnosed with the human immunodeficiency virus, emotional disturbance, and substance abuse). Because quality-of-life outcomes are described as having major importance, these authors used measures such as the SF-36 (Ware & Sherbourne, 1992) and the Brief Symptom Inventory (Derogatis, 1992).

Royle and Moynihan found that major modifications in implementation of these measures were required to recruit subjects for their study in a real-world setting. Trade-offs often were made between measuring "nothing well and something poorly" as patients found participation in studies threatening, burdensome, and time-consuming. Therefore, the researchers chose to obtain limited information on as many patients as possible. They modified the measures by making them as brief and simple as possible, writing them in the languages appropriate to the population, distributing them when patients were a "captive" audience, and providing fiscal incentives. They also note the emotional impact these measures can have on chronically or terminally ill individuals. For example, to alleviate patient anxiety regarding certain questions about possible bodily deterioration greatly feared by patients who have a life-threatening illness, research assistants read the questions, thereby relating more personally to patients. When possible, they also used additional sources of information such as case records and staff ratings to corroborate and confirm client responses.

These design modifications resulted in greater success in the numbers of patients recruited at their site compared with other sites that did not accommodate patients in these ways. Royle and Moynihan discuss the cost of these modifications. This study provides new insights and information about the use of such measures with culturally diverse individuals. It also demonstrates the necessity of using standardized measures when attempting to study patients in multiple institutional sites. Continued efforts to apply these measures with diverse populations is an important direction for social work.

Identifying the Cost of Social Work Services

Another outcomes measurement theme articulated by studies described in part IV was the importance of social work services for management and administrative purposes. Two of these studies compared the cost of two intervention models or approaches. Generally, in current practice, such management-focused studies do not use standardized measures. Rather, typical measures assess productivity such as numbers of cases, patient contacts, and hours spent providing services; work processes such as assessment, counseling, education, and discharge planning; availability of resources such as home care, hospice, day hospital, and discharge planning teams; staffing patterns, which include numbers and location of social work staff; and leadership that defines the administrative auspices and direction of social work services.

Key measures used in these studies are financial, measuring the cost of care especially as determined by number of hospital days or the number of staff required for the number of patients served and whether and how long the patient remains an inpatient or is moved to ambulatory care status. Although quality of care as viewed by the patient and staff may be evaluated, the most frequent outcomes measure is cost of service. Studies also focused on treatment and health care processes such as the timeliness and appropriateness of the discharge plan and the number of discharge delays as a result of social or family circumstances. Many of these results feed back into continuous quality improvement systems and are used for service improvements and cost reductions. All the authors thought their investigations had been effective in demonstrating to hospital administrators the ability to decrease costs.

Dimond and Roca clearly describe the ethical dilemmas such studies can create for social workers because the outcomes are tailored specifically to the needs of the organization. They focus on research that examines more rapid discharge to save costs. The social workers raised ethical concerns about the impact on ill patients of faster movement to the home and the consequent burden of that care on the patients and family caregivers. This concern was handled inventively by having social workers redesign the focus of their interventions to include preparation of patients and families before admission and the development of ambulatory care service approaches that would address patients' needs after discharge.

What is often missing from these management-focused studies is an explicit identification of the possible effect of less costly alternatives on quality of life or patient satisfaction. This issue has been raised over discharging new mothers from the hospital within 24 hours. It may be less costly in the short run, but is it safe and how does it affect the quality of life of the patient and of the family? Is it really cost-effective in the long run? Thus, by adding quality-of-life and patient satisfaction variables to cost, outcomes variables make management studies more comprehensive. Social workers continue to struggle with how they can address these sometimes conflicting patient and system needs.

What about Randomized Clinical Trials?

Finally, Epstein, Zilberfein, and Snyder question the appropriateness of outcomes measures derived from randomized clinical trials for many psychosocial services. They provide an excellent discussion of the value of randomized clinical trials to answer such questions. They strongly recommend the use of existing, routinely gathered data for outcomes measurement as an alternative to randomized clinical trials. In their study of patients who had liver transplants, information had been gathered by multiple disciplines for seven years. The authors intend to analyze the patterns of patient selection for liver transplants and to correlate these patterns with patients' medical and psychosocial outcomes.

These authors advocate that the use of existing data is an approach that looks at services in the real world. They argue that this approach has a host of advantages over expensive and—in their view—rarely competently implemented randomized clinical trials. However, as they acknowledge, the study of existing data can only be as good as the quality of the information available. In planning for usage of data systems, research needs must be considered in advance. For example, having quality-of-life data from the SF-36 questionnaire routinely obtained at critical points in the transplant process would support outcomes measurement of this type of study. The quality and usefulness of existing data depend on planning in advance and more extensive routine use of efficient standardized measures. Such planning may also optimally include regular quality-of-life assessments of family members as well as patients.

Conclusion

The studies presented in part IV demonstrate the remarkable growth and productivity of social work and health care research efforts that are in large part—but not entirely—directed by the demand for cost reductions. For example, Royle and Moynihan strove to increase use of services by a patient population that traditionally underuses services.

Several important themes emerged from the studies presented in the health section. Certainly affirmation of the commitment to obtaining the patients' views of medical and psychosocial outcomes is one theme that is welcomed by social work. Standardized measures of patients' quality of life and satisfaction with services were emphasized as essential to comparing outcomes of social work services across populations and improving the credibility of claims that social work services can reduce health care costs and improve quality of life. However, important barriers to the use of such measures exist, and strategies to overcome these barriers should be implemented. Part IV authors suggest several ways to improve the use of standardized measures:

- More support should be given to social work efforts to refine and use existing measures in clinical practice and research settings as well as to develop new standardized measures. The studies should include both cost reduction and cost-effectiveness analyses and quality-of-life measures to gain acceptance of services in such a cost-controlled health care environment so that a demonstrable value is added by these services.
- Measures must be standardized with culturally and economically diverse and vulnerable populations as noted by Coulter, Royle, and Moynihan.
- Social work graduate and postgraduate education should increase the teaching of research methods and address attitudinal barriers to the use of these methods.
- Considering ways to resolve the ethical dilemmas these studies raise may also help in overcoming barriers to their implementation.

Social work managers are under increasing pressure to conduct studies with cost control as an outcome. This pressure has led to an expansion of social work research efforts in hospital settings as reflected by the studies presented in part IV. However, social workers can and should include quality-of-life and patient satisfaction outcomes where possible to clarify the total cost, including the cost to quality, of service reductions or changes.

Because the studies described in part IV are context based, they examined interventions with individuals, considering the family, larger social support network, and multiple aspects of the environment. A question for future research is whether these outcomes measures can also be used to assess individual- and family-focused interventions. It is clear that serious efforts are being made to apply these measures at individual, program, and policy levels.

References

Derogatis, L. R. (1992). *BSI: Administration, scoring and procedures manual—II.* Baltimore, MD: Clinical Psychometric Research.

Ware, J. E., & Sherbourne, C. D. (1992). The MOS 36-item short-form health survey (SF-36). *Medical Care, 30,* 473–483.

CHAPTER 30

Concluding Comments

EDWARD J. MULLEN

JENNIFER L. MAGNABOSCO

This book and the symposium on which it is based were designed to examine the following questions:

- How can outcomes measurement be usefully reconceptualized and placed in historical, public policy, administration, practice, and research contexts? What is the legislative and public policy context of outcomes measurement? Why should outcomes be addressed in a measurable way?
- What approaches to outcomes measurement are being promulgated? What can be said about the reliability, validity, and quality of existing approaches to outcomes measurement and their relevance for social work interventions?
- What are the implications for future research?
- What are the implications for social programs and for practitioners of the increasing attention to outcomes measurement?

Each contributor considered these questions when preparing his or her chapter and symposium presentation. Consequently, a variety of perspectives and answers to these and related questions and issues has been provided. Drawing from the ideas expressed by the book's contributors, in this concluding chapter, we comment on the implications for the future as presented in the last two questions.

What Approaches to Outcomes Measurement Are Being Promulgated? What Can Be Said about the Reliability, Validity, and Quality of Existing Approaches to Outcomes Measurement and Their Relevance for Social Work Intervention?

Outcomes measurement researchers have developed an impressive array of instruments with respectable reliability and validity as described in many of the chapters throughout this book. Although considerable progress has been made in the development of a range of discrete outcomes measures, their incorporation into outcomes measurement systems is only beginning. Similarly, the development of outcomes measurement and management systems, which may also use newly developed measures, is in the beginning stages. The current wealth of instruments available for outcomes measurement purposes is continuously being expanded by groups other than traditional academic outcomes measurement researchers. These groups include governmental bodies, policymakers, behavioral health care and managed care organizations, insurance companies, independent consultants, human service providers, and consumers. The current rush to measurement (see Hudson, chapter 5) and pushes toward cost containment, results-based accountability, managed care, and outcomes measurement for use in policymaking are rapidly reshaping the practice and delivery of human services in an undirected fashion. However, such a general emphasis on proven accountability can improve the quality and delivery of human service practices, programs, and systems. Nonetheless, debates about how this should and can be done will not result in decision making that will satisfy all stakeholders on the use of outcomes measures and systems. Consequently, the inclusion of stakeholder perspectives into the developmental processes of outcomes measurement is one pressing priority. In addition, a careful examination of both new and old outcomes measures, outcomes management systems, and the consequences that imposing outcomes measurement requirements on human services can have on service delivery should be done. This type of assessment is fundamental to quality-based, efficient, and cost-effective care that the outcomes measurement movement in the human services seeks to achieve.

What Are the Implications for Future Research?

Collectively, the contributors have generated an ambitious agenda for outcomes measurement research. In this section we identify those research questions pertaining to five topics: (1) levels of analysis, (2) population, (3) methodology, (4) conceptualization, and (5) use.

LEVELS OF ANALYSIS QUESTIONS

Current managed care and results-based accountability efforts have stressed measuring outcomes at individual, group, and program levels. Such aggregate assessment has been used for program accountability, profiling, development of report cards, program improvement, and individual and practitioner outcomes. Many of these outcomes measures have not been validated for use at the case level, although practice and treatment decisions are made on a daily basis without standardized information. The design and use of case or program outcomes measures can no longer be detached from services delivery system issues. Human service delivery system reform efforts are currently targeted at all three levels of analysis and seek to integrate these multiple levels to provide better services. How can outcomes measurement systems be designed to be of use at the case and program levels? What types of outcomes measurement systems are required to capture case, program, and system levels of analysis?

Chapter 7 provides a context in which to begin to answer such questions. Shern and Trabin identify development of methods and outcomes-oriented accountability strategies for monitoring the overall well-being of populations, including services used across the range of human service systems (rather than within a program-budget category) as a research agenda. It proposes that future research seek an understanding of comprehensive service use patterns. Such research should document cost shifting across human service domains and develop cost estimates to establish rates for integrative treatment and support services. Finally, it calls for research examining the impacts of varying organizational forms and financing strategies on the broad social good.

With the increasing shift toward devolution of human services, states and localities should consider outcomes measurement systems capable of monitoring this broadly conceived "social good." Accordingly, chapter 14 calls for research on the challenges and opportunities that states face in designing, implementing, and sustaining results-based accountability initiatives in different contexts is timely. Weiss suggests that research about political, technical, and resource challenges across contexts is essential for planning, implementing, and sustaining results-based accountability systems.

Some contributors have described issues pertaining to the specificity of outcomes measures at various levels of outcomes assessment (for example, individual consumer, program, community, or broader population levels). Examples of highly specific measures are rapid assessment instruments (RAIs) and outcomes modules, whereas examples of broad measures are report cards and community and social indicators. Typically, RAIs are used to assess specific, time-limited changes in individuals resulting from direct counseling. Such instruments measure the effect of a specific program intervention designed to achieve a specific intervention objective. Similarly, the outcomes modules described by researchers associated with the Arkansas Center for Outcomes Research and Effectiveness are designed to measure individual patient change in specific diagnostic areas associated with program-level interventions. Alternatively, at a much broader level, chapter 16 describes outcomes measures developed in Los Angeles County, California, designed to monitor changes in county-level populations such as indicators of child well-being. Chapter 1 describes some community-level efforts and concludes that research should assess the use of individual-level in contrast to community- or system-level measures. Even at the individual level, there is a need for research that examines whether human service outcomes measurement should focus on all aspects of the clients' conditions or focus more narrowly on outcomes relating to specific services. Among the questions here is the level of accountability as well as the level at which the intervention is thought to have an effect. Clearly, some outcomes indicators such as infant mortality are generally considered to be affected by many factors rather than a single agency's program. Research should sort out the many questions pertaining to levels of analysis.

POPULATION QUESTIONS

Research regarding the sensitivity and relevance of outcomes measures for various population and stakeholder groups is essential, especially for consumers. Chapter 3 calls for research examining how stakeholder and consumer preferences can be accommodated. The authors see a need for research assessing adaptation of outcomes measures to vulnerable populations. Similarly, chapter 18 proposes a broad research agenda examining instrument reliability and validity across varying populations, with questions focused on the use of cross-cultural measures in countries around the world and in the United States. Research pertaining to development of culturally sensitive instruments is necessary with testing over a wide spectrum of social categories.

METHODOLOGICAL QUESTIONS

Because outcomes measurement methodology is emerging as a specialized research area, many methodological questions should be addressed. These questions pertain to sampling, research design, methods, analytic techniques, focus of instrument development, and barriers to measurement.

In the human services a frequent criticism of outcomes measures is that they are too complex, lengthy, and demanding of time and methodological expertise for their administration, analysis, and interpretation. This criticism pertains especially to outcomes measures originally designed for use in social or behavioral science research where efficiency of administration is not always required. Many contributors see problems with these measures and call for outcomes measures that are simple, easily and inexpensively administered, and directly interpretable so that they can be used in routine practice without undue interference with service.

Chapter 18 describes research occurring at RAND that is focusing on redesigning instruments to increase their efficiency without significant loss of information. The work pertaining to RAIs further illustrates needed methodological research on this topic. Chapter 14 calls for the development of outcomes measures that can be used by practitioners and line workers in results-based accountability efforts. Chapter 15 is especially critical of studies that have used cross-sectional designs to examine questions regarding characteristics of broad child welfare populations and calls for future research that avoids the selection bias of cross-sectional designs and that uses statistical models "that reveal the structure and pattern in the experiences of children" (p. 187). Chapter 6 sees a similar need for improved statistical methods in the analysis of behavioral health care outcomes data. In behavioral health research, Chapter 3 enumerates many methodological questions: Should outcomes measurement systems be disorder-specific or rely on generalized assessments? Should measures be of samples or of entire populations? Should measures be of tracer conditions, or should all disorders be assessed? Should brief assessments or more precise, multidimensional measures be used? How can assessment logistics be improved? How can initial dissimilarities be controlled in outcomes measurement systems? Chapter 1 encourages the development of sampling methods that enhance response rates to minimize the selection bias resulting from poor response rates evident in much outcomes research. Related to this selection bias are the problems resulting from measuring outcomes at the wrong time. Research should carefully track methodological artifacts associated with the measurement of outcomes at varying intervals after intervention.

It is likely that the current emphasis on cost containment—as well as the growth of a concern for quality of life—will underscore methodologies that appropriately reflect progress and desired outcomes of human services and also underscore efforts to prevent human service–related problems. Real world cost-containment efforts have rarely been driven by the humanitarian and scientific values or theoretical bases that are fundamental to developing such appropriate measures. In a pragmatic, cost-conscious society, if outcomes are more appropriately measured by a cost-effectiveness framework (that is, trade-offs between costs and nonmonetary units of analysis) as opposed to a cost-minimization or cost–benefit framework (that is, trade-offs between dollars of cost and dollar benefit units of analysis), then many conflicting questions arise (Gramlich, 1990). Cost-containment initiatives as applied to social policies and programs may be driven more by assessment of measures that reflect only costs per service delivered than by other measures that may be as important to consider when providing human services; for example, how did the treatment methods used help the client's progress compared with its cost of provision? Investments in prevention will be subject to critical review, and they should stand the test of measurable outcomes. No greater challenge to outcomes measurement methodology may exist than the development of assessments capable of measuring outcomes associated with prevention efforts. (For a review of preventive intervention research, see Mrazek & Haggerty, 1994.)

CONCEPTUAL QUESTIONS

The conceptual and theoretical dimensions of outcomes measurement in the human services are only beginning to be studied. Perhaps this delay is a result of the dominance of practical considerations and the proximity of this type of research to the press of accountability. Nevertheless, rich research traditions have developed in the various fields associated with outcomes measurement such as those found in organizational and management theories (for example, continuous quality improvement [CQI]), empirical practice theories (for example, behavioral and cognitive theories), and evaluation research (for example, Rossi & Freeman, 1993).

Although conceptual or theoretical research questions have not been extensively addressed in this book, several important conceptual issues have been identified by contributors. Chapter 15 expresses concern that research in child welfare has too often studied children out of context, especially out of the context of their geographic communities. Wulcyzn calls for future research to contextualize child and family services by creating what he calls *geographic sensitivity*. This suggestion is clearly in keeping with what would appear to be an increasing move toward local, community-based human services. The chapter sees the need for contextualizing research as counter to the traditional "reductionist" tendencies of viewing individuals in isolation from their environments. Outcomes measurement capable of contextualizing services and consumers presents a major but relevant challenge.

Related to the issue of contextualization is the concern expressed by some contributors that outcomes measures should not be too narrowly crafted or limited only to models where there has been some degree of successful measurement (for example, medical models), especially when measurement is applied to broad social work and human service domains. For example, in child and family services some contributors have cautioned against the wholesale adoption of measures found useful in health and behavioral health. McGowan and Cohen reflect the concern of many when they note the conceptual split within child and family services between those who would base outcomes measurement on a family preservation framework and those who would use a protective services approach is discussed in chapter 28. Clearly, depending on which approach one used, different outcomes measures would be indicated. Research should address this tough conceptual problem that has practical consequences.

An important conceptual issue to address pertains to how a human service field's particular outcomes are conceptualized, that is, the classification systems on which outcomes measures are to be based. Chapter 3 calls for future outcomes measurement research that addresses nosological questions. Related to this is the need for careful development of indicator systems capable of assessing whatever classification systems are used.

Basic to outcomes measurement in the human services is the development of improved theories on how interventions can affect change in the myriad problems addressed. As noted in chapter 6, little research exists on the assessment, explanation, and prediction of clinical change in mental health and substance abuse, and little is known about the treatment of mental health and substance abuse disorders in the real world. Chapter 6 calls for future behavioral health research capable of specifying patient, treatment, and systems factors that account for improvement. This call for research that will contribute to an understanding of change and how to promote change in human service problems is important.

USE QUESTIONS

Outcomes measurement in the human services is undertaken for practical reasons. Data are produced for use in decision making for policy and program redesign, resource allocation, and consumer service choice. Yet, the history of research use has shown that findings often are not used. The contributors have identified use issues and questions that require attention in future outcomes research. (For discussions of past efforts to use research in social work, see Grasso & Epstein, 1992; Task Force on Social Work Research, 1991; Videka-Sherman & Reid, 1990.)

Typically, human service organizations have existing information systems that serve various functional requirements but often are not set up for or do not include capacities for outcomes measurement efforts. The addition of an outcomes measurement system may be experienced as yet another demand on resources. Furthermore, with multiple information systems it may be difficult to properly interpret outcomes data out of context. Accordingly, some contributors call for research examining how outcomes measurements can be integrated into existing information systems. Although an integrated system may facilitate use, alone it does not guarantee the proper interpretation, management, and monitoring of outcomes data. Several contributors call for research examining how statistical systems can be strengthened to enhance usability and interpretability.

Although outcomes data can be used to improve services, they also can be misused if understood simplistically or if used to limit service access. Research should examine both the benefits of outcomes measurement on service quality and efficiency and examine misuse by consumers, providers, managers, payors, and policymakers. Weiss notes that although policymakers and practitioners assume that outcomes initiatives (for example, results-based accountability) produce efficiency and effective services, evidence should show this. Furthermore, although the experiences with these initiatives in the private sector may be positive, research that will assess how elements of such initiatives work in the public sector to make decisions about budgeting and program continuation is needed.

What Are the Implications for Social Programs and for Practitioners of the Increasing Attention to Outcomes Measurement?

RELEVANCE OF AVAILABLE MEASURES

Chapter 19 discusses the importance of adapting instruments developed outside of social work for use in social work settings. Such adaptation requires careful review of the measurement needs of the particular setting. According to chapter 10, in the past 20 years the exponential growth of sound and useful measurement tools has occurred, although these measures have not been incorporated into practice. Chapter 5 indicates that additional psychometric work should be done, but Hudson believes the greatest need is the development of additional assessment and evaluation tools that will provide "broader coverage of the measurement constructs that are useful to clients and service delivery personnel" (p. 74). On a related note, Chapter 18 expresses particular concern about the validity of existing measures for minority populations and sees this as a challenge for future research. Clearly, the extension of outcomes measures for use with minority populations should be a priority for the human services including social work.

STANDARDIZATION

Outcomes measurement in the human services must necessarily stand the test of public accountability. Stakeholders—whether they be providers, payers, consumers, or policymakers—place greater value on human services that take accountability seriously and that provide evidence of proven outcomes. Nevertheless, the outcomes measurement movement results, and will continue to result, in significant changes in practice and in agency organization. Among these changes none is more significant for social agencies and social work than measurement standardization. In this era of simultaneous development and use of outcomes measures in social work and other human service practices, the purposes underlying any push for centralized standardization of outcomes measures across settings and populations is foremost among those issues that require deeper consideration. Managed care companies, accreditation, and other standard-setting bodies and government initiatives are increasingly requiring standardized quantitative outcomes measures that address what these groups consider important and that permit aggregation of data and comparisons across settings. What are the implications of centralized standardization of such measures, especially in a market-driven, proprietary environment? In particular, what are the implications for a profession such as social work that has stressed the importance of individualized personal services? Historically, social work has resisted standardization and quantitative measurement. It has been argued that social work services are too personalized, relationship-based, and subjective to permit standardized, quantitative measurement. The confidentiality and privacy of the relationship and communication between a client and a practitioner has been valued and protected. Yet, as public accountability and standardized, quantitative outcomes measurement requirements become part of human service practice, the need to individualize services and protect confidential relationships may clash, demanding fresh solutions. Human service professionals should better define their roles in this endeavor at both macro and micro levels. Specifically, human service professionals should better determine how to maintain an appropriate focus on ethics and standardization as pushes for accountability continue.

SYSTEMATIC, ROUTINE, AND CONTINUOUS EVALUATION

Early evaluations of social work and other human service experiments begun during Lyndon Johnson's Great Society program in the late 1960s reported only modest effectiveness. In one of the landmark assessments at that time Mullen, Dumpson, and associates (1972) concluded, "We stand convinced that program evaluation must be built into all major organized interventive efforts, and feedback should be part of the ongoing process of all agency systems. Professional accountability demands systematic evaluation. We should not have to rely on infrequent reports of field experiments to learn of intervention effectiveness" (pp. 253–254). This warning to the human service field nearly 25 years ago was only one among many heard then. The need for systematic evaluation of the human services was heard as early as 1931 when in his presidential address to the National Conference of Social Work, Cabot (1931) challenged the field: "Let us criticize and reform ourselves before a less gentle and appreciative body takes us by the shoulders and pushes us into the street" (p. 24).

Currently, Cabot's (1931) "less gentle and appreciative body" is prevalent everywhere. Despite these and other warnings such as those in previous chapters, few human service programs and few communities have built routine, systematic, ongoing evaluation into their programs. Recent cost-containment and accountability initiatives have the potential to permanently reshape human services and are already institutionalizing outcomes measurement into provision of care. As previously noted, funding decisions are increasingly based on measured outcomes. Human service programs no longer have the option of putting off *regular, ongoing, systematic outcomes measurement*. Outcomes measurement systems are now required for organizational, professional, and community survival. This does not mean simply the gathering of data now and then as requests are presented or issues move into the spotlight. Rather, it means that outcomes data must be routinely collected so that they are readily available for both external accountability and for internal learning and redesign.

Beyond producing data, outcomes management systems must provide for competency in data interpretation and presentation, a point amplified by many contributors to this book. Human service organizations and communities should have the capacity to analyze, interpret, and communicate the outcomes data they are collecting (Coulton, 1995). Otherwise the data will be unintelligible or misused to the disadvantage of the human services. It is no longer a matter of an organization or community conducting a study periodically, nor is it a matter of routinely collecting and storing some service statistics. Rather, information technologies should be integrated into the organizational and community fabric providing systematic and ongoing feedback on performance and outcomes at all levels of organizational and community life.

PARTNERSHIPS IN OUTCOMES MEASUREMENT

Few members of human service organizations are unaware of the importance of people in various organizational roles and levels working together to accomplish goals. Building outcomes measurement into human service practice and policies is no exception. It takes a unified effort and a partnership of practitioners, administrators, and researchers within human service organizations and among other important stakeholders (for example, consumers, insurance companies) to make outcomes measurement systems an integral part of organizational life. In the past it has been difficult for professionals to collaborate in research, and much has been written about the practitioner–administrator–researcher *gap*. This gap has not been bridged in human service organizations. A recent assessment of this gap identified differences in relational, organizational, philosophical, political, and ethical dimensions as reasons for the continuing divisions among these groups (Hess & Mullen, 1995). Based on that assessment, Hess and Mullen concluded, "Social agencies must continue to move toward incorporating systematic reflection, knowledge development, and research in the professional social worker's role. . . . Although the pressures on staff time and the scarcity of agency resources present formidable obstacles to these efforts, continuing the *status quo* will result in inadequate resources being made available for knowledge development. As a result, service quality and effectiveness will suffer" (p. 270).

In the past the partnership between practitioners and researchers has been fostered and advocated because it has been seen as the road to practice–knowledge development. However, in the context of the outcomes measurement movement, knowledge development is no longer the only issue, nor the only goal. Rather, the partnership goal, namely, the measurement and effective communication of quantitative information about human service outcomes for use by organizations competing for scarce resources among policy and service options as well as for use by practitioners and consumers in decision making, is also practical. The urgent questions driving human service outcomes measurement are practical questions of relative performance and how this performance is valued by key stakeholders given the costs. This gives a different meaning and urgency to the practitioner–administrator–researcher partnership agenda. This partnership is an organizational and professional necessity driven by the pragmatic goal of survival. Although the practitioner–researcher partnership has been advocated for decades (see Hudson, chapter 5), the new accountability context may quickly achieve what decades of teaching and writing have failed to accomplish regarding the integration of research into human service practice.

Unless more appropriate care is taken, the pushes for accountability and various outcomes measurement efforts can further distance the fragile partnerships formed among practitioners, consumers, administrators, and researchers. For example, in previous chapters several contributors taking the practitioner stakeholder perspective argue for the importance of outcomes measures that are sensitive to individual practitioner–client transactions used to monitor and assess change and progress toward goal attainment at the case level. The primary users of such outcomes measures are the practitioner and the client, although data aggregation for use at the program level is also possible. This use of measurement has been an ideal and a rationale sustaining the empirical practice movement (for example, chapters 5, 10, 11, and 17). (For an examination of the empirical practice movement in social work, see Book Forum on the Scientist–Practitioner, 1996; and Reid, 1994. For an example of how a practitioner would use such data on an ongoing basis to develop practice guidelines, see Mullen, 1978.) Other contributors have emphasized outcomes measurement systems that do not easily incorporate direct use by individual practitioners or consumers such as when outcomes data are produced in aggregate form to measure gross or net program impact; to measure outcomes at various governmental, geographic, or network levels; or to trace an organizations performance such as through measuring tracer conditions. Some contributors have noted the unreliability of many such outcomes measures when they are disaggregated and used at the individual case level.

Given these varying approaches to outcomes measurement, unless the information needs of different stakeholders are carefully considered, more fracturing could occur that could drive the outcomes measurement communities in divergent directions. Outcomes measurement and management systems founded on results-based continuous quality improvement (CQI) frameworks can help avoid this fracturing of the stakeholder partnership. In a CQI framework, outcomes measures and systems are used to provide routine and systematic monitoring and improvements within the human service organization. The organization must develop a "learning organization" model, that is, a learning capacity to innovate, experiment, and share ideas, because its foundation better positions human service organizations to deal with the demands of external and internal pushes for accountability. In a CQI context, outcomes measurement information is collected and systematized considering the needs and interests of both internal stakeholders (for example, practitioners, consumers, administrators) and external stakeholders (for example, funding, governmental, or accreditation bodies). This framework is discussed by several contributors to this book. (For an examination of related ideas in the human services, see Martin & Kettner, 1996.)

IN WHOSE BEST INTEREST: OUTCOMES FOR WHOM?

Although organizational and professional survival and learning are important reasons for developing outcomes measurement systems, quality human services must eventually meet the test of benefiting citizens. Not all human service organizations should survive. Clearly, scarce resources should not simply be allocated to the most competitive and powerful organizations or the organizations that offered the least costly services without consideration of societal benefits. This is the danger of a one-sided cost-containment approach to resource allocation and the danger of treating human services like commodities. The justification for human services must be found in their value to the actual and potential recipients of those services. Accordingly, community- and client-based outcomes measures should become the pivotal focus. Whether considered outcomes measures or not, client–consumer satisfaction measurement must be an important part of any outcomes measurement system. Several authors in this book have been major contributors to the development of such measures, and most chapters attest to the importance of these measures. Efforts by organizations such as the National Alliance for the Mentally Ill and the Center for Mental Health Services are strengthening the role of the consumer perspective in outcomes measurement and in the report card movement (Center for Mental Health Services, 1995). The significance of the mental health consumer movement and the importance of highlighting the client–consumer's interests and perspective are emphasized in chapter 13. Consumer-centered outcomes measurement promises to offset the sharp edge of cost containment as the human services are reshaped.

Social work—because of its broad focus, its orientation to individuals as well as programs and systems, and its value-based pragmatic concern for human welfare—is well positioned to be a leader in using the outcomes measurement movement to strengthen human services. As noted in chapter 7, if the social work profession is willing to adapt to the rapid changes occurring in the human services, social work in particular is well positioned to lead the effort in both research and practice in system design and in forming interdisciplinary research teams. Accordingly, the profession of social work can have a "profound effect on the shape of these reforms and ultimately on the overall public health." Social work is also well positioned to assemble various stakeholder groups to "reconcile needs and interests over positions" so that outcomes measurement initiatives in the human services result in the most efficient, cost-effective, and satisfying quality-based care. Forging such "zones of agreement" is an important step in defining how the outcomes measurement movement in the human services is reshaping the provision and delivery of care (Chandler, 1990)

The Ultimate Test

The human services and social work have as a central goal the facilitation of a just society, especially for the most vulnerable and powerless populations. A recent study (see chapter 4) investigating the delivery of health services found that those who are sicker and either poorer or older do less well under managed care health plans than under traditional fee-for-service plans. These findings highlight a serious problem associated with the shift of human services into the managed care delivery frameworks of for-profit contracts—the emergence of populations for whom the provision of services is not profitable. What will happen to needy popula-tions whose care is not profitable? What stakeholder group will have sufficient interest and power to ensure that needed human services are provided to these groups? What political processes will ensure that needed resources are allocated? Whose outcomes measurement system will report on the status of the most vulnerable and underserved populations? Undoubtedly, profit-seeking efforts have motivated many payers and providers to engage in hurried outcomes measurement and new ways of providing services. Providing services based on profit motives or cost-containment efforts may also dictate the use of outcomes measurement systems that isolate unprofitable groups into risk categories to be avoided. Will the ultimate test of outcomes measurement systems in the human services be how such systems can be used to ensure that quality-based services are provided equitably to all in need, even to populations without resources and for whom service provision is not profitable?

References

Andrews, G., Peters, L., & Teeson, M. (1994). *The measurement of consumer outcome in mental health: A report to the National Mental Health Information Strategy Committee.* Sydney, Australia: Clinical Research Unit for Anxiety Disorders.

Bloom, M., Fischer, J., & Orme, J. G. (1995). *Evaluating practice: Guidelines for the accountable professional.* Boston: Allyn & Bacon.

Book forum on the scientist–practitioner (1996, June). *Social Work Research, 20* (2), 67–118.

Cabot, R. C. (1931). Treatment in social casework in the need of criteria and of tests of its success or failure. *Proceedings of the National Conference of Social Work, 58,* 3–24.

Center for Mental Health Services. (1995). *Stakeholder perspectives on mental health performance indicators.* Rockville, MD: Author.

Chandler, S. M. (1990). *Competing realities: The contested terrain of mental health advocacy.* New York: Praeger.

Corcoran, K., & Fischer, J. (1995). *Measures for clinical practice.* New York: Free Press.

Coulton, C. J. (1995). Research for initiatives in low-income communities. In P. Hess & E. J. Mullen (Eds.), *Knowledge for practice* (pp. 103–121). Washington, DC: NASW Press.

Gramlich, E. M. (1990). *A guide to benefit–cost analysis.* Englewood Cliffs, NJ: Prentice-Hall.

Grasso, A. J., & Epstein, J. (Eds.). (1992). *Research utilization in the social services.* New York: Haworth.

Hess, P., & Mullen, E. J. (Eds.). (1995). *Knowledge for practice.* Washington, DC: NASW Press.

Hudson, W., & Nurius, P. S. (1993). *Human services: Practice, evaluation, and computer.* Pacific Grove, CA: Brooks/Cole.

Martin, L. L., & Kettner, P. M. (1996). *Measuring the performance of human service programs.* Newbury Park, CA: Sage Publications.

Mrazek, P. J., & Haggerty, R. J. (Eds.). (1994). *Reducing risks for mental disorders: Frontiers for preventive intervention research.* Washington, DC: National Academy Press.

Mullen, E. J. (1978). The construction of personal models for effective practice: A method for utilizing research findings to guide social interventions. *Journal of Science Research* [Special Issue on New Models of Social Service Research], *2,* 45–63.

Mullen, E. J., Dumpson, J. R., & Associates. (1972). *Evaluation of social intervention.* San Francisco: Jossey-Bass.

Pecora, P. J., Fraser, M. W., Nelson, K. E., McCroskey, J., & Meezan, W. (1995). *Evaluating family-based services.* New York: Aldine de Gruyter.

Reid, W. J. (1994). The empirical practice movement. *Social Service Review, 68,* 165–184.

Rossi, P. H., & Freeman, H. E. (1993). *Evaluation: A systematic approach.* Newbury Park, CA: Sage Publications.

Task Force on Social Work Research. (1991, November). *Building social work knowledge for effective services and policies: A plan for research development.*

Videka-Sherman, L., & Reid, W. J. (Eds.). (1990). *Advances in clinical social work research.* Silver Spring, MD: NASW Press.

Weiss, H., & Jacob, F. H. (Eds). (1988). *Evaluating family programs.* New York: Aldine de Gruyter.

INDEX

C

D

E

I

K, L

M

N

O

P

Q

R

S

T

U

THE EDITORS

Edward J. Mullen, DSW, is the Willma and Albert Musher Professor, Columbia University School of Social Work, and director, Center for the Study of Social Work Practice. He is director of the National Institute of Mental Health Services Research Doctoral Program at the School of Social Work, Columbia University. He was formerly professor, University of Chicago and Fordham University, and director, Institute of Social Welfare Research, Community Service Society of New York.

Jennifer L. Magnabosco, MA, MPhil, is former director of administration and operations, Center for the Study of Social Work Practice, and a PhD program candidate in Social Policy Administration at the Columbia University School of Social Work. During the past several years, she has held various management, research, and practice positions in the field of mental health.

THE CONTRIBUTORS

Robert Abramovitz, MD, is chief psychiatrist, Jewish Board of Family and Children's Services, New York, New York.

Rami Benbenishty, PhD, is professor, Paul Baerwald School of Social Work, Hebrew University, Jerusalem, Israel.

Barbara Berkman, DSW, is the Helen Rehr and Ruth Fizdale Professor of Health and Mental Health, Columbia University School of Social Work, New York, New York.

William H. Berman, PhD, is associate professor, Department of Psychology, Fordham University, Bronx, New York, and president, Behavioral Health Outcomes Systems (BHOS, Inc.), White Plains, New York.

Rita Beck Black, PhD, is associate professor, Columbia University School of Social Work, New York, New York.

Brenda M. Booth, PhD, is associate professor, Department of Psychiatry, University of Arkansas for Medical Sciences, Little Rock; in the HSR&D Field Program for Mental Health, Little RockVA Medical Center; and Center for Outcomes Research and Effectiveness, University of Arkansas for Medical Sciences, Little Rock.

M. Audrey Burnam, PhD, is senior scientist, RAND Corporation, Santa Monica, California.

Barbara J. Burns, PhD, is professor, Department of Psychiatry and Behavioral Sciences, Duke University Medical Center, Durham, North Carolina.

Lisa Caraisco, MS, CSW, is a social worker, Intensive Psychiatric Community Care, FDR Veterans Administration Hospital, Montrose, New York.

Grace H. Christ, DSW, is associate professor, Columbia University School of Social Work, New York, New York.

Steven D. Cohen, MPA, is associate executive director, Jewish Board of Family and Children's Services, New York, New York.

Kevin Corcoran, PhD, JD, is professor, Graduate School of Social Work, Portland State University, Portland, Oregon.

Ian D. Coulter, PhD, is health consultant, RAND Corporation, Santa Monica, California, and professor, School of Dentistry, University of California, Los Angeles.

Margaret Dimond, ACSW, is assistant administrator of the Bone and Joint Center and Neurology Department, Henry Ford Health System, Detroit, Michigan.

Irwin Epstein, PhD, is the Helen Rehr Professor of Applied Social Work Research (Health), Hunter College School of Social Work, New York, New York.

Marianne C. Fahs, PhD, MPH, is associate professor and director of Health Policy Research Center, New School for Social Research, New York, New York.

Ronald A. Feldman, PhD, is dean, Ruth Harris Norman Centennial Professor, Columbia University School of Social Work, New York, New York.

Ellen P. Fischer, PhD, is assistant professor, VA HSR&D Field Program for Mental Health and Department of Psychiatry and Behavioral Sciences, University of Arkansas for Medical Sciences, Little Rock.

David Gitelson, DSW, is chief, Social Work Service, FDR VA Hospital, Montrose, New York.

Sherri Sheinfeld Gorin, PhD, is associate professor, SUNY Stony Brook, Stony Brook, New York, senior research associate, Hunter College School of Social Work, and senior partner, Management Horizons, New York, New York.

Harry P. Hatry is director, Public Management Program, The Urban Institute, Washington, DC.

Marilyn J. Henderson, MPA, is assistant branch chief, Survey and Analysis Branch, Division of State and Community Systems Development, Center for Mental Health Services, Substance Abuse and Mental Health Services Administration (SAMHSA), Rockville, Maryland.

Walter W. Hudson, PhD, is professor, School of Social Work, Florida State University, Tallahassee.

Stephen W. Hurt, PhD, is associate professor of clinical psychology, Cornell University Medical College, White Plains, New York, and executive vice president, Behavioral Health Outcomes Systems (BHOS, Inc.), White Plains, New York.

André Ivanoff, PhD, is associate professor, Columbia University School of Social Work, New York, New York.

Ronald W. Manderscheid, PhD, is branch chief, Survey and Analysis Branch, Division of State and Community Systems Development, Center for Mental Health Services, Substance Abuse and Mental Health Services Administration (SAMHSA), Rockville, Maryland.

Jacquelyn McCroskey, DSW, is associate professor, School of Social Work, University of Southern California, Los Angeles.

Brenda G. McGowan, DSW, is professor, Columbia University School of Social Work, New York, New York.

Rami Mosseri, PhD, is director, Residential Treatment Facilities, Jewish Board of Family and Children's Services, New York, New York.

Sr. Rosemary T. Moynihan, PhD, ACSW, is supervisor, Mental Health Program Comprehensive Care Center for HIV, St. Joseph's Hospital and Medical Center, Paterson, New Jersey.

Paula S. Nurius, PhD, is professor, School of Social Work, University of Washington, Seattle.

Anne O'Sullivan, MPH, is a consultant and executive director, RSVP International, New York, New York.

Penny Goldberg Roca, MS, is assistant director of social work, Memorial Sloan-Kettering Cancer Center, New York, New York.

Peter H. Rossi, PhD, is the Stuart A. Rice Professor of Sociology Emeritus and Director Emeritus, Social and Demographic Research Institute, University of Massachusetts, Amherst.

Kathryn M. Rost, MSW, PhD, is associate professor, The Center for Outcomes Research and Effectiveness, National Institute of Mental Health, Center for Rural Mental Healthcare Research, and Department of Veteran's Affairs Health Services Research and Development Field Program for Mental Health, Department of Psychiatry, University of Arkansas for Medical Sciences, Little Rock.

Marjorie H. Royle, PhD, is coordinator of research and evaluation, Department of Psychiatry, St. Joseph's Hospital and Medical Center, Paterson, New Jersey.

Arthur Russo, MSW, is program director of Intensive Psychiatric Community Care, FDR VA Hospital, Montrose, New York.

Steven P. Segal, ACSW, PhD, is professor and director, Mental Health and Social Welfare Research Group, School of Social Welfare, University of California, Berkeley.

David L. Shern, PhD, is dean and professor, Florida Mental Health Institute, University of South Florida, Tampa.

Alan B. Siskind, PhD, is executive vice president, Jewish Board of Family and Children's Services, New York, New York.

G. Richard Smith, Jr., MD, is vice chairman and professor, Department of Psychiatry, University of Arkansas for Medical Sciences, Little Rock; HSR&D Field Program for Mental Health, Little Rock VA Medical Center; and Center for Outcomes Research and Effectiveness, University of Arkansas for Medical Sciences, Little Rock.

Stephen L. Snyder, MD, is clinical assistant professor of psychiatry, Mount Sinai Hospital School of Medicine, New York, New York.

Tom Trabin, PhD, MSM, is vice president, The Partnership for Behavioral Healthcare, CentraLink, and research director, Institute for Behavioral Healthcare, Tiburon, California.

Betsy S. Vourlekis, PhD, ACSW, is associate professor, Department of Social Work, University of Maryland, Baltimore County.

Kathleen Wade, MSW, is assistant director, Social Work Services, Columbia Presbyterian Medical Center, New York, New York.

John E. Ware, Jr., PhD, is senior scientist, The Health Institute, New England Medical Center, Boston, Massachusetts.

Mona Wasow, PhD, is professor, School of Social Work, University of Wisconsin, Madison.

Heather B. Weiss, EdD, is director, Harvard Family Research Project, Harvard University, Cambridge, Massachusetts.

Fred H. Wulczyn, PhD, is assistant professor, Columbia University School of Social Work, New York; and Research Fellow, Chapin Hall Center for Children, University of Chicago, Chicago, Illinois.

James R. Zabora, MSW, is director, Patient and Family Services, Johns Hopkins Oncology Center, Baltimore, Maryland.

Felice Zilberfein, PhD, is preceptor, Department of Social Work Service, and instructor, Department of Community Medicine, Mt. Sinai Hospital, New York, New York.

Outcomes Measurement in the Human Services: Cross-Cutting Issues and Methods

Cover design by Gehle Design

Interior design by Anne Masters Design, Inc.

Typeset in Bodoni and Futura by Wolf Publications, Inc.

Printed by Automated Graphic Systems, Inc., on 60# Williamsburg